T0323392

# Zero Interest Policy and the New Abnormal

# Zero Interest Policy and the New Abnormal

*A Critique*

MICHAEL BEENSTOCK

# OXFORD
## UNIVERSITY PRESS

Great Clarendon Street, Oxford, OX2 6DP,
United Kingdom

Oxford University Press is a department of the University of Oxford.
It furthers the University's objective of excellence in research, scholarship,
and education by publishing worldwide. Oxford is a registered trade mark of
Oxford University Press in the UK and in certain other countries

Published in the United States of America by Oxford University Press
198 Madison Avenue, New York, NY 10016, United States of America

British Library Cataloguing in Publication Data
Data available

Library of Congress Control Number: 2022930915

ISBN 978–0–19–284966–3

DOI: 10.1093/oso/9780192849663.001.0001

Printed and bound by
CPI Group (UK) Ltd, Croydon, CR0 4YY

# Preface

When in the wake of the Subprime Crisis, which broke out in 2008, the Federal Reserve and many other central banks took the unprecedented step of setting their policy rates to zero, I expected this to be temporary, as most did. By 2014 it became increasingly clear that a sea change had occurred. Not only did ZIP (zero interest policy) persist in the US and elsewhere, it was globally contagious. Other countries, including Israel and Australia, adopted ZIP despite the fact that their economies were not affected by the Subprime Crisis and were not even in crisis. Moreover, other unorthodox macroeconomic policies were adopted, including quantitative easing and the unbridled growth in debt-to-GDP ratios induced by large budget deficits. The Washington Consensus had been overturned. Previous anathemas had become conventional wisdom. The "New Normal" had arrived.

While all this was happening in the world of policy makers, academia had been under attack for its failure to predict the Subprime Crisis and the ensuing recession. Indeed, many blamed neoclassical macroeconomic orthodoxy for what happened. New intellectual brooms swept clean. Behavioral macroeconomics was in the ascendancy, while macroeconomists belonging to the DSGE (dynamic stochastic general equilibrium) movement attended to their intellectual bruises by patching up their models where they had failed. The lights were going out over macroeconomic orthodoxy.

I saw a connection between ZIP and the New Abnormal, as I refer to it, with the turmoil in academia. By 2015 I decided to start work on the present monograph, which would challenge the sustainability of the New Abnormal by appealing to orthodox macroeconomics. I hadn't made much progress with this revisionist project when the Federal Reserve began to raise its policy rate in 2016. I thought that this was the beginning of the end for the New Abnormal, and that it was a matter of time before other central banks followed the Federal Reserve. So I abandoned my monograph more in hope than in sorrow.

I was wrong. Other central banks persisted with ZIP and the New Abnormal, and in September 2019 the Federal Reserve started cutting its policy rate. So in December 2019 I returned to my monograph notes. Then came Covid-19.

The lockdowns of 2020 provided the perfect opportunity to work undisturbed on the monograph. Also, the hysterical reactions of policy makers to the pandemic seemed to enhance the relevance of the project; macroeconomic policy became increasingly abnormal. The first draft was completed by June 2021.

There is a risk in writing a monograph like this because by the time it is published central bankers might have upstaged me by raising interest rates. If they do, as I hope, all is not lost because the monograph is as much concerned with macroeconomic theory and what I call "postmodernism" in applied macroeconomic analysis, as it is about monetary policy in particular and macroeconomic policy in general. In any case it will take many years to undo the damage wrought by ZIP and the New Abnormal. So far there are no signs that I am about to be upstaged, despite growing calls for the Federal Reserve to lead the way by raising its policy rate to combat inflation.

Some of the material, such as the critique of New Keynesian theory and the DSGE movement, is unavoidably technical. I have tried to make my critique of the New Abnormal more accessible to general readers by summarizing the main arguments in synopses at the end of each chapter.

I wish to thank Paul Wachtel for his endorsement, Avichai Rozencraft for his assistance with data and graphics, Rosie Canaan for her artwork, and three reviewers for their helpful comments.

While correcting the final proofs in April 2022 the Federal Reserve raised its policy rate to 0.25 percent and the Bank of Israel raised its policy rate to 0.35 percent. Hopefully, this is the beginning of the return to normality, which is advocated in this book.

Michael Beenstock

*Jerusalem*
*February 2022*

# Contents

# List of Figures

## Chapter 1

## Chapter 2

## Chapter 3

## Chapter 4

## Chapter 5

## Chapter 6

## Chapter 7

# Chapter 8

# Chapter 9

# Chapter 10

# 1

# The New Abnormal

In 2009 Mohamed El-Erian, former CEO of Pimco, introduced the "New Normal" into the vernacular of macroeconomists in general, but especially in central banks, ministries of finance and international organizations such as the International Monetary Fund (IMF) and the Organization for Economic Cooperation and Development (OECD). El-Erian was referring to the prospect that economic growth in the United States (US) during the twenty-first century would not be as impressive as it was in the twentieth century, a view that was subsequently given academic legitimacy by Gordon (2016). New normals are typically negative. For example, doctors warn patients with heart disease that they should avoid stress in their new normal, and psychologists refer to trauma as the new normal after sudden bereavement. Subsequently, reference to the New Normal has spread and embraced further phenomena, including the widespread practice of zero interest policy (ZIP) by central banks, and debt-to-GDP ratios that were prohibitive under the Old Normal prior to 2009.

At first, the New Normal was used to justify or apologize for unorthodox fiscal and monetary policies, which under the Old Normal would have been deemed to be abnormal if not anathema. However, with the passage of time the world accustomed itself to these unorthodox policies to the point that reference to the New Normal began to drop out of the vernacular; the New Normal had acquired normal status.

New normality implies that these phenomena are here to stay; they have become structural if not immutable features of global macroeconomics. It is as if the laws of economics that underpinned the Old Normal are no longer relevant, or have at least been suspended. My purpose here is to argue that the New Normal is newspeak for a system of political economy that is profoundly flawed, socially damaging, and unsustainable. Indeed, although ZIP may last for decades, as it has in Japan since 1996, it cannot last forever. And when it eventually comes to an end, governments such as in Japan will be unable to service their burgeoning national debt and cope with the kinetic inflation that has accumulated through unorthodox monetary policies, such as quantitative easing (QE). ZIP is like a time bomb, which must eventually explode. There will be no soft landing unless steps are taken to return to the orthodoxies of the Old Normal. ZIP induces "existential risk" because

*Zero Interest Policy and the New Abnormal.* Michael Beenstock, Oxford University Press. © Michael Beenstock (2022).
DOI: 10.1093/oso/9780192849663.003.0001

the political economy upon which it is based is destined to collapse in due course; it sows the seeds of its own destruction.

The New Normal is more aptly the "New Abnormal," because ZIP, spiraling debt-to-GDP ratios, the collapse of financial distancing between central banks and the private sector through QE, and massive increases in the quantity of money are not only highly abnormal, they are dangerous. Longstanding categorical imperatives such as fiscal and monetary orthodoxy, as enshrined in the Maastricht Treaty and in the Washington Consensus, have become taboo since 2010. Indeed, the transition to the New Abnormal was rapid and contagious.

Proponents of the New Abnormal point to the absence of inflation as evidence that the laws of economics that applied under the Old Normal are no longer relevant. They claim that spiraling debt-to-GDP ratios and rapid rates of growth in money supply that should have induced inflation according to macroeconomic orthodoxy have failed to do so under the New Normal. Indeed, in some countries such as Japan inflation has been negative despite the best efforts of the authorities to induce inflation through operating ZIP and increasing fiscal deficits. These proponents have failed to understand that when the rate of interest is zero the demand for money becomes infinitely elastic, as a result of which rapid rates of money supply growth have no inflationary implications.

## Liquidity Trap

Indeed, this constellation of events was fantasized by Keynes (1936 p 207) in his liquidity trap theory. "There is a possibility ... that, after the rate of interest has fallen to a certain level, liquidity-preference may become virtually absolute in the sense that almost everybody prefers cash to holding a debt which yields so low a rate of interest. In this event the monetary authority would have lost control over the rate of interest. But whilst this limiting case might become practically important in the future, I know of no example of it hitherto. Indeed, owing to the unwillingness of most monetary authorities to deal boldly in debts of long term, there has not been much opportunity for a test. Moreover, if such a situation were to arise, it would mean that the public authority itself could borrow through the banking system on an unlimited scale at a nominal rate of interest." Keynes' fantasy has become reality.

Or in the words of Hicks (1937 pp 469–70) in his influential interpretation and popularization of Keynes, "A liquidity trap may be defined as a situation in which conventional monetary policies have become impotent, because nominal interest rates are at or near zero; injecting monetary base into the economy has no effect because base and bonds are viewed by the private sector as perfect substitutes."

The liquidity trap will play a central but not exclusive role in our critique of ZIP. As pointed out by Patinkin (1966 pp 349–55) among others, liquidity trap theory requires that not only must the policy rate be zero or near zero, so must other rates of interest, such as on bonds. This will only happen if the central bank engages in massive open-market purchases of bonds, "It follows that if the government is willing to pursue a sufficiently vigorous open-market policy—one that encompasses private as well as government bonds—there is no reason why it should not be able to drive interest down as low as it wants." Patinkin noted that such a policy, "... negates the whole institutional meaning of a policy designed to enable government to influence the over-all level of economic activity in the economy with a minimum of direct intervention."

Patinkin's caveat constitutes another central role in the present critique of ZIP. Newspeak for the open-market operations to which he referred is "quantitative easing." What turned fantasy into reality is that ZIP and aggressive QE eventually forced other rates of interest into line with the zero policy rate (Chapter 5). The political economy of ZIP starts with central bank policy rates that are zero. Frustrated by their inability to cut interest rates further, central banks turn to limited QE involving purchases of government bonds, which reduces the yield on bonds. Next, QE is extended to corporate bonds. Finally, QE is extended to equity and made unlimited. At each stage bond yields are forced down, as predicted by Patinkin, and the liquidity trap gets stronger until monetary policy becomes increasingly impotent. During this process, the public, which might have initially expected ZIP to be temporary, increasingly expects ZIP to be permanent. In Chapter 5 we relate how these expectations flattened yield curves and drove bond yields to zero.

In summary, the absence of inflation when central banks operate ZIP is perfectly consistent with orthodox macroeconomic theory. If ZIP does not last forever, two seismic events are predicted to occur according to macroeconomic orthodoxy. First, the cost of servicing public debt will increase as a percentage of GDP. For example, if debt is 100 percent of GDP, a return to normal interest rates of, say, 3 percent must directly increase the cost of debt service from zero to 3 percent of GDP. Governments have three ways to finance the increase in the cost of debt service. They may reduce the primary fiscal deficit by cutting spending and increasing taxes. They may debt-finance the increase in the cost of debt service, which would increase the cost of debt service beyond 3 percent of GDP. Finally, they may simply print money. Second, because the rate of interest is positive, the demand for money decreases, and ceases to be infinitely elastic because the economy is no longer in the liquidity trap. The latter releases kinetic inflation, which will most probably be compounded by the resort by governments to print their way out of bankruptcy.

## Existential Risk

Existential risk arises when the existence of an entire system of political economy is expected to end at an unknown date in the future. The end is inevitable, but its timing is uncertain. Existential risk is different to systemic risk, which has entered the vernacular since the Subprime Crisis. Whereas systemic risk refers to the epidemiology of risk in a given economic system induced by networks between banks, financial institutions and economic sectors, existential risk is about the existence of the system in which systemic risk arises. Whereas systemic risk and other types of risk are immanent, existential risk is not. In the nature of things, it arises infrequently. For example, the Bretton Woods system of fixed exchange rates based on a dollar standard, established after World War Two and administered by the International Monetary Fund, was exposed to existential risk. Critics such as Peter Kenen (1960) and Robert Triffin (1960) reasoned that the system would break down sooner or later because the US could not support the use of US dollars as a reserve currency indefinitely. In the 1950s there was a worldwide dollar shortage, and central banks were happy to hold their reserves of gold and foreign exchange in US dollars. The dollar was as good as gold. The Bretton Woods system became a source of seigniorage, which transferred resources to the US from the rest of the world. Critics argued that the system was fundamentally flawed because it was incentive incompatible. They were right. In 1971 the US devalued the dollar in relation to gold, and the Bretton Woods system collapsed. This is an example of Herbert Stein's Law that "... if something cannot go on forever, it will stop."

The cartoon depicts the spirit of existential risk. The subject's demise is inevitable. Meanwhile, all seems well, but the laws of gravity must win out. In the case of the New Abnormal, time passes more slowly. It may seem that the laws of economics have been suspended. However, the end is a matter of time, although its timing is harder to predict than in the cartoon. Versions of this cartoon date back to the nineteenth century (https://quoteinvestigator.com/2019/03/09/fall/) to depict optimism. Here we use it to depict short-sightedness bordering on stupidity. Indeed, it depicts the leitmotiv for the first five chapters.

First adopted by Japan in 1996, ZIP spread throughout the developed world in the wake of the Subprime Crisis that broke out in 2008. It was adopted by several central banks in 2008–9, including the Federal Reserve and the Bank of England, and by the European Central Bank in 2013. By 2015 twelve out of the forty central bank members of the Bank for International Settlements had adopted ZIP. By May 2021 this number had increased to twenty. In 2016 the Federal Reserve began to raise its rate of interest, and it looked as though ZIP was about to come to an end. However, these hopes were dashed when the Federal Reserve began to cut interest rates again in September 2019. Indeed, this strengthened the belief that ZIP is here to stay and that the New Abnormal is indeed normal. These hopes were further dashed when, faced with the Covid-19 pandemic in early 2020, the Federal Reserve returned to ZIP in March 2020, while it and other central banks engaged in unprecedented QE.

ZIP creates the illusion that debt service is cheap and even costless. As a result, governments run fiscal deficits that would have been unthinkable under the Old Normal, and their debt-to-GDP ratios increase. In Japan, this ratio has grown from

**Cartoon 1**  Existential Risk

50 percent in 1990 to 260 percent in 2021. In the US and elsewhere, debt-to-GDP ratios have increased less spectacularly, but had climbed even before the Covid-19 crisis to levels that were unthinkable before 2008. Some countries, such as the UK and France, have fought to prevent their debt ratios from getting out of hand, while

other countries, such as Italy, Spain and Portugal, have failed in this endeavor. The existential risk of ZIP has been compounded by spiraling debt-to-GDP ratios.

## Academic Macroeconomics in Crisis

Prior to the Subprime Crisis, macroeconomics had become consensual in academia and in the practical world. Keynesian and classical macroeconomists understood where they disagreed, rather as Protestants and Catholics do about Christianity. However, they belonged to the same church. Keynesians thought that there was enough nominal rigidity to justify proactive fiscal and monetary policy, while their classical colleagues did not. There was no deep disagreement about principles. In the practical world the so-called Washington Consensus served as the holy grail; debt-to-GDP ratios should be sustainable, the private sector should serve as the engine of growth, exchange rates should be flexible, and interest rates should follow Taylor rules. In Europe, the Maastricht guidelines attached importance to fiscal orthodoxy; fiscal deficits should be limited to 3 percent of GDP and debt-to-GDP ratios should not exceed 60 percent.

All this changed with the Subprime Crisis, which broke out in August 2007 and progressed in 2008. The consensus collapsed. Macroeconomics was attacked from within and without. The attack from within came with the rise of behavioral economics, which eschewed the axiom of rationality upon which consensual macroeconomics was based (and microeconomics too). This has given rise to popular courses on behavioral macroeconomics in leading universities. The attack from without has come from practitioners in central banks, finance ministries, and policy makers in general, who consider that macroeconomics under the Old Normal was discredited by the Subprime Crisis.

The Subprime Crisis was a parochial US affair. A house price bubble resulted from the aggressive marketing of mortgages provided by the Federal Home Loan Mortgage Corporation (Freddie Mac) and the Government National Mortgage Association (Ginnie Mae), intended to encourage home ownership. These mortgages were securitized with triple A credit ratings, despite their subprime status. When the bubble burst, home owners defaulted. What should have been a US crisis turned global because the securitized mortgages had been marketed globally.

But for the Subprime Crisis and its aftermath, it is doubtful that the present book would have been written. The New Normal would not have entered the vernacular, and the political economy of ZIP would not have established itself. The Old Normal would have continued, and the crisis in macroeconomic theory would not have broken out. The American tendency to see the world in US-centric terms applies also to academia. Global macroeconomics is in crisis. When the US sneezes, the world catches a cold.

As we shall see, global macroeconomics was not in crisis. The Old Normal continued outside North America and Europe. However, the political economy of ZIP spread globally (rather like Covid-19) because in small open economies central bankers targeted exchange rates in the mistaken belief that embracing ZIP would weaken their exchange rates.

Trends in macroeconomic policy cannot be divorced from developments in macroeconomic theory and macro-econometrics. The Keynesian revolution had a profound influence on macroeconomic policy in the 1950s and 1960s, as did the Neoclassical Counterrevolution, led by Milton Friedman and others, on macroeconomic policy subsequently. I shall argue that the intellectual foundations of the New Abnormal may be found in "New Keynesian" or Neo-Wicksellian macroeconomics in particular and in the dynamic stochastic general equilibrium (DSGE) movement in general (Woodford 2003, Walsh 2017). Keynes was right in believing that the madmen in high places are the slaves of defunct academic scribblers. However, Neo-Wicksellian monetary theory became detached from the original (Wicksell 1898) by overlooking the pivotal importance of the natural rate of interest.

Following Patinkin (1966) I shall argue that the natural rate of interest is measured by the return on fixed capital assets. By ignoring the natural rate of interest, Neo-Wicksellian macroeconomics is like Hamlet without the Prince of Denmark. This omission led policy makers astray. They attached importance to output gaps and inflation gaps but they ignored the gap between the natural rate of interest and the money rate of interest adjusted for inflation. We shall see that this interest rate gap is empirically very large; the return on fixed assets greatly exceeds the money rate of interest adjusted for inflation, and the gap has widened during the New Abnormal in most OECD countries (Chapter 4).

This development should have rung alarm bells, but it didn't for two reasons. First, because there were no good measures of the rate of return on fixed assets. Second, because the natural rate of interest went largely ignored in twenty-first century macroeconomic theory. In short, DSGE and related models were fundamentally flawed because the natural rate of interest had no explicit role. The outcome was that if the "divine coincidence" (Blanchard and Gali 2007) arose in which the output and inflation gaps happened to be zero under ZIP, it must be the case that the natural rate of interest equals the target rate of inflation. If the target rate of inflation is zero, the natural rate of interest must also be zero, by implication.

But the natural rate of interest measured by the return on fixed assets has been large and positive during the New Abnormal, and remains so. I propose, therefore, that the divine coincidence is conceptually inadequate and misleading, and should be replaced by a "holy trinity" in which the gap between the natural rate of interest and the real rate of interest constitutes a third gap alongside the output and inflation gaps. The holy trinity would imply that the natural rate of interest is zero under ZIP if, in addition to the divine coincidence, the gap between the natural rate of interest and the money rate of interest is zero too. Otherwise, the sanctity of the divine coincidence is suspect. True sanctity involves the holy trinity. I shall argue that contemporary macroeconomic theory went astray by failing to be truly Wicksellian. The "neo" in Neo-Wicksellian monetary theory is its casual treatment of Wicksell's major contribution to macroeconomic theory, the natural rate of interest.

In Chapter 2 Neo-Wicksellian monetary theory is reconstructed by making the natural rate of interest explicit and endogenous. I believe that, had this reconstructed model been canonical, policy makers would not have made the mistake of thinking that the divine coincidence under ZIP implied that the natural rate of interest was zero or close to it. They would have realized instead that the natural rate of interest is too large for comfort. They would not have been misled into adopting ZIP, and the New Abnormal might not have come about.

Not only was contemporary monetary theory flawed, empirical methodology in macroeconomics became increasingly postmodern (Chapter 3). Instead of trying to falsify macroeconomic theory in the modernist tradition, which dates back to David Hume, macroeconomists increasingly assumed their models to be true, but used empirical data to parametrize them using heterodox methods such as calibration and indirect estimation. The legitimate criticism raised by Lucas and others that "too many good models were being rejected by the econometricians" ironically culminated in "too many bad models being accepted by their calibrators." The combination of flawed macroeconomic theory and postmodern macro-econometrics was scientifically disastrous and paved the way for the New Abnormal.

My message here is revisionist. Not only shall I argue that the New Normal is very abnormal, socially harmful and unsustainable, I shall argue that Old Normal macroeconomics provides all the insights to understand how the New Abnormal took hold after 2008, and why this political economy failed to deliver economic growth. The laws of economics that appear to have been suspended, especially in terms of the absence of inflation, have simply been misunderstood. Moreover, Old Normal macroeconomics helps policy makers find their way out of the New Abnormal with minimal damage. Instead of a hard landing, a return to the Old Normal in which interest rates are normalized may be achieved gently, as discussed in Chapter 10.

The normalization of interest rates is of major social importance too, because under ZIP future pensioners will get no return on their savings. Current pensioners have benefited from positive rates of return during their working lives. Matters are different for their children and grandchildren, who since 2008 have saved under ZIP. They face a major cut in their standard of living when they retire because their pension will be worth less and because their life expectancy on retirement is expected to be greater. Since current pensioners belong to the generation of baby boomers and subsequent cohorts belong to Generations X, Y(millennials) and Z, our subject matter is relevant to the growing intergenerational tension between boomers and subsequent generations, which has attracted the attention of sociologists.

Central banks may target inflation and the output gap, but they have not targeted interest rates. As long as inflation and output are on track under ZIP, central bankers see no reason to change the rate of interest. This blinkered view of their purpose is inducing intergenerational inequity because current pensioners benefit at the expense of future pensioners. Some argue that ZIP also induces intragenerational inequity because it benefits capitalists (borrowers) at the expense of workers (savers).

Future pensioners have lost out since ZIP was adopted. So far, in many countries, this has not been for too long. However, in Japan it has been for a quarter of a century. Indeed, we shall use Japan as a crystal ball for learning about the political economy of the New Abnormal, and its social cost (Chapter 8). We shall see that the Japanese economic miracle, which ended in the late 1980s, laid the seeds of its own destruction in terms of inefficiency, cartels, corruption, and a breakdown in trust. After the "lost decade" in which Japan eschewed reforms, it adopted ZIP in 1996 and tried to spend its way out of recession. Since 1996 completed fertility in Japan has fallen dramatically from 2.1 children to 1.2 children. We shall attribute some of this decrease to existential risk; young couples who are fearful of the future are reluctant to bring children into the world (Chapter 6). Indeed, this phenomenon has occurred elsewhere. We shall also compare the pensions of Japanese people who retired before 1996 with pensioners who retired more recently (Chapter 7).

Just as young couples have been reluctant to invest in children, so have business people been reluctant to invest in the future. Existential risk has induced them to insist on higher risk premiums on their investments, with the result that the return on fixed assets has increased sharply relative to interest rates (Chapter 4). Economic theory predicts that interest rates and the return to fixed assets are related in the long run. We show that this historical relationship has broken down under the New Abnormal. Whereas in the past the return to fixed assets exceeded interest rates by a stable risk premium, since 2008 matters have been different. Specifically, ZIP was supposed to have encouraged business investment, which should have lowered the return on fixed assets. This did not happen. Instead, either the return on fixed assets did not change, or it even increased. Instead of ZIP encouraging business investment, it either made no difference, or had the opposite effect. My interpretation is that investors perceived ZIP as an expression of panic by central bankers. Indeed, the more central bankers turned to QE and other unorthodox measures, such as negative interest on bank reserves, to keep interest rates down, the more this propagated existential risk among investors.

Under the New Abnormal, monetary policy has not just become impotent because interest rates have a natural zero bound, it has become self-defeating. If they could, central bankers would operate negative interest rates, but they cannot. Central banks can charge banks for holding reserve assets, and they can pay banks to borrow from them, but they cannot set negative interest rates on money itself. This means that banks can borrow from central banks at negative rates of interest and simply hold their reserves in cash, which is infinitely elastic in supply under ZIP. Central bank attempts to apply negative interest rates simply enhance bank arbitrage profits at the expense of the public.

Since negative interest rate policy is not feasible, central banks have engaged, out of desperation, in unorthodox measures such as QE. Having spent all their ammunition, they have taken to throwing brickbats and stones. This eccentric behavior compounds existential risk, which further frightens the business community into cutting back on investment. The cost of raising capital in terms of gross redemption yields on commercial bonds is almost zero in some countries, and some junk bonds even have negative returns. Grotesque. Something is profoundly wrong. Company treasurers may be taking advantage of this cheap capital to restructure their debt, but it makes no difference to business investment.

I argue that cryptocurrency should be understood in terms of the New Abnormal (Chapter 10). Indeed, it is no coincidence that the New Abnormal and cryptocurrencies have established themselves since 2010. The abuse of monetary policy under the New Abnormal has enhanced the attraction of currency that is not subject to political manipulation. After a slow start, the cryptocurrency market became more active after 2014, when it became clear that ZIP and the New Abnormal were here to stay. Indeed, cryptocurrency provides insurance against existential risk. The traditional role of gold as a hedge against economic instability is being replaced by cryptocurrency, which has the advantage of being a medium exchange.

Future economic historians will no doubt be fascinated and puzzled by the New Abnormal. It will be regarded as a unique aberration in economic history. Global macroeconomic history has known vicissitudes and episodes such as the Great Depression, the Gold Standard, trade wars and inflation. However, the New Abnormal is different because it abjures fundamental economic principles that, in one form or another, have guided mankind for almost three centuries.

## Globalism v Parochialism and other Dichotomies

The New Abnormal is global in the sense that it has been adopted by most OECD countries. However, its etiology is essentially parochial rather than global. Just because a large number of countries happen to behave in a similar way does not necessarily mean that they are responding to common global factors. The Organization of the Petroleum Exporting Countries (OPEC) oil price shocks generated worldwide stagflation in the 1970s because crude oil was a global common factor. Global studies of the world economy (Beenstock 1984, Bruno and Sachs 1985, Goodhart and Pradhan 2020) stand back in search of these common factors; they are top–down rather than bottom–up. They focus on the forest rather than the trees. Although the present study is concerned with a global phenomenon, the New Abnormal, it does not adopt a global perspective to study it; it is parochial or bottom–up and the forest emerges from the individual trees. Each tree or country had its own particular reasons for adopting the New Abnormal, starting with Japan in 1996 and ending with Australia in 2019. On the other hand, the New Abnormal was and remains contagious, so when one country adopted it, it spread to others. However, this does not detract from the essential parochiality of the New Abnormal.

It has been argued that slower economic growth in OECD countries has been induced by a growing conflict of interest between senior business management and shareholders (Smithers 2013). In theory, chief executive officers (CEO) should act as agents of their principals, their shareholders. If CEOs were loyal agents, they would promote economic growth because it is in the interest of shareholders. The principal – agent problem arises when agents have different agendas from their principals. Smithers argues that for many different reasons shareholders have lost control over CEOs, who have been more concerned with their short-term career development than with the long-term interest of shareholders. This is an example of a parochial theory turned global. The agency problem has increased in each country for reasons which are common across countries.

Econometricians have usefully clarified the conceptual difference between the global and the parochial. The "reflection problem" identified by Manski (1995) distinguished between two possible reasons why individuals might behave similarly. The first is "contextual": common exogenous variables influence their behavior. The second is "endogenous": the individuals concerned happen to influence one another. In the first there is no causal relationship between individuals, but matters are different in the second. Endogeneity might arise for many different reasons, including herding, social rivalry, and externalities of various forms. Spatial econometricians distinguish between strong and weak spatial dependence (Chudik, Pesaran and Tosseti 2011, Beenstock and Felsenstein 2019, Chapter 10). Spatial dependence is "strong" when the correlation between them is independent of distance, which arises when spatial units are influenced by common factors with heterogeneous factor loadings. Spatial dependence is "weak" when the correlation between them varies inversely with distance and tends to zero. When dependence is strong there is no causal relation between spatial units. Matters are different under weak dependence.

The parochial perspective of global developments implies endogenous reflection or weak spatial dependence. The global perspective of global developments implies contextual reflection or strong spatial dependence. According to the latter, the advent of ZIP stems from a decrease in the world rate of interest

(Goodhart and Pradhan 2020), whereas, according to the former, ZIP became global through contagion.

A related dichotomy concerns "real" versus "nominal" or "monetary" theories of global developments. For example, inflation ceased to be an issue in OECD countries until 2022. Goodhart and Pradhan explain this development in terms of real theory; China's integration into the world economy increased global aggregate supply, which moderated world inflation. By contrast, I explain this phenomenon in terms of monetary theory; ZIP generated a liquidity trap so that inflation ceased to be an issue. As for the future, Goodhart and Pradhan envisage a resurgence of inflation because of a "great demographic reversal," a real phenomenon, whereas I envisage a resurgence because of the release of kinetic inflation, a monetary phenomenon. However, other aspects of the New Abnormal have real rather than monetary roots. For example, Japan's inability to carry out structural reforms (Chapter 8), which led into the New Abnormal, is a real phenomenon, as is the inability of the US to carry out structural reforms in its banking and financial institutions.

A further dichotomy concerns the development of an overarching theory of the New Abnormal versus the generation of empirical evidence in its favor. I am mainly concerned with the former rather than the latter, although I am obviously not indifferent to providing persuasive empirical evidence. The development of coherent theory comes before econometric evidence to corroborate it. A peculiar characteristic of the New Abnormal is the absence of inflation despite expansionary fiscal and monetary policies. Another peculiar characteristic is the coexistence of large and even increasing rates of return on fixed assets (capital), despite the fact that, thanks to ZIP and QE, the real cost of long-term capital is almost zero and even negative. To account for these peculiarities, I revive liquidity trap theory and propose a new theory of existential risk. I also use this theory to account for the decrease in fertility in many countries, along the same lines as the decrease in capital investment.

I hope this theory is persuasive. I also hope that it is empirically convincing. I therefore provide supportive empirical data, but I avoid here detailed econometric analysis and hypothesis testing. It is especially difficult to test the existential risk hypothesis while the New Abnormal is still in force (Chapter 5). So, if some readers feel unconvinced by some of my empirical analysis, they might nevertheless appreciate the broad theoretical perspective that I propose. At the very least, I hope they will appreciate my attempt to make sense of the New Abnormal in terms of orthodox economic theory, and to take seriously the prospect that it is living on borrowed time.

## Covid-19 Pandemic

This book was planned and designed before the outbreak of the Covid-19 pandemic in early 2020. In fact, I planned to write it in 2016, but abandoned it when the Federal Reserve began to raise interest rates under the chairmanship of Janet Yellen. I thought that this heralded the beginning of the end for the New Abnormal. It would be a matter of time until other central banks raised interest rates. I was wrong on three counts. First, other central banks did not end ZIP. Second, the Federal Reserve began to cut its interest rates in September 2019. Third, further central banks, such as Australia in 2019, joined ZIP. So, in December 2019 I returned to my original plan. Then came Covid-19.

This isn't the first pandemic with which the world has had to cope. In previous pandemics business carried on as usual. By April 2020 it became clear that this time business would not carry on as usual. It also became clear that Covid-19 mortality mainly involved older people with limited life expectancy due to background morbidity. If ever there was a case for business to carry on as usual, it was Covid-19, because the economic and social cost of lost life years was small relative to other pandemics in which younger people were at risk. In Chapter 9 I estimate the economic cost per life year saved through lockdowns and other mitigation policies. It is enormous. So, what was different about Covid-19? The answer is that it is part of the New Abnormal. Had Covid-19 broken out in, say, 2005, it would most probably have been dealt with like swine flu, which broke out in 2009. Business would have carried on as usual. Indeed, experience of the New Abnormal prior to Covid-19 prepared the ground for "curve flattening" in 2020.

If this book was justified before Covid-19, it is all the more justified afterwards. During the Covid-19 crisis, deeply indebted governments became even more indebted as a result of double-digit fiscal deficits. During 2020, debt-to-GDP ratios increased by between 10 and 30 percentage points, reflecting the increase in fiscal deficits and the decrease in GDP. Changes on this scale, which normally take a decade, occurred in less than a year. Central banks would have cut their interest rates if they could, but, with the exception of the Federal Reserve and Bank of New Zealand, there was nothing to cut. So, they engaged in massive QE in the hope that this might help, as if there was insufficient liquidity in the first place. For the first time in its history the Federal Reserve broke precedent by buying junk bonds in the hope that this might improve the survival chances of their issuers. Central banks that had limited QE to the purchase of treasury securities broke precedent with respect to financial distancing between central banks and businesses by extending QE to the purchase of commercial securities. Furthermore, whereas previously central banks announced the scale of QE in advance so that it was understood that it would not be open ended, in July 2020 the Bank of Japan announced that henceforth QE was to be unlimited.

The New Abnormal became yet more abnormal with the Covid-19 pandemic. If the political economy of ZIP was already deeply entrenched by 2020, it was even more deeply entrenched by 2022. There can be no doubt that the Covid-19 pandemic has reduced the prospects for an orderly exit from ZIP in particular and the New Abnormal in general. As discussed in Chapter 9, the return to normality has suffered a major but not lethal setback, which makes the design of normalization policy more complex than it was before the pandemic.

Fiscal deficits induced by the Covid-19 pandemic are different from regular fiscal deficits; they should not be judged on the same basis as fiscal deficits in normal times. They may be justified in terms of Rawlsian distributive justice. Rawls (1971) surmised that before they are born people would agree to redistribute income to their worst-off cohort members. Before they are born, individuals are under a veil of ignorance, and wish to insure themselves against the risk of being worst-off. This second principle of distributive justice (the first being equality before the law) lies at the heart of social insurance theory. Although this principle has been challenged (Nozick 1974), we accept it uncritically for the present.

By similar argument, unborn cohorts should agree to an insurance policy to cover themselves against natural disasters, such as the Covid-19 pandemic. It is in the interests of future generations to pool the risks of natural disasters with the current generation. It implements Rawls' second principle of justice intergenerationally rather than intragenerationally.

Viewed in this way, it is intergenerationally just to finance the Covid-19 pandemic by increasing public debt, which will be paid off by future generations. In any case, provided economic growth continues, future generations will be better off than the current generation, and will be more able to afford the cost of the pandemic.

## Behavioral Macroeconomics

As mentioned, macroeconomic orthodoxy has been attacked from without by behavioral economists as well as from within. Our critique of ZIP and the New Abnormal is addressed exclusively to the attack from within. Behavioral economists draw attention to empirical "anomalies," which appear to be inconsistent with the axiom of rationality upon which modern economic theory is based. Subsequently, they seek to evince rules to predict anomalous behavior without recourse to rationalism. This is an almost impossible challenge because, whereas rationality is finite and well defined, irrationality is open ended. There is only one rational answer to the sum 1 + 1, but there is an infinity of irrational answers. Whereas all rational theories are similar, all behavioral theories differ in their own ad hoc, irrational way. Prospect theory (Kahneman and Tversky 1979), based on endowment effects and framing, sought to explain anomalies in consumer behavior, but progress has been disappointing.

There has also been a basic misunderstanding about axiomatic science. Axiomatic science is tested not by challenging its axioms, but by trying to falsify its predictions (Popper 1963; Friedman 1953). For example, utility theory predicts that consumers buy less when prices are raised. It is based on rationality and the axiom that there is an unobservable phenomenon such as utility. Failure to falsify the theory empirically means that the theory is corroborated. It does not mean that the theory and its axioms are correct. It simply means that it is as if consumers are rational and experience utility.

Nor does it mean that all consumers are rational and experience utility. This is because hypotheses are tested by frequentist methods based on probability theory. An empirical test with a p-value of 0.05 means that there are individuals who are anomalies. There would be no anomalies only if p-values were zero. Just as one or more swallows do not make a spring, a number of anomalies do not mean a hypothesis is rejected. Matters would naturally be different if there were too many anomalies. But in such cases p-values would be too high, and the hypothesis would be falsified. Much of modern medicine would be cast aside if we took the methodology of anomalies seriously. The fact that aspirin doesn't cure headaches for some does not mean that the pharmacological theory behind aspirin is false.

In summary, behavioral economics is based on a misunderstanding about hypothesis testing, and in the absence of axioms, it has failed to develop useful theory. For these reasons, there is no need to rebut the attack from without from behavioral economics. Matters are different regarding the attack from within, to which the present critique of ZIP is addressed.

## Theory in Brief

In 1996 Japan was the first country to adopt ZIP in more than three centuries of central bank history (Chapter 5). Central bank policy rates had been small and even less than 1 percent, but they had never been zero. This unprecedented action was a desperate response to a real cause: the end of the Japanese economic miracle. In 2008 the Federal Reserve adopted ZIP in response to the Subprime Crisis. ZIP was not adopted because global interest rates suddenly become zero. Rather, global interest rates tended to zero because of ZIP.

Once countries had adopted ZIP, conventional monetary policy was no longer feasible. Because the rate of interest on currency is zero, central bank policy rates cannot be negative unless central banks pay interest to banks for borrowing from them. So central bankers engaged in QE to fill the void. In doing so, they flattened yield curves so that long-term rates of interest tended to zero too.

As interest rates in general become zero, Keynes' liquidity trap theory predicts that expansionary monetary policy cannot be inflationary because the demand for money is infinitely elastic. Money and bonds become perfect substitutes. The public is prepared to hold infinite amounts of liquidity without spending it.

Because interest rates are zero, the service cost of public debt is zero. This encourages governments to run fiscal deficits, as result of which debt-to-GDP ratios increase. For example, "The world has changed. In a very low interest-rate environment like we're in, what we're seeing is that even though the amount of debt relative to the economy has gone up, the interest burden hasn't ... But right now, with interest rates at historical lows, the smartest thing we can do is to act big." (Janet Yellen, Congressional Hearing, January 19, 2021).

The New Abnormal combines ZIP with fiscal deficits and mounting debt-to-GDP ratios without inflation. It turns the Old Normal on its head, as if your dietician told you that if you eat as much as possible fast enough, you won't put on weight because you ingest faster than your metabolism can respond.

If ZIP could be maintained forever, the New Abnormal might be sustainable. However, this would mean that the central bank eventually owns all the financial and real assets of the economy (as pointed out by Patinkin (1966)), which would be incompatible with free market democracy. Since interest rates won't remain zero forever, existential risk is induced about when the New Abnormal will break down. Existential risk adversely effects business investment, which reduces economic growth. It also increases the risk premium on fixed assets so that their rate of return is positive, despite the fact that the cost of capital is zero. The rate of return on fixed assets is the "natural" rate of interest. Just as business investors are frightened of the future, so are prospective parents. Fertility is expected to be low under the New Abnormal.

The New Abnormal self-destructs because, with the passage of time, debt-to-GDP ratios increase and the velocity of circulation of money decreases, hence existential risk gets progressively larger. The former puts upward pressure on interest rates directly, and the latter increases kinetic inflation, which puts upward pressure on interest rates indirectly. At some point, the central bank will no longer be able to withstand upward pressure on interest rates, the dam will burst, ZIP will end, and so will the New Abnormal.

Yellen's words at her Congressional Hearings are somewhat disinguous. The cost of debt service is low because the Federal Reserve has flattened interest rates through ZIP and massive QE. The Federal Reserve and the Treasury are acting together. The low interest rate environment is not the *deus ex machina* that she presumes.

## The Chapters Ahead

We begin in Chapter 2 by setting out the macroeconomic theory for understanding ZIP. A central theme is that since the 1990s a dominant macroeconomic paradigm has emerged, which has been adopted by practitioners, especially in central banks, such as the Federal Reserve, the European Central Bank and the Bank of England. It has also been adopted in smaller central banks, including the Bank of Israel. This paradigm goes by various names, including Neo-Wicksellian macroeconomics, New Keynesian macroeconomics, and dynamic stochastic general equilibrium (DSGE) macroeconomic theory. There are three common denominators to these schools of macroeconomic theory. The first is that the operating instrument for monetary policy is the rate of interest set by central banks, rather than the quantity of money. The second concerns the primary role of the "natural rate of interest," originally proposed by Wicksell in his *Interest and Prices* published in 1898, in the determination of macroeconomic activity. The third, is the assumption that prices and nominal wages are sufficiently inflexible or sticky to enable central banks to influence macroeconomic activity through their interest rate policy. There is a fourth common denominator, which is methodological, and which is the focus of Chapter 3.

We use the term Neo-Wicksellian macroeconomics to embrace New Keynesian and DSGE models because, in principle, the natural rate of interest should play a key role in these models. New Keynesian models embody equations for aggregate demand, inflation and a Taylor rule for the rate of interest set by the central bank. When inflation is on target and the output gap is zero, the rate of interest set by the central bank should equal the natural rate of interest plus the target rate of inflation. Aggregate supply is determined outside the model; New Keynesian models do not articulate the relation between aggregate supply, capital accumulation, and the difference between the money and natural rates of interest.

DSGE models combine New Keynesian elements regarding aggregate demand, inflation and the rate of interest set by the central bank, and they draw on Real Business Cycle theory to determine aggregate supply within the model. In the latter, capital accumulates if the natural rate of interest as expressed by the return to capital exceeds the real cost of capital. Also, intertemporal substitution in labor supply implies that employment is procyclical. Aggregate supply varies directly with capital and employment. Consequently, the output gap is endogenous in DSGE models, and the natural rate of interest features in the Taylor rule for the rate of interest set by the central bank, as well as in the process of capital accumulation and aggregate supply.

Chapter 2 provides the theoretical background to Neo-Wicksellian macroeconomics. The crucial issue concerns the empirical representation of Wicksell's natural rate of interest in Neo-Wicksellian theory. We explain that there are two rival representations, which have radically different implications for the design of monetary policy. The first in order of chronology is due to Patinkin (1966). The second is due to Woodford (2003). Both authors named their books after Wicksell's. Patinkin's is *Money, Interest and Prices*, and Woodford's *Interest and Prices* is identical to Wicksell's. This is no coincidence. Because Wicksell was writing in 1898, he referred to capital rather differently to how it was defined in the twentieth century. Patinkin (a Talmudical scholar used to interpreting ancient texts) interpreted the natural rate of interest as the return on fixed capital assets. Woodford interpreted it as the rate of interest that would be observed if wages and prices were perfectly flexible. To be fair to Woodford, he also referred to this interest rate by the "equilibrium" rate of interest.

The thesis in Chapter 2 is that Patinkin was right and Woodford was wrong. The theoretical implications of this mistaken identity are a central feature in Chapter 2. Indeed, a generation of economists and central bankers have followed Woodford. This has led them down the road to ZIP in the mistaken belief that the natural rate of interest is in fact zero. The irony is that these economists refer to themselves as Neo-Wicksellian, despite their ignoring Wicksell's natural rate of interest.

Chapter 2 recalls Keynes' liquidity trap and reminds readers that, if interest rates are zero, monetary growth is not inflationary. Monetary expansion is like "full gas in neutral" because the demand for money becomes infinitely elastic as the rate of interest tends to zero. This simple theory explains the puzzle why there has been no inflation since the adoption of ZIP. The absence of inflation does not prove that orthodox macroeconomic theory has broken down. On the contrary, orthodox macroeconomic theory explains why ZIP is not inflationary. It also implies that when ZIP eventually comes to an end the kinetic inflation built up under ZIP threatens to become actual.

Since central banks cannot cut interest rates under ZIP, they have found a new purpose in QE. Under the Old Normal, QE would have similar monetary effects to open-market operations: aggregate demand would increase. However, under ZIP these effects disappear because the economy is stuck in a liquidity trap in which the demand for money is infinitely elastic. Increasing liquidity through QE or other methods makes no difference to aggregate demand, as predicted by Keynes (1936). In the early stages of ZIP, QE might continue to have some effect on aggregate demand because the public might expect ZIP to be temporary. However, once the public understands that ZIP is here to stay, QE turns out to be a mere window-dressing operation in which the central bank buys bonds, which have a zero return, with high-powered money, which has a zero return.

More importantly, QE has broken the institution of financial distancing between central banks and the public. Central bank purchases of commercial bonds, including junk bonds, has crossed a red line that is as old as central banking itself in the Anglo-American tradition. By contrast, the Bank of Japan and the Deutsche Bundesbank were more traditionally involved in directing credit to the business sector.

Chapter 2 discusses the relation between fiscal deficits and ZIP. The obvious point is that under ZIP the cost of debt service tends to zero. Whereas under the Old Normal the cost of debt service reduced the primary deficit, under ZIP almost all the deficit constitutes the primary deficit. ZIP has contributed, in part, to spiraling debt-to-GDP ratios because governments feel that issuing debt does not cost anything, as per Janet Yellen's remarks above. Of course, this would be true if ZIP lasted forever. However, if ZIP comes to an end, the cost of debt service would be prohibitive, as noted.

Chapter 2 concludes with a critique of Interest Parity Theory (IPT), which has been a major influence on the conduct of monetary policy, especially by central banks in small open economies. IPT has played a central role in the epidemiology of ZIP because it implies that, if these economies do not adopt ZIP, their exchange rates will appreciate permanently. IPT implies that international capital flows are perfectly elastic; if the rate of interest in a country plus the expected rate of appreciation of its currency happened to be fractionally larger than interest rates abroad, *all* the world's capital would immediately flow into the country. If, more realistically, *some* of the world's capital flowed into the country, i.e., IPT is relative rather than absolute, interest rate policy has only a temporary effect on the exchange rate.

This result was well-known before absolute IPT was adopted by the New Keynesian, Neo-Wicksellians and the DSGE movement, but has been forgotten. Indeed, central banks in small open economies that adopted ZIP to protect their exchange rates discovered that their exchange rates weakened temporarily as predicted by relative IPT instead of permanently as predicted by absolute IPT. Had they understood this in advance, they might not have adopted ZIP in the first place.

Whereas Chapter 2 is theoretical, Chapter 3 is largely methodological. It describes how empirical methods in macroeconomics have become looser and less rigorous, while in microeconomics empirical methods have become more rigorous. Indeed, applied macroeconomics has become increasingly postmodern, while the opposite has happened in microeconomics. What passes for hypothesis testing in macroeconomics has become lax to the point where most of the time macroeconomic models are used to provide narratives about macroeconomic developments. More seriously, these narratives are not just retrospective, they are also prospective.

Postmodern macroeconomists believe that their New Keynesian and DSGE models are true. However, they use data to set their unknown parameters, rather in the way that climate scientists do to parametrize their models (Beenstock, Reingewertz and Paldor 2016). They use methods of calibration or various Bayesian methods to "fit" their models to data. This kind of approach is based on the principle of "indirect estimation," which, as we shall see, is akin to "extraordinary" least squares.

We argue that in 1980 macroeconomics underwent a methodological crisis from which it has not yet fully recovered. Prior to 1980 there was broad methodological agreement between macroeconomists about how to test macroeconomic theory. Subsequently, three methodological developments emerged. The first was atheoretical and purely statistical, based on vector autoregression (VAR) models. The second went to the other extreme: the models were theoretically sophisticated, but their respect for data was secondary if not minimal. The third retained the modernist methodological tradition of before 1980. The strongest of these developments in macroeconomics was the second, and remains so today. Indeed, institutions such as the International Monetary Fund provide technical assistance to finance ministries in member countries (such as Georgia and Armenia), with training in the construction of New Keynesian and DSGE models.

ZIP is in part born out of the second, postmodern, tradition. Belief in narratives is dangerous because after some time their narrators believe in them absolutely. Instead of modernist scientific skepticism, according to which hypotheses are regarded as null hypotheses to be refuted by data, in the sense proposed by David Hume and Karl Popper, they are taken instead to be true. Moreover, when events cease to fit the narrative, the models are not rejected. Instead, they are patched up piecemeal to account for the aberration until the next aberration arises, as we explain in Chapter 3.

In Chapter 3 we also describe some important recent methodological developments concerning "indirect inference" intended to bridge the gap between postmodern macroeconomics in the New Abnormal and modernist macroeconomics under the Old Normal. Influential critics of the Old Normal, including a number of Nobel laureates, might have had a point that what passed for modernist methodology prior to 1980 rejected "too many good models" because it failed to see the big picture embodied in macroeconomic models. As described in Chapter 3, they argued that the standards of frequentist, classical econometrics were too strict, and they proposed looser criteria for model evaluation. However, during the last forty years, they have failed to formalize what these looser criteria should be.

Indirect inference is a methodology for the empirical testing of models, such as DSGE models, whose parameters have been chosen through various methods of indirect estimation, including calibration and Bayesian methods. Indirect inference is not frequentist in the sense that the goodness of fit is compared with the actual data. Instead, the sophistication of indirectly estimated models is compared with a naïve alternative, such as a simple VAR model. The latter is a "no brainer" model, whereas the former is rich in macroeconomic theory. The basic idea is that sophisticated, structurally specified DSGE models, rich in economic theory, should outperform "no brainer" VAR models in explaining the data. In summary, indirect inference establishes empirical criteria for the evaluation of DSGE and other models that are based on heterodox indirect methods of estimation.

We report tests based on indirect inference, which overwhelmingly reject the influential Smets-Wouters (2007) DSGE model of the US economy. These tests are much looser than standard frequentist tests. Indirect inference formalizes the looser criteria mentioned above. It constitutes a modern method of evaluation for postmodern macroeconomic models. It tests these models in the looser terms proposed by the DSGE movement.

In summary, the thesis in Chapter 3 is that ZIP has been embraced by central banks in part as a result of methodological laxity in macroeconomics. This criticism is taken up specifically in Chapter 4 with respect to the role of the natural rate of interest in Neo-Wicksellian monetary policy. Chapter 4 begins with a literature review regarding the measurement of the natural rate of interest, which has been exclusively concerned with Woodford's definition. We note that New Keynesian and DSGE models do not specify the natural rate of interest even by proxy, so it is treated as a missing variable. This is an important variable to omit, especially in models that are supposed to be Neo-Wicksellian. Since this omitted variable is expected to be correlated with output, inflation, and other included variables, its omission most probably induces model mis-specification.

Putting this criticism to one side, if inflation is on target and the output gap is zero, the rate of interest that induces this "divine coincidence" must be the natural rate of interest. If the divine coincidence occurs when the rate of interest is zero, it must be the case that the natural rate of interest is zero. This simple but flawed logic has had a major influence on the descent into ZIP by many central banks. This is rather like a blind man inferring that there is no tiger in the room because it hasn't attacked him yet.

The main new contribution of Chapter 4 is the focus on the Wicksell-Patinkin definition of the natural rate of interest, which refers to the return on fixed capital assets. It is surprising that in only three countries, the US since 1960, Israel since 1980 and the UK since 2019, do the statistical authorities systematically publish data on the rate of return on fixed assets in the business sector. For other countries, we have tried to construct these data. These data show that the natural rate of interest is large and positive. In New Keynesian and DSGE models, it is assumed that, when central banks cut their rate of interest, business investment should increase, as a result of which the rate of return on capital should decrease and the capital–output ratio should increase. In the long run the real rate of interest and the return on capital should move together.

The adoption of ZIP was expected to boost business investment, increase the capital–output ratio and lower the rate of return on capital. None of these events took place. Either the return to capital did not change, or it increased. It is as if the risk premium on business investment increased as a result of ZIP. This would be consistent with the hypothesis that ZIP increased existential risk. Investors are frightened by the abnormality of ZIP, and instead of inducing them to invest, it deters them. They understand that ZIP cannot last, so they cut back on investment to reduce their risk exposure. When ZIP eventually ends, there will be a hard landing because, apart from anything else, debt-laden governments, which benefited from zero debt-service costs under ZIP, will be unable to service their debts once the rate of interest is positive.

Had central banks focused on the return to capital as the natural rate of interest, they might have understood that something had gone seriously wrong. ZIP was having no effect on the natural rate of interest. More than half a century of US data shows that the gap between the return on fixed assets and the rate of interest set by the Federal Reserve had never been greater. This should have served as an alarm bell. With almost no exception, nobody paid any attention to the real economy and the return on capital. The divine coincidence should be replaced by the "holy trinity": the central bank does not need to change its rate of interest provided inflation is on target, the output gap is zero, and its rate of interest plus target inflation equals the natural rate of interest as measured by the return to capital.

In summary, Neo-Wicksellian macroeconomic theory has benignly neglected the role of the natural rate of interest. As a result, macroeconomic theory has turned into Hamlet without the Prince. This has happened because in New Keynesian models the specification of aggregate supply is determined outside the model. DSGE models combine New Keynesian elements on aggregate demand and inflation, and Real Business Cycle elements on capital accumulation and the natural rate of interest. Although the natural rate of interest is determined inside DSGE models, in practice it has been treated as a nuisance parameter, which may be ignored. Had macroeconomists attached importance to the return on capital as a measure of the natural rate of interest, it is unlikely that the descent into ZIP would have occurred by default.

Chapter 5 focuses on four aspects of the New Abnormal. We begin by chronicling the global descent into ZIP, starting with Japan in 1996 and ending with Australia in 2019 and New Zealand in 2020. The reasons for Japan and Australia are very different from each other, but the Subprime Crisis serves as the common denominator for the Federal Reserve and the Bank of England. So far, no central bank has managed to extricate itself from ZIP. Janet Yellen, as chairperson of the Federal Reserve, attempted to extricate the Federal Reserve in 2016, but for reasons discussed in Chapter 5, the Federal Reserve began to cut interest rates in 2019, and reinstated ZIP with the outbreak of the Covid-19 pandemic in 2020.

Other central banks, including the Bank of Israel, adopted ZIP temporarily, then subsequently readopted it permanently. These events occurred despite the fact that Israel was not affected by the Subprime Crisis, and its economy was stable and strong with no inflation. Moreover, natural gas discoveries in the Eastern Mediterranean turned Israel into an energy producer. There were no objective reasons for Israel's descent into ZIP. A case history for Israel is provided, which draws on the exchange rate theory presented in Chapter 2. Governor Karnit Flug of the Bank of Israel reduced interest rates in the mistaken belief that this would weaken the shekel. She also undertook massive forex intervention to weaken the shekel with no effect. Thus did Israel descend into ZIP because of a simple misunderstanding about the difference between absolute and relative interest parity theory and its implications for the operation of foreign exchange markets.

To place the abnormality of the New Abnormal in its historical perspective, we record the interest rates set by the Bank of England since its foundation in 1694. For more than three hundred years this rate of interest was never less than 2 percent. So, when the Bank of England adopted ZIP in 2009, it broke with historical precedent and entered into uncharted macroeconomic waters. We also provide historical data for younger central banks, such as those of Norway and

Switzerland, which date back to the nineteenth century, and the Federal Reserve, which dates back to the twentieth century.

What matters for investment is the long-term real cost of capital rather than the current inflation-adjusted policy rate. We trace the relation between the latter and the former through the forward rates implied by the yield curves on treasury securities, and the spreads between the yields to redemption on corporate and treasury securities. At first, ZIP was expected to be temporary because long-term forward rates remained unchanged. Indeed, it took a few years before long-term forward rates began to decrease. This interpretation is also supported by the futures prices of treasury securities. However, even as of mid-2020 long-term forward rates exceeded 1 percent, suggesting perhaps that at some point over the next twenty years ZIP is expected to come to an end.

The second aspect of the New Abnormal concerns the resort to QE by almost all central banks. These central banks turned to QE out of frustration. Having thrown away their main operating instrument of monetary policy by descending into ZIP, they tried to reinvent themselves through QE. For some of them the scale of QE has been staggering, as recorded in Chapter 5. At first QE was limited in scale (a fixed amount announced in advanced) and scope (treasury bonds only). More recently, QE has become open ended and has been extended to corporate bonds and equity. The latter has broken the categorical imperative of Anglo–US banking regarding financial distancing between central banks and the non-bank private sector.

The third aspect of the New Abnormal is spiraling debt-to-GDP ratios fueled by oversized fiscal deficits as a percentage of GDP. Under the Old Normal there was a consensus regarding the importance of fiscal probity, especially between business cycles. Indeed, the Maastricht Treaty of 1992 set targets for debt-to-GDP ratios at 60 percent, but almost nobody cares about this now. Even before the Covid-19 pandemic, the debt-to-GDP ratio exceeded 200 percent in Japan, was 150 percent in Italy, and was almost 100 percent in the US.

The fourth aspect of the New Abnormal is the rapid growth in money supply induced by QE and the long-term commitment to ZIP, which implies that the supply of base or high-powered money is infinitely elastic. Liquidity trap theory implies that, when the rate of interest is zero, money supply growth has no effect on aggregate demand and inflation. The scale of this abnormality is measured by the income velocity of circulation of money. Prior to the New Abnormal, velocity tended to increase globally because of fintech improvements that enabled the public to manage its affairs with less money. Subsequently, velocity has ceased to increase, and has even decreased significantly in countries after adopting ZIP.

Kinetic inflation may be measured by the percentage decrease in velocity under the New Abnormal. For example, if velocity decreased by 50 percent, kinetic inflation would be approximately 50 percent. This inflation ceases to be kinetic when ZIP ends.

In summary, the purpose of Chapter 5 is simply to document the scale of the New Abnormality in its four aspects. Although the main focus is on developments before the Covid-19 pandemic, these abnormalities became yet more abnormal subsequently. Central banks have massively increased their QE programs. Indeed, in some countries, such as Japan, QE has become open ended and unlimited. Finance ministries have been running larger budget deficits. The Covid-19 pandemic has made this book more relevant than before because many countries have dug themselves ever deeper into the ZIP trap, from which escape becomes ever harder.

Had the Covid-19 pandemic broken out under the Old Normal, one suspects that governments, as in the past, might have reacted more conservatively by running smaller budget deficits, and central banks might have reacted by reducing interest rates without recourse to ZIP and QE. The heterodox fiscal and monetary policies under the New Abnormal most probably induced policy makers to undertake more radical action in response to the Covid-19 pandemic.

Chapter 4 showed that the natural rate of interest as measured by the return to capital has increased relative to the real cost of capital under the New Abnormal. We attributed this phenomenon to an increase in the risk premium required on business investment induced by the emergence of existential risk under the New Abnormal. Business investors are more fearful of the future, and are frightened of investing despite the fact that the cost of capital is cheap. In Chapter 6 we ask whether the same phenomenon applies to fertility. Are parents reluctant to bring children into the world because they are fearful of the future? Just as existential risk induced by the New Abnormal deters business investment, perhaps it also adversely affects fertility. If it does, then the New Abnormal will have adverse consequences for secular economic growth for two reasons. It reduces capital accumulation and it also reduces the growth in employment through negative demographics.

During the New Abnormal in Japan, since the 1990s, fertility has almost halved. At the same time longevity has continued to increase. As a result, the dependency ratio (the ratio of pensioners to workers) has increased because there are more pensioners and fewer workers. The socio-economic implications of the demographic imbalance in Japan (OECD 2019) have become a major concern of public policy. In Chapter 6 we ask whether the New Abnormal is partly responsible for this socio-economic crisis. In doing so, we draw on the quantity–quality theory of fertility (Becker 1992), according to which parents trade off the quantity of children that they have with the human capital invested in each child. The theory predicts that if the return to human capital increases or its cost decreases, parents will curtail their fertility because they substitute quality for quantity. Since ZIP directly reduces the cost of investing in human capital, it should discourage fertility. It also predicts that, if parents benefit directly or indirectly from the income of their children, existential risk induced by the New Abnormal will tend to reduce fertility.

Chapter 6 elaborates on the theoretical relationship between existential risk and fertility in terms of quantity–quality theory. It compares the fertility rates in countries that adopted ZIP with the rates in those that did not, and it compares fertility rates in countries that adopted ZIP sooner with the rates in countries that adopted ZIP later.

Chapter 6 is more speculative than other chapters. Its purpose is to suggest a potential theoretical connection between global fertility decline and the New Abnormal. If this connection can be established empirically, its implications would be far-reaching. Existential risk induced by the New Abnormal not only reduces capital accumulation through its adverse effect on business investment, it also reduces the growth of labor supply through its adverse effect on fertility. A downward spiral in economic growth is generated, which exacerbates existential risk.

In Chapter 7 we examine some of the socio-economic implications of ZIP and the New Abnormal. We begin by discussing the implications for pensions, and then turn our attention to economic inequality and insurance. Pensioners are expected to be worse off under ZIP when they retire because the return on their savings is obviously lower. It may also be that they save less towards their pension because the return is lower. Baby boomers retired before ZIP and the New Abnormal. They benefited from the economic stability under the Old Normal. Their children (Generation X and especially Millennials) will have spent most of their working lives under the New Abnormal. Their pension income is likely to be smaller than their baby-boomer parents' income because of ZIP. Most probably, Generation X and Millennials are destined to live under the shadow of the New Abnormal. If and when the New Abnormal ends, baby boomers' grandchildren (Millennials) will be the chief beneficiaries.

Under the Old Normal, insurance companies obtained positive returns on their premium income, so that insurance premia varied inversely with market rates of interest. Under ZIP and the New Abnormal, insurance premia are expected to increase because insurance companies get no return on invested premia. In Chapter 7 we discuss the theoretical implications of ZIP for insurance pricing, and investigate empirically the effects of ZIP on insurance premia.

Chapter 7 also considers the implications of the New Abnormal for economic inequality. Specifically, the theory of the factorial distribution of income proposed in Chapter 4 is related to the Gini coefficient, which measures the personal distribution of income. This relation depends critically on the elasticity of substitution between labor and capital, which in turn depends on the technology of production.

Chapter 8 is devoted to a detailed case study of Japan's descent into ZIP in 1996 and to subsequent developments under the New Abnormal. In particular, we focus on the "tar baby effect," according to which the longer Japan has been entrapped by ZIP, the more stuck it has become. Indeed, currently the prospects of Japan ever escaping from ZIP are very remote. Our case study begins with Japan's economic miracle after World War Two, which ended suddenly in the 1980s. This miracle was corporatist in the sense that the keiretsu (industrial conglomerates such as Mitsubishi), government ministries, such as the Ministry of Finance and the Ministry of International Trade and Industry, and the Bank of Japan were all heavily involved with each other. This corporatist model of economic development was very different from the Anglo-Saxon model, which attached importance to financial distancing between business, the state, and the central bank on the one hand, and the banking system, the state, and the central bank on the other. Also, the Anglo-Saxon model attached importance to the divide between workers and firms, or between labor and capital, whereas in Japan life-long relations between workers and firms were the norm. In Japan, workers and firms cooperated, whereas elsewhere they antagonized. Finally, the Liberal Democratic Party (LDP) had been in continuous power since the end of hostilities, and was seen as a source of stability and wisdom.

Not only did Japan achieve extraordinary rates of economic growth, it also came out very well from the OPEC oil price hikes in 1973–4 and 1979. Whereas the increases in oil prices halted postwar economic growth in most OECD countries, Japan proved to be a rare exception. Indeed, Japan's corporatist economic model became an attractive rival to the Anglo-Saxon model (Bruno and Sachs 1985).

There is an irony in the affairs of state that when modes of statehood are singled out for praise, shortly afterwards they prove to be failures, as in Japan. At first, 1985–95 was referred to as the "lost decade," suggesting Japan's economic troubles were temporary. These troubles largely revolved around a breakdown in trust. Government officials and central bank personnel were involved in corruption scandals. Accounting firms were misrepresenting company accounts. Banks were concealing zombie assets to which regulators turned a blind eye. Cosy corporatism, which might have suited Japan's postwar recovery, had turned into an incentive incompatible system, which was no longer appropriate as the twenty-first century approached.

The "lost decade" turned into the "lost decade and half," during which Japan descended into ZIP in 1996 and the "New Normal." Prime minister Koizumi (2001–6) realized that Japan had to change in favor of the Anglo-Saxon model. He demoted conservative members of his party (LDP) and undertook reforms, which are detailed in Chapter 8. He was unpopular within the party and with the public, and retired from politics in 2009. Koizumi was Japan's last chance for change. Subsequently, Japan has become increasingly trapped in a ZIP equilibrium, accompanied by spiraling debt-to-GDP ratios, largely negative rates of economic growth, open-ended QE and massive monetization.

Successive studies of the Japanese economy end with the common mantra that, although Japan has thus far failed to reform, it is likely that reform will occur during the next decade. However, with the passage of each decade, the mantra does not change. Chapter 8 looks for a deeper structural reason for Japan's inability to reform in terms of "face-saving" in Japanese culture. Many of Japan's economic traditions, such as lifetime employment, seniority-related pay and mandatory retirement may be regarded as face-saving phenomena, as may other practices, including misreporting company accounts, and the importance of hierarchy in businesses and the public service. This interpretation of Japan's failure to reform suggests that reform in the future is improbable. Japanese culture, which enabled the postwar economic miracle, does not suit the twenty-first century.

In Chapter 9 it is argued that government responses to the Covid-19 pandemic should be regarded as part of the New Abnormal. Pandemics have happened before, but this is the first time that governments have tried to "flatten the curve" of morbidity by undertaking mitigation policy in the form of nationwide lockdowns and other restrictions. This development has incurred enormous economic costs and governments have run historically large fiscal deficits because of increased public expenditure and loss of tax revenue. It is argued that, but for the New Abnormal, governments might have responded more conservatively as they did in the past. Had the Covid-19 pandemic broken out in 2000 instead of 2020, presumably mitigation policy would have been far less radical.

Chapter 9 begins with the Rawlsian case for sharing the cost of the pandemic with future generations in the name of intergenerational equity. This case runs against the grain of the traditional stance on intergenerational equity of global warming and sovereign funds, where the present generation should protect future generations, rather than seeking assistance at the expense of the unborn.

The main focus of Chapter 9 is on the cost per life year saved by mitigation policy. Estimating this cost is methodologically difficult because it is necessary to estimate the counterfactual loss of life that would have occurred in the absence of mitigation. Chapter 9 is devoted to this problem. A theory of mitigation policy is proposed in which the authorities attempt to minimize the joint cost of economic lockdown and loss of life. Matters are complicated by the fact that it takes time for mitigation policy to reduce morbidity and mortality. This generates the phenomenon of instrument instability, which expresses itself in waves of morbidity and mortality on the one hand, and episodes of mitigation policy followed by its relaxation on the other. This theory is applied to estimate the counterfactual loss of life in Israel.

The cost per life year saved is estimated for Israel during the first wave of mitigation policy in the spring of 2020. This cost turns out to be out of all proportion in relation to the shadow value per life year used in the determination of investment in national health. This excess cost measures the abnormality in mitigation policy. Dying from Covid-19 is implicitly given a much larger value than dying from other causes. It measures the hysterical response of the Israeli government to the pandemic. Presumably, the Israeli government is not alone. The excess cost is most probably a lower bound, because it excludes the social cost to children of school closures, the cost of social isolation to the elderly, and the social cost of uncertainty to the public at large.

We also point out that Covid-19 mortality is most probably overestimated. Whereas doctors tend to attribute causes of death from influenza to background illnesses, they apply different criteria to patients who die with Covid-19. The cause of death for patients with chronic heart disease who die with influenza will most probably be attributed to heart disease. The cause of death for patients with chronic heart disease who die with Covid-19 will most probably be attributed to Covid-19. On the other hand, Covid-19 mortality will be underestimated if patients die of Covid-19 at home rather than in hospital. These data problems have led epidemiologists to use "excess mortality" estimates rather than official mortality data for Covid-19 (Karlinsky and Kobak 2021). A surprising and unreasonable result is that excess mortality in some countries, such as Australia, Japan and New Zealand, is negative. In Chapter 9 we explain how this false paradox may arise.

Chapter 9 concludes with a cross-country survey of macroeconomic policy during the pandemic, with special emphasis on New Abnormal phenomena such fiscal deficits, debt-to-GDP ratios, central bank policy rates and QE. The New Abnormal intensified during the pandemic, making it even harder to exit the New Abnormal in 2022 and beyond than it was in 2019 before the outbreak of the pandemic.

Finally, Chapter 10 is concerned with the escape from ZIP and the New Abnormal. It begins with the question, "Can the New Abnormal last forever, as suggested by the experience of Japan?" Our answer is no, because the New Abnormal sows the seeds of its own destruction. Macroeconomic theory (Patinkin 1966) suggests that eventually the central bank must acquire all the economy's financial assets for ZIP to last forever, and the money supply tends to infinity through QE. The central bank becomes the sole owner of all financial and real assets, as a result of which private enterprise breaks down. It also implies that the public is prepared to accumulate money balances forever. The central bank owns all the assets, and in return the public become paper millionaires. At some point the public will increase its spending, and kinetic inflation will break out. This theoretical solution is a politically impossible backstop in democratic societies.

Another preliminary issue concerns the economic status of public sector debt, which has accumulated under the New Abnormal. The common view is that this debt will eventually have to be redeemed in the future at the expense of the public. According to Ricardian equivalence theory, the public regards government debt as a future tax liability, which affects current spending and not merely future spending. According to this view, deficit-financed government spending has no effect on current aggregate spending; it is equivalent to tax-financed government spending. It also means that public debt does not matter per se because the public is indifferent between a "haircut," which would reduce tax liability, and an increase in taxation to reduce public debt. Ricardian equivalence implies that public debt is

not an issue in itself; the real issue is that the public discounts the future tax burden of public debt. We argue, as did Ricardo himself, that Ricardian equivalence
is empirically false and that public debt matters.

Chapter 10 discusses Krugman's (1998) liquidity trap model for terminating
ZIP. However, Krugman ignored public debt, and he probably did not imagine
in 1998 that Japan would still have ZIP in 2020. On the other hand, Krugman's
model might be relevant for economies that are not heavily indebted and which
adopted ZIP relatively recently (such as Israel and Australia). In Chapter 10 we
extend the theory of the descent into ZIP presented in Chapter 2 to the ascent
or escape from ZIP for the case where there is no background morbidity in the
form of huge public indebtedness. Next, we consider the case with background
morbidity (high debt-to-GDP ratios and kinetic inflation).

An exit strategy from the New Abnormal has to deal with three problems.
First the cost of debt service may become prohibitively large, both economically
and politically, especially for countries with large debt-to-GDP ratios. Second,
kinetic inflation may be large. Third, asset prices are expected to fall when ZIP
ends and interest rates become positive. Although the decrease in house prices
is welcome, mortgagees will suffer from higher interest payments and capital
losses.

There are four broad exit strategies. First, governments may cut public sector
debt through "haircuts," as in the private sector. Second, the exit from ZIP will release kinetic inflation, which will reduce debt-to-GDP ratios because public debt
is not indexed to inflation. Third, central banks reverse QE by selling off the assets that they acquired through QE, which should reduce kinetic inflation. Fourth,
governments might engage in tight fiscal policy over several decades until debt-to-
GDP ratios return to sustainable levels. (See Chapter 5 on the US after World War
Two and Israel after the Yom Kippur War).

The third strategy is the least disruptive and conventional. However, it is most
probably not feasible for Japan where the debt-to-GDP ratio is so large. The escape
from ZIP is more difficult the greater is the debt-GDP ratio and kinetic inflation.
We therefore distinguish between countries that have descended into ZIP more recently and have less background morbidity (high debt-to-GDP ratios and kinetic
inflation), such as Israel and Australia, and countries such as Japan, which have extensive background morbidity. Our premise is that ZIP and the New Abnormal are
unsustainable despite the fact the Japan has survived twenty-five years under ZIP.
In any case, survival under ZIP comes at a price: background morbidity eventually
becomes chronic.

In the absence of background morbidity, the escape from ZIP turns out to be
relatively simple. If the public expects ZIP to persist, it will persist. If the public expects ZIP to end, it will end. There are many examples in macroeconomic history
where expectations become self-fulfilling. Inflations have been stopped almost
overnight, by coordinated monetary policy and fiscal policy, such as in Weimar

Germany in 1923 and in Israel in 1985. Once the public truly believes that these policies are going to be implemented, their success becomes self-fulfilling. If central banks announce with conviction that they intend to raise interest rates, it will happen with minimal collateral damage. Indeed, Janet Yellen, chairperson of the Federal Reserve, proved the feasibility of this policy in 2016.

Chapter 10 includes a discussion of cryptocurrencies such as Bitcoin, which have evolved during the New Abnormal. Since the launch of Bitcoin in 2009, cryptocurrencies have established themselves, despite the skepticism voiced by most economists (including eight Nobel laureates). They have particularly consolidated their status since the outbreak of the Covid-19 epidemic. By contrast, we take the cryptocurrency market seriously, and suggest that its meteoric rise is a response to existential risk associated with the New Abnormal. Fears of kinetic inflation and the chaotic collapse of the New Abnormal have caused a flight from fiat money to cryptocurrency. Indeed, cryptocurrency is superior to gold as a safe haven for the simple reason that it is increasingly used in transactions as more and more goods and services are priced in cryptocurrency. Also, fintech developments in the cryptocurrency market have increased their attraction as credit markets and derivatives have developed.

If Gresham's Law implies that cryptocurrencies will eventually drive out fiat money, this would be a major game-changer. In Chapter 10 we stop short of this brave new world by reworking some of the monetary theory presented in Chapter 2 when fiat money and cryptocurrency coexist. An important theoretical result is the "mining irrelevance theorem," according to which the mining costs of cryptocurrency, which are large, do not matter for macroeconomic equilibrium. Another important result is that the price of cryptocurrency varies directly with existential risk. If the New Abnormal ends chaotically, cryptocurrency will survive and have value, whereas fiat money may become worthless with the release of kinetic inflation.

## Synopsis

The New Abnormal is a form of political economy in which central banks set their policy rate to zero, and finance ministries run large budget deficits as a result of which debt-to-GDP ratios increase. Japan adopted the New Abnormal in 1996, the US and UK in 2009, and many other OECD countries subsequently.

Central banks took to QE as their instrument of monetary policy, since their policy rate of interest has a lower bound of zero. QE led to massive expansions in money supply.

Proponents of the New Abnormal point to the absence of inflation to justify it. They have not understood that, according to Keynes' liquidity trap theory, money supply growth is not inflationary when the rate of interest is zero.

Since the New Abnormal is not sustainable, it generates existential risk, which depresses business investment because entrepreneurs are fearful of the future. Existential risk might also be a factor in the global decline in fertility; parents, like entrepreneurs, are fearful of what will happen when the New Abnormal eventually comes to an end, so they have fewer children.

The thesis in this book is revisionist. Orthodox macroeconomic theory explains the rise of the New Abnormal. There is no need for heterodox macroeconomic theory. Also, orthodox macroeconomic theory lights the way out of the New Abnormal back to the Old Normal, in which central banks operate positive policy rates of interest and finance ministries run sustainable fiscal deficits.

The next chapter presents a critique of contemporary macroeconomic theory, which underpinned the descent into the New Abnormal.

# 2

# Where Macroeconomic Theory Went Wrong

This chapter deals with the macroeconomic theory that underpins the chapters ahead. It begins by recalling Wicksellian theory upon which the theory of monetary policy under the Old Normal is based. Whereas macroeconomic textbooks typically refer to money supply as the operating instrument of monetary policy, and economists such as Milton Friedman (1969) advocated base money as the operating instrument for monetary policy, central bankers universally use interest rates rather than base money as their operating instrument. Ever since its establishment as the first central bank in 1694, the Bank of England has used "bank rate" and its successors (minimum lending rate) as its operating instrument.

These operating instruments, base money and interest rates, are mutually exclusive. If base money is the operating instrument, the rate of interest is left to be determined by market forces. If the rate of interest is the operating instrument, the base money stock is left to be determined by market forces. The laws of supply and demand mean that it is impossible to control prices and quantities. These laws also apply to monetary policy. Poole (1970) has discussed the pros and cons of the rival operating instruments. If the demand for money is empirically more stable with respect to output and interest rates than is aggregate demand, then base money is a more efficient operating instrument than the rate of interest. We do not enter into this debate. Instead, we simply accept the reality, that, for better or worse, interest rates serve as the operating instrument of monetary policy universally.

Neo-Wicksellian macroeconomic theory (Woodford 2003, Walsh 2017) has typically focused on the stabilization of output and inflation under the assumption that the "cumulative process" hypothesized by Wicksell (1898) in his *Interest and Prices* is empirically valid. According to this process, investment in fixed assets continues until the "natural" and "money" rates of interest converge. It is no coincidence that Woodford chose *Interest and Prices* for a title. We drew attention in Chapter 1 to the breakdown in this empirical process under the New Abnormal, and its implications for the future of ZIP. Hence, Wicksell's cumulative process shall be a major focus in this chapter

Second, a theoretical framework is proposed to handle the analysis of ZIP and other features of unorthodox monetary policy, such as quantitative easing. In this

*Zero Interest Policy and the New Abnormal.* Michael Beenstock, Oxford University Press.
© Michael Beenstock (2022). DOI: 10.1093/oso/9780192849663.003.0002

framework we add an "intermediate" rate of interest to Wicksell's natural and money rates, which refers to the rate of interest determined through financial intermediation. This minimalist model jointly determines the structure of parallel interest rates, money supply, credit, savings and investment, and the return on fixed assets. Note that Wicksell himself identified the money rate of interest with our intermediate rate of interest, represented by the rate of interest on credit. However, neo-Wicksellians identify it with the rate of interest set by the central bank.

Third, Keynes' liquidity trap theory is recalled to remind us why, under ZIP, monetary growth does not induce inflation. It is no surprise, therefore, that inflation has remained stable under ZIP. Far from the absence of inflation refuting orthodox macroeconomic theory, as purported by proponents of the New Abnormal, orthodox macroeconomic theory predicts the absence of inflation under ZIP, and its outbreak when ZIP ends.

Fourth, we focus on the role of the natural rate of interest in the design of Taylor rules for monetary policy. In Taylor's original rule (Taylor 1993) the natural rate of interest was implicitly fixed (at 2 percent). Subsequently, its role in empirical Taylor rules fell into obscurity, although attempts were made to resuscitate it (Laubach and Williams 2003, Beenstock and Ilek 2010). This development, as we shall see, has played a central role in the political economy of ZIP. The disappearance of the natural rate of interest from empirical Taylor rules has misled central bankers into thinking that there is no social cost to the level of interest rates. Just as there is a cost to output and inflation gaps, so is there a cost to gaps between the natural and money rates of interest.

Fifth, a theory of existential risk is proposed in which the risk premium is the willingness to pay to extricate oneself from exposure to this risk. Existential risk arises when a system of political economy is not sustainable, and its collapse is a matter of time. For example, it was a matter of time before the Bretton Woods system collapsed, or the Soviet Union collapsed. It might be a matter of time before the political economy of ZIP and the New Abnormal collapse. In the nature of things, the existential risk premium is negligible at first, but it increases with the passage of time. It is also influenced by external events in both directions. In the life cycle of existential risk, the risk premium may be negligible for a long time, but it approaches infinity towards the end. Indeed, the end, when it comes, can be sudden.

Sixth, standard macroeconomic theory for open economies is based on absolute interest parity theory, in which financial assets in domestic and foreign currency are assumed, for simplicity, to be perfect substitutes. We show that relative interest parity theory, according to which financial assets in domestic and foreign currency are imperfect substitutes, implies that lower interest rates weaken exchange rates temporarily rather than permanently. This crucial theoretical difference between absolute and relative interest parity will play a central role in understanding the epidemiology of ZIP among central banks.

Finally, the arithmetic relation between debt-to-GDP ratios and fiscal policy is presented, and its implications for the so-called "unpleasant monetary arithmetic" are discussed.

The central theme of this chapter is that contemporary macroeconomic theory has gone astray in two respects. The first concerns the role of the natural rate of interest in New Keynesian and DSGE models. Although the natural rate of interest plays a pivotal role in Wicksell (1898), ironically it has been neglected and even overlooked in Neo-Wicksellian monetary theory. Indeed, influential textbooks such as Walsh (2017) do not refer to it at all. Nor does Woodford (2003), who refers instead to the "equilibrium rate of interest," which turns out to be conceptually different to the natural rate of interest. Another influential textbook (Romer 2019) refers to the equilibrium rate of interest as the natural rate of interest. This oversight has sown confusion, especially in central banks, where the fallacy of the "divine coincidence" (Blanchard and Gali 2007) has led central bankers to believe that if inflation is on target and the output gap is zero under ZIP (when the policy rate of the central bank is zero), it must be the case that the natural rate of interest is zero, or almost so. This fallacy lies at the foundation of the New Abnormal and its associated political economy. This fallacy is exposed and corrected.

The second concerns the confusion between relative and absolute interest parity theory (IPT) in open economy DSGE and New Keynesian models. In the original Mundell-Fleming theory of open economy macroeconomics, developed in the early 1960s (Mundell 1963, Fleming 1962), capital was imperfectly mobile between countries because exchange rate risk implied that assets in different currencies were imperfect substitutes for risk-averse individuals. Influential textbooks such as Parkin and Bade (1988) were based on relative IPT (RIPT), which implied that if the central bank in a country raised its rate of interest it would attract finite capital inflows from abroad. It also implied that international interest rate differentials adjusted for expected exchange rate changes were not necessarily zero because of risk premia. Countries exposed to more exchange rate risk pay a risk premium when they borrow from abroad.

By contrast, absolute IPT (AIPT) makes the simplifying assumption that investors are risk neutral rather than risk averse. AIPT implies that if the central bank raises its interest rate it would attract an infinite capital inflow. This would induce an appreciation of the exchange rate, which would immediately restore uncovered interest rate parity. AIPT has a pedagogic advantage over RIPT in that it is easier to teach and simplifies textbooks on open economy macroeconomics. There is no doubt that it is easier to teach open economy macroeconomics based on AIPT than RIPT. Gradually, RIPT disappeared from macroeconomic curricula. Importantly in the present context, AIPT was adopted by Svensson (2000) in open economy New Keynesian theory and it was adopted by the DSGE movement.

Maybe AIPT simplifies the teaching of open economy macroeconomics, but the simplifying assumption of risk neutrality is unlikely to be empirically useful.

In Chapter 3 we describe how hypothesis testing in macroeconomics has become increasingly subjective to the point that false hypotheses are regarded as true. This explains how AIPT replaced RIPT. An important implication of this aberration is that central bankers mistakenly believed that if they cut their policy rates, it would weaken their exchange rate permanently. By contrast, we show that under RIPT exchange rates weaken temporarily. This simple theoretical insight will play a central role in the global epidemiology of ZIP. Countries, such as Israel and Australia, which were not affected by the Subprime Crisis or indeed any other crisis, kept cutting their policy rates because their central banks targeted their exchange rates. Since RIPT implies that interest rate cuts weaken exchange rates temporarily, they continued cutting until their policy rates of interest were zero.

## Wicksell's Cumulative Process

### "Natural" Rate of Interest

The concept of the natural rate of interest has been a focus of confusion in the history of economic thought and in contemporary macroeconomic theory. Wicksell (1958 p 84, 1946, p 205) attributed this concept to Böhm-Bawerk's "epoch making" *Capital and Interest* published in 1888 (Böhm-Bawerk 1959). According to Wicksell (1898, p 102) the natural rate of interest "is necessarily the same as the rate of interest which would be determined by supply and demand if no use was made of money and all lending were effected in the form of real capital goods. It comes to much the same thing to describe it as the current value of the *natural rate of interest on capital*" (italics in original). According to Woodford (2003, p 248) the natural rate of interest is "the equilibrium rate of return in the case of flexible prices." Both definitions are counterfactual. In Wicksell's case the counterfactual arises because money exists. In Woodford's case it arises if prices are not flexible. Woodford's definition is conceptually different to Wicksell's because if prices were flexible Woodford's natural rate of interest would be observable but Wicksell's would not. To observe Wicksell's definition, we require an economy without money.

"By the 'natural rate' is meant not a rate quoted upon in a market, but the investors' rate of return on capital in the commodity market." (Patinkin 1966, p 368). This interpretation is also adopted in some modern textbooks (Handa 2009, Chapter 2) where capital refers to fixed assets, symbolized by economists as K. This definition of K is different to Wicksell's (Wicksell,1898, pp 129–30), for whom capital refers to the finance required to cover the "period of production" or the gestation lag in investment. Hence, Wicksell's K includes fixed assets as well as outlays on wages and raw materials during the gestation period. This makes his lengthy discussion in Chapter 9, part A in *Interest and Prices* of the determinants of the natural rate of interest difficult to follow by the modern reader. In any case, for reasons to which we shall return, Wicksell decided to assume that the natural rate of interest plays only a supporting role in his theory of interest and prices, the main actor being the money rate of interest.

Patinkin's interpretation is supported by Wicksell (1958), written just prior to the publication of his *Interest and Prices* in 1898, and in his *Lectures on Political Economy*, originally published in Swedish in 1906 "... there is always a certain rate of interest, at which the exchange value of money and the general level of commodity prices have no tendency to change. This can be called *the normal rate of interest* [italics in original]; its level is determined by the *current* [italics added] natural rate of interest, the real return on capital in production, and must rise or fall with this." (Wicksell 2018, chapter 2). Also, "The natural rate of interest, the real yield of capital in production, is, like everything else, exposed to changes ..." (Wicksell 1946, Volume 2, p 205). Wicksell's natural rate of interest is not an equilibrium concept. It becomes an equilibrium concept only when it equals the "normal rate." Since Wicksell spends so much time explaining how money and natural rates of interest take time to adjust to each other, it is obvious the he did not see the natural rate of interest as an equilibrium phenomenon. This interpretation is further supported in Wicksell's book review of Ludwig von Mises' *The Theory of Money and Credit* translated into English in 1999 (Wicksell 1999, Volume 2, chapter 33).

Perhaps some of the misunderstanding that the natural rate of interest is necessarily an equilibrium phenomenon associated with price stability may be attributed to Friedman (1968) and Phelps (1968), who borrowed Wicksell's terminology for the "natural rate of unemployment" as an analogue to Wicksell's natural rate of interest. Whereas the natural rate of unemployment is an equilibrium phenomenon, Wicksell clearly did not consider the same for the natural rate of interest.

Keynes (1930 Chapter 13) extolled the virtues of Wicksell's natural rate theory at a time when there was no English translation. He referred to the natural rate of interest as the rate of interest, which equates saving with investment. When this equality holds, the rate of return on capital in the commodity market equals the rate of interest on savings. For Keynes, the natural rate of interest is an equilibrium phenomenon; it equates saving with investment. Although he did not change his definition of the natural rate of interest, Keynes (1936 p 243) subsequently declared, "I am now no longer of the opinion that the concept of a 'natural' rate, which previously seemed to me a most promising idea, has anything very useful or significant to contribute to our analysis. ... If there is any such rate of interest which is unique and significant, it must be the rate which we might term as the *neutral* rate of interest, namely, the natural rate ... which is consistent with *full* employment ..."

This "neutral" rate of interest would have been identical to Wicksell's "normal" rate of interest had Keynes written instead, "... consistent with full employment and price stability." It is no coincidence that Keynes omitted "prices" from the title of his *General Theory of Employment, Interest and Money*. The motivation behind this omission has been discussed by Patinkin (1976) and Beenstock (1980). This omission turns the general theory into a particular theory or partial equilibrium theory because the determination of the general level of prices is left out of the analysis. Nevertheless, Keynes recognized in 1936 that the natural rate of interest is not necessarily an equilibrium phenomenon. However, we disagree with him that it does not have "anything very useful or significant to contribute." Perhaps Keynes would have felt differently had he attached importance to the price level, as in his *Treatise on Money*.

Confusion over what Wicksell meant by the natural rate of interest persists. For example, Vines and Wills (2018) misquote Wicksell (1898 p 102) as stating that the natural rate of interest is "... the real rate of interest that would prevail in the absence of price rigidities." In the moneyless economy to which Wicksell referred, there can be no general price level, nor can there be nominal rigidities. Wicksell was referring instead to the natural rate of interest as the return on capital, as interpreted by Patinkin, which is most probably why Wicksell chose to italicize this. Vines and Wills seem to be referring to Woodford's "equilibrium rate of return in the case of flexible prices."

In summary, the natural rate of interest is measured by the return to capital, and the natural rate of interest is not an equilibrium phenomenon. In equilibrium, the natural rate of interest equals the normal rate of interest. In our critique of ZIP, we think that it is helpful to separate the issues of how the natural rate of interest should be measured from how it behaves in equilibrium. We follow Wicksell in hypothesizing that, through the process of capital accumulation, it takes time for the natural rate of interest to converge on Wicksell's normal, or equilibrium, rate of interest. This process turns out to be central to Real Business Cycle theory, as we discuss.

## The Natural Rate of Interest in the Neoclassical Growth Model

The determination of interest rates in economies with money is essentially different to its counterpart in economies without money (Johnson 1967, Foley and Sidrausky 1970). Figure 2.1 compares the determination of interest rates in the neoclassical growth model with and without money. The vertical axis measures GDP per unit of labor efficiency ($y$) and the horizontal axis measures capital per unit of labor efficiency ($k$). The growth rate of the population is denoted by $n$ and technical progress grows at the rate $a$, hence efficiency units of labor ($\tilde{L}$) grow at the rate of $n + a$. Schedule OY is determined by the neoclassical production function, which is concave because of constant returns to scale, and its tangent measures the marginal product of capital, which varies inversely with $k$. Schedule OS is the

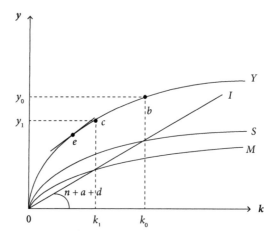

**Fig. 2.1** The Natural Rate of Interest in the
Neoclassical Growth Model

savings schedule, which is a proportion (s) of schedule OY. Finally, the slope of
schedule OI equals n + a + d, where d denotes the rate of capital depreciation.
This schedule subtends the volume of investment that is required to maintain a
constant capital–labor ratio in terms of units of labor efficiency.

In the standard neoclassical growth model, it is well known that the steady-state
equilibrium is determined by the intersection of schedules OI and OS, at which
the capital–labor ratio is $k_0$ and the marginal product of capital is determined by
the tangent at point b, and the rate of interest is equal to the marginal product of
capital minus the rate of capital depreciation. Since the marginal product of capital
varies inversely with k, so does the rate of interest. This is Wicksell's "natural rate
of interest"; it is the rate of interest that would be determined "if no use was made
of money." In this equilibrium the growth rates of GDP and capital equal n + a.

Suppose the economy was out of its steady-state equilibrium and k happened to
be greater than $k_0$. In this case, the marginal product of capital would be smaller
than at point b, and the capital–labor ratio would begin to contract because saving
is insufficient to sustain this larger value of k. The contraction in k continues until
the economy returns to its steady-state equilibrium at point b. During this process,
the marginal product of capital decreases until it returns to what it was at point b.

How should we refer to the marginal product of capital out of equilibrium? Following Patinkin, we refer to it as the natural rate of interest because it is "investors'
rate of return on capital". Insisting that the natural rate of interest is an equilibrium phenomenon is counterproductive; it confuses measurement with market
behavior.

In the neoclassical growth model, savings are invested in capital. In a monetary economy, savings are also used to acquire money (M). Hence, investment

(I) equals savings (S) minus $\dot{M}/P$ where P denotes the price level. The demand for money is assumed to be standard:

$$\ln\frac{M}{P} = \alpha lnY - \beta\left(r + \pi\right) \tag{1.1}$$

It varies directly with GDP and inversely with the nominal rate of interest (i) equal to the real rate of interest (r) plus inflation ($\pi$). Equation (1.1) implies, setting $\alpha = 1$ for simplicity, that:

$$\frac{\dot{M}}{P\tilde{L}} = y\left(a + n + \pi\right)e^{-\beta(r+\pi)} \tag{1.2}$$

Equation (1.2) states that real monetary savings per capita in terms of efficiency units vary proportionately with y, where the proportion varies directly with population growth (n), technical progress (a) and inflation ($\pi$). The latter is induced by the inflation tax, where the tax base varies inversely with inflation. At high rates of inflation, the inflation tax becomes negative (Bruno and Fischer 1990) because the tax base contracts faster than it increases revenue. Here, however, inflation is assumed to be relatively low.

Schedule OM in Figure 2.1 is constructed by deducting equation (1.2) from schedule OS. It measures investment in terms of efficiency units. Its relation to schedule OY is $s - (a + n + \pi)\exp[-\beta(r + \pi)]$. Since in equilibrium the real rate of interest equals the marginal product of capital net of the rate of capital depreciation ($r = MPK - d$), this relation is not strictly proportional, as in the case of schedule OS. Instead, the ratio of OY to OM varies directly with k because r varies inversely with k, i.e. at lower interest rates the demand for money increases.

When there is money, the neoclassical growth equilibrium is determined by the intersection of schedules OI and OM, at which the capital–labor ratio is $k_1$, which is smaller than $k_0$, and the marginal productivity of capital, determined by the tangent at c, is larger than at b. Consequently, in a monetary economy the rate of interest is larger, and GDP per efficiency unit is smaller. This is Woodford's "equilibrium rate of interest," which is larger than Wicksell's "natural rate of interest." The reason for this is simple; some savings are diverted into money, which reduces savings for the purposes of capital accumulation.

The monetary equilibrium in Figure 2.1 would have occurred at an even greater rate of interest had the interest elasticity of demand for money been larger. This happens because schedule OM would have been lower than drawn in Figure 2.1, as a result of which schedule OI would have intersected schedule OM closer to the origin, and the marginal product of capital would have been larger than c. The same happens if inflation increases. Inflation lowers schedule OM by the inflation tax paid by the public as it attempts to maintain the real amount of money it wishes to hold.

## The Dynamics of the Natural Rate of Interest

Consider a moneyless economy in which the central bank sets its rate of interest at r percent, i.e. the central bank lends and borrows Wicksell's real capital goods at this rate of interest. This is obviously a hypothetical construct because it implicitly assumes that the central bank has unlimited reserves of capital goods. Nevertheless, this abstraction is made for heuristic purposes only. To make matters even more heuristic, there is no population growth (n = 0) and no technical progress (a = 0), but capital depreciates (d > 0). In this economy, net investment occurs when the marginal product of capital (MPK) exceeds the cost of capital (r + d). However, in common with much of investment theory, fixed assets are costly to adjust.

The production function is assumed to be $Y_t = AK_t^\alpha L^{1-\alpha}$ where Y denotes GDP or output, K denotes the capital stock measured at the beginning of period t, and total factor productivity (A) and employment (L) are fixed and normalized to 1. Hence, the MPK is $\alpha K_t^{\alpha-1}$. Net investment equals gross investment (I) minus capital depreciation. The dynamics of the capital stock are governed by:

$$\dot{K}_t = I_t - dK_t = \gamma[MPK_t - (r + d)] \tag{1.3}$$

where $\gamma$ is infinite if adjustment costs are zero, and $\gamma$ is zero if adjustment costs are infinite. According to equation (1.3), net investment depends on the difference between the marginal product of capital and its cost. Since the marginal product of capital varies inversely with the stock of capital, equation (1.3) is a nonlinear differential equation in K, for which the general solution is:

$$K_t = \left[\frac{Ae^{-\gamma t} + r + d}{\alpha}\right]^{\frac{1}{\alpha-1}} \tag{1.4}$$

where A is a constant of integration determined by initial conditions. A is negative (positive) if the capital stock is initially low (high), as a result of which MPK is large (small). Because the root is stable, the capital stock accumulates or decumulates to its equilibrium value. The speed of convergence varies directly with $\gamma$, as expected, and it varies inversely with $\alpha$ (because MPK diminishes more rapidly). Equation (1.4) implies, as expected, that the capital stock varies inversely with the cost of capital (r + d). It also implies that the marginal productivity of capital converges to its cost (r + d).

Figure 2.2 illustrates this Wicksellian cumulative process through which the marginal product of capital converges to the cost of capital, where schedule W plots the inverse relation between MPK and the capital stock. The slope of schedule W varies directly with $\alpha$. The speed of adjustment varies directly with $\gamma$. For

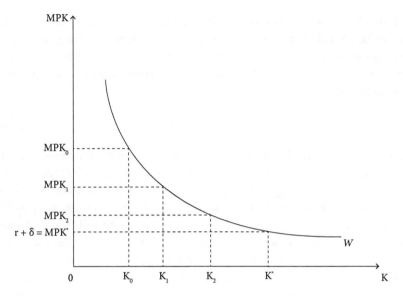

**Fig. 2.2** Convergence between the Natural and Money Rates of Interest

example, if the marginal product is initially large ($MPK_0$) and the capital stock is initially small ($K_0$) the number of steps (3 in Figure 2.2) required for the capital stock to converge on $K^*$ would have been larger had $\gamma$ been smaller. If MPK was initially small and K initially large, convergence would have been from below instead of above. Also, convergence would be asymmetrical if increasing the capital stock is more or less costly than decreasing it.

Wicksell's natural rate of interest, as represented by MPK, converges upon the rate of interest rate set by the central bank (plus d). This same process occurred in Figure 2.1 in the transitional dynamics between steady state equilibria. We may therefore speak of Wicksell's natural rate of interest in and out of equilibrium. In equilibrium, it converges to r + d. However, out of equilibrium it may be larger or smaller, and is essentially dynamic.

The process that we have just described lies at the heart of Real Business Cycle theory, according to which business cycles are induced by the dynamic adjustment of investment to shocks to the cost of capital, as here, as well as to shocks to productivity etc. (Romer 2019, Chapter 5). Wicksell was aware of this process (Wicksell 1898, p 143) but decided to ignore it on the questionable grounds that it was of secondary importance to his main argument, to which we now turn.

## Accumulation with Money

Of course, central banks do not have reserves of capital goods. They can borrow and lend fiat money at the money rate of interest that they set. We denote this nominal or money rate of interest by i. Whereas in the previous moneyless sub-section inflation could not exist, matters are different here. We denote the rate of inflation by π, so the real rate of interest is $r = i - \pi$, and the natural rate of interest by $r_n$. Wicksell argued that inflation depends on the difference between the natural rate of interest and the real rate of interest:

$$\pi = \theta\left(r_n - r\right) \tag{1.5}$$

He argued that, when the natural and real rates are the same, the demand for output in the economy equals its supply, in which event producers have no incentive to change their prices. Aggregate demand, as represented by investment plus consumption, exactly equals aggregate supply. If the real rate of interest is less than the natural rate, investment will increase and consumption will increase because households save less, so aggregate demand increases. If investment increases it might be expected that aggregate supply will increase too. However, Wicksell decided to ignore this effect on the grounds that, "Such changes require time to be affected ... or that at the most ... there is a certain non-cumulative increase in production, of which the influence on price is not *progressive* and will therefore be neglected." (Wicksell 1898, p 143). Henceforth, we shall refer to this as Wicksell's "neglect" clause, which implies that aggregate demand increases relative to aggregate supply. This "... will cause the general level of prices to rise to an unlimited extent in a continuous and more or less uniform manner." (Wicksell 1898, p 100).

Equation (1.5) implies the following relation between inflation and the natural and money rates of interest:

$$\pi = \frac{\theta}{1 - \theta}\left(r_n - i\right) \tag{1.6}$$

which implies that inflation would explode if θ happened to be 1, and prices eventually explode if θ is less than 1. This dramatic result has naturally attracted a great deal of attention, and as we shall see, underpins the so-called New Keynesian Phillips curve, which is the cornerstone of the New Keynesian model (NKM) of monetary policy. This model has had a major influence on the theory of macroeconomic policy in academia and on policy makers for almost thirty years. We shall argue, however, that the NKM has led policy makers astray and has played a negative role in the New Abnormal.

Not all economists have been impressed. "Wicksell's 'cumulative process' is not the unstable process that almost all later commentators have tried to make of it, but a stable equilibrating process whose function it is to achieve the long-run equality of the money and natural rates of interest. This is not a quibble. For the commonly accepted interpretation of Wicksell completely overlooks the central problem with which he was concerned. And it thereby overlooks the vital key which he provides to an understanding of one of the central themes of classical interest theory." (Patinkin 1966, pp 368–9).

Patinkin is referring here to Chapter 10 in Wicksell (1898), in which the cumulative process is studied in an open economy. The increase in prices eventually forces banks to raise money interest rates in line with the natural rate of interest to prevent a drain on their reserves of gold, which brings the cumulative process to a natural end. The unstable cumulative process described in Chapter 9 refers to a pure credit economy, which was set up by Wicksell as a strawman to be knocked down. See further Patinkin (1966, pp 238–41), where he shows that money and natural rates converge more generally.

Whereas Patinkin was concerned with the convergence of the money rate to the natural rate, the discussion in the previous section suggests that the natural rate may converge to the money rate. The cumulative process implies that the capital stock will tend to increase over time, which will reduce the natural rate of interest. Suppose that the change in the natural rate varies inversely with the gap between the natural and real rates of interest:

$$\dot{r}_n = -\omega \left( r_n - r \right) \tag{1.7}$$

Equations (1.5) and (1.6) imply that the general solution for the natural rate of interest when the money rate of interest is fixed is:

$$r_{nt} = \frac{Ae^{-\omega t}}{1 - \theta} + i \tag{1.8}$$

where $A$ is an arbitrary constant. Hence the natural rate converges to the money rate provided $\theta$ is less than 1. Wicksell's "neglect" clause prevented him from entertaining this type of resolution to the cumulative process because he assumed that the natural rate of interest is independent of the money rate of interest.

In summary, we follow Patinkin in identifying the natural rate of interest with the rate of return on capital, or fixed assets. Both inflation and investment depend on the gap between the money and natural rates of interest. Wicksell had in mind two cumulative processes. The first anticipates the Phillips curve: inflation varies directly with the difference between the natural and money rates of interest. The second anticipates Real Business Cycle theory: capital accumulation driven by investment varies directly with the difference between the natural and money rates of interest. Both cumulative processes are convergent because the gap between the natural and money rates of interest tend to zero over time.

## The New Keynesian Model

As we shall see, New Keynesian economics is neo-Wicksellian because the money rate of interest serves as the operating instrument of central banks, and inflation is specified in terms of a cumulative process (Walsh 2017). In fact, because central banks face no limitations on the amount of base money that they can issue, they can set money rates of interest in the same way as banks do in Wicksell's pure credit economy. Despite Patinkin's reservations, the strawman assumes relevance once more, even if the actors are different.

The NKM has several components. Firms engage in imperfect competition. In each period a proportion of firms change their prices (Calvo pricing). The labor market is competitive. In the basic NKM wages are flexible. Agents have rational expectations of future output and inflation. The central bank sets its interest rate following a Taylor rule. What makes NKM "Keynesian" is the assumption that prices are not perfectly flexible, as a result of which aggregate demand does not necessarily equal aggregate supply, i.e. there is an output gap (y), which on average is zero. We follow the version of NKM in Walsh (2017, Chapter 5), which also provides the theoretical underpinnings of equations (2.1).

The current output gap is assumed to depend upon the current expected value of next period's output gap, and to vary inversely with the expected real rate of interest:

$$y_t = \gamma E_t y_{t+1} - \left(i_t - E_t \pi_{t+1} - r_{nt}\right) \tag{2.1}$$

where $\gamma = 1$. Note that Walsh omitted the natural rate of interest from equation (2.1), which, as we shall argue, is an oversight that is not innocent. Current inflation is assumed to depend on expected future inflation and the output gap:

$$\pi_t = \beta E_t \pi_{t+1} + \theta y_t \tag{2.2}$$

where $\beta$ is less than 1 (but close to 1) because it is the discount rate for utility from consumption. Equation (2.2) is the New Keynesian Phillips curve. There is an obvious resemblance between equation (2.2) and (1.5). If $\gamma = \beta = 0$, they would be identical. The model is closed by a Taylor rule for the rate of interest, which obeys the Taylor principle according to which the central bank raises its interest rate by more than inflation, and it lowers interest rates when the output gap is negative:

$$i_t = r_{nt-1} + \pi_t + \lambda \left(\pi_t - \pi_t^*\right) + \chi y_t \tag{2.3}$$

where $\pi^*$ denotes the target rate of inflation. If inflation and output are on target, equation (2.3) implies that the money rate of interest equals the natural rate of interest plus target inflation. Walsh omitted the natural rate of interest from equation (2.3), which also turns out to be not innocent. According to equation (2.3), it takes the central bank one period to adjust its policy rate to the natural rate of interest.

The heart of NKM consists of equations (2.1) and (2.2). Exploring the implications of interest rate policy for inflation and the output gap involves two stages. In the first, we derive the rational expectations for inflation and the output gap, i.e. $E_t\pi_{t+1}$ and $E_t y_{t+1}$. In the second, these rational expectations are substituted into equations (2.1) and (2.2). In the first stage, equations (2.1) and (2.2) are lagged one period and expectations are taken at time t:

$$\begin{bmatrix} 1-\beta L^{-1} & -\theta \\ -\alpha L^{-1} & 1-\gamma L^{-1} \end{bmatrix} \begin{bmatrix} E_t\pi_t \\ E_t y_t \end{bmatrix} = \begin{bmatrix} 0 \\ -\alpha E_t\left(i_t-r_{nt}\right) \end{bmatrix} \tag{2.4}$$

where L is the lag operator (hence $L^{-1}$ is a lead operator). The roots of the coefficient matrix are:

$$\rho = \frac{\beta+\gamma+\alpha\theta \pm \sqrt{\left(\beta-\gamma\right)^2 + 2\alpha\theta\left(\beta+\gamma+\dfrac{\alpha\theta}{2}\right)}}{2\beta\gamma} \tag{2.5}$$

These roots are real, but one root ($\rho_1$) exceeds 1 while the other ($\rho_2$) is a positive fraction. For example, when $\alpha = 0.3$, $\beta = 0.97$, $\gamma = 1$, $\theta = 0.2$ the roots are $\rho_1 = 1.29$ and $\rho_2 = 0.79$. When $\theta = 0.4$ the roots are $\rho_1 = 1.45$ and $\rho_2 = 0.69$. As expected, the cumulative process is unstable for inflation if there is a gap between the money and natural rates of interest. The general solutions for the rational expectations of inflation and the output gap are:

$$E_t\pi_t = \frac{-\alpha\theta E_t\left(i_t-r_{nt}\right)}{\left(1-\rho_1 L^{-1}\right)\left(1-\rho_2 L^{-1}\right)} + A\rho_1^t + B\rho_2^t \tag{2.6}$$

$$E_t y_t = -\alpha\frac{E_t\left(i_t-r_{nt}\right) - \beta E_t\left(i_{t+1}-r_{nt+1}\right)}{\left(1-\rho_1 L^{-1}\right)\left(1-\rho_2 L^{-1}\right)} + C\rho_1^t + D\rho_2^t \tag{2.7}$$

where A, B, C, and D are arbitrary constants. We use the partial fraction decomposition for products of inverted polynomials:

$$\frac{1}{\left(1-\rho_1 L^{-1}\right)\left(1-\rho_2 L^{-1}\right)} = \frac{1}{\rho_1-\rho_2}\left[\frac{\rho_1}{1-\rho_1 L^{-1}} - \frac{\rho_2}{1-\rho_2 L^{-1}}\right]$$

Hence equation (2.6) may be rewritten (ignoring A and B) as:

$$E_t\pi_t = \frac{-\alpha\theta}{\rho_1-\rho_2}\sum_{j=0}^{\infty}\left(\rho_1^{j+1} - \rho_2^{j+1}\right) E_t\left(i_{t+j}-r_{nt+j}\right) \tag{2.8}$$

Since $\rho_1 > \rho_2$ expected inflation varies inversely with the expected future differences between the money and natural rates of interest. Inflation is expected to be zero if these differences are expected to be zero, or their weighted average is expected to be zero. Notice that since $\rho_1 > 1$ and $\rho_2 < 1$ these weights ($w_j$) increase with j through the New Keynesian cumulative process, since:

$$\frac{dw_j}{dj} = \rho_1^{j+1} \ln \rho_1 - \rho_2^{j+1} \ln \rho_2 > 0$$

Equation (2.7) may be rewritten (ignoring C and D) as:

$$E_t y_t = \frac{-\alpha}{\rho_1 - \rho_2} \sum_{j=0}^{\infty} \left( \rho_1^{j+1} - \rho_2^{j+1} \right) E_t \left[ (i_{t+j} - r_{nt+j}) - \beta (i_{t+j+1} - r_{nt+j+1}) \right] \qquad (2.9)$$

In equation (2.9) the weight on the expected differential between the money and natural rates of interest j periods ahead is $\rho_1^{j+1} - \rho_2^{j+1} - \beta \left( \rho_1^j - \rho_2^j \right)$ which is positive for two reasons. First, because $\beta < 1$ and second because $\rho_1^{j+1} - \rho_2^{j+1} > \left( \rho_1^j - \rho_2^j \right)$. Hence, the expected output gap varies inversely with future expectations of the difference between the money and natural rates of interest. This completes stage 1.

In stage 2 we use equations (2.8) and (2.9) to substitute for expected inflation in equation (2.1) and the expected output gap in equation (2.2) by leading equations (2.8) and (2.9) one period forward. For example, the solution for inflation is:

$$\pi_t = -\alpha\theta \left( i_t - r_{nt} \right) - \frac{\alpha\theta}{\rho_1 - \rho_2} \left[ (\beta + \gamma + \alpha\theta) \sum_{j=0}^{\infty} \left( \rho_1^{j+1} - \rho_2^{j+1} \right) E_t \left( i_{t+j+1} - r_{nt+j+1} \right) \right.$$

$$\left. -\beta E_t \left( i_{t+j+2} - r_{nt+j+2} \right) \right] \qquad (2.10)$$

Inflation varies inversely with the current difference between the money and natural rates of interest as well as expected future differences. The central bank controls inflation through its current monetary policy ($i_t$) and through forward guidance, which frames expectations of future monetary policy. In doing so the central bank must assess the current and future outcomes for the natural rate of interest.

## Taylor Rule

The discussion so far has assumed that the central bank's interest rate policy is discretionary. What happens if instead it follows a Taylor rule such as equation (2.3)?

The counterpart to equation (2.5) is:

$$\rho = \frac{\beta + \gamma + \alpha\theta + \alpha\beta\chi \pm \sqrt{(\beta + \gamma + \theta + \alpha\beta\chi)^2 - 4\beta\gamma\left[1 + (1 + \lambda)\alpha\theta + \alpha\chi\right]}}{2\beta\gamma} \tag{2.11}$$

In contrast to equation (2.5) where the roots are real, the roots of equation (2.11) may be complex, especially if the central bank leans hard into the wind (i.e. if $\lambda$ is large). Also, both roots may be larger than 1. Assuming $\lambda = 0.2$, $\chi = 0.1$ and the other parameter values are as in equation (2.5), the roots are $\rho_1 = 1.5733$ and $\rho_2 = 0.5495$. Both roots exceed 1 when the square root in equation (2.11) is close to zero (about to turn complex). These unstable roots ($\rho_1$ and $\rho_2$) are "bubble" roots, which are common in rational expectations models. For example, whimsical expectations of inflation might become irrationally self-fulfilling. Whereas it was rational in the previous sub-section to expect inflation to be unstable when monetary policy is discretionary, matters are different when the central bank commits to a Taylor rule, which embodies an inflation target. Indeed, this is why New Keynesian monetary policy attaches central importance to Taylor rules over discretionary monetary policy.

Bubble roots are suppressed by using their forward solutions (Sargent 1979, pp 194–5):

$$\frac{1}{(1 - \rho_1 L)(1 - \rho_2 L)} = \frac{\frac{1}{\rho_1 \rho_2} L^{-2}}{\left(1 - \frac{L^{-1}}{\rho_1}\right)\left(1 - \frac{L^{-1}}{\rho_2}\right)} = \frac{L^{-2}}{\rho_2 - \rho_1}\left[\frac{\rho_1^{-1}}{1 - \frac{L^{-1}}{\rho_1}} - \frac{\rho_2^{-1}}{1 - \frac{L^{-1}}{\rho_2}}\right] \tag{2.12}$$

These forward solutions imply that the counterpart to equation (2.8) is:

$$E_t\pi_t = \frac{\alpha\theta}{\rho_2 - \rho_1}\sum_{j=0}^{\infty}\left(\frac{1}{\rho_1^{j+1}} - \frac{1}{\rho_2^{j+1}}\right)\left(\lambda E_t\pi^*_{t+j+2} + \alpha E_t\Delta r_{nt+j+2}\right) \tag{2.13}$$

Expected inflation varies directly with the expected inflation target and with expectations of changes in the natural rate of interest. Notice that this result does not depend on which root is larger. The natural rate of interest would not have featured in equation (2.13) had the central bank adjusted its rate of interest to the natural rate instantaneously. In summary, commitment to the inflation target and fulfillment of the Taylor principle ensures that expected inflation depends on the target, and the bubble roots are prevented from driving inflation to plus or minus infinity. It also implies that the unconditional expectation of inflation equals the inflation target.

The counterpart to equation (2.10) is:

$$E_t y_t = \frac{\alpha\lambda}{\rho_2 - \rho_1} \sum_{j=0}^{\infty} \left( \frac{1}{\rho_1^{j+1}} - \frac{1}{\rho_2^{j+1}} \right) \left[ (1-\beta)\, E_t \pi^*_{t+j+2} - \beta\Delta E_t \Delta\pi^*_{t+j+3} \right.$$

$$\left. + \alpha[(1-\beta)\, E_t \Delta r_{nt+j+2} - \beta E_t \Delta^2 r_{nt+j+3)} \right] \tag{2.14}$$

So, the expected output gap varies directly with expected inflation target and it varies inversely with expected changes in the inflation target. It also varies directly with expected changes in the natural rate of interest and inversely with acceleration in the natural rate of interest. Substituting equations (2.13) and (2.14) into equations (2.1) and (2.2) would show that inflation and the output gap vary directly with rational expectations of target inflation and changes in the natural rate of interest.

The important result here is that in the NKM the natural rate of interest and expectations of the natural rate of interest play a crucial role in the business cycle and inflation. This role varies directly with the time it takes the central bank to adjust its policy rate to the natural rate of interest.

## The Missing Link in New Keynesian Theory

So far, we have been concerned with the canonical NKM represented by equations (2.1), (2.2), and (2.3). In many respects NKM is virtual because it is driven by virtual variables such as expectations and the output gap, which are not variables for which data are provided by the statistical authorities. The same applies to the natural rate of interest. Indeed, inflation is the only variable for which data exist. This criticism is reminiscent of Dennis Robertson's criticism of virtual phenomena, which he likened to the Cheshire cat's grin, which fades away as you look at it (Robertson 1939). Indeed, there is much of Alice in Wonderland in NKM.

NKM has many variants (Walsh 2017). Some versions allow for wage stickiness as well as price stickiness. Others allow for combinations of rational and adaptive expectations, which induces autoregressive behavior in output and inflation. Open economy versions of NKM have been developed too. Although all these versions are claimed to be neo-Wicksellian, none attach importance to the natural rate of interest, or even bother to mention it. For example, the "natural rate of interest" is not even mentioned in Walsh (2017).

A central theme in this critique is that this omission is a case of Hamlet without the Prince of Denmark. In their neglect of the natural rate of interest, New Keynesian macroeconomists have created an intellectual fantasy, which has led central bankers astray. Equations (2.1) to (2.14) have reinstated the natural rate of interest as an exogenous variable. The solution for inflation in the conventional NKM in which the natural rate of interest is ignored is obviously different to its counter-part in equation (2.10). Specifying the natural rate of interest in NKM ties down the real rate of interest to real variables in a way that should have pleased Dennis Robertson.

What would happen to NKM if the natural rate of interest was endogenous, as in equations (1) instead of exogeneous as in equations (2.1) to (2.14)? To answer this question, we first need to recall how the output gap is calculated by New Keynesians.

## Filtered Output Gaps

The output gap (y) is defined as the percentage difference between total final ex-penditure (consumption C and investment I) and full employment output, i.e. $y = \log(C+I) - \log Q$. In practice, New Keynesians have applied time series meth-ods to filter out business cycles, represented by y, from secular trends in the economy. In the simplest case, if secular GDP follows a fixed linear time trend, $\log GDP_t = a + bt + u_t$, then y is represented by the residual error (u). The out-put gap is positive when u is positive and is negative when u is negative, and u is positively autocorrelated. Several methods allow for time trends, which vary. By way of illustration, we focus on the popular Hodrick-Prescott (HP) filter (Ho-drick and Prescott 1997), in which the trend in GDP is denoted by $\mu_t$, which is chosen to minimize a loss function (z) that penalizes changes in the time trend:

$$z = \sum_{t=1}^{T} (Y_t - \mu_t)^2 + \lambda \sum_{t=2}^{T-1} (\Delta^2 \mu_{t+1})^2 \qquad (3.1)$$

where the penalty is denoted by $\lambda$, and the output gap is $Y_t - \mu_t$. Minimizing z with respect to $\mu_t$ implies the following first-order condition:

$$\frac{\partial z}{\partial \mu_t} = -2(Y_t - \mu_t) + 2\lambda \left[ (\mu_{t+2} - 2\mu_{t+1} + \mu_t) + \right.$$

$$\left. + (\mu_t - 2\mu_{t-1} + \mu_{t-2}) - 2(\mu_{t+1} - 2\mu_t + \mu_{t-1}) \right] = 0 \qquad (3.2)$$

Equation (3.2) is a center-weighted difference equation involving two lags and two leads of $\mu_t$, which implies the following relation between GDP and its trend:

$$F(L)\mu_t = [\lambda L^{-2} - 4\lambda L^{-1} + 1 + 6\lambda - 4\lambda L + \lambda L^2] \mu_t = Y_t \qquad (3.3)$$

If $\lambda$ is zero, equation (3.3) implies that $\mu_t = Y_t$, i.e. trend GDP changes in each period. If $\lambda$ is infinite, it implies that $\Delta \mu_{t+1} = \Delta \mu_t$ in which case the trend is constant or linear. This shows that $\lambda$ smooths the trend. Finally, the output gap generated by the HP filter turns out to be a fourth-order center-weighted moving average process:

$$u_t = Y_t - \mu_t = [\lambda L^{-2} - 4\lambda L^{-1} + 6\lambda - 4\lambda L + \lambda L^2] \mu_t = MA(4) \qquad (3.4)$$

Equation (3.4) shows that the output gap is autocorrelated and cyclical, and its unconditional expectation is zero, as befits a variable that is supposed to represent the business cycle. Suppose, however, that in truth there are no business cycles. The HP filter nevertheless generates a statistical artifact, which is necessarily cyclical (Harvey and Jaeger 1993), and is mistakenly interpreted by the unassuming as representing the business cycle. Suppose instead that business cycles exist. The HP filter implies that the length or persistence of business cycles varies directly with $\lambda$. However, the choice of $\lambda$ is arbitrary, in which case the estimated business cycle may be too long or too short. In summary, the HP filter may induce fake business cycles.

Software such as Eviews recommends defaults for $\lambda$, which vary inversely with the frequency of the data. For example, $\lambda = 100$ is recommended for annual data, 1,600 for quarterly data, and 14,400 for monthly data. Of course, these recommendations are entirely arbitrary. This critique of filtered business cycles is generic and applies to various alternatives to the HP filter. The macroeconomic literature is replete with filtered business cycles that most probably have little to do with reality.

## Output Gap and Natural Rate Theory

NKM is incomplete because it ignores the natural rate of interest and it is deficient because of its reliance on filtered output gaps. In this subsection we endogenize the natural rate of interest and the output gap when the latter is defined according to theory rather than arbitrary filters. However, for expositional clarity we ignore the determination of inflation and expectations in NKM. We focus instead on the dynamic relation between the natural and real rates of interest and the role of capital accumulation in determining the output gap.

Suppose that an exogenous increase in the natural rate of interest increases net investment (gross investment exceeds replacement investment) when the real rate of interest (r) is fixed. The increase in investment raises aggregate demand indirectly, but it also raises aggregate supply, which varies directly with the capital stock. However, we show that in the short run the former will exceed the latter so that the output gap (y) increases, but in the longer run, the latter will exceed the former. As the capital stock accumulates the natural rate of interest decreases, until eventually it reverts to its original level. These phenomena are entirely overlooked by New Keynesians. Walsh (2003, p 231) observes that this convention "... follows McCallum and Nelson (1999), who argue that little is lost for the purposes of short-run business-cycle analysis by assuming an exogenous process for the capital stock." As already noted, Wicksell too decided to overlook these phenomena in his cumulative process by applying Wicksell's "neglect" clause. The fundamental issue here is whether it makes sense to detach trends from cycles, or the short run from the long run. Our contention is that this false dichotomy has turned out to be deleterious for policy makers as well as academia.

In what follows, lower case letters refer to logarithms of their higher case counterparts, e.g. $k = \log K$. For expositional simplicity, we assume that employment and total factor productivity are fixed so that aggregate supply (Q) depends entirely on capital, hence $q = \alpha k$. Aggregate demand comprises investment (I) and consumption (C), hence the output gap (y) is $y = \log(I + C) - q$. Net investment as a percentage of the capital stock, $(I - dK)/K = \dot{k}$, is assumed to vary directly with the difference between the natural and real rates of interest (r), where the former is represented by the MPK and the cost of capital includes the rate of depreciation (d):

$$\dot{k} = \phi \left( mpk - \ln \left( r + d \right) \right) \tag{3.5}$$

where $\phi$ varies inversely with the cost of adjustment of the capital stock, and $r_n = mpk = \log \alpha + (\alpha - 1)k$. Gross investment is $I = \left( \dot{k} + d \right) K$. Without loss of generality set $d = 1$ so that $\ln I = k + \dot{k}$, and $\ln \left( r + d \right) = r$. Finally, consumption is assumed to depend on aggregate supply, which is smoother than aggregate demand, hence $c = bq$. The output gap is:

$$y = w \left[ k + \phi \left( mpk - r \right) \right] + \left( 1 - w \right) bq - q \tag{3.6}$$

where w is the share of investment in aggregate demand. Since the output gap must be zero when $mpk = r$, the income elasticity of demand for consumption must be $b = (\alpha - w)/\alpha(1 - w)$. An increase in the natural rate of interest increases aggregate demand through mpk in equation (3.6) but it increases aggregate supply through equation (3.5). The general solutions for capital and the output gap are:

$$k_t = Ae^{-\phi(1-\alpha)t} + \frac{\ln \alpha - r}{1 - \alpha} \tag{3.7}$$

$$y_t = w\phi \left( \ln \alpha - r \right) + \Omega k_t \tag{3.8}$$

$$\Omega = w \left[ 1 + \phi \left( \alpha - 1 \right) \right] + \alpha \left[ \left( 1 - w \right) b - 1 \right] \tag{3.9}$$

Substituting for b in equation (3.9) implies that $\Omega = -w\phi(1-\alpha)$. Since $mpk = \log \alpha + (\alpha - 1)k$, equation (3.7) implies that mpk tends to r and the natural rate of interest as represented by MPK tends to 1 + r, as expected. Therefore, equations (3.7) and (3.8) imply that the output gap tends to zero, as expected. It also implies that the output gap varies inversely with the capital stock.

A reduction in the real rate of interest directly raises the output gap through equation (3.8), but it indirectly reduces it through equation (3.7). It is this latter effect that is ignored by the New Keynesians. They also ignore the fact that the effect of the rate of interest on investment and aggregate demand gets weaker over time as the natural rate of interest decreases towards the lower real rate of interest.

The empirical importance of the role of capital accumulation and the natural rate of interest depends mainly on the speed of adjustment of investment, represented here by $\phi$. If the adjustment is very slow, maybe Wicksell, McCallum, and Nelson had a point in neglecting capital accumulation. Matters would be different if the adjustment takes a few years. In any case, since the long run is a sequence of short runs, sooner or later capital accumulation cannot be ignored. We shall argue that these oversights or omissions played a central role in the political economy of ZIP.

In summary, the natural rate of interest suffered from benign neglect in the highly influential New Keynesian model. Since NKM was popular among central bankers, so did policy makers neglect the natural rate of interest. It went under the radar of the dashboard of indicators, which informed monetary policy. Also, NKM is almost entirely virtual. Its key variables include expectations and output gaps, which are not directly observable; the only observable variables are inflation and the policy rate of the central bank. As we shall see in Chapter 3, the role of virtual variables in NKM is related to the rise of postmodernism in applied macroeconomics.

## Walras' Law

At about the same time, or slightly before, that Wicksell was developing his theories of monetary policy, Léon Walras (in Lausanne) was pioneering general equilibrium theory, which was to revolutionize economic theory during the twentieth century. At about the same time that Walras was launching general equilibrium theory, Alfred Marshall sang the praises of partial equilibrium theory in his famous textbook, *Principles of Economics*, first published in 1890 and which ran to eight editions by 1925. Whereas partial equilibrium theory focuses on a narrow number of markets, ignoring what happens in the rest of the economy, general equilibrium theory considers all markets together. Whereas in general equilibrium everything depends on everything else, in partial equilibrium it does not. This makes theory easier.

Wicksell, for example, may be characterized as a partial equilibrium theorist. In his *Interest and Prices*, one is never quite sure how, apart from interest and prices, employment and output are determined. Indeed, it took more than 50 years for this to be clarified in Patinkin's *Money, Interest and Prices*, in which he integrated money and value theory in general equilibrium, and where there are fascinating appendices on Walras as well as Wicksell. General equilibrium theory is especially relevant to macroeconomics because it is concerned with the notion that everything affects everything else.

Walras' law states that if N − 1 markets are in equilibrium, so must the N'th market be in equilibrium. A corollary of Walras' law is that if there are N markets there are only N − 1 relative prices. If N = 2 and there are only apples and oranges, and the supply of apples equals the demand for apples, so must the supply of oranges equal the demand for oranges. There is only one relative price, which simultaneously clears both markets: the relative price between apples and oranges.

In closed economy macroeconomics without a banking system there are four main markets: GDP, labor, bonds, and money (as in Patinkin 1966, Part 2). According to Walras' law, if three of these markets are in equilibrium, so must be the fourth. They are brought into equilibrium by three relative prices: wages, the general price level (the relative price of money), and the rate of interest on bonds. If, in addition, there is a banking system, there are two more markets: for bank credit and base money. There are also two more relative prices: the rate of interest on bank credit, and the rate of interest set by the central bank on base money (as in equations 5 below). This economy has three rates of interest, a general price level, and a wage rate, which establish general equilibrium in six markets.

In the NKM there is an explicit market for GDP (equation 2.1) and an implicit bond or capital market in which the rate of interest is set by the central bank (equation 2.3). There are two relative prices: the rate of interest and the price level (or inflation). How does this fit in with Walras' law? Outside the model there is also a market for money and a labor market, so there are four markets and three relative prices (price level, wages, and the rate of interest). Suppose the market for GDP is in equilibrium (the output gap is zero) and inflation is on target at zero, as in the "divine coincidence." If the money and labor markets are in equilibrium, this would imply according to Walras' law that the rate of interest equals the natural rate of interest, as commonly assumed by Neo-Wicksellians.

Matters would obviously be different if the money and labor markets are out of equilibrium. If they are, the supposition that the "divine coincidence" implies that the rate of interest must equal the natural rate of nterest would be wrong. It would be just as arbitrary to suppose that the market for labor must be in equilibrium as it is to suppose that the rate of interest must equal the natural rate of interest. Walras' law has been misapplied.

## Existential Risk

Imagine a world in which an event is going to occur with certainty but its timing is uncertain. For example, we all must die sooner or later, but in the absence of life tables we would be unable to calculate survival probabilities. In the Jewish tradition we all must die by 120, the age at which Moses died. The calculation of life assurance premiums becomes very difficult under this type of uncertainty because there is no empirical data on the hazard of death. To fix ideas, suppose that people live two periods so that if they survive period 1 they must die in period 2. If they die in period 1 they want their inheritors to receive a benefit of $x. What is the competitive premium that a life assurance company would request at the beginning of period 1 to pay $x in period 2?

For simplicity, suppose the rate of interest is zero. In the absence of life tables, it might be reasonable to suppose that, since the insured must die in period 1 or period 2, half will die in period 1. In this case the premium would be $½x. Premium income is N$½x in the first period and life assurance claims are ½N$x in the second, where N is the number of insured, so the life assurance companies just break even. If, however, all the insured die in period 1 they will have to pay out N$x in the second period, in which event they will lose ½$x. If instead none die in the first period, they will gain ½$x because they do not have any claims. Since everyone might die in period 1, it was not reasonable to assume that only half might die in period 1.

The problem here is that we are dealing with Knightian uncertainty, which arises when probabilities cannot be assigned to potential outcomes. Uncertainty creates ambiguity; all might die in period 1 but all might die in period 2. A conservative solution to ambiguity is to minimize the maximum loss (Manski 2008): the so-called minimax solution. Since the maximum claim against the life assurance company is Nx$1, i.e. when all die in period 1, the premium must be $1 instead of 50 cents. The minimax premium means that life assurance is not worthwhile because the premium per dollar claimed is one dollar. As expected, when death is certain but its timing is uncertain, life assurance would not be feasible. Thanks to life tables the timing of death is not uncertain; it is risky and insurance is feasible.

There have been many events in history that were certain and inevitable but their timing was uncertain. Wars, for example, do not last forever. The Thirty Years' War came to an end after thirty years and the Hundred Years' War ended after a century. However, the Six-Day War only lasted six days. The same applies to political regimes as well as economic regimes. Economists such as Triffin (1960) and Kenen (1960) predicted that the Bretton Woods system of fixed exchange rates against the US dollar and policed by the International Monetary Fund must come to an end sooner or later because a US dollar crisis was a matter of time. The US current account deficits required to supply international reserves of foreign exchange would eventually cause the US to devalue the dollar against gold. This event happened in 1971 and the Bretton Woods system collapsed. Even in 1970 the Bretton Woods system seemed sound. The collapse came suddenly, as did the collapse of the former Soviet Union.

ZIP has so far lasted twenty-five years in Japan and twelve years in the UK. However, interest rates will not remain zero forever. Sooner or later ZIP will come to an end. Indeed, the end might come suddenly. However, there is no actuarial basis for estimating the probability of its demise; the timing is shrouded in Knightian uncertainty. As in the example of life assurance, it is impossible to insure against the ending of ZIP.

To fix ideas, we assume that business investors are risk-averse and have CARA (constant absolute risk aversion) utility functions with absolute risk aversion $\alpha$, i.e. their utility function is:

$$u = -\frac{1}{\alpha}e^{-\alpha y} \tag{4.1}$$

where y denotes profit, which equals the marginal revenue product of capital minus its cost:

$$y = K(MPK - r - d) \tag{4.2}$$

and d denotes the rate of capital depreciation. The marginal product of capital is risky. It equals $MPK_H$ with probability p and it equals $MPK_L$ with probability $1 - p$. where H refers to "high" and L refers to "low." The production function is assumed to be $Q = AK^\gamma$ where A denotes total factor productivity, which equals $A_H$ or $A_L$, and $\gamma$ is less than 1 but positive so that the marginal product of capital, which equals $\gamma AK^{\gamma-1}$, varies inversely with capital.

Since probabilities (p) are ascribed to different states of the world for total factor productivity, the marginal product of capital is risky rather than uncertain. Uncertainty arises when probabilities cannot be ascribed to total factor productivity. Before discussing the case in which the marginal product of capital is uncertain, we investigate the case in which it is risky.

Investors are assumed to maximize expected utility equal to $E(u) = pu_H + (1-p)u_L$. It may be shown that the first-order conditions for a maximum are:

$$\frac{p}{1-p}\frac{\gamma^2 A_H K^{\gamma-1} - r - d}{\gamma^2 A_L K^{\gamma-1} - r - d}e^{\alpha\gamma(A_L-A_H)K^\gamma} = -1 \tag{4.3}$$

Since equation (4.3) is nonlinear in K, it does not have an analytical solution for the optimal capital stock, which maximizes expected utility. Table 2.1 reports numerical solutions for different rates of interest and total factor productivity. Since

Table 2.1  Investment under Existential Risk

| r | $A_H$ | $A_L$ | K | MPK |
|---|---|---|---|---|
| 0.05 | 2 | 1 | 8.173 | 0.170 |
| 0.04 | 2 | 1 | 10.813 | 0.143 |
| 0.06 | 2 | 1 | 6.440 | 0.196 |
| 0.05 | 2.5 | 1 | 8.610 | 0.192 |
| 0.05 | 1.5 | 1 | 7.015 | 0.155 |
| 0.05 | 2 | 1.5 | 12.371 | 0.154 |
| 0.05 | 2 | 0.5 | 4.612 | 0.200 |

Notes: α = 0.8, p = 0.5, d = 0.1, γ = 0.4

p = 0.5, high and low total factor productivity are just as likely. This may sound as if investors are uncertain about these states of the world, but it simply means that their priors are diffuse. Belief that states of the world are just as likely does not mean that they are uncertain, as we shall see.

Row 1 in Table 2.1 serves as the base case, in which the marginal product of capital is 17 percent. Since the rate of depreciation is 10 percent and the rate of interest is 5 percent, the risk premium on fixed assets is 2 percent. In row 2 the rate of interest is reduced to 4 percent, the capital stock increases, the return to capital decreases to 14.3 percent and the risk premium on fixed assets decreases to 0.3 percent. Rows 2 and 3 show that the risk premium varies directly with the rate of interest. In row 4 the good state of the world becomes better, the capital stock as well as its return increase, and the risk premium increases from 2 percent to 4.2 percent. In row 5 the good state of the world is worse, so the opposite happens but it is asymmetrical. Finally, in row 6 the bad state of the world becomes better, and in row 7 it worsens. The latter establishes that when the worse state of the world worsens, investment is reduced, the return on capital increases (to 20 perent), and the risk premium increases from 2 percent to 5 percent.

Totally differentiating equation (4.3) with respect to K and r + d, implies:

$$\frac{dK}{d(r+d)} = \frac{\Omega_1}{\Omega_2} \tag{4.4}$$

$$\Omega_1 = \frac{\gamma MPK_H - r - d}{\gamma MPK_L - r - d} - 1$$

$$\Omega_2 = \gamma^2 \left\{ (1-\gamma) \frac{\gamma MPK_H - r - d}{\gamma MPK_L - r - d} + (\gamma - 1) \frac{MPK_H}{\gamma K} \right.$$
$$\left. + \alpha (A_L - A_H)(\gamma MPK_H - r - d) \right\}$$

From the second-order conditions, $\Omega_1/\Omega_2$ is negative. Hence, as expected, equation (4.4) implies that the capital stock varies inversely with the cost of capital.

Equation (4.4) implies that the effect of the cost of capital on its marginal product is:

$$\frac{dMPK}{d(r+d)} = \gamma(\gamma-1)K^{\gamma-2}\frac{\Omega_1}{\Omega_2} >; 0 \tag{4.5}$$

which, as expected, is positive because $\gamma$ is less than 1. It may be shown, as in Table 2.1, that equation (4.5) implies that MPK exceeds the cost of capital, and that the difference between them varies directly with the cost of capital.

Under uncertainty, probabilities cannot be assigned to states of the world, not even diffuse probabilities as in Table 2.1. The minimax solution involves maximizing profits in the worst state of the world. Hence:

$$K = \left(\frac{\gamma A_L}{r+d}\right)^{\frac{1}{1-\gamma}} \tag{4.6}$$

is the minimax capital stock, which according to row 1 in Table 2.1 would be 5.128, and the return to capital is 15 percent (not shown). Because investors expect the worst, they invest less than in row 1. Hence, uncertainty frightens investors by more than risk, even when the latter is diffuse. Note that, since the return to capital and the cost of capital are 15 percent, this does not mean that the risk premium is zero. The return to capital has a lower bound of 15 percent, but in practice it will be greater than this, because on average the worst state of the world does not arise. On average, therefore, the risk premium on capital (more strictly the uncertainty premium) will exceed its 2 percent counterpart in row 1 because the capital stock is only 5.128 instead of 8.173.

Strictly speaking, existential risk is existential uncertainty. This uncertainty intensifies when $A_L$ decreases, which in the nature of things varies directly, but nonlinearly, with the duration of the New Abnormal. According to equation (4.6), business investment is expected to decrease, and the ex-post risk premium on capital increases. The similarity between this and row 7 in Table 2.1 suggests that the implications of risk and uncertainty are observationally equivalent. In both cases, existential risk adversely affects investment and it increases the risk premium on capital. However, our purpose here is not to suggest empirical tests to distinguish between risk and uncertainty. Instead, it is to establish that, when existential risk is uncertain, it adversely affects investment and increases the risk premium on capital.

The implications of existential risk are summarized in Figure 2.3 where the cost of capital to firms is measured on the vertical axis and their fixed assets are measured on the horizontal. Schedule $I_0$ denotes the inverse relation between fixed assets and the cost of capital in a risk-free and certain environment. Notice that in this case equation (4.3) implies, as expected, that the marginal product of capital equals its marginal cost (MPK = r + d). If the cost of capital is $r_0$, fixed assets will be $K_0$. As in Figure 2.2, it generally takes time for the capital stock to adjust to the rate of interest, and for the money and natural rates of interest to converge. In Figure 2.3, the money and natural rates of interest are assumed to be the same; they have converged.

In a risky environment, firms will be unable to borrow at $r_0$, which is the risk-free rate of interest. Suppose that they can borrow at $r_1$ where the difference between $r_1$ and $r_0$ is the risk premium for commercial borrowers. In Figure 2.3 we ignore the possibility that this risk premium may vary with K. Also, firms will demand a risk premium on their business investment because the return on fixed assets is not risk-free. In Figure 2.3 this business risk premium is represented by the vertical difference between schedules $I_0$ and $I_1$, which according to equation (4.5) varies inversely with the capital stock. For convenience it has been assumed that schedule $I_1$ is linear, despite the fact that equation (4.4) suggests otherwise. Fixed assets contract from $K_0$ to $K_1$, the business risk premium equals bc, firms borrow at $r_1$ and the return on fixed assets increases from a to c. Therefore, in a risky environment fixed capital decreases and the return on fixed assets increases. This happens for two reasons: the cost of capital is larger and firms are more cautious.

Suppose next that the central bank cuts its interest rate so that the cost of capital to firms decreases from $r_1$ to $r_2$. If the rate of interest is cut to a normal level, the new equilibrium will be determined at point d, and fixed assets will increase from $K_1$ to $K_2$. If instead the rate of interest is cut permanently to an abnormal level of

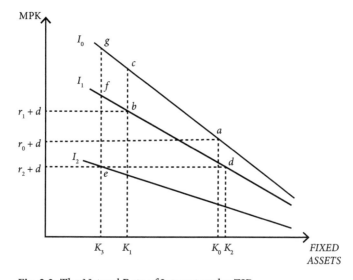

**Fig. 2.3** The Natural Rate of Interest under ZIP

zero, i.e. ZIP, existential risk will be induced. In Figure 2.3, this is represented by the vertical difference between schedules $I_1$ and $I_2$. The equilibrium stock of capital or fixed assets is determined at point e. Figure 2.3 is drawn with $K_3$ less than $K_1$ to underscore the possibility that ZIP may induce a reduction in fixed assets instead of an increase. In this equilibrium the return on capital is determined at point g, i.e. it increases. The business risk premium is fg and the existential risk premium is ef.

Had Figure 2.3 been drawn with schedule $I_2$ steeper, $K_3$ could have been greater than $K_1$, in which event ZIP would have increased the capital stock instead of the opposite. This might happen at first if ZIP is perceived to be a temporary phenomenon. However, as ZIP persists and the New Abnormal becomes even more abnormal, existential risk is expected to intensify, so that schedule $I_2$ tends to flatten over time, as drawn in Figure 2.3.

In summary, because ZIP is abnormal, the return on capital might increase instead of decreasing as in normal times. Investors hedge existential risk by investing less so that the rate of return on capital increases. ZIP deters business investment instead of promoting it.

## Quantitative Easing

Under ZIP, central bankers have almost become obsolescent. Long have gone the days when monetary policy committees met to set the rate of interest for the next month. At first, they met to decide that the rate of interest will remain zero. But after some time, they realized that there was no point in meeting to pronounce month after month that the rate of interest will remain zero. The media understandably lost interest in the monthly meetings of monetary policy committees. Presumably, MPC members continued to draw their emolument.

There seems to be a law according to which institutions reinvent themselves when their original purpose becomes obsolete. For example, the IMF's original purpose was to police the Bretton Woods system of fixed exchange rates. After the Bretton Woods system collapsed in 1971 and exchange rates were no longer fixed, the IMF reinvented itself with structural adjustment lending to assist economies in implementing macroeconomic policy. The IMF was not closed down; on the contrary, it has continued to find new tasks until today. The World Bank was established at Bretton Woods in 1944. Originally, its main purpose was to provide temporary loans, especially for low-income countries, while international capital markets recovered after World War Two. By the 1960s it looked as though the World Bank had served its purpose; the chaos in international capital markets had abated. However, Robert McNamara (appointed president in 1968) ironically exploited the recovery of international capital markets by issuing World Bank bonds to expand lending to developing countries. The World Bank was not closed down;

on the contrary, it not only competed with private financial institutions to provide loans to so-called "middle-income developing countries," it also competed with the IMF in structural adjustment lending.

In 1948 the Organization for European Economic Cooperation (OEEC) was established to oversee the Marshall Plan for postwar economic construction in western Europe. By 1960 the OEEC had served its purpose. The OEEC was not closed down; in 1961 it morphed instead into the Organization for Economic Co-operation and Development (OECD), which attracted member countries from outside Europe. The functions of the OECD today are essentially similar to what they were in the 1960s (writing country reports and analyses of the world economy, and making non-binding policy recommendations). Interestingly, Luis Buñuel included a scene filmed in the OECD building in Paris in his *Discreet Charm of the Bourgeoisie*, showing actor Fernando Rey sniping at an amorous couple strolling in the Rue de Franqueville below.

Old soldiers might fade away, but economic institutions do not. So was it that central bankers discovered an alternative raison d'être in the form of quantitative easing, or QE (see cartoon) after adopting ZIP.

Central bankers engage in QE when they buy securities, such as government and commercial bonds, from the public. QE entered into the vernacular in the late 1990s after Japan adopted ZIP in 1996. As we shall see, QE is euphemistic newspeak for when central banks "print money."

It is important to distinguish between open market operations, an orthodox activity of central banks of long standing, from QE, which is a recent heterodox activity. Central bankers engage in open market operations when they buy and sell treasury bills to control the volume of liquidity in money markets. Central banks implement their monetary policy through open market operations. If the money markets are short of liquidity and interest rates are above the central bank's target, it buys treasury bills. Their price increases and their return decreases in line with the central bank's interest rate policy. It sells treasury bills if the money markets are too liquid, and interest rates are too low.

Historically, central banks such as the Federal Reserve, the Bank of England, and the European Central Bank have kept the private sector at arm's length. They do not lend directly to the public for good reason. Instead, they operate through the banking system. Banks may borrow directly from central banks, but not the public. There are prudential reasons for this tradition, for otherwise central bankers might be pressurized by persons in the private sector seeking preferential treatment. Financial distancing is in the public interest. In Chapter 8 we shall describe what happened in Japan, where financial distancing was not practiced. QE should be regarded as a manifestation of the breakdown in financial distancing, because central banks must decide which commercial bonds to buy. The walls separating central banks and the private sector have been breached. Moral hazard is rife.

**Cartoon 2.**  Quantitative Easing

The present discussion of QE has positive and normative components. The former naturally comes after the latter. We begin by discussing how interest rate policy, represented by i in equation (2.1), affects the supply of money. Next, we focus on what happens as the rate of interest approaches zero. This part of the discussion is related to Keynes' "liquidity trap"; as the rate of interest tends to zero, the demand for money becomes infinitely elastic. As far as Keynes was concerned, this was a theoretical possibility, now turned into reality under the New Abnormal. This sets the theoretical scene for discussing QE, which turns out to be "full gas in neutral." In short, the positive effects of QE are neutral, as Keynes foresaw. However, the normative effects of QE are harmful and induce existential risk because, like ZIP, it is interpreted by the public as an act of desperation.

A minimal model is proposed to analyze the positive economics of QE in which there are three sectors: a banking sector, a private sector, and a central bank. In the background there is also the government or public sector. We begin by defining the balance sheets of each sector. Then we propose a theoretical model in which the central bank sets the interest rate at which banks may borrow reserves from the central bank. Banks intermediate between the central bank and the private sector by supplying bank credit. The model solves for the rate of interest on bank credit and reserves borrowed from the central bank. By implication it also solves for money supply. The model is used to investigate the theoretical effect of QE on the private and banking sectors when the central bank's rate of interest is positive. Finally, we investigate this effect when the central bank's interest rate tends to zero.

## Balance Sheets

The money stock (M) is defined as bank deposits (D) plus notes and coin held by the public ($C_p$). Bank reserves (R) are borrowed from the central bank (BR) at rate of interest i, while other reserves are non-borrowed (NBR), including notes and coin and bank balances at the central bank. Hence, R = BR + NBR. Base money ($M_0$) is defined as non-borrowed reserves plus notes and coin held by the public. Hence, $M_0$ = NBR + $C_p$. The "money multiplier" (m) is defined by the ratio between money and base money ($M/M_0$). Hence:

$$m = \frac{D + C_p}{C_p + NBR} \tag{5.1}$$

Bank reserves are also equal to required reserves (RR) and free or excess reserves (FR). Hence, R = RR + FR = BR + NBR. Following Meigs (1962), these definitions imply that equation (5.1) may be rewritten as:

$$m = \frac{1 + c_p}{c_p + \rho + f} \tag{5.2}$$

where $c_p = C_p/D$ denotes the "cash ratio," $\rho = RR/D$ denotes the required reserve ratio, and $f = (FR - BR)/D$ denotes the "free reserves" ratio. The cash ratio depends on fintech; it decreases as society becomes more cashless. In the past, $\rho$ was set by the central bank, but with financial liberalization banks set their own requirements on prudential grounds. Finally, the business of banking revolves around $f$ for free reserves don't earn profits, and borrowed reserves have a profit margin of $i_b - i$, where $i_b$ denotes the rate of interest on bank credit. Note that if BR exceeds FR, $f$ is negative. The money multiplier varies inversely with all the ratios in equation (5.2). Here we focus on the free reserves ratio because banks can borrow as many reserves as they wish from the central bank since the rate of interest is fixed. The more they borrow, the greater is the money multiplier.

The balance sheet of the banking system is $L + NBR = D + BR$, where $L$ denotes bank loans to the private sector. The balance sheet of the central bank is $BR + Q + TB_b = C + D_b$ where $TB_b$ denotes treasury bills purchased through open market operation, $D_b$ denotes bank deposits at the central bank (a component of reserves) and $Q$ denotes assets acquired through QE, which is normally zero. The borrowing requirement of the government equals its fiscal deficit (DEF). The borrowing requirement of the central bank equals its income from assets minus its operating cost $(Y_{cb})$ plus its open market purchases $(\Delta TB_b)$ and $\Delta Q = QE$. The consolidated borrowing requirement of the government and the central bank is $DEF + \Delta TB_{cb} + QE - Y_{cb} = PSBR$, often referred to as the public sector borrowing requirement. Finally, the public sector borrowing requirement is financed by issuing bonds (B), treasury bills, and base money. Hence, $PSBR = \Delta B + \Delta TB + \Delta M_0$ where $\Delta M_0 = \Delta NBR + \Delta C_p$. Insofar as the public sector borrowing requirement is not funded in the bond and bill markets, it must be funded by expanding the money base, or high-powered money. Since $QE = \Delta B_{cb}$ it would be self-defeating to fund QE by issuing treasury bonds. In practice, QE is funded through increasing base money.

## Money and Credit

The money supply is by definition equal to the money base times the money multiplier, hence $M^S = mM_0$. The demand for money is hypothesized, as usual, to vary inversely with the nominal rate of interest represented here by $i_b$:

$$ln M^D = \alpha + \frac{\beta}{i_b} \tag{5.3}$$

where $\alpha$ refers to nominal income, which for present purposes is determined outside the model, and the absolute interest elasticity of demand for money decreases with the rate of interest. Indeed, the demand for money becomes infinitely elastic as the rate of interest tends to zero. This is the "liquidity trap" imagined by Keynes in 1936, but now turned reality. When the rate of interest is zero, money has no opportunity cost, so there is no point in economizing on the quantity of money balances. Since money does not bear interest, and financial assets do not bear interest, money and financial assets tend to become perfect substitutes. In normal times, when interest rates are positive, this of course does not apply.

The demand for bank credit by the public is assumed to vary inversely with its rate of interest:

$$\ln L^D = \gamma - \delta i_b \tag{5.4}$$

where $\gamma$ represents off-model factors such as economic activity that affects the demand for bank credit. The supply of bank credit is implied by the balance sheet of the banking sector:

$$L^S = BR + \left(\frac{1}{\rho + f} - 1\right) NBR \tag{5.5}$$

The supply of bank credit varies directly with non-borrowed reserves (since the term in brackets is positive) and inversely with the required reserve ratio. Since borrowed reserves vary directly with the margin of intermediation ($i_b - i$) and f varies inversely, the supply of credit varies directly with the rate of interest on bank credit ($i_b$) and inversely with the rate of interest set by the central bank (i).

Figure 2.4 depicts the joint equilibrium in the market for money and credit. The demand schedules for money and credit slope downwards and their locations depend on $\alpha$ and $\gamma$ respectively. The supply schedules for money and credit slope upward. The location of the former varies directly with base money and inversely with the currency ratio and the central bank's interest rate. The location of the latter depends on non-borrowed reserves and varies inversely with the currency ratio and the central bank's interest rate. In equilibrium, bank credit is $L_a$, the money stock is $M_a$ and the rate of interest on bank credit is $i_{ba}$, which will be greater than the central bank's interest rate (i). By implication the equilibrium demand for borrowed reserves is $BR_a = L_a + NBR - (M_a + C_p)$.

The demand for money becomes infinitely elastic as the rate of interest tends to zero. The same does not apply to the demand for bank credit. As interest rates tend to zero the margin of intermediation contracts, as a result of which the supply of bank credit becomes, if anything, less interest elastic. The slope of the supply schedule for money in terms of its semi-elasticity is $-\frac{1}{c_p + \rho + f}\frac{\partial f}{\partial i_b} > 0$ since f varies inversely with $i_b$. This semi-elasticity varies inversely with f. Note that, although

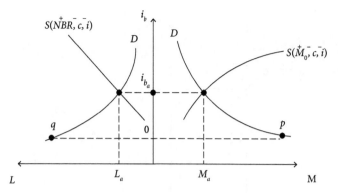

**Fig. 2.4** Equilibrium in Money and Credit Markets

the supply of borrowed reserves is infinitely elastic, the supply of money is not. The slope of the supply schedule for credit is $-\dfrac{NBR}{(\rho+f)^2}\dfrac{\partial f}{\partial i_b} + \dfrac{\partial BR}{\partial i_b} > 0$, which also varies inversely with f.

A credit squeeze induces an increase in f, inducing a leftward shift in the supply schedules for money and credit in Figure 2.4, as a result of which the rate of interest on bank credit increases, and both money and credit contract. QE increases non-borrowed reserves, inducing rightward shifts in the supply schedules for money and credit, and a lower rate of interest on bank credit. Therefore, QE may offset the adverse effects of a credit squeeze. The same would apply, however, to open market operations, or, for that matter, any other action that increased the money base.

## The Bond Market

The previous discussion refers to a partial equilibrium setting in which the endogenous variables are money, bank credit and the rate of interest on bank credit. Other asset markets, including treasury bills and bonds, were left outside the model. In principle these assets might have been handled in a general equilibrium setting, but in practice basic economic principles are often more transparent in the Marshallian tradition of partial equilibrium.

QE involves the purchase of financial securities, which mostly include treasury bonds, but in practice, as discussed in Chapter 4, central banks have also purchased corporate bonds and even equity. QE increases asset prices, which lowers their return. In the case of treasury bonds, QE lowers their gross redemption yields. Figure 2.5 is the partial equilibrium counterpart to Figure 2.4, in which the market for bank credit is off-stage and the bond market is given a leading role. The right-hand panels of Figures 2.4 and 2.5 are the same, but the left-hand panels

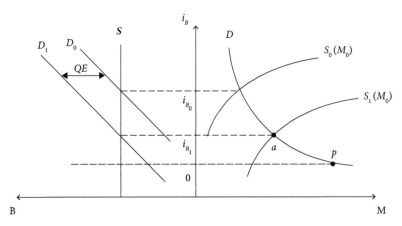

**Fig. 2.5** Equilibrium in Money and Bond Markets

are different. In Figure 2.5, B denotes the stock of bonds and their return is de-noted by $i_B$ (not to be confused with $i_b$ in Figure 2.4). The public's demand to hold bonds as part of their wealth varies directly with their return; hence, schedule D slopes upward. However, as their return approaches zero, so does their demand. Nevertheless, the public may wish to hold bonds even if their return is negative.

The stock of bonds is fixed in the immediate term; hence, the supply schedule (S) is vertical. Initially, their equilibrium rate of return is $i_{B0}$ at which the supply of money equals demand (and off stage the market for bank credit is in equilibrium). QE raises the demand schedule for bonds from schedules $D_0$ to $D_1$ and lowers their return. Because QE is financed by base money, the supply schedule for money (and credit) expands to the right, from schedule $S_0$ to $S_1$. The new partial equilibrium is determined at point a, at which the demand for money equals supply and the demand for bonds equals supply at interest rate $i_{B1}$. QE lowers interest rates and increases money supply and credit.

## Quanatitive Easing under Zero Interest Policy

Figures 2.4 and 2.5 are drawn for normal times when rates of interest are positive. What happens in abnormal times when the rate of interest is zero? In this case, the supply schedule for money intersects the demand schedule at a point such as p, and the supply schedule for credit intersects the demand schedule at a point such as q in Figure 2.4. Since the rate of interest is zero, the central bank has lost its main operating instrument; it has run out of ammunition.

Suppose that out of frustration it engages in QE. Equating equation (5.3) for the demand for money equal to the supply of money ($mM_0$), it may be shown that the marginal effect of base money on market interest rates, represented by $i_b$ or $i_B$, is:

$$\frac{di_b}{dM_0} = -\frac{1}{M_0}\left[\frac{1}{\dfrac{\beta}{i_b^2} - \dfrac{1}{c_p+p+f}\dfrac{\partial f}{\partial i_b}}\right] \qquad (5.6)$$

Since f varies inversely with $i_b$, equation (5.6) is negative as expected. However, as $i_b$ tends to zero, so does equation (5.6) because the denominator in square brackets approaches infinity. Since $dM_0$ = QE, this means that QE cannot affect market interest rates under ZIP. In summary, QE has no economic effect. All that happens is that the public simply adds the liquidity created by QE to its money balances because the demand for money is infinitely elastic in the liquidity trap. In fact, since risk-adjusted interest rates are zero everywhere, money, bonds, securitized mortgages, etc. are perfect substitutes for each other; they are all equally liquid. If so, QE is equivalent to buying an asset, such as treasury bonds, with base money when base money and bonds are perfect substitutes. In the limit under ZIP, QE is equivalent to treading water, or rather liquidity. QE is equivalent to full gas in neutral.

If QE makes no difference, why has it become the central operating instrument of central banks under ZIP? It won't be the first time that central banks have behaved irrationally. First, treading liquidity occurs in the limit under ZIP. If the limit has not been reached, QE may succeed in increasing liquidity, albeit by not very much. However, the more it does so, the closer it approaches the limit. Second, QE might be motivated to combat market failure in the financial system. For example, a credit crunch arises when banks refuse to lend even when borrowers are prepared to pay higher rates of interest to compensate for credit risk (Diamond and Dygbiv 1983). Due to asymmetric information, banks cannot assess credit risk properly, so they apply credit limits to their customers, instead of charging them higher rates of interest as assumed in our analysis. By flooding financial markets with liquidity through QE, central bankers might think it will break the log jam; banks will relax their credit limits. Third, a related argument arises when QE involves corporate bonds and equity. In a severe bear market, central bankers believe that the public is behaving irrationally and that QE will stabilize asset prices. In short, market failure justifies QE.

## Krugman's Zero Interest Policy Model

As noted in Chapter 1, Japan was the first country to adopt ZIP, in 1996, an event which prompted Krugman (1998) to ask whether monetary policy could affect inflation in the liquidity trap. As a matter of historical record, Krugman's pronouncement in reference to the liquidity trap that "it's baack" is over-dramatic because, even according to Keynes, it was never there in the first place. Keynes invented liquidity trap theory in 1936, but during the 1930s the Bank of England's bank rate was never less than 2 percent. Indeed, as noted in Chapter 1, Keynes did not think that the liquidity trap was relevant to his time, but he thought it might become relevant at some future time. This time came in 1996, when the Bank of Japan became the first central bank to adopt ZIP in several centuries of central banking.

Krugman's answer, described nicely by Romer (2019, section 12.7) and discussed further in Chapter 10, concurs with our own: ZIP implies that open market operations make no difference, unless the public perceives that ZIP is temporary. "Our analysis implies that one approach to stimulating the economy in a liquidity trap is to change expectations about what monetary policy will be once the economy is out of the trap." (Romer 2019, p 625). For example, the government should adopt a higher inflation target. Or the central bank engages in forward guidance by announcing its commitment to ZIP in the hope that this will increase expected inflation.

Even if ZIP is expected to be temporary, such policies may be time-inconsistent. When ZIP ends and inflation increases, the public might reasonably expect the government to revert to its pre-ZIP inflation target. If so, announcing higher inflation targets or engaging in forward guidance are unlikely to be credible. Indeed, such policy proposals recall the result that time-inconsistent policy is not optimal. Crying wolf undermines confidence in forward guidance. More importantly, when the public no longer believes that ZIP is temporary, these policies are irrelevant. Indeed, forward guidance on ZIP will most probably strengthen the belief that ZIP is permanent.

In 1998 only two years had passed since ZIP was adopted in Japan. The idea that ZIP would still be operating in Japan in 2022 would have sounded fantastic. Therefore, Krugman's proposals to break out of the liquidity trap are no longer relevant. Nor are they relevant elsewhere where several years have passed under ZIP. They might have been relevant during the first year of ZIP, but not subsequently. We shall return to this issue in Chapter 10.

## Normative Economics of Quantitative Easing

So far, we have been solely concerned with the positive economics of QE in terms of its effect on economic activity, which tends to zero in the limit. There are two key normative issues. The first concerns the end of financial distancing between central banks and the nonbank private sector. The second concerns the long-term implications for private enterprise.

As we shall see in Chapter 8, the Bank of Japan was historically directly involved with the nonbank private sector. There was no tradition of financial distancing. On the contrary, the central bank and the business sector were heavily involved with each other as a matter of policy. The Bundesbank in West Germany was also directly involved with the business sector during the 1950s and 1960s, but after the postwar reconstruction the Bundesbank reduced its involvement. By contrast, the Anglo-Saxon model of central banking is based on financial distancing with respect to the nonbank private sector. Central banks deal with their banking systems, and banking systems deal with their nonbank private sectors. This separation is intended to establish an arm's-length relation to protect central bankers from vested business interests. Indeed, as we shall see in Chapter 8, officials at the Bank of Japan succumbed to pressures from these vested interests.

As chronicled in Chapter 5, Anglo-Saxon central banks have increasingly extended QE to the purchase of corporate bonds and more recently to corporate equity. In doing so, they have broken the taboo of financial distancing. Which bonds should they buy? How can they remain neutral? The central banks involved have thus far tried to limit their QE to baskets of corporate bonds with specific grades. However, it is impossible for them to ensure that their corporate bond purchases are neutral with respect to specific businesses. Surely it is a question of time before companies begin to lobby central bankers, as they do ministries of finance, to include their corporate bonds on the shopping lists of central banks? The moral hazard issues involved in the extension of QE to corporate bonds loom large.

As explained in Chapter 5, central banks have used QE to flatten yield curves. At first, ZIP steepened yield curves because short-term interest rates decreased by more than long-term rates. Subsequently, long-term rates started to decrease when the markets realized that ZIP was not temporary, and yield curves became less steep. QE finally served as the *coup de grace* to flatten yield curves by massive purchases of long-term bonds. In doing so, central banks are implementing a form of political economy, fantasized by Patinkin (1966), in which they eventually own all corporate bonds to keep yield curves flat. This eventuality, as noted by Patinkin, is inconsistent with the future of private enterprise, and the traditional role of central banks as the guardians of liquidity.

## Fiscal Policy

In this section we begin by introducing the accounting mechanics of the ratio of public debt to GDP. Since accounting identities are truisms, they are very useful in setting ground rules over which there can be no argument. However, they are vacuous in the sense that they do not embody any economic theory. We introduce two components of economic theory. The first is concerned with the so-called "unpleasant monetary arithmetic" (Sargent and Wallace 1981), which applied under the Old Normal when interest rates were positive. The second is concerned with ZIP, where we show that much of this unpleasantness disappears when interest rates are zero.

## Accounting Identities

Let d = B/Y denote the ratio of nominal public debt (B) to nominal GDP (Y). Hence:

$$\dot{d} = \frac{\dot{B}}{Y} - \frac{B}{Y^2}\dot{Y} = def - dg \tag{6.1}$$

where def denotes the ratio of the fiscal deficit to GDP and g denotes the rate of growth of nominal GDP. In equation (6.1) it is assumed for the moment that the fiscal deficit is entirely financed by debt; none of it is monetized. Dividing equation (6.1) by d implies that the rate of growth of the debt-to-GDP ratio equals def/d−g. If the debt-to-GDP ratio is 100 percent (d = 1), its rate of growth is the difference between the fiscal deficit as a percentage of GDP and the rate of economic growth. If the former exceeds the latter, the debt-to-GDP ratio grows by the difference. If the latter exceeds the former, the debt-to-GDP ratio decreases by the difference. When the difference is zero, the debt-to-GDP ratio remains stable.

Suppose there are two economies, A and B, in which their nominal economic growth and their fiscal deficits as a percentage of GDP are 3 percent per year. In country A, debt is 100 percent of GDP but in B it is 50 percent. Equation (6.1) implies that in economy A the debt-to-GDP ratio is stable whereas in B it grows by 3 percent per year. If debt was 200 percent of GDP in country B its debt-to-GDP ratio would decrease by 1.5 percent per year. This may sound counterintuitive, but it is not. A thin person who overeats puts on weight faster than a fat person because to maintain a stable weight the fat person needs to eat more than the thin person. Heavily indebted countries such as Japan, where the debt-to-GDP ratio is approaching 300 percent, can afford to run larger fiscal deficits as a percentage of GDP than Germany, where the debt-to-GDP ratio is 60 percent. Japan is obese in debt whereas Germany is skinny.

Notice that, whereas d and def are real variables, the growth rate (g) refers to nominal GDP, where g = q + π is the real rate of growth (q) plus inflation (π). Equation (6.1) implies that, if the deficit as a percentage of GDP happens to be fixed, the debt-to-GDP ratio varies inversely with inflation. The reason for this is that public debt is not indexed to the general price level. So, as far as the debt-to-GDP ratio is concerned, the decomposition of nominal income growth does not matter. Matters would be different in countries such as Israel, in which a large proportion of public sector debt is indexed to the rate of inflation. If all the debt is index-linked, what matters is q. If none is index-linked what matters is g. If some is index-linked what matters is a combination of g and q.

If the rate of nominal GDP growth happens to be fixed as well as the deficit-to-GDP ratio, the general solution to equation (6.1) is:

$$d(t) = d_0 e^{-gt} + \left(1 - e^{-gt}\right) \frac{def}{g} \tag{6.2}$$

where $d_0$ denotes the initial debt-to-GDP ratio. Equation (6.2) implies that in the steady state the debt-to-GDP ratio is def/g in which case the primary fiscal deficit is defp = def(1-i/g), i.e. the primary fiscal deficit varies inversely with the rate of interest and directly with the rate of growth of nominal GDP. If the rate of interest exceeds the rate of growth of nominal GDP, the primary fiscal deficit is negative if the fiscal deficit is positive. For example, if the rate of nominal income growth equals the deficit as a percentage of GDP, the debt-to-GDP ratio tends to 100 percent. If nominal income grows at half the rate of the fiscal deficit, the debt-to-GDP tends to 200 percent. In the absence of nominal income growth, the debt-to-GDP ratio tends to infinity. Also, if the nominal rate of interest equals the rate of growth of nominal GDP, the primary deficit tends to zero in the steady state; the deficit is comprised entirely of debt interest. Matters are different if the rate of interest is less than the growth of nominal GDP because i/g < 1.

The change in the debt-to-GDP ratio is:

$$\dot{d}(t) = \left(def - gd_0\right) e^{-gt} \tag{6.3}$$

According to equation (6.3), the debt-to-GDP ratio grows if the term in brackets is positive. The debt-to-GDP ratio is more likely to grow in countries where deficit-to-GDP ratios are large relative to the initial level of debt, and where nominal income growth is smaller.

Thus far we have assumed that the government targets the fiscal deficit rather than the primary fiscal deficit. We have also assumed that the fiscal deficit is entirely bond-financed; the authorities do not "print" money to finance the deficit. Relaxing these assumptions implies that equation (6.1) becomes:

$$\dot{d} = defp - \mu + (r - q) d \tag{6.4}$$

where $\mu = \dot{M}_0/Y$ denotes the monetization rate, and r = i − π denotes the real rate of interest on public debt. If the primary deficit and monetization rates happen to be fixed as well as the real rates of interest and economic growth, the general solution to equation (6.4) is:

$$d(t) = d_0 e^{-(q-r)t} + \left(1 - e^{-(q-r)t}\right) \frac{defp - \mu}{q - r} \tag{6.5}$$

If q > r, equation (6.5) implies that in the steady state the debt-to-GDP ratio tends to $\frac{defp - \mu}{q-r}$; it varies directly with the primary deficit relative to GDP and the real rate of interest, and it varies inversely with the real rate of interest and the rate of monetization. The overall percentage fiscal deficit in the steady state is:

$$def = \frac{(q - \pi)\, defp - (r - \pi)\, \mu}{q - r} \tag{6.6}$$

In the absence of inflation, the coefficient of defp is q/(q − r) > 1 because q > r, in which event the fiscal deficit is a multiple of the primary fiscal deficit, and the co-efficient on the rate of monetization is a negative multiple. Hence, the fiscal deficit varies directly with primary fiscal deficit and inversely with the rate of monetiza-tion. Moderate inflation reduces the coefficients, and if inflation exceeds the rate of growth and the real rate of interest, these coefficients become negative.

If, instead, q < r, the debt-to-GDP ratio is unstable. Note that when the fiscal deficit is targeted the root of equation (6.1) is g. When the primary fiscal deficit is targeted the root of equation (6.4) is q − r = g − i.

We have assumed thus far that the rate of interest on public sector debt is in-dependent of the debt-to-GDP ratio. If, instead, the rate of interest varies directly with the debt-to-GDP ratio, e.g. $r = r_0 d^a$, the cost of debt interest as a percentage of GDP would be $r_0 d^{1+a}$ where the exponent must exceed 1. In this case, it is obvious that if there is a steady-state debt-to-GDP ratio it must be larger than its counter-part in equation (6.5), where it was assumed that a = 0. Moreover, at some point r will exceed q and the debt-to-GDP ratio will tend to explode.

The monetization rate equals the inflation tax, or central bank seigniorage, as a percentage of GDP. Hence $\mu = (\pi + q)M_0/Y$, which in the absence of inflation varies directly with the rate of growth and inversely with the velocity of circulation of base money. The Maastricht fiscal guidelines set d at 0.6 (debt-to-GDP ratio of 60 percent) and the fiscal deficit at 3 percent of GDP. Under the assumption that q = π = 0.06 this implicitly assumes that μ = 0.012, and the velocity of base money equals 5.

If the real rate of interest on public debt happens to be zero, as it is under ZIP, the real cost of debt service is zero. This enables the government to run larger primary fiscal deficits. In the numerical example, the primary fiscal deficit would be 3 percent of GDP instead of 1.8 percent even when μ = 0. At least this would have been the case assuming that the rate of economic growth was still 3 percent. However, existential risk induced by the New Abnormal is expected to lower the rate of economic growth.

## Unpleasant Monetary Arithmetic

Suppose in the previous numerical example that $\mu = 0$ so that fiscal deficits are entirely funded in the bond market rather than being partially monetized. If the debt-to-GDP ratio is growing, the ratio of government debt to base money must be growing even faster. Intuitively, the rate of interest on public debt will tend to increase as the public holds ever-larger shares of its wealth in treasury bonds. The cost of debt service becomes ever-larger too. As long as the government does not cut its primary deficit by ever-larger amounts, the cost of debt service will eventually threaten the solvency of the government. Eventually, the unpleasant monetary arithmetic (UMA) predicts that the government will be forced into monetizing the deficit. According to UMA, persistent and unsustainable fiscal deficits eventually have to be monetized, and are consequently inflationary.

This does not mean that, before UMA kicks in, funding the deficit in the bond markets has no inflationary implications. This fiscal theory of the price level may be seen in Figure 2.4. Funding deficits increases the stock of bonds, which increases $i_B$ and reduces the demand for money. Unless the central bank raises its interest rate, the supply schedule for money continues to be $S_0$. The excess supply of money over demand induces an increase in prices, which reduces the real value of bonds. The latter induces a leftward movement in the demand schedule for bonds, which partially offsets the initial increase in $i_B$. In the new equilibrium, both prices and $i_B$ are larger than at the beginning.

Monetizing deficits implies that schedule S in the bond market remains unchanged, while schedule S in the market for money shifts to the right because the money base is larger. This is inflationary because the price level must increase until the excess supply of money is eradicated. According to UMA, monetization is induced when the deficit can no longer be funded in the bond market because $i_B B_g$ is too large relative to GDP. This discussion of UMA refers to conditions under the Old Normal when interest rates were positive.

## Unpleasant Monetary Arithmetic and Zero Interest Policy

What happens to UMA under ZIP? Under ZIP the cost of debt service tends to zero by definition. In the bond market, schedules S and D in Figure 2.4 intersect at rates of interest, which are almost zero if not zero. The same applies to the intersection of schedules S and D in the market for money. Moreover, the location of schedule S reflects the fact that the central bank's rate of interest is zero too. Monetizing the deficit shifts the money supply schedule S to the right. However, because the demand for money is infinitely elastic there can be no excess supply of money, and consequently no inflation. This explains the coexistence of rapidly expanding money supplies with no inflation, discussed in Chapter 5. If the deficit is funded instead, schedule S in the bond market shifts to the left. The demand schedule for bonds is elastic too, so the rate of interest on bonds scarcely changes. Indeed, money and bonds have become close if not perfect substitutes, so it makes no difference whether the deficit is funded or monetized. In either case there are no inflationary implications.

In summary, UMA ceases to apply under ZIP, and because the demand for money is infinitely elastic, its supply can increase without inflationary consequences. Governments can run large deficits without unpleasantness. Maybe this is why ZIP has become so popular.

The suspension of UMA can be made more formally by obtaining the counterpart of equation (5.6) for the price level (P) instead of $i_b$:

$$\frac{dP}{dM_0} = \frac{1}{M} \left[ \frac{1}{\frac{1}{P} - \left( \frac{\beta}{i_g^2} + \frac{1}{\mu} \frac{\partial \mu}{\partial i_g} \right) \frac{\partial i_g}{\partial P}} \right] \tag{6.7}$$

Since, as noted, the partial derivative of the rate of interest on public debt $i_g$ with respect to the price level is negative, monetizing deficits normally increases price levels, as expected. However, as the rate of interest tends to zero, so does the term in square brackets, in which event equation (6.7) tends to zero. UMA is suspended.

In summary, ZIP creates a world in which the laws of economics seem to be suspended. It costs nothing to run fiscal deficits. There is no inflation. All assets assume the characteristics of money insofar as they too bear no interest. The world of ZIP, however, is not sustainable because its architecture is flawed. Capital markets lose their meaning. Incentives to save disappear. Monetary policy is of no consequence. It can't last.

## Exchange Rates and Interest Rates

Equations (2.1–2.3) refer to the NKM for a closed economy, which was adequate to make the point that in practice the natural rate of interest has been overlooked and even mismeasured. In this section we deal with open economy aspects of the NKM (Svensson 2000), which have had a major influence on central banks, especially in small open economies. Specifically, the New Keynesian adoption of interest parity theory (IPT) has induced central banks to cut their interest rates simply because ZIP was adopted by dominant players such as the Federal Reserve, the European

Central Bank, and the Bank of England. According to IPT, the foreign interest rate ($i^*$) equals the local interest rate (i) plus the expected rate of exchange rate appreciation:

$$i_t^* = i_t + E_t\left(e_{t+1}\right) - e_t \qquad (7.1)$$

where e denotes the logarithm of the exchange rate (e increases with appreciation as in the case of sterling). If the economy is small and open, equation (7.1) seems to suggest that if ZIP is applied abroad ($i^*$ is set to zero), but the central bank does not cut its rate of interest, the exchange rate will appreciate. If the central bank is targeting the exchange rate, it will adopt ZIP too in order to prevent the revaluation of the exchange rate.

Many central bank governors, including the governor of the Bank of Israel, fell into this trap and adopted ZIP as if it were *force majeure*. The only reason why they adopted ZIP was because it was adopted elsewhere. There was no inherent justification for ZIP, such as a financial crisis, which induced foreign central banks to adopt ZIP in the first place. In summary, IPT is a driving force in the global epidemiology of ZIP.

We do not ask why these smaller central banks should have targeted their exchange rates, although it is usually to protect exporters from international com-petition under floating exchange rates. Instead, we focus on positive rather than normative economics by asking whether interest rate policy has lasting effects on exchange rates both in theory and in practice.

We start with the accounting identity for the balance of payments, according to which the current account balance (CA) plus the capital account balance (CAP) equals the purchases of foreign exchange by the central bank (Z), where Z rep-resents foreign exchange intervention. The change in foreign exchange reserves equals Z plus interest and capital gains on the reserves. The current account bal-ance varies inversely with the exchange rate because devaluation makes exports more expensive abroad and imports cheaper at home. Hence $CA_t = c_t - \alpha e_t$ where c denotes other factors influencing the current account balance, including the volume of world trade and relative price levels at home and abroad.

The net stock of foreign capital (F) is hypothesized to depend on the expected return to investing capital in the economy minus the return to investing abroad. Hence, $F_t = \beta\left[i_t + E_t e_{t+1} - e_t - i_t^*\right]$. Interest rates, announced in advance, are fixed at the beginning of period t. Since the capital account balance during period t is defined as $F_{t+1} - F_t$, the balance of payments identity may be written as:

$$-\alpha e_t + c_t + \beta\left[E_{t+1} e_{t+2} - E_t e_{t+1} + \Delta\left(i_{t+1} - i_{t+1}^* - e_{t+1}\right)\right] = Z_t \qquad (7.2)$$

Equation (7.2) constitutes the equilibrium condition in the forex market. It implies that the current exchange rate depends on the rational expectations of $e_{t+1}$ and

$e_{t+2}$, on interest rate differentials at time t and t+1, as well as on $c_t$ and forex intervention ($Z_t$).

To solve for the current exchange rate, we apply the same procedures used for equations (2.1) and (2.2). We begin by lagging equation (7.2) two periods, taking expectations as of time t (since according to the law of iterated expectations $E_t(E_{t+1})e_{t+j} = E_t(e_{t+j})$), dividing through by $\beta$ and reorganizing generates a second-order stochastic difference equation in the expected exchange:

$$\left(1 - \frac{\alpha}{\beta}\right)E_t e_{t-2} - 2E_t e_{t-1} + E_t e_t = E_t x_{t-2} \tag{7.3}$$

where:

$$x_t = \frac{Z_t - c_t}{\beta} + \Delta\left(i^*_{t+1} - i_{t+1}\right) \tag{7.4}$$

The roots of equation (7.3) are:

$$\rho = 1 \pm \sqrt{\alpha/\beta} \tag{7.5}$$

Hence, one root ($\rho_1$) is less than 1 and $\rho_2$ is greater than 1, where $\rho_2$ is the bubble root. If capital account transactions are more exchange rate sensitive than trade transactions, then $\alpha/\beta$ is a fraction. For example, if this fraction is one half, $\rho_1 = 0.2929$ and $\rho_2 = 1.7071$, and the inverse of the bubble root is 0.5858. Applying the forward solution to the inverse of the bubble root implies the following general solution to the rational expectation for the exchange rate:

$$E_t e_t = \rho_1 E_t e_{t-1} - \frac{\rho_2^{-1} E_t x_{t-1}}{1 - \rho_2^{-1} L^{-1}} + A\rho_2^{-t} \tag{7.6}$$

It has an autoregressive component through $\rho_1$ and, as expected, a forward-looking component through the inverse of $\rho_2$:

$$-\sum_{j=0}^{\infty} \rho_2^{-(j+1)} E_t x_{t+j-1} \tag{7.7}$$

Equation (7.7) implies that current expectations of the exchange rate vary inversely (weaker exchange rate) with expected forex intervention and expected increases in interest rates abroad, and they vary directly (stronger exchange rate) with expectations of benign current account shocks (c), such as oil and gas discoveries, and tighter monetary policy at home. This completes stage 1 in solving rational expectations models.

In stage 2, equation (7.6) is used to obtain the one step ahead rational expectations for the exchange rate, $E_t e_{t+1}$ and $E_{t+1} e_{t+1}$, which are substituted into equation (7.2). Before doing so, however, we note that these rational expectations imply that interest rate policy has only a passing or temporary influence on the exchange rate. Indeed, a permanent change in the interest rate can have no long-term effect on the exchange rate because what matters in equation (7.6) is the change in interest rates rather than the level. For example, equation (7.5) implies that a cut in the rate of interest of 1 percent induces a devaluation of less that 1 percent. It equals $\rho_2^{-1}$ percent or only 0.5858 percent according to our numerical example. Moreover, this effect dissipates subsequently.

The only permanent influences on the exchange rate are related to the current account balance through c, which strengthens the exchange rate, and forex intervention, which weakens it. If, however, forex intervention is intended to smooth the exchange rate, current intervention will be expected to be reversed, in which case the effect of intervention will be seriously mitigated (Beenstock 1983).

The general solution for the exchange rate obtained by substituting for the expected exchange rates into equation (7.2) is:

$$e_t = \rho_1 e_{t-1} + \frac{\Omega_t + \left(\frac{1}{\rho_2} - 1\right) x_{t-1}}{1 - \rho_1} \tag{7.8}$$

$$\Omega_t = \sum_{j=0}^{\infty} \rho_2^{-(j+1)} \left(E_t x_{t+j} - \rho_2 E_{t+1} x_{t+j}\right) \tag{7.9}$$

As expected, the exchange rate is a first-order autoregression with stable root $\rho_1$. The coefficient of $x_{t-1}$ in the numerator of equation (7.8) is negative because $\rho_2$ exceeds 1. Hence, contemporaneous interest rate policy strengthens the exchange rate. In equation (7.9), $\Omega$ decreases if expectations of x are revised upward. For example, if the public revised upward its expectations of forex intervention by the central bank, the current exchange rate would weaken. This effect is weaker if these revisions refer to the more remote future. If the public revises upward its expectations of tighter monetary policy in the future (increase in i) the current exchange rate strengthens on anticipation. However, these effects are transient because what matters is the change in interest rates rather than the level (since in equation (7.4) x depends on $\Delta i_{t+1}$).

Equation (7.9) focuses on monetary policy and exchange rate policy. As expected, the exchange rate is autoregressive, forex intervention weakens the exchange rate, and tighter monetary policy has the opposite effect. $\Omega$ captures the effect of expectations. For example, an increase in the rate of interest expected three periods hence (t + 3) induces an exchange rate appreciation at time t:

$$\frac{\partial e_t}{\partial \Delta i_{t+3}} = -\frac{p_2^{-3}\left(1 - p_2^{-1}\right)}{1 - p_1} = -0.283 \tag{7.10}$$

Continuing with the numerical illustration, an increase in the current rate of interest appreciates the exchange rate by 0.5858 percent. If instead, the tightening of monetary policy is expected to occur three periods hence, the current exchange rate appreciates by only 0.283 percent.

IPT assumes that international capital movements are perfectly elastic or $\beta = \infty$. In this case, equation (7.2) reverts to equation (7.1), and forex intervention and current account shocks cannot affect the exchange rate. If, in general, international capital movements are more elastic than international trade but are nevertheless imperfectly elastic, the implications of monetary policy for exchange rates are radically different. Changes in interest rates have a less than proportionate effect on exchange rates in the short run and no effect at all in the long run.

## Relative and Absolute Interest Parity

IPT is a simplifying pedagogic assumption that makes it easier to teach open economy macroeconomics. The assumption that $\beta$ is infinite means that assets in domestic and foreign currency are perfect substitutes. Even if assets happen to be riskless in terms of their currency of denomination, they involve exchange rate risk since exchange rates cannot be predicted perfectly. Assuming that $\beta$ is infinite also means that if interest parity did not hold, either all the world's capital would flow instantaneously into the country concerned, or all its capital would flow out. It also means that phenomena such as home currency preference would not exist (Beenstock 1980). Finally, it means that what happens to the current account of the balance of payments cannot directly affect the exchange rate. In summary, when $\beta$ is infinite IPT is absolute in the same way that absolute purchasing power parity theory (PPP) assumes that goods and services from different countries are perfect substitutes. Absolute PPP implies that $\alpha$ is infinite. Absolute IPT implies that $\beta$ is infinite.

The counterpart to relative PPP, where goods and services from different countries are imperfect substitutes, is relative IPT where capital assets from different countries are imperfect substitutes, i.e. where $\beta$ is infinite. Textbooks such as Parkin and Bade (1988), in which international capital movement are imperfectly elastic, are considerably more complicated because they do not assume absolute IPT. The assumption that $\beta$ is finite means that the effect of the current account on the exchange rate cannot be ignored, which is why open economy macroeconomics is much more difficult to teach.

The exchange rate theory proposed here refers to the general case of relative PPP and relative IPT because α and β are assumed to be finite. Of course, the model also generates the limiting special cases when either α or β tend to infinity, or both α and β tend to infinity.

In summary, whereas absolute interest rate parity theory implies that interest rate policy has permanent effects upon exchange rates, relative interest parity theory implies that these effects are temporary. When the Federal Reserve, the Bank of England, and the European Central Bank (as well as some minor central banks) adopted ZIP in the aftermath of the Subprime Crisis, exchange rates in small open economies elsewhere tended to appreciate. To prevent their exchange rates from appreciating their central banks cut interest rates in the belief that interest rate parity theory is absolute as in the NKM. In Chapter 5 we explain that, because interest rate parity theory is relative rather than absolute, these cuts in interest rates had only temporary effects on exchange rates. Consequently, these central bankers continued to cut interest rates until they cut them to zero. They descended into ZIP despite their immunity from the Subprime Crisis due to a basic and simple misunderstanding about the difference between relative and absolute interest parity.

## The Dynamic Stochastic General Equilibrium Movement

The NKM, represented by equations (2.1) to (2.3), is minimalistic. Equation (2.2) does not distinguish between consumption and investment; there is no labor market, and aggregate supply is determined outside the model. The output gap in NKM is assumed to be a measure of aggregate demand. DSGE models may be regarded as an attempt to add flesh to NKM by specifying equations for consumption, investment, labor supply, labor demand, and aggregate supply. The basic DSGE model (Romer 2019, Chapter 7) assumes that there is a representative consumer and a representative producer who are fully rational. The representative consumer dynamically optimizes utility in terms of consumption and labor supply. The representative producer dynamically optimizes profits in terms of investment and employment. Apart from this, DSGE models take on board the NKM Phillips curve (equation 2.1) and close the model by a Taylor rule for interest rate policy such as equation (2.3). Open economy versions of DSGE assume the exchange rate is determined by equation (7.1) according to absolute IPT.

DSGE models are eclectic. They borrow ideas from New Keynesian theory such as imperfect competition and Calvo pricing to motivate price stickiness. They also borrow ideas from Real Business Cycle theory along the lines of equations (2.3) above. The basic insight of Real Business Cycle theory is that, because of adjustment costs, it takes time for firms to change their capital stocks. During this adjustment process the marginal product of capital differs from the cost of capital. This may sound as if Wicksell's natural rate of interest theory is also adopted by the DSGE movement. As we shall see, this impression is correct in principle but not in practice. The DSGE movement has overlooked the natural rate of interest despite the fact that the movement is Neo-Wicksellian.

The guiding principle of the DSGE movement is that the "deep" structural parameters of macroeconomic models should be clearly specified and be based on clear microeconomic foundations. In the next chapter we explain that this principle was intended as a (misguided) response to the Lucas critique (Lucas 1976). The term "movement" is used advisedly. There is a rich variety of DSGE models, all of which adopt the principles of the movement in terms of microfoundations. The DNA of DSGE models vary in the way that frictions are introduced into the determination of prices, wages, investment, and capital markets. Also, DSGE models have relaxed the representative agent principle by allowing for risk averse and risk neutral agents, as well as rational and irrational agents. As described in the next chapter, these piecemeal developments have been motivated to make DSGE models fit the data better. Members of the DSGE movement tweak the DNA of their models to "explain" new features of the data; they are always one step behind.

The DSGE movement has played a dominant role in macroeconomics since 2000. Romer (2019, pp 364–5) refers to optimists who believe that the DSGE movement is on the "right track" as well as pessimists who think that the movement "has put macroeconomics back into a position similar to where it stood in the early 1970s." The optimists believe that piecemeal improvements will eventually lead to macroeconomic models that respond to the Lucas critique. The pessimists believe that "there is greater value of working on new issues in narrower models."

As explained in the next three chapters, the dichotomy is not between optimism and pessimism. The dichotomy is methodological; it is about how hypotheses should be tested in macroeconomics. The DSGE movement has strayed from classical econometric methods to the point where the model is assumed to be the truth and the empirical data are used to populate its unknown parameters. Revisionist critics of the DSGE movement call for a return to classical hypothesis testing using methods of indirect inference, designed to test entire models. The author is on the side of the revisionists.

Vines and Wills (2018) have sought to "rebuild macroeconomic theory" following the failure of DSGE models to predict the Subprime Crisis of 2008 and the Great Depression that followed in its aftermath. They seem to think that macroeconomic theory is synonymous with the DSGE movement, and ask what modifications should be made to DSGE models so that they would have predicted the Subprime Crisis and its aftermath. Vines and Wills are good examples of tweakers who are always one step behind reality. By the time that they have resuscitated their DSGE model, its next failure has already occurred.

Thus do successive generations of DSGE models stagger from one failure to the next. There is, of course, much more to macroeconomic theory than DSGE models.

The methodological heterodoxy of the DSGE movement has played a major role in the development of the New Abnormal. Policy makers have fallen under the influence of narratives generated by DSGE models, as recounted in the next chapter.

## Synopsis

Contemporary Neo-Wicksellian macroeconomic theorists have misunderstood Wicksell's natural rate of interest, which refers to the return on fixed capital assets. They have also misunderstood that the natural rate of interest is not an equilibrium phenomenon. In practice, they have overlooked the natural rate of interest as a key variable in their theory. This omission is important because zero interest policy has widened the gap between the natural rate of interest and the real rate of interest. This interest rate gap is also omitted from the dashboards at central banks and policy makers.

The concept of existential risk is introduced and developed. Existential risk arises when a form of political economy, such as the New Abnormal, does not last forever but the timing of its demise is uncertain. Since business investment varies inversely with existential risk, the interest rate gap tends to widen because the existential risk premium is reflected in the natural rate of interest. The increase in the existential risk premium hastens the end of political economies, e.g. the collapse of the Bretton Woods system in 1971. Sooner or later the New Abnormal will end.

The natural rate of interest, which has been overlooked in New Keynesian and DSGE models, is reinstated into the influential NKM. Whereas in the NKM there is an output gap and an inflation gap, in the reinstated model there is also an interest rate gap (the difference between the natural rate of interest measured by the return on fixed capital assets and the rate of interest minus the rate of inflation). Whereas according to the NKM, if output and inflation are on target (the so-called divine coincidence) the interest rate gap must be zero, matters are different in the reinstated model because this gap is measured directly. In the absence of measures of the natural rate of interest, central bankers have concluded mistakenly that the natural rate of interest must by default be zero, or close to it, if output and inflation are on target when the rate of interest is zero. This theoretical flaw has been instrumental in the widespread international adoption of the New Abnormal.

Keynes' liquidity trap theory is used to explain why, as the rate of interest tends to zero, monetary growth induced by quantitative easing cannot induce inflation. This argument overturns those of the proponents of the New Abnormal, who have argued that, because inflation has been almost zero under the New Abnormal, orthodox macroeconomic theory must be wrong. Liquidity trap theory also explains why the Unpleasant Monetary Arithmetic, one of the pillars of macroeconomic orthodoxy, has been temporarily suspended. Once rates of interest cease to be zero, however, inflation, which has been kinetic, is expected to break out.

It is no coincidence that the New Abnormal was adopted by countries such as the US and the UK following the Subprime Crisis. It is more difficult to explain why other countries, which were not directly or indirectly involved in the Subprime Crisis, nevertheless adopted ZIP and the New Abnormal. A simple theoretical model is proposed to account for the epidemiology of ZIP based on the difference between absolute and relative interest rate parity theory under floating exchange rates. The former assumes that international capital is perfectly mobile. The latter assumes that it is imperfectly mobile. Exchange rates in these countries appreciated following the adoption of ZIP in the US, UK, and elsewhere. Central banks cut interest because they were targeting their exchange rates. Whereas absolute interest parity implies that a once and for all cut in interest rates will depreciate the exchange rate permanently, relative interest parity implies that interest rate cuts have only a temporary effect on exchange rates. Failing to understand the difference between relative and absolute interest parity theory, central bankers kept cutting interest rates until they could do so no longer, because the rate of interest reached the lower bound of zero.

Under the New Abnormal, debt-to-GDP ratios have spiraled out of control in many countries, including the US, Japan, and Italy. The arithmetic of the dynamics of debt-to-GDP ratios is examined when interest rates are positive and zero, when nominal income grows faster or slower than the fiscal deficit as a percentage of GDP, when inflation is greater or smaller than the rate of interest, when the government targets the primary deficit rather than the overall deficit, when the central bank monetizes the deficit etc.

# 3

# Postmodern Macroeconomics

## The Postmodern Revolt against Science

Modernism began in the seventeenth century with the rationalism of Francis Bacon and René Descartes, continued in the eighteenth century with the deductive theories of knowledge of David Hume, expressed itself in the nineteenth century through the Enlightenment movement, and was consolidated in the twentieth century by the epistemology of Karl Popper, Rudolph Carnap, and others. The modernist credo is to push back the frontiers of ignorance through rational scientific inquiry. This process involves the development of falsifiable hypotheses, which are rejected if they fail to be empirically corroborated and are provisionally accepted otherwise. Advances in science and technology bear witness to the success of the modernist movement. Mankind is better off today than before Francis Bacon (Mokyr 2002).

Economists took to modernism like a duck to water. They developed their theories axiomatically, based on axioms such as rationality, expressed them mathematically to avoid ambiguity, and, in the absence of experimental data, developed the discipline of econometrics to test their hypotheses with observational data. Axiomatic theory is not falsified by rejecting its axioms, but by its failure to predict reality. Nor does corroboration imply that axioms are true.

We do not judge here whether modernist economics turned out to be a successful project, and whether or not "Funeral by funeral, does economics makes progress. Darwinian impact of reality melts away even the prettiest of fanciful theories and the hottest of ideological frenzies." (Samuelson 1997, p 159). Instead, we focus on how postmodernism has challenged economics as a discipline. Postmodernism started out as a critique of art, literature, architecture and culture, but it soon turned its back on the Enlightenment and the belief that, funeral by funeral, mankind makes progress. As far as science is concerned, postmodernists questioned whether we can learn anything from empirical testing. "The anti-empiricist stance adopted by epistemological postmodernists means that the importance which has traditionally been attached to research methodology becomes suspect. Indeed, skeptical postmodernists rarely do empirical work of any kind as they deny the possibility of an empirical social science." (Johnson and Duberley 2000, p 104). They believe that the search for "truth" is sisyphic, and that

*Zero Interest Policy and the New Abnormal.* Michael Beenstock, Oxford University Press. © Michael Beenstock (2022).
DOI: 10.1093/oso/9780192849663.003.0003

knowledge is ultimately relativistic (Fuller 2015). The utterances of pretenders to knowledge are merely narratives about the world. It is a matter of taste which narratives are preferred. Their narrators involve themselves in "discourses" (in the sense of Michel Foucault), which are usually disjointed. Narrators may "deconstruct" (in the sense of Jacques Derrida) the narratives of their rivals with the result that discourses remain mutually exclusive.

This revolt against empirical orthodoxy led to the "Science Wars" of the 1990s (Fuller 2015). Modernist objections to postmodern relativism were simply deconstructed away, except for the Sokal Hoax. In 1996 physicist Alan Sokal published a fabricated postmodern critique of physics, entitled, "Transgressing the boundaries: towards a transformative hermeneutics of quantum gravity," in a leading postmodernist journal. He peppered his critique with scientific errors, but crafted it in postmodern jargon. After the bluff was called, the editors blamed the referees. Signally, his postmodern critics did not resort to postmodern methods to deconstruct him. Nevertheless, Fuller (2015, p 266–9) offers a belated postmodern defense.

Surprisingly, the social sciences have largely escaped the attention of the postmodernists. However, a small minority of economists (Johnson and Duberley 2000, Amariglio, Cullenberg and Ruccio 2001 Ruccio and Amariglio 2004) have extended a welcome to the postmodernist agenda. "The postmodern turn within economics is beginning to reshape the way economists relate to what they do, especially the modernism that characterizes most twentieth century economics" (Ruccio 1991, p495). Foucault might have regarded neoclassical, post-Keynesian and behavioral economics as separate discourses. He might also have interpreted the formalization of mainstream economics as an attempt by its founders to acquire "power" by making it inaccessible to the verbal public, and by endowing it with artificial scientific esoterics. Amariglio, Cullenberg and Ruccio quote David Kreps to this effect with respect to economists' use of mathematics. The same would apply to econometrics with sub-discourses for time series data, cross-section data and panel data.

Amariglio, Cullenberg and Ruccio side with McCloskey (1985, 1994), who argued that economists do not practice what they preach. They use their technical skills for rhetorical purposes and to back up their advocacy with pseudo-scientific support. Modernism is a fig leaf for justifying preconceived narratives. These postmodern economists do not criticize orthodox econometrics per se, but they call for heterodoxy in empirical inquiry. Indeed, this postmodern perspective on hypothesis testing in economics constitutes the major theme in this chapter. In this context, Fuller (2015, pp 273–4) regards the practice of counterfactual simulation using computer models as a form of postmodern expression. Instead of real experiments in the laboratory, computer experiments are used to acquire virtual knowledge. "Leading the postmodern revival of counterfactual reasoning has been the proliferation of computer models in scientific research. Interestingly, journalists were among the first to herald the increasing use of such models as marking the end of the strict modernist divide between the scientific and the artistic mindsets, as actual reality comes to be reabsorbed as just one of the many versions of virtual reality contained within a computer model. ... The simulation of global climate change over the centuries is the most notorious contemporary icon of this sensibility ..." (Fuller 2015 pp 278–9).

Fuller's criticism also applies to much of macroeconomics, including Real Business Cycle models, and DSGE models. Indeed, Kydland and Prescott, who pioneered Real Business Cycle theory (Kydland and Prescott 1982), expressly imported into economics the computer simulation methods used by climate scientists. They argued that, just as climate scientists write down the laws of physics in their computer models, so should economists write down the laws of economics.

## Econometric Orthodoxy

As mentioned, mainstream economics has been, and continues to be, unapologetically modernist. A major methodological breakthrough was the instrumental variables estimator developed in the 1930s and 1940s, which enabled the identification of causal effects in observational studies (Morgan 1990). In the 1980s, this was refined into the generalized method of moments (GMM).

From the beginning, econometrics was guided by the epistemology of David Hume and Karl Popper, who were cited in the introductions to econometric textbooks. During the second half of the twentieth century, the econometric analysis of time series data and cross-section data became specialized sub-disciplines. Since macroeconomic data are time series, macroeconometrics and microeconometrics went their separate ways. Microeconometrics became increasingly rigorous (Cameron and Trivedi 2005), raising the methodological bar for identifying causal effects, and was characterized by continuity and development. It remained modernist.

By contrast, macroeconometrics split into three branches. One branch remained modernist, drawing on radical developments in the econometric analysis of nonstationary time series (Hendry 1995). A second branch rejected the principle of hypothesis testing altogether and concerned itself with statistical forecasting (Sims 1980). A third branch adopted the opposite strategy of the second. Whereas the second branch eschewed economic theory but glorified data, the second branch eschewed data but glorified economic theory. The third branch is postmodern in the sense that models are assumed to be correct. The role of data is not to test theory, but to inform its parameters through calibration and related unorthodox techniques. Model proprietors assume the role of narrators who use their models to provide narratives. The model is the message.

The second branch has lost much of its importance after a heyday in the 1980s and 1990s. The first branch continues to survive and develop. However, the third branch has dominated empirical macroeconomics for 20 years (Canova 2007, DeJong and Dave 2012). New Keynesian and DSGE models have constituted the workhorses of this branch. Moreover, these models have turned out to be popular in central banks. As a result, postmodernism has been influential in high places.

These methodological developments in macroeconomics have provided fertile ground for the evolution of ZIP. ZIP is the consequence of narratives in which narrators have persuaded themselves that the natural rate of interest is zero. If inflation and output are on target when the rate of interest is zero, then the natural rate of interest must be zero. This is so even if other data, such as the return to fixed assets, suggests the opposite. This kind of false reasoning echoes Pirsig (1974, p 102), "If the horn honks, and the mechanic concludes that the whole electric system is working, he is in deep trouble." In the next chapter we show that rates of return on fixed assets are large and positive, and are inconsistent with the hypothesis that the natural rate of interest is zero.

## The Revolution of 1980

In the beginning there were large-scale macroeconometric models (Klein and Goldberger 1955, de Leeuw and Gramlich 1968), which failed to predict the increase in inflation in the 1970s and the slowdown in economic growth. These models focused on Old Keynesian income-expenditure mechanisms in the determination of aggregate demand, but ignored aggregate supply, and they assumed that expectations of such variables as inflation were adaptive. During the 1970s macroeconomists belatedly discovered rational expectations (which had been around since 1961), and the Lucas critique (Lucas 1976) became a methodological challenge to macroeconometricians. A sort of Catch-22, this critique predicts that if policy makers try to base policy on observed statistical relationships, rational expectations may cause these relationships to break down. Econometricians developed methodological solutions to the Lucas critique by developing econometric methods for estimating models with rational expectations (Pesaran 1978). They also developed methodological solutions, based on cointegration theory (Engle and Granger 1987), to the spurious regression and nonsense regression problems (Yule 1897, 1926) that had dogged the econometric analysis of nonstationary time series since the beginning. Modernism thrived.

Sims (1980) launched the counter-modernist revolution. He argued that hypothesis testing was too difficult, if not impossible, due to the role of virtual variables such as expectations, problems associated with nonstationary time series such as macroeconomic time series, and because macroeconomic theory itself was often vague, especially regarding the speed of adjustment processes. Consequently, the parameters of macroeconomic models cannot be identified. He proposed instead that macroeconomists might occupy themselves with the estimation of statistical vector autoregressions (VAR), which may be used to predict macroeconomic variables such as inflation and economic growth. These VAR models are entirely atheoretical; they have no structural pretentions. However, they were not useful to policy makers because they did not seek to identify the causal effect of policy on the macroeconomy.

A generation of macroeconomists responded to Sims' iconoclasm. VAR models became immensely popular, and not just in macroeconomics. VAR models are used to calculate impulse responses, which describe how VAR innovations, e.g. for monetary policy, affect state variables such as inflation and output over time. It was tempting to attribute causality to such impulse responses, despite the fact that VAR models are concerned with prediction rather than causality. To attribute causality, structural VAR models (SVAR) were proposed in which untestable restrictions were imposed to justify causal attributions (Beenstock and Felsenstein 2019, Chapter 6). To convey this, consider the following simple model of supply and demand, in which P denotes price and Q denotes quantity:

$$Q_t^D = -\beta P_t - \lambda P_{t-1} + \gamma Q_{t-1} + d_t \tag{1.1}$$

$$Q_t^S = \theta P_t + \phi P_{t-1} + \mu Q_{t-1} + s_t \tag{1.2}$$

Equations (1.1) and (1.2) are first-order dynamic structural equations in demand and supply, in which iid demand shocks are denoted by d and iid supply shocks by s. Equations (1.1) and (1.2) involve eight structural parameters, including the variances of d and s. Since supply and demand depend on current price, there is an obvious identification problem that needs to be solved by proposing instrumental variables for supply and demand.

The SVAR solution to this problem is as follows. The VAR is obtained by setting supply equal to demand and solving for the final forms for Q and P:

$$Q_t = \pi_{11} P_{t-1} + \pi_{12} Q_{t-1} + u_t \tag{1.3}$$

$$\pi_{11} = \frac{\phi\beta - \theta\lambda}{\beta + \theta} \quad \pi_{12} = \frac{\gamma\theta + \beta\mu}{\beta + \theta} \quad u_t = \frac{\theta d_t + \beta s_t}{\beta + \theta}$$

$$P_t = \pi_{21} P_{t-1} + \pi_{22} Q_{t-1} + v_t \tag{1.4}$$

$$\pi_{21} = -\frac{\phi + \lambda}{\beta + \theta} \quad \pi_{22} = \frac{\gamma - \mu}{\beta + \theta} \quad v_t = \frac{d_t - s_t}{\beta + \theta}$$

The VAR delivers estimates of four $\pi$'s as well as three elements of the variance-covariance matrix of the VAR innovations:

$$\sigma_u^2 = \frac{\theta^2 \sigma_d^2 + \beta^2 \sigma_s^2}{(\beta + \theta)^2} \quad \sigma_v^2 = \frac{\sigma_d^2 + \sigma_s^2}{(\beta + \theta)^2} \quad \sigma_{uv} = \frac{\theta \sigma_d^2 - \beta \sigma_s^2}{(\beta + \theta)^2} \tag{1.5}$$

These seven VAR objects almost solve for the eight structural parameters in equations (1.1) and (1.2). There is an identification deficit of 1. To close the deficit, SVAR enthusiasts impose untestable restrictions. For example, setting $\beta = 0$ in equation (1.1) makes the model recursive, in which supply is determined before demand. In SVAR terminology this is known as a Cholesky decomposition, which closes the identification deficit. There are obviously numerous other arbitrary restrictions that close the deficit, all of which are consistent with different structural models. If $\beta = \mu = 0$, the identification deficit is $-1$, i.e. the structural parameters are over-identified.

If the supply and demand shocks happened to be correlated, the identification deficit would have been 2 instead of 1 because their covariance would need to be identified. The identification deficit increases with the number of state variables. For example, when there are three state variables instead of two, the identification deficit increases from 1 to 4. The number of arbitrary identifying restrictions is at least 1 and varies directly with the number of state variables.

In macroeconomic VAR models the identification deficit is often closed by assuming that central macroeconomic hypotheses are true. For example, the price level is assumed to be proportional to the quantity of money in the long run, and inflation and unemployment are assumed to be independent in the long run. Instead of testing these auxiliary hypotheses, they are assumed to be correct. These restrictions turn statistical impulse responses into causal narratives. Since these restrictions are untestable, SVARs are a postmodern development. Interpreting impulse responses is rather like interpreting tea-leaf patterns in a cup. Much depends on viewer subjectivity.

One wonders whether the Revolution of 1980 could have occurred ten years later in 1990, by which time methodological problems associated with the Lucas critique and spurious regression had been resolved. These methodological developments apparently came too late to stem the tide in favor of VARs and SVARs. My contention is that SVARs constituted the first step into postmodern macroeconomics, which paved the way for a bolder second step. This step had a very different agenda. Instead of starting out with data and applying untestable macroeconomic theories to interpret it, as in SVAR, it started out with macroeconomic theory, and used data to window-dress it empirically. Specifically, New Keynesian models described in Chapter 2 were calibrated to data. Subsequently, DSGE models were calibrated to data. The role of data was not to test these models empirically, but to show that they were broadly consistent with "stylized facts," such as pro-cyclicality or anti-cyclicality, or positively or negatively correlated with income.

## Calibration, Bayesian Priors, and Indirect Estimation

In what follows, "indirect estimation" refers to the estimation of model parameters by unorthodox methods rather than by classical, frequentist methods such as least squares and maximum likelihood. Indirect estimation includes calibration, and Bayesian estimators including Markov Chain Monte Carlo methods (MCMC) discussed below. "Indirect inference" refers to the empirical testing of models whose parameters are obtained through indirect estimation (Gourieroux, Montfort and Renault 1993).

Whereas regression methods estimate parameters directly, calibration and related methods estimate parameters indirectly. For example, in the model $y = a + bx + u$, where $u$ is a residual error, the unknown parameters $a$ and $b$ may be estimated by ordinary least squares (OLS) by regressing $y$ on $x$. The OLS formula assumes that the classical assumptions apply to $u$. Suppose the OLS estimates are $a = 2$ and $b = 3$, which are best linear unbiased estimates. Calibrators guess different values of $a$ and $b$ and pick the combination that satisfies some statistical criteria. If the criterion is to minimize the error sum of squares, they should eventually get close to estimating $a = 2$ and $b = 3$. They might also have some priors about the values of $a$ and $b$. For example, they are positive and take values between 1 and 4.

The use of calibration is trivial here because OLS is the obvious estimator. If, however, the model comprises a number of nonlinear simultaneous equations with cross-equation restrictions, classical methods of inference are less straightforward. Take for example, the six parameters of the New Keynesian model in equations (2.1–2.3) in Chapter 2. These equations constitute a coherent system or model. They hang or fall together. It would not help if one equation was rejected by direct inference. The model must be judged integrally and not severally. Interviewed in 2005, Thomas Sargent recalled that Robert Lucas had said "... your likelihood ratio tests are rejecting too many good models." He meant that models are wholes, which are more than the sum of their parts, and should be judged differently to models based on an incoherent group of equations. This point is related to the criticism of full information maximum likelihood (FIML), where an entire model may be rejected because of a statistically weak component. The baby should not be thrown out with the bath water.

Calibration was imported into macroeconomics from climate science by Prescott in the 1980s (Kydland and Prescott 1982), who likened "economic laws" to the laws of atmospheric physics embodied in calibrated climate models. As an aside, the laws of physics embodied in calibrated global climate models do not do a good job of tracking the history of global temperature (Beenstock, Reingewertz and Paldor 2016). As we shall see, nor do calibrated macroeconomic models do a good job of tracking macroeconomic history. Calibration has turned out to be very popular in macroeconomics (Canova 2007, Chapter 7, DeJong and Dave 2007, Chapter 6).

Calibration usually begins by setting priors for model parameters, such as those in the New Keynesian model. These priors may be based on empirical studies for other countries, or they may be informed by empirical studies of specific parameters, such as the slope of the New Keynesian Phillips curve. Often priors are based on theoretical beliefs, such as there is no money illusion, or the natural rate of unemployment is independent of monetary policy in the long run. These priors are typically used informally by experimenting with parameter values that are similar to them. Calibration involves repeated simulation of the model until it has "plausible" properties. In practice, calibrators tweak parameters until the model gives the results that were sought in the first place. This possibly cynical view of calibration regards it as a window-dressing exercise rather than motivated by proper hypothesis testing. The medium of the model embodies the message intended.

The calibrated model is "validated" by comparing the empirical variance-covariance matrix of the data, with its counterpart generated by the model. Provided the former is sufficiently close to the latter, the model is declared to be consistent with the data. The trouble is that observationally similar models might have completely different parameters. If so, why should the calibrated model be taken seriously? The art of tweaking lies behind different calibrated models.

Other calibrators use their priors more formally and rely on Bayesian methods to impose discipline on the art of tweaking. To fix ideas, suppose a parameter $\theta$ has a prior of 10 with variance 2. However, according to data $\theta$ is 20 with variance 4. The Bayesian or posterior mean and variances are:

$$posterior\ mean = \frac{\frac{1}{4}20 + \frac{1}{2}10}{\frac{1}{4} + \frac{1}{2}} = 13.33$$

$$posterior\ variance = \frac{1}{\frac{1}{4} + \frac{1}{2}} = 1.33$$

The posterior mean weights the prior mean and the sample mean by the inverse of their variances; as expected, it gives more weight to the more certain mean. If the prior variance is zero, the posterior mean would be 10 regardless of data. The facts don't matter for religiously held priors. Moreover, suppose the variance of $\theta$ in the data happened to exceed 4. The posterior mean would be closer to the prior, but the posterior variance would be larger. Ironically, priors gain salience when the empirical evidence refutes them.

Suppose new data have become available and the sample moments are recalculated. Suppose further that the sample mean continues to be 20 and the variance is still 4. To a classical or frequentist statistician this is good news because the sample moments haven't changed. By contrast, Bayesians update their priors according to the posterior moments (13.33 and 1.33) from the original data so that the posterior mean from the new data is 14.995 with variance 0.998. If yet more new data become available, the posterior moments from the previous new data become the priors for further Bayesian updating. If the sample moments remain unchanged, the new posterior mean is 15.995 with variance 0.7998. With each round of updating the posterior mean gets closer to the sample mean, and the variance decreases. It may be shown asymptotically that the posterior mean equals the sample mean of 20 but the variance gets smaller until it converges on its asymptote.

A frequentist might wonder, why engage in Bayesian updating when asymptotically it converges on the frequentist solution based on the sample mean of the data? The reply is that Bayesians have priors whereas frequentists do not. What is important here is that the priors influence the posterior moments in finite samples. Therefore, in practice Bayesian updating produces different results to frequentism. In practice Bayesian calibrators do not engage in numerous rounds of updating. They typically engage in a single round, as a result of which the posteriors are heavily influenced by the priors.

The postmodern issue here involves beliefs about priors. The posterior moments of model parameters are a blend of belief and data. Bayesians believe that their model is correct, but use data to update their priors. Suppose in our numerical illustration that the sample variance was large. If its standard deviation exceeded 10.2 it would not be significantly different from zero. A frequentist could not reject the null hypothesis that $\theta$ is zero. By contrast, a Bayesian would give almost no weight to the data, so that the posterior mean would be slightly above 10 and would reject the null hypothesis. For Bayesians, the model is always correct. They are postmodernists. For frequentists, the data must reject the null hypothesis that the model is wrong. They are modernists.

In the numerical example, the moments of the posterior density were easy to calculate. In many cases these moments have to be computed numerically because the joint distribution of the model parameters and data is either unknown or too intractable to carry out the necessary integration. Suppose we draw random samples of y and x from the joint population (y, x) when the joint distribution is intractable or unknown. If the conditional distributions $f(y/x)$ and $f(x/y)$ are known and simple enough, the Gibbs sampler may be used as follows. Draw $x_0$ in the range of x/y. Then draw $y_0$ given $x_0$, and draw $x_1$ given $y_0$ and so on. Repeating these steps several thousand times eventually delivers a random sample from the joint distribution. The Markov chain component in MCMC refers to conditioning on the previous draws of y and x and the Monte Carlo component refers to the initial draws of $x_0$ and $y_0$.

Suppose next that $\beta$ denotes a vector of n population parameters with covariance matrix $\Sigma$. The Metropolis-Hastings (MH) algorithm (Berg 2004) assumes priors for $\beta$ and $\Sigma$ and exploits the Gibbs sampler to resample for the parameter estimates and the data (Canova 2007, Chapter 9, DeJong and Dave 2007, Chapter 9). MATLAB and other statistical software have made MCMC-MH available to economists and epidemiologists (Beenstock and Dai 2020) among others. MCMC-MH should be regarded as a sophisticated method of calibration or indirect estimation because it starts out with priors, which are updated by maximum likelihood estimates of the parameters of the model. The special role of MCMC-MH is to solve for the moments of the posterior distribution, which would otherwise be unfeasible. MCMC-MH has given Bayesian methods a major boost because it has rendered feasible what was previously impossible.

We complete this subsection with quotations from four important commentators:

"The lack of formal model validation does not seem to bother some researchers. Kydland and Prescott (1991, 1996), for example, emphasize that the trust a researcher puts in an answer given by the model does not depend on a statistical measure of discrepancy, but on how much she believes in the economic theory used and in the measurement undertaken – in other words, trust could be an act of faith.

Nowadays, most calibrators informally compare the properties of the simulated data with a set of stylized facts of the actual data. Such an approach is also in fashion with econometric skeptics: simple sample statistics are believed to be sufficient to do the job since 'either you see it with the naked eye or no fancy econometrics will find it'. The choice of stylized facts obviously depends on the question asked but one should be aware that there are many ways to summarize the outcome of a calibration exercise and some may be more informative than others for comparison purposes."

(Canova 2007, p 260)

"The models constructed within this theoretical framework are necessarily highly abstract. Consequently, they are necessarily false, and statistical hypothesis testing will reject them. This does not imply, however, that nothing can be learned from such quantitative theoretical exercises."

(Prescott 1986, p 10)

"...calibration exercises can certainly serve as an effective means of making headway in empirical applications involving general equilibrium models ... That being said, the lack of statistical formality associated with calibration exercises imposes distinct limitations upon what can be learned and communicated via their use. Moreover, the particular approach advocated by Kydland and Prescott for addressing empirical questions in the absence of a formal statistical framework has been criticized on a variety of fronts."

(DeJong and Dave 2007, p 142)

"Regarding the problem of choosing among given theories, there is no doubt that from a classical hypothesis testing perspective, under which one model is posed as the null hypothesis, this is complicated by the fact that the models in question are 'necessarily false'...Moreover, this problem is not an issue given the adoption of a Bayesian perspective ... Under this perspective, there is no need for the declaration of a null model; rather, all models are treated symmetrically, and none are assumed a priori to be 'true.'"

(DeJong and Dave 2007, p 143)

"Even the most complicated models of fluctuations are grossly simplified descriptions of reality. It would be remarkable if none of the simplifications had quantitatively important effects on the models' implications. But given this, it is hard to determine how informative the fact that a model does or does not match aggregate data is about its overall usefulness.

It would be a mistake to think that the only alternative to calibration is formal estimation of fully specified models ... Unfortunately, there is little evidence concerning the relative merits of different approaches to evaluating macroeconomic models. ... At this point choices among these approaches seem to be based more on researchers' 'tastes' than on a body of knowledge about the strengths and weaknesses of the approaches. Trying to move beyond this situation by developing evidence about the merits of different approaches is an important and largely uncharted research area."

(Romer 2019, p 220)

These quotations express the postmodern muddle into which applied macroeconomics has fallen. The first muddle is epistemological. The fact that theory is abstract does not mean that it is necessarily false. This applies not only to macroeconomics, but to economics as a whole, as well to the natural sciences. All models are proposed as simplifications of a complex world, so by this criterion no model should be corroborated by data. In any case, according to deductive epistemology dating back to David Hume and Karl Popper, axiomatic theory is not judged empirically by its axioms, but by its ability to predict data. As long as a theory is empirically corroborated, the axioms upon which it is based are useful. Applying this principle to DSGE models means that their axioms are useful provided the theory is empirically corroborated. In this case it would not matter that there is no artefact, such as a representative agent. The representative agent is an axiom that helps us understand the real world. Matters would be different, of course, if the theory were falsified empirically. Friedman (1953) restates this view without reference to Hume and Popper.

Nor are corroborated models necessarily true. They simply have not been falsified. The history of science is replete with corroborated theories that were eventually falsified (Kuhn 1970). Einstein's theory eventually replaced Newton's. It is a matter of time before Einstein's theory will be replaced.

The second muddle is practical. If a model is falsified by empirical data, how can it be "useful" to policy makers, or anyone else? It might be useful to theoreticians who use numerical methods instead of analytical methods to make their arguments. Or it might be useful to professors to convey ideas to their students. But faith in a model will not convince the practical men and women in high places, especially when it cannot explain the past. In any case, faith is entirely subjective and metaphysical. It should play no part in scientific discourse.

The third muddle is methodological. Calibration and Bayesian methods are seen as methodological alternatives to the system-of-equations approach to econometrics, which was classical and frequentist, and was reputed to have failed to predict US stagflation in the 1970s. Modernist economists, including myself (Beenstock 1984) and Bruno and Sachs (1985), attributed this failure to a misunderstanding of the role of energy prices in supply side economics. Others jumped to the conclusion that the Lucas critique was to blame, despite the fact that super-exogeneity tests (Ericsson and Irons 1994) showed that it wasn't. Proponents of indirect estimation threw out the baby with the bath water. Instead of improving the system-of-equations approach, they turned their back on it. Forty years on, they have still failed to provide a methodological basis for the empirical testing of indirect estimation.

Would DSGE models have predicted stagflation in the 1970s? Did DSGE models predict the Subprime Crisis and the Great Recession in 2008 and thereafter? The sudden abandonment of frequentist econometrics in the name of the Lucas critique and the failure to predict stagflation proved to be a serious misjudgment.

## A Critique of the Lucas Critique

The Lucas critique implies that if policy makers try to take advantage of observed statistical relationships, effects operating through rational expectations may cause these relationships to break down. This "Catch 22" phenomenon arises because agents with rational expectations take into account how they expect policy makers to behave. Sophisticated policy makers should therefore allow for these rational expectations when designing their policy, otherwise economic outcomes of interest may turn out to be different from what they were intended.

The Lucas critique led to two methodological responses. First, macroeconomic models should specify rational expectations for inflation and the output gap, as in the New Keynesian and DSGE models described in the previous chapter. Methodological research into the specification and econometrics of rational expectations has been usefully reviewed by Pesaran (1978), and many textbooks, such as Maddala (2001, Chapter 10) and Hansen and Sargent (1991) cover the econometric analysis of rational expectations. Second, economic models should specify "deep" structural parameters such as utility and production functions. These deep structural parameters induce cross-equation restrictions between the variables in the model, implying that models cannot be estimated equation by equation by limited information methods. Instead, the equations of the model have to be estimated jointly as an integrated system by full information methods.

The first response is well taken. It is no coincidence that in the aftermath of the Lucas critique econometricians developed methods for estimating models with rational expectations, especially during the 1970s. It is with the second response that we take issue, because it has led to reductive concepts such as representative agent macroeconomics. The price of deep structuralism has been to ignore the fact that economies comprise numerous types of individuals and firms. Elegant DSGE models with deep structures may have their pedagogic use in textbooks, but they should not be taken too seriously in central banks and ministries of finance. Indeed, empirical tests of some flagship DSGE models reported below show that they do not fit the data better than atheoretical statistical VAR models.

Suppose policy makers wish to stabilize state variable Y, which depends on X in the following rational expectations model:

$$Y_t = \beta E_t Y_{t+1} + \lambda Y_{t-1} + \theta X_t + u_t \tag{2.1}$$

where X and u are stationary iid random variables. If $\beta > 1 - \lambda$ one of the roots ($\rho_1$) of equation (2.1) exceeds 1 while the other ($\rho_2$) is a positive fraction. Since X and u are stationary, so must Y be stationary. As we saw in Chapter 2, bubble roots such as $\rho_1$ tend to arise in rational expectations models. Such roots imply that Y is nonstationary, despite the fact that the fundamentals, X and u, are stationary. The standard solution (applied in Chapter 2) is to obtain forward solutions in which expectations of the exogenous variables (X and u) are weighted by the inverse bubble root. This solution method uses the fact that, since $\rho_1$ exceeds 1, its inverse is a positive fraction.

Following the same solution procedures in Chapter 2, equation (2.1) is lagged one period, reorganized and expectations are formed in period t (using the law of iterated expectations):

$$\beta E_t Y_t - E_t Y_{t-1} + \lambda E_t Y_{t-2} = -\theta E_t X_{t-1} - E_t u_{t-1} \tag{2.2}$$

Equation (2.2) is a second-order stochastic difference equation in the rational expectation $E_t Y_t$. Its two roots are:

$$\rho = \frac{1 \pm \sqrt{1 - 4\beta\lambda}}{2\beta} \tag{2.3}$$

Hence, $\rho_1$ exceeds 1 when $\beta > 1 - \lambda$. Equation (2.2) is led one period and expressed in terms of its roots:

$$(1 - \rho_1 L)(1 - \rho_2 L) E_t Y_{t+1} = -\theta E_t X_t - E_t u_t \tag{2.4}$$

The bubble root is re-expressed in terms of its forward solution:

$$\frac{1}{1 - \rho_1 L} = -\frac{\frac{1}{\rho_1} L^{-1}}{1 - \frac{1}{\rho_1} L^{-1}} \tag{2.5}$$

where $L^{-1}$ is a first-order lead operator and L is its first-order lag counterpart. Dividing both sides of equation (2.4) by equation (2.5) and reorganizing gives the rational expectation for $E_t Y_{t+1}$:

$$E_t Y_{t+1} = \rho_2 Y_t + \frac{\theta}{\rho_1} \sum_{i=0}^{\infty} \frac{1}{\rho_1^i} L^i E_t X_{t+1+i} \tag{2.6}$$

Equation (2.6) states that at the end period t the expected value of $Y_{t+1}$ mean-reverts with respect to its current value (because $\rho_2$ is a positive fraction) and it varies directly with a declining weighted average of current expectations of future values of X. Since the expected value of u is zero, it does not feature in equation (2.6). This completes stage 1.

In stage 2, equation (2.6) is substituted for $E_t Y_{t+1}$ in equation (2.1) to provide the general solution for $Y_t$:

$$Y_t = \frac{1}{1 - \beta\rho_2} \left[ \lambda Y_{t-1} + \theta X_t + u_t + \frac{\beta\theta}{\rho_1} \sum_{i=0}^{\infty} \frac{1}{\rho_1^i} E_t X_{t+1+i} \right] \tag{2.7}$$

Equation (2.7) states that $Y_t$ mean-reverts with respect to its previous value, it varies directly with the current value of X and its expected future values, and it varies directly with $u_t$. Since Y is stationary, the single root in equation (2.7) must be less than one, i.e. $\lambda/(1 - \beta\rho_2) = \psi < 1$.

According to equation (2.7), the impact effect on $Y_t$ of a temporary increase in $X_t$ is $\theta/(1 - \beta\rho_2)$, which after j periods decreases to $\psi j\theta/(1 - \beta\rho_2)$ before eventually tending to zero. The impact effect of a permanent increase in X from period t and beyond is $\theta\frac{1+\beta/(\rho_1-1)}{1-\beta\rho_2}$, which after j periods builds up to $\theta\frac{(1-\psi^{j+1})(1+\beta)}{(1-\psi)(\rho_1-1)(1-\beta\rho_2)}$.

The Wold representation (infinite moving average representation of an autoregressive process) of equation (2.7) is:

$$Y_t = \sum_{j=0}^{\infty} \psi j \left[ \theta_{t-j} + u_{t-j} + \frac{\beta\theta}{\rho_1}\tilde{X}_{t-j} \right] \tag{2.8}$$

where $\tilde{X}_t = \sum_{j=0}^{\infty} \frac{1}{\rho_1 j} E_t X_{t+1+j}$ denotes the current weighted average of expected future values of X. Equation (2.8) implies that the variance of Y is:

$$\sigma_Y^2 = \frac{1}{1 - \psi 2} \left[ \theta^2 \sigma_X^2 + \sigma_u^2 + \left(\frac{\beta\theta}{\rho_1}\right)^2 \sigma_{\tilde{X}}^2 + 2\frac{\beta\theta^2}{\rho_1} \sigma_{X\tilde{X}} \right] \tag{2.9}$$

Equation (2.9) expresses the volatility of Y in terms of its components where u and X are assumed to be independent. It states that volatility varies directly with $\psi$, $\beta$, $\theta$ and the variances of X, u and the forward components of X as well the covariance between X and its forward component, which is likely to be positive. It also states that volatility varies inversely with $\rho_1$.

Suppose a policy maker wishes to reduce the volatility of Y in equation (2.9) with policy instrument Z, which might be positive or negative. A naïve policy maker might "lean into the wind" by reducing Z when Y is high relative to the mean and increasing it when Y is low using the rule:

$$Z_t = -\eta \left( Y_{t-1} - \bar{Y} \right) + z_t \tag{3.1}$$

where z denotes policy noise. Adding Z to equation (2.1) implies that Y equals:

$$Y_t = \beta E_t Y_{t+1} + \lambda Y_{t-1} + \theta X_t + Z_t + u_t \tag{3.2}$$

Substituting equation (3.1) into equation (3.2) implies:

$$Y_t = \beta E_t Y_{t+1} + (\lambda - \eta) Y_{t-1} + \theta X_t + \eta\bar{Y} + u_t + z_t \tag{3.3}$$

Our naïve policy maker thinks that, because the autoregressive coefficient is smaller, $(\lambda - \eta)$ is smaller, as a result of which the variance of Y must be smaller in equation (2.9). Although naïve, our policy maker is not stupid and understands that the variance of z will increase volatility. With sufficient forward guidance about z, the stabilization policy might reduce volatility.

According to the Lucas critique, what is naïve here is that our policy maker has assumed that expectations of $Y_{t+1}$ will remain unchanged. If expectations are rational these expectations will change because the roots become:

$$\rho = \frac{1 \pm \sqrt{1 - 4\beta\left(\lambda - \eta\right)}}{2\beta} \tag{3.4}$$

instead of what they were in equation (2.3). The unit root condition becomes $\beta > 1 - \lambda + \eta$, so a unit root is less likely. In fact, both roots may be less than 1, in which event forward solutions are no longer relevant. The message of the Lucas critique is not that the stabilization policy will be counterproductive; it is that it will be different to what our naïve policy maker expected. He may be pleasantly surprised; on the other hand, he might be regretful.

A sophisticated policy maker would set Z by minimizing the variance of Y subject to rational expectations where the public builds this policy into their expectations. A backward-looking policy maker would optimize with respect to $\eta$, i.e. he sets a policy rule for leaning into the wind. A forward-looking policy maker would set Z discreetly without setting rules. This is not the place to enter into the debate about rules v discretion in policy making and the related issue of time-inconsistency and optimality (Minford and Peel 2019). The first main point is that sophisticated policy makers need to know the deep structural parameters $\beta$, $\lambda$ and $\theta$ when designing their policy. The second main point is that econometricians who estimate equation (3.2) will obtain some estimate for the coefficient on Z, which reflects the average effect of policy on Y during the sample period, but is meaningless for providing policy makers with advice how to change their policy.

In summary, the Lucas critique makes enormous demands on econometricians. They must provide information on the deep structural parameters so that sophisticated policy makers can design efficient policies. To identify these parameter estimates, it is necessary to use econometric methods designed for models with rational expectations (Pesaran 1978), such as the substitution method and instrumental variables methods designed for single equations, and FIML methods designed for systems of equations. It also makes enormous demands on policy makers, who may not be sufficiently sophisticated. No wonder postmodernism has become attractive; simply calibrate the deep structural parameters in a DSGE model, assume that the model embodies the "truth," then use the model to design sophisticated policy.

We conclude this critique with a skeptical discussion of the empirical relevance of the Lucas critique. To set the scene, we recall the concepts of weak, strong and super exogeneity in the econometric analysis of time series data (Hendry 1995). Suppose that an economist has used time series data to estimate the effect of policy variable Z on outcome Y, which also depends on X. For expositional simplicity, we assume that $\beta = \lambda = 0$ in equation (3.2) and the coefficient of Z is denoted by $\mu$.

$$Y_t = \theta X_t + \mu Z_t + u_t \qquad (4.1)$$

where:

$$X_t = \delta Y_{t-1} + v_t \qquad (4.2)$$

and:

$$u_t = \rho u_{t-1} + \gamma v_t + \varepsilon_t \qquad (4.3)$$

and $\varepsilon$ and $v$ are iid disturbance terms. It is obvious that $X_t$ is not strongly exogenous in equation (4.1) because it depends on $Y_{t-1}$ in equation (4.2). Nor is $X_t$ weakly exogenous, because it is contemporaneously correlated with $u_t$ via $\gamma$, and because it depends on $u_{t-1}$ via $\delta$, but so does $u_t$ depend on $u_{t-1}$ via $\rho$. Hence $X_t$ is not independent of $u_t$. Matters would be different, however, if $\rho = \gamma = 0$, in which case $X_t$ would be weakly exogenous for $\beta$ in equation (4.1). What matters for the identification of causal parameters in time series data is weak exogeneity rather than strong exogeneity where $\delta = 0$ (Hendry 1995). The choice of "weak" here is unfortunate because $\beta$ is fully identified; there is no need for instrumental variables as there would be in cross-section data because $X_t$ and $u_t$ are by definition independent in equation (4.1). In time series data, the sequencing of the observations matters for identification. Under weak exogeneity, X during period t is independent of $u_t$, which satisfies the classical conditions for causal identification.

What about $\mu$, which refers to the effect of policy on Y? If Z is determined according to equation (3.1), the conditions for weak exogeneity would be the same as for X because both Z and X depend on lagged Y, i.e. $z_t$ and should be directly and indirectly independent of $u_t$. However, if the model includes rational expectations, as in equation (3.2), $\mu$ would not be identified according to the Lucas critique because it depends on the way policy makers have optimized Z to achieve objectives for Y and perhaps other variables too. In general, $\mu$ depends on the deep structural parameters as well as the moments of $v$ and $\varepsilon$ and perhaps other variables determined outside equation (4.1). The Lucas critique may or may not be valid in practice; it is simply a hypothesis about how policy makers behave. It needs to be tested empirically against the null hypothesis that the Lucas critique is just another theoretical proposition, which happens to be empirically irrelevant.

Suppose the auxiliary hypothesis for Z is:

$$Z_t = Q_t \eta + z_t \tag{4.4}$$

where Q is a vector of variables hypothesized to influence policy makers, such as period dummy variables for potential regime changes, as well as lags of Z and other variables, and z captures unobservable factors that influence policy as in equation (3.3). Next, re-estimate equation (4.1) using the estimated moments of z:

$$Y_t = \theta X_t + \mu Z_t + \sum_{m=1}^{M} \phi_m \hat{z}_t^m + u_t \tag{4.5}$$

If $\phi_m = 0$ according to a chi-square test with M degrees of freedom, then Z is "super exogenous" for $\mu$, in which event the Lucas critique is empirically invalid (Hendry 1995). Ericsson and Irons (1994) show that in most cases the Lucas critique is empirically invalid. Provided Z is super exogenous, econometric estimates of $\mu$ are meaningful; they represent the average effect of policy on state variables such as Y.

The Lucas critique has been exploited by theoreticians to terrorize econometricians intellectually. It has been exploited by enthusiasts of the DSGE movement to justify their heterodox descent into postmodern macroeconomics.

## Indirect Inference

Applied macroeconomists have largely abandoned the frequentist methods developed by the founding fathers of econometrics. On the extreme left wing, VAR macroeconomists abandoned hypothesis testing altogether. Subsequently, SVAR macroeconomists introduced postmodern narratives into VAR models. On the extreme right wing, calibrators engaged in indirect estimation, which euphemistically refers to "... a way of ignoring the fact that the data do not fit your model, and proceeding as if it did." (Blanchard). The model is always right even if it doesn't fit the data (see cartoon).

Because of these developments, which are peculiar to macroeconomics, there has been an almost complete breakdown in the modernist empirical tradition. If Lucas feared that too many good models are being rejected, maybe too many bad models have been accepted as a result of the DSGE movement. The descent into ZIP and the New Abnormal is inextricably intertwined with the rise of postmodernism in applied macroeconomics. Particularly, the New Keynesian model has misled central bankers into believing that if the "divine coincidence" (output and inflation are on target) occurs when the rate of interest is zero, it must be the case

**Cartoon 3.**  Even His Clothes Don't Fit

that the natural rate of interest is zero. In the next chapter we show that the natural rate of interest is in fact large and positive even under the divine coincidence.

We now turn to recent developments in the empirical testing of models estimated by indirect estimation. These developments are intended to restore modernism and empirical scrutiny to applied macroeconomics. It turns out that a number of well-known and influential models estimated by indirect estimation methods fail to pass basic empirical criteria. Indeed, supposedly "good" models are not so good after all.

Canova (2007) thinks that using frequentist methods to test models estimated by indirect methods sets an almost impossible standard. New Keynesian and DGSE models stand almost no chance against the data because they are too simple and stylized. He suggests instead comparing the impulse responses of models constructed by indirect estimation with the impulse responses of VAR models. Since VAR models are entirely naïve, whereas DSGE models are supposed to be sophisticated, it is natural to ask whether there is empirical value added to sophistication. In this case, the impulse responses generated by VAR models should be compared to the impulse responses generated by DSGE or other models estimated by indirect methods. In what follows, unrestricted VAR models estimated with actual data shall serve as auxiliary models for testing DSGE and other structural models that have been estimated by indirect methods.

The proposal to test DSGE models against VAR models rather than against the data constitutes a serious admission of defeat. Just because a DSGE model happens to outperform the auxiliary VAR model does not mean that it would satisfy classical frequentist criteria for hypothesis testing. It simply means that the DSGE model is superior to its VAR comparator; the VAR model is worse than the DSGE model, which is rejected by the data. On the other hand, if the DSGE model is rejected by the VAR model, this would be very bad news. Indirect inference sets a low bar for hypothesis testing.

Suppose, for example, that the structural parameters in equations (1.1) and (1.2) have been calibrated or estimated by some method of indirect estimation, such as MCMC-MH. The structural model may be expressed as a VAR model as in equation (1.3) and (1.4). We shall refer to this by the SVAR model, which embodies the restrictions in the structural model according to which the $\pi$ parameters and innovations u and v are related to the structural parameters. Equations (1.3) and (1.4) may be estimated as an ordinary VAR model in which the $\pi$ parameters and u and v are freely estimated. We shall refer to this by the unrestricted VAR model. Suppose that the SVAR $\pi$s happen to be identical to their unrestricted VAR counterparts. This would imply that the structural model replicates the empirical VAR parameters, which represent the data. In equations (1.3) and (1.4) we noted that there are seven VAR parameters. If they are all equal to their SVAR counterparts, this would constitute complete empirical success for the structural model.

Notice that this test refers to the inside-sample past rather than outside-sample future. Models that fail to predict the past are unlikely to predict the future. It would be peculiar if a model that failed to predict the past succeeded in predicting the future. Model testing necessarily begins inside-sample before it is tested outside-sample. Therefore, the tests of indirect inference refer exclusively to inside-sample.

Obviously, complete success is unlikely. Ideally, a test statistic is required to differentiate between success and failure in probabilistic terms. Common sense suggests that the greater the distance between the SVAR and unrestricted VAR parameters, the more likely it is that the structural model should be rejected. In a series of papers, Meenagh, Minford and Wickens have developed this idea further and have formalized frequentist test statistics for structural models estimated by indirect methods. We begin by recalling these test statistics and then discuss their application to a leading DSGE model estimated by indirect methods.

Continuing with our example of supply and demand, let $\Sigma_R$ denote the variance-covariance matrix of the innovations of the SVAR model as in equations (1.5), i.e. using the structural parameters obtained through indirect estimation, and let $\Sigma_U$ denote the variance-covariance matrix of the unrestricted VAR innovations, i.e. when u and v are freely estimated. The likelihood ratio (LR) statistic for the difference between the restricted and unrestricted VAR models is:

$$LR = T\left[\ln|\Sigma_R| - \ln|\Sigma_U|\right] \sim \chi_n^2 \qquad (5.1)$$

where T denotes the number of time series observations and n denotes the number of restrictions. If the identification deficit is negative, the number of structural parameters is n less than the number of VAR parameters. If the identification deficit is positive, the unrestricted model uses fewer degrees of freedom than the SVAR. This (LR) test compares the likelihood of the SVAR model derived for the DSGE model whose parameters were obtained through indirect estimation with the likelihood of a freely estimated VAR model. It does not compare the goodness-of-fit of the SVAR model with actual data, although this information is contained in $\Sigma_R$. If the VAR model happens to fit the data poorly, it won't be too much of a consolation to learn that LR is less than its critical value.

Suppose that LR = 0; the restricted SVAR model is statistically equivalent to the VAR, i.e. $|\Sigma_R| = |\Sigma_U|$. In the example of supply and demand this means that:

$$\frac{\sigma_{QR}\sigma_{PR}}{\sigma_{QU}\sigma_{PU}} = \sqrt{\frac{1 - \rho_U^2}{1 - \rho_R^2}} \qquad (5.2)$$

where, for example, $\sigma_{QR}$ denotes the standard deviation of the quantity innovation from the SVAR, or $\sigma_u$ in equation (1.5), and $\rho_R$ denotes the correlation between the quantity and price innovations from the SVAR, or $\sigma_{uv}/\sigma_u\sigma_v$ in equation (1.5). If $\rho_R$ is less than $\rho_U$ equation (1.7) is a fraction, the goodness-of-fit of the SVAR, as measured by the product of standard deviations, is inferior to the VAR. This serves to remind us that the LR test compares the likelihood of the structural model with its VAR counterpart. The structural model may fit the data better or worse than the VAR. Even if it fits the data better, $\sigma_{QR}$ and $\sigma_{PR}$ may be impractically large because the VAR fits the data poorly.

An alternative test of indirect inference proposed by Le, Meenagh, Minford and Wickens (2011) is a Wald test, which we continue to illustrate with our simple example of supply and demand. It has the following steps:

1. Solve for the demand and supply innovations ($d_t$ and $s_t$) using the indirectly estimated structural parameters in equations (1.1) and (1.2).

2. Resample from the empirical distribution function for d and s obtained from step 1 to construct simulated time series data for Q and P through equations (1.3) and (1.4).
3. Use the simulated time series generated by step 2 to estimate an unrestricted VAR, and save the estimates of the four $\pi$ parameters.
4. Repeat steps 2 and 3 $\tau$ times where $\tau$ is large and is the number of Monte Carlo trials.
5. Use the results from step 4 to construct the Monte Carlo sample means of the four $\pi$ parameters, denoted by N (= 4) length vector $\pi_R$.
6. Use the results from step 4 to construct the NxN variance-covariance matrix (V) of the parameter estimates of the $\pi$ parameters.
7. Estimate an unrestricted auxiliary VAR from the actual data with parameters $\pi_U$.
8. Calculate the Wald statistic:

$$W = \left(\pi_R - \pi_U\right)' V^{-1} \left(\pi_R - \pi_U\right) \sim \chi_n^2 \tag{5.3}$$

If W exceeds its critical value, the indirectly estimated structural parameters are rejected when the auxiliary model is an unrestricted VAR.

Step 3 and 4 rerun history $\tau$ times under the assumption that the structural model is true. Each trial constitutes a potential history or narrative according to the structural model. If these narratives happen to be consistent with the empirical description according to the auxiliary VAR model, then the structural model that produced these narratives is consistent with the data in the same way that $\tau$ experiments would be consistent with the data. We do not require that all $\tau$ experiments should succeed, but we do require that, say, 95 percent of them should be successful.

Table 3.1 conveys this idea, where the percentages refer to the accuracy of the structural parameters in descending order, and the table records the rejection

**Table 3.1** The Power of Indirect Inference

| N | p | Wald | | | LR | | |
|---|---|---|---|---|---|---|---|
| | | 3% | 7% | 10% | 3% | 7% | 10% |
| 3 | 1 | 36.1 | 98.1 | 100 | 21.8 | 58.9 | 84.0 |
| 3 | 2 | 35.5 | 96.9 | 100 | 20.7 | 57.6 | 82.9 |
| 5 | 1 | 85.5 | 100 | 100 | 22.4 | 68.6 | 89.6 |
| 7 | 3 | 99.2 | 100 | 100 | 10.6 | 46.3 | 83.2 |

Based on Minford and Peel (2019, Chapter 17) and Meenagh et al (2019) p 29. N number of variables. p order of VAR. T = 200 for Smets and Wouters (2007) DSGE model for US.

rates of the structural model. For example, using the Wald statistic to test the Smets-Wouters model with a three-variable first-order VAR has a rejection rate of 36.1 percent when the structural parameters are least inaccurate, increasing to 100 percent when they are more inaccurate. As expected, the rejection rate varies directly with the inaccuracy of the structural parameters. The same pattern applies to the LR test, but the power is systematically smaller. Increasing the number of variables increases the power of both tests, but especially for the Wald statistic. Table 3.1 also suggests that increasing the VAR order induces a minor reduction in power.

Power varies directly with the number of variables because it increases the opportunities for false models to reveal themselves. Since there are nine state variables in the Smets-Wouters model, rejection rates approach 100 percent when slightly more than half of them are included in the test. Indeed, the combination of variables included in the test makes little difference to the rejection rates.

The Wald test assumes that the restricted model, represented by the structural model, is true, and constitutes the null hypothesis to be tested. In step 2 the simulated data would be observed if the structural model is true. In step 4 the moments of the VAR parameters are generated under the assumption that the structural model is true. Finally, the estimated $\pi$ parameters that would have been estimated had the structural model been true are compared with their counterparts generated by the data.

Note that this Wald test is conceptually different from a conventional Wald test that is directly related to LR and Lagrange multiplier tests. Whereas LR tests compare restricted and unrestricted models and LM tests assume that the unrestricted model is correct, Wald tests assume that the restricted model is correct. A standard Wald test would compare the restricted $\pi$ parameters from equations (1.3) and (1.4) with those obtained from an unrestricted VAR. In equation (5.3) the restricted model is used to generate $\pi_R$ and V through Monte Carlo simulation.

Equation (5.3) may be defined in terms of average impulse responses instead of VAR parameters. In this case, $\pi_R$ and $\pi_U$ would be replaced by vectors of impulse responses, and V would be the variance-covariance matrix of impulse responses. Indeed, any sufficient statistic for auxiliary VAR models may be used in equation (5.3).

Smets and Wouters (2003, 2007) used indirect estimation methods to construct DSGE models for the EU and the US, in which the state variables include consumption, investment, Tobin's q, capital stock, inflation, wages, employment, GDP, and the central bank's rate of interest. The model is New Keynesian because prices and wages are sticky, and it incorporates Real Business Cycle features. Indirect estimation methods based on calibration and Bayesian methods were used to construct their DSGE model for the US using quarterly data during 1966–2004. They used various filtering methods to ensure the stationarity of these time

**Table 3.2** VAR Parameters for the Smets-Wouters DSGE Model for US

| π | VAR$_U$ | Lower bound | Upper bound |
|---|---|---|---|
| **Output-output** | 0.99908 | 0.71104 | 0.96272 |
| **Output-investment** | 0.22591 | −0.27355 | 0.18519 |
| **Output-consumption** | 0.10174 | −0.07815 | 0.02091 |
| **Interest-consumption** | −0.5553 | −0.83083 | −0.2264 |
| **Consumption-investment** | −0.4296 | −0.36543 | 0.08677 |
| **Variance-interest** | 0.65276 | 0.19035 | 0.56812 |
| **Variance-consumption** | 10.3888 | 6.19987 | 45.31804 |

Source: Le et al (2011) Table 3. Variables: output, consumption, investment, inflation, interest rate.

series where necessary. Their DSGE model has had a major influence on applied macroeconomics and is heavily cited.

Le et al (2011) carried out 1,000 Monte Carlo trials to calculate the within-sample indirect inference Wald statistic in equation (5.3). Instead of using the chi-square distribution to set critical values, they used Monte Carlo methods to simulate critical values for finite samples. They found that the Smets-Wouters model for the US was strongly rejected by indirect inference. In 100 percent of trials the Smets-Wouters model was rejected.

The first five rows of Table 3.2 report some of the twenty-five VAR coefficients for the Smets-Wouters model. For example, the autoregressive coefficient for output in the unrestricted VAR is 0.99908. The 95 percent confidence interval for its Smets-Wouters counterpart falls short of its true value. The same applies for the VAR coefficients for output on lagged investment, output on lagged consumption, and consumption on lagged investment. In fact, this applies to no less than nine out of twenty-five VAR coefficients. The VAR coefficient for interest on lagged consumption falls in the middle of the bounds. The penultimate row in Table 3.2 shows that the variance of the rate of interest exceeds the Smets-Wouters bounds, while the variance of consumption is close to the lower bound.

In general, the Smets-Wouters model generates VAR coefficients, which are very different to their unrestricted counterparts. This is why the Wald percentile is maximal at 100. The results in Table 3.2 refer to a first-order VAR. Had the Wald statistic in Table 3.2 failed to reject the Smets-Wouters model, there would have been a point in using a second-order VAR. Since the first-order Wald statistic categorically rejects the Smets-Wouters model, there is no point in calculating a second-order Wald statistic.

The Wald statistic in Table 3.2 refers to five key variables. The results in Table 3.2 are robust to increasing the number of variables, by including, for example, Tobin's q. However, reducing the number of variables tends to reduce the failure rate. For example, the effect of consumption shocks on labor supply and productivity reduces the rejection rate to 34 percent. Although statistically significant, this rejection rate is less draconian. On the other hand, the rejection rate is 100 percent for the effect of monetary policy shocks on government spending, investment, and labor productivity and supply.

There is a tendency among calibrators and with indirect estimation in general to add new features to DSGE models when the previous version of the model failed to capture a new phenomenon, such as the Subprime Crisis. One suspects that something similar will happen following the Covid-19 pandemic. These "patches" use up degrees of freedom and introduce further complexity into the model. Patching up models might fix matters by explaining the slow recovery in the wake of the Subprime Crisis, but this would not be justified unless it improved the Wald statistic. Meenagh et al (2019) report two "patches" to the Smets-Wouters model. The first introduces a banking sector. The second extends the first by introducing collateral lending and taking account of ZIP so that the rate of interest has a zero lower bound. The rejection rate for the first in a three-variable first-order VAR (output, inflation and interest) varies between 99.9 percent when T = 200 and 79.7 percent when T = 75. The rejection rates for the second are 100 percent and 98.1 percent respectively.

Other examples of patches include introducing more than one representative agent into the model, where for example one agent is rational and the other is not. Patching up the DSGE model in an effort to make it more realistic is arguably against the spirit of the DSGE movement. In any case, making DSGE models more realistic does not apparently improve them. Patching up might fix the job in hand, but it comes at the expense of using up degrees of freedom.

It is ironical that DSGE models, whose deep parameters and treatment of rational expectations were intended to respond to the Lucas critique, should be passed off as too simple and stylized to be tested against actual data. However, even the less severe Wald statistic in which the auxiliary model is a naïve VAR suggests the Smets-Wouters DSGE model for the US has little to do with US macroeconomic realities.

## Return to Econometric Orthodoxy

Some economists think that macroeconomics has gone backwards for three decades under the malign influence of Lucas and Prescott (P. Romer 2016). Calibration, indirect estimation and the DSGE movement have been scientific dead ends because they have ceased to be scientific, and they should be seen instead as postmodern developments. The methodology of indirect inference should be seen as an attempt to put the DSGE movement onto a more orthodox methodological footing. However, the results so far have been very disappointing. DSGE models may be elegant but they have little to do with the real world. Nevertheless, policymakers in general and central bankers in particular continue to be influenced by them. Indeed, their fall into the ZIP vortex is partly related to the lack of empirical scrutiny of their postmodernism.

Following the Revolution of 1980, classical econometric theory continued to develop. As far as macroeconometrics is concerned, there were major developments in the econometric analysis of time series, which are entirely overlooked in macroeconometric textbooks (Canova 2007, DeJong and Dave 2007). The first refers to the econometric analysis of nonstationary time series and cointegration theory. The second refers to the econometric analysis of rational expectations. Both of these developments are highly pertinent to the DSGE movement.

## Integrating the Secular and the Cyclical

Most macroeconomic time series are nonstationary; however, they tend to be stationary in log first differences. Macroeconomics has bifurcated into growth theory and business cycle theory. For growth economists, the business cycle is a nuisance parameter. For business cycle economists, secular economic growth is a nuisance parameter. Although there are some exceptions, growth economists assume that economic growth and business cycles are independent. Almost without exception business cycle economists make the same assumption. For example, Smets and Wouters used various filters, such as the Hodrick-Prescott filter criticized in chapter 2, to winnow the secular chaff from the cyclical wheat. We have already shown how the popular Hodrick-Prescott filter may induce fake cycles. Another motivation behind the use of filters is that filtered time series tend to be stationary, which greatly simplifies statistical inference and hypothesis testing.

Cointegration theory integrates the secular with the cyclical. Take for example an economy with a Cobb-Douglas technology:

$$lnQ_t = A_t + \alpha lnK_t + (1 - \alpha) lnL_t + u_t \tag{6.1}$$

where $A = lnTFP$, assumed here to be determined outside the model. Profit maximization implies that the demand for labor is:

$$lnL_t^D = lnK_t + \frac{1}{\alpha} \left[ ln(1 - \alpha) + A_t - lnw_t \right] + v_t \tag{6.2}$$

where w denotes the real wage. The supply of labor is hypothesized to be proportional to the population of working age and to vary directly with the real wage:

$$lnL_t^S = lnPOP_t + \beta lnw_t + \omega_t \tag{6.3}$$

Finally, the capital stock at the beginning of period t is:

$$K_t = I_{t-1} + \delta K_{t-1} \tag{6.4}$$

where $\delta$ denotes the rate of depreciation and I denotes investment. Equating the supply and demand for labor implies that the real wage equals:

$$lnw_t = \frac{\alpha}{1 + \alpha\beta}\left[ ln\frac{K_t}{POP_t} + \frac{1}{\alpha}\left( ln\left(1 - \alpha\right) + A_t\right) + v_t - \omega_t\right] \tag{6.5}$$

The model contains several variables, which are typically nonstationary: the logs of Q, K, w, L, A, POP and I. We could extend the model to include an equation for investment, as in Chapter 2, where net investment depends on the difference between the marginal product of capital and the cost of capital. However, we shall stop here. These equations are key components of the RBC model.

The theory implies that the six time series embody three cointegrating vectors. The production function, equation (6.1), has a cointegrating vector comprising A and the logs of Q, K and L. The employment function, equation (6.2), has a cointegrating vector comprising A and the logs of L, K and w. Alternatively, equation (6.3) has a cointegrating vector comprising the logs of L, POP and w. Finally, the real wage function, equation (6.5), has a cointegrating vector comprising A and the logs of w, K and POP. The cointegration methodology of Johansen (1995) may be used to test for the presence of these three cointegrating vectors.

Suppose the nonstationary variables in equation (6.1) are cointegrated, i.e. u is stationary. Then u may be interpreted as the "output gap," which is supposed to be stationary, and the secular component of output is $A_t + \alpha lnK_t + (1 - \alpha)lnL_t$. Suppose further that the nonstationary variables in equation (6.2) are cointegrated, i.e. v is stationary. Since employment has a stationary component a more refined definition of the output gap might be $A_t + \alpha lnK_t + (1 - \alpha)(lnL_t - v_t)$. Since lnL is difference stationary and v is stationary by definition, this refinement has no asymptotic importance, but it might matter in finite samples. Further refinements may be applied to the stationary component of real wages from equation (6.5).

In summary, we have generated output gaps, wage gaps, etc. without resorting to filters. There are different estimation methods for cointegrating vectors (Beenstock and Felsenstein 2019, Chapter 2, Hamilton 1994), which need not concern us here. Since cointegrated variables are dynamically related through error correction, the error correction models for wages, output, and so on may be New Keynesian, New Classical, Real Business Cycle, etc. Error correction models typically include expectations of future inflation or economic growth.

For example, the error correction models for output and employment might be:

$$\Delta lnQ_t = aE_t\Delta lnQ_{t+1} + b\Delta lnQ_{t-1} + \Delta lnL_{t-1} + d\Delta A_t + e\Delta lnK_t + fu_{t-1} + \varepsilon_t \tag{6.6}$$

$$\Delta lnL_t = gE_t\Delta lnw_{t+1} + h\Delta lnL_{t-1} + i\Delta A_t + j\Delta lnK_t + kv_{t-1} + \zeta_t \qquad (6.7)$$

where $\varepsilon$ and $\zeta$ are assumed to be iid. Note that all the variables in equations (6.6) and (6.7) are stationary because the data are difference stationary and u and v are stationary by definition. Error correction implies that f and k are negative. If f = a = 0 then equation (6.6) would constitute one of the equations in a first-order VAR for the logs of w, Q, and L. However, if the variables in equation (6.1) are cointegrated, they have to be related through error correction, so f is not expected to be zero.

Equations (6.6) and (6.7) are specified in terms of actual data instead of virtual data, such as filtered output gaps. We do not specify here error correction models for real wages, i.e. the counterparts of equation (6.6) for these variables. The error correction term for wages would be $v_{t-1} - \omega_{t-1}$. Together with equations (6.6) and (6.7), they form a vector error correction model (VECM), which by definition encompasses the VAR model. The VECM integrates the secular with the cyclical because it solves for the nonstationary and stationary components of the state variables.

Economic theory does not suggest that secular growth depends on expectations of future growth. This is why $E_t lnQ_{t+1}$ is not specified in equation (6.1). Matters are different in error correction models such as equation (6.6). The Lucas critique attaches importance to the way in which rational expectations might affect the impulse responses of shocks to the exogeneous variables. Several econometric methods have been proposed for rational expectations of state variables such as $E_t\Delta lnw_{t+1}$ in equation (6.7). Limited information methods are based on the idea that the prediction errors of rational expectations should be unpredictable, i.e. $\Delta lnw_{t+1} - E_t \Delta lnw_{t+1} = r_{t+1}$ should be serially uncorrelated and independent of relevant information for predicting the real wage that was available in period t. Substituting $\Delta lnw_{t+1} - r_{t+1}$ for $E_t\Delta w_{t+1}$ in equation (5.7) implies:

$$\Delta lnL_t = g\Delta lnw_{t+1} + h\Delta lnL_{t-1} + i\Delta A_t + j\Delta lnK_t + kv_{t-1} + e_t - gr_{t+1} \qquad (6.8)$$

Since r is serially uncorrelated it must be independent of all the right-hand side variables in equation (6.8), with the exception $\Delta lnw_{t+1}$ with which it is negatively correlated. Hence, the estimate of g embodies attenuation bias. This "errors in variables" problem may be solved using instrumental variables for wages, which were available in period t (McCallum 1976, Wickens 1982).

Rational expectations for output growth in equation (6.6) involve more complex issues because, unlike in equation (6.7), they refer to a dependent variable.

It is obviously not possible to substitute expected output growth with actual output growth, because the latter is the dependent variable. The substitution method suggests that an auxiliary autoregressive model be estimated in which output growth is regressed on the relevant information set. The one step ahead prediction from the auxiliary model is used to substitute for expected future output growth.

Limited information methods, as described, provide consistent estimates of the VECM parameters. More efficient estimates may be obtained by applying full information methods (Pesaran 1978). In this case the VECM is seeded with rational expectations obtained using limited information methods. Then the VECM Is used to solve for rational expectations for output growth, wage growth, etc. These expectations are used to re-estimate the VECM. The re-estimated VECM is used to solve for rational expectations, and re-estimated once again. This iterative procedure provides FIML estimates of the VECM and its rational expectations. FIML is more efficient than limited information maximum likelihood (LIML) because, unlike the substitution method, it uses the parameter estimates of the model to generate rational expectations. Of course, if part of the VECM is misspecified, FIML will induce specification error elsewhere in the VECM. As usual, FIML is only advisable for well-specified models.

This VECM methodology seems to deal with the Lucas critique because the cointegrating vectors embody deep parameters and rational expectations are featured in the VECM. In summary, the secular and cyclical are integrated and classical frequentist methods are used to estimate the VECM parameters. There is no need for virtual variables, such as filtered output gaps; there is no need for indirect estimation methods such as calibration and Bayesian methods; and there is no need for indirect inference. The VECM methodology constitutes a modernist methodological agenda.

There are only two deep parameters in our illustrative example: the production function parameter $\alpha$ and the participation parameter $\beta$. The DSGE movement would insist on imposing the cross-equation restriction in equations (6.1)–(6.5). Suppose, empirically, that the output equation happened to be Cobb-Douglas, but the labor demand equation happened to be CES. That is, the elasticity of demand for labor with respect to the real wage does not equal $-1/\alpha$ as it should, if the cross-equation restriction were imposed. Indeed, empirical estimates suggest that the absolute wage elasticity is less than 1, whereas according to Cobb-Douglas it should be greater than 1. Suppose further that the rejection of the cross-equation restriction is statistically significant and has a small p-value.

How should we relate to this apparent inconsistency? If, indeed, the economy consisted of a single representative firm, it would be difficult to justify. But the economy does not comprise a single representative firm. Aggregation theory does not necessarily imply that the wage elasticity of demand for labor must be $-1/\alpha$.

Consistency should not be the enemy of empirical relevance. In macroeconomic models we should learn to live with what would be inconsistent in a representative agent model.

The same flexibility should apply to consumer behavior and labor supply. Since consumers and suppliers of labor refer to the same agents, equation (6.3) should be consistent with the consumption function, which was not specified in the illustrative example, or the investment equation should be consistent with the labor demand equation. Insisting on consistency would most probably reject too many good models. A similar criticism has been voiced by Wren-Lewis (2018), who refers to the "micro-foundations hegemony," where the holy grail of cross-equation restrictions is imposed regardless of empirical considerations. Perhaps "tyranny" is more apt than "hegemony." Like us, Wren-Lewis also calls for combining micro-foundations with structural equation modeling. The search for a model that has coherent micro-foundations and is also coherent with the data promises to be endless. The challenge is to find a wise balance between atheoretical data-driven models on the one hand, and theory-driven models on the other that have little to do with macroeconomic reality.

When I was working on Beenstock and Ilek (2010), Smets and Wouters sent me their unpublished solutions for the natural rate of interest from their DSGE model for the US. Strictly speaking, these solutions referred to Woodford's equilibrium rate of interest (the real rate of interest generated by perfect price flexibility). These solutions ranged unreasonably between 15 percent and minus 25 percent, and were very volatile. The tyranny of cross-equation restrictions can have unpleasant and unintended consequences.

In summary, a return to modernism should satisfy the original aspirations of the DSGE movement, with the exception of the imposition of cross-equation restrictions. This agenda builds on developments in econometric theory that were largely unknown in the Revolution of 1980. Given the poor empirical performance of DSGE models, there is no alternative to this agenda. It is easy to specify DSGE models and to use Bayesian methods for their indirect estimation. These methods, as we have seen, are bound to "succeed" even if they do not fit the data. Indeed, the worse the fit the greater the weight attributed to the priors in the posterior distribution. The postmodernist agenda is win-win. A model emerges when the empirical evidence rejects its hypothesis and when it does not.

By contrast, the modernist agenda involves much hard work.

## Synopsis

Applied macroeconomics during the last quarter of a century has undergone a postmodernist revolution, imported into economics by Prescott and Kydland from computer models of global climate change. Under this revolution DSGE models are assumed to be the "truth," their parameters are calibrated to data by methods of indirect estimation, after which policy narratives are told about past and future economic developments. These models are not formally tested as they would have been under the modernist agenda, which dates back to Francis Bacon, René Descartes, David Hume, and Karl Popper.

This revolution was intended as a response to the Lucas critique, according to which econometricians have been unable to identify deep structural macroeconomic parameters required for policy analysis forecasting. Lucas himself thought that econometricians were rejecting too many "good models." It is ironical, therefore, that the spread of indirect estimation has led to the failure to reject too many "bad" models.

These bad models have led central bankers astray, and contributed to the intellectual environment that justified the eventual adoption of ZIP. The emergence of the New Abnormal cannot be disconnected from the spread of postmodernism in applied macroeconomics. Central bankers found narratives to justify their behavior, especially in terms of the divine coincidence (output and inflation on target under ZIP).

Indirect estimation applies cross-equation restrictions using methods such as calibration where structural parameters are chosen by tweaking them until the model as a whole fits the data to some satisfactory subjective degree. More sophisticated methods apply Bayesian priors to the structural parameters and obtain their posterior counterparts using MCMC methods. These methods of indirect estimation are essentially different to the frequentist methods of classical statistics and econometrics.

A parallel development to indirect estimation has been the use of vector autoregressions in applied econometrics. VAR models are purely statistical descriptions of the data, and are not intended to test hypotheses (indeed structural parameters are under-identified). They arose out of frustration with the difficulty of testing macroeconomic models in the frequency tradition. The first postmodernist development was to impose untestable restrictions on VAR models (SVAR models) in an attempt to give them structural interpretations.

Since 1993, frequentist methods of indirect inference have been developed to test empirically models based on indirect estimation. Indirect inference restores classical discipline in the testing of DSGE and other indirectly estimated models. These methods treat the DSGE model as the null hypothesis, which is tested against a rival VAR model rather than the data. If the DSGE model is rejected by the VAR model, it shows that the theoretical sophistication of the DSGE model adds no further empirical understanding than a "no-brainer" VAR model. This result applies to the seminal DSGE model of the US economy developed by Smets and Wouters.

The chapter concludes with a call to return to classical econometric methods for time series data, which have undergone major developments since the Lucas critique. The first concerns the development of econometric methods (in the 1970s and 1980s) for testing hypotheses with rational expectations. The second concerns the development of econometric methods (in the 1980s and 1990s) for testing hypotheses with nonstationary time series data. The third concerns the development (in the 1980s) of tests for weak, strong and super exogeneity, where the latter provides an empirical test of the Lucas critique which is largely rejected. The fourth concerns the development of tests for indirect inference (see above). Had these developments occurred ten years earlier, macroeconomic postmodernism might have been nipped in the bud.

Many macroeconomists (author included) think that, despite its pedagogic advantages in classrooms, the DSGE movement and its emphasis on postmodern narratives has been unfruitful. Some macroeconomists have criticized the hegemony of cross-equation restrictions imposed in DSGE models despite their badness of fit. Macroeconometric models relevant to policy must fit the data well, even if this is at the cost theoretical esthetics. After all, estimating and testing macroeconometric models is an agenda requiring humility; it is nothing short of fantastic.

# 4

# The Natural Rate of Interest

In Chapter 2 we noted that the natural rate of interest, which lies at the heart of neo-Wicksellian monetary policy, was neglected and almost forgotten by macroeconomic theorists and practitioners. Just as it would be inconceivable for labor economists to overlook the natural rate of unemployment, so it is inconceivable that monetary economists should have overlooked the natural rate of interest. Just as targeting unemployment below its natural rate is bound to destabilize the macroeconomy, so does targeting the rate of interest below or above its natural rate.

To be fair, the natural rate of interest has attracted some empirical attention, but, as we shall see, much of this attention was misguided, including the author's (Beenstock and Ilek 2010). In this chapter, we follow Patinkin's interpretation of Wicksell in Chapter 2, according to which the natural rate of interest should be measured by the return to capital, or the marginal product of capital net of depreciation. According to this measure, we shall show that the natural rate of interest is currently large in most countries, despite the fact that according to the New Keynesian and DSGE schools the natural rate of interest is zero or near zero. Indeed, in some countries the natural rate of interest has been increasing despite the fact that the money rate of interest set by central banks under ZIP has been decreasing. According to Wicksell, the money and natural rates of interest are expected to move together in the longer term. ZIP should have induced a reduction in the natural rate of interest, but, if anything, the opposite happened.

Instead, the natural and money rates of interest have become disconnected. Central banks have cut their interest rates without regard to the natural rate of interest, while the natural rate of interest seems to disregard the money rate of interest set by central banks. In Chapter 2 we pointed out that, because the return on capital is risky whereas the money rate of interest set by the central banks is riskless, we should expect that in equilibrium the natural rate to exceed the money rate (in real terms) by a risk premium. The gap between the natural and money rates has widened because the money rate fell to zero under ZIP while the natural rate even increased. This widening gap implies that the risk premium has been increasing. It also means that, instead of ZIP inducing more business investment, which would have reduced the natural rate of interest as measured by the return to

*Zero Interest Policy and the New Abnormal.* Michael Beenstock, Oxford University Press. © Michael Beenstock (2022).
DOI: 10.1093/oso/9780192849663.003.0004

capital, the opposite has happened. Business investment has decreased, resulting in an increase in the return to capital.

The increase in the risk premium is consistent with the hypothesis that ZIP has increased existential risk in the New Abnormal (Chapter 2). Instead of encouraging business investment as intended, it has scared off investors. This explains why the return to capital failed to decrease and even increased. By failing to monitor the return to capital, central bankers forced the money rate of interest to run loose from its anchor, the natural rate of interest. Their monetary policy lost contact with reality. Instead, they tried to persuade themselves that the natural rate of interest was close to zero, and that ZIP is justified on Wicksellian grounds. In reference to the natural rate of interest, Janet Yellen, as chairperson of the Federal Reserve, declared at a conference in May 2015 that, "Under assumptions that I consider more realistic under present circumstances, the Taylor rule calls for the federal funds rate to be close to zero."

Until the Covid-19 crisis struck in early 2020, stock markets were buoyant and bullish, even though many economies were lackluster. This apparent paradox is explained by the fact that, as the return to capital increases in the face of existential risk, so do equity prices. This effect is in addition to the standard inverse relation between equity prices and interest rates through which ZIP inflated equity prices directly. However, this effect is insufficiently important to account for the increase in equity prices.

We ask of economists who disagree with Patinkin that the natural rate of interest is measured by the return on fixed capital, and who conclude that the natural rate of interest is zero if output and inflation happen to be on target under ZIP, should it worry them that the return on fixed capital is high? It should not worry them if the high return on fixed capital assets happens to be an equilibrium phenomenon. A central theme in this chapter is that the high return on capital should worry them for two reasons. First, because they might have mistaken the identity of the natural rate of interest, and second, because the high return on capital should have served as an alarm bell that their model is wrong. It should not have predicted the high return on capital; on the contrary, the return on capital should have decreased.

In summary, our contention is that the natural rate of interest as measured by the return on fixed assets has not tended to zero as predicted by the New Keynesian and DSGE schools. On the contrary. However, a rose by any other name would smell just as sweet. Even if they happen to object to Patinkin's definition of the natural rate of interest, central bankers should have asked themselves why the return on capital behaved in contradiction to expectations. Our answer is simple: for most central bankers the return on capital is below their statistical radar. Indeed, in most countries data for the return to capital do not even exist.

This chapter begins with a critical review of a handful of studies that have attempted to measure the natural rate of interest. As mentioned, these studies were misguided because their concept of the natural rate of interest had little to do with Wicksell's. Since Wicksell's is based on the return to capital, we recall some basic theory about the determinants of the return to capital. Then we discuss how to measure the natural rate of interest with empirical data. Next, we construct time series data for the return to capital, also known as the natural rate of interest, for a number of key OECD countries. Finally, we calculate the implicit risk premium between the natural and money rates of interest for the countries in the study. We also show that increases in the return to capital resulted from a reduction in business investment.

## Literature

It is unfortunate that studies of the natural rate of interest have focused exclusively on Woodford's definition, discussed in Chapter 2, rather than Wicksell's definition as interpreted by Patinkin. To recall, Woodford's natural rate of interest is the rate of interest that would be generated if wages and prices were perfectly flexible. Since wages and prices are not perfectly flexible, Laubach and Williams (2003) suggested that the natural rate of interest may be estimated by filtering it from a New Keynesian model when the output and inflation gaps (see Chapter 2) are zero. Consider equations (3.1) and (3.2) in Chapter 2, in which the natural rate of interest ($r_{nt}$) is a latent variable. Suppose that we have econometric estimates of the parameters of the model, $\alpha$, $\beta$, $\gamma$ and $\theta$. Let the inflation target be $\pi^*$. Let $r = i - \pi^*$ denote the central bank's real rate of interest given the inflation target, which must equal $r_n$ if inflation and output are on target. By reverse engineering, and setting y and $\pi$ to their target values, we may solve implicitly for the unknown latent variable, $r_n$. Alternatively, one may use Kalman Filter methods to infer $r_n$ from data for the output gap (y) and inflation.

According to this view, the natural rate of interest is doubly virtual; it is a virtual variable generated by yet other virtual variables, such as the output gap and expected inflation. Apart from this, the parameters of the New Keynesian model, $\alpha$, $\beta$, $\gamma$ and $\theta$, were estimated ignoring the natural rate of interest. Presumably, their estimates would have been different had there been data for the natural rate of interest because the natural rate of interest is unlikely to be independent of other variables in the model. Therefore, a variant of the Lucas critique applies to Laubach-Williams estimates of the natural rate of interest.

The Laubach-Williams method has been used quite widely in various forms, especially in central banks (Barsky et al 2014, Holsten et al 2016, Wynne and Zhang 2017, and Elkayam and Segal 2018). See also Brand, Bielecki, and Penalver (2018) for a review of various forms of the Laubach-Williams method, including short-term and long-term estimates of the natural rate of interest, all of which indicate that the natural rate of interest has decreased over the last fifteen years.

A conceptually different approach to estimating the natural rate of interest was proposed by Beenstock and Ilek (2010). According to equation (3.3) in Chapter 2, New Keynesian models are completed by a Taylor rule for monetary policy in which the central bank reacts to the natural rate of interest as well as output and inflation gaps. Beenstock and Ilek showed that the Bank of Israel behaved as if it was using the gross redemption yield on long-term index-linked treasury bonds to represent the natural rate of interest. The natural rate of interest is supposed to reflect the underlying real return to capital, so perhaps this gross redemption yield serves as a plausible proxy for the long-run natural rate of interest. Matters would be different for non-indexed bonds because their gross redemption yields depend on expected inflation over their lifetime, which is unknown. Very few countries have developed indexed bond markets, but matters have been different in Israel since 1960, the UK since 1980 and the US since 2002.

Suppose that the Bank of Israel in fact referred to the return on indexed bonds to represent the natural rate of interest. This, of course, does not prove that the gross redemption yield on indexed bonds is the natural rate of interest, or is even a good proxy for it. The Bank of Israel may simply have chosen the wrong anchor to represent the natural rate of interest. So, this line of research is not fruitful either. In any case, as discussed in Chapter 5, quantitative easing undertaken by the Bank of Israel in the indexed bond market has driven down gross redemption yields on index-linked treasury bonds. Since the natural rate of interest is conceptually supposed to be independent of the central bank, long-term gross redemption yields on indexed treasury bonds do not satisfy the criteria of the natural rate of interest. Instead of the anchor stabilizing the ship, the ship drags the anchor.

A separate but related literature has tried to explain why interest rates have fallen across the world. Some have suggested that declining birth rates, combined with greater longevity, might have created a savings glut, which has depressed interest rates (Bacchetta and Benhima 2015, Carvalho, Ferrero, and Nechio 2016). Others have suggested that a scarcity of safe assets contributed to the fall in interest rates (Caballero, Farhi, and Gourinchas 2016). Earlier, the same authors attributed the fall in interest rates to growing global income inequality (Caballero, Farhi, and Gourinchas 2008). For one reason or another, these and related studies treat central banks as reacting to global developments.

According to this view, the sudden and almost simultaneous adoption of ZIP by the Federal Reserve, the Bank of England and other central banks (Switzerland and Sweden) in 2008–9 resulted from global trends in international capital markets. The same applies to other central banks, such as the European Central Bank, which adopted ZIP in 2013, the Bank of Israel, which adopted ZIP in 2014, and the Reserve Bank of Australia, which adopted ZIP in 2019. All these central banks just happened to be prisoners of global circumstances beyond their individual control. They were simply submitting to market forces, albeit sequentially. This unlikely argument could not have applied to the Bank of Japan, which has operated ZIP since 1996, before global interest rates were supposed to have declined.

Our thesis is that ZIP was the cause and not the effect. ZIP has been responsible for the decline in international interest rates as suggested by Borio et al (2019). When the major central banks of the world commit themselves to ZIP, market forces bow to the inevitable financial tsunami. It is no coincidence that in North America and Europe interest rates decreased after 2008. In Chapter 5 we show that, at first, the fall in short-term interest rates was not accompanied by a decrease in long-term interest rates. However, when it was understood that ZIP had become a permanent feature of the New Abnormal, long-term interest rates followed short-term interest rates downwards. We also show that latecomers to ZIP such as Israel and Australia experienced normal interest rates until they joined the ZIP club. In summary, the argument that ZIP is an effect rather a cause is not persuasive.

Patinkin's definition of the natural rate of interest as the marginal product of capital net of depreciation is real rather than virtual because it is observable. As discussed below, the return to capital may not be free of measurement problems, but it is palpable. However, this definition has been ignored in the literature; Woodford's definition has attracted all the attention. Our purpose in this chapter is to resuscitate Patinkin's definition. We show that the natural rate of interest as measured by the marginal product of capital has behaved completely differently to Woodford's measure. In fact, the natural rate of interest has not decreased. It is far from zero, and it has even been increasing in some countries. Woodford measures based on Laubach-Williams have lulled central banks into believing that ZIP is a normal state instead of a pathological one; it has led them to chase their own shadow. All is well and natural under ZIP because the natural rate of interest is zero.

However, the opposite is true. The natural rate of interest is normal. It is therefore ironical that Marx, Mojon, and Velde (2018) ask "why have interest rates fallen far below the return on capital?" Like us, they observe that the return on capital has behaved normally. Unlike us, they believe that ZIP has emerged because Woodford measures of the natural rate of interest have fallen towards zero. The answer is that the natural rate of interest is the return on capital, which is normal. What is abnormal is not the return on capital, but ZIP. Central banks, misguided by Woodford's definition, have created an artificial cleavage between the money rate of interest and the natural rate of interest. Ironically, Neo-Wicksellians are not Wicksellian.

## Theory

Value added (Q) is produced by labor (L) and capital (K). The Cobb-Douglas production function has served as a workhorse in economics in general and macroeconomics in particular for almost a century:

$$Q = AK^{\alpha}L^{\beta} \tag{1.1}$$

where A denotes total factor productivity (TFP) and return to scale equals $\alpha + \beta$. Returns to scale are constant when $\alpha + \beta = 1$; hence we set $\beta = 1 - \alpha$. The marginal product of capital (MPK) is:

$$MPK = \alpha\, Ak^{\alpha-1} = \alpha\frac{Q}{K} \tag{1.2}$$

where k denotes the capital–labor ratio. As expected, MPK varies inversely with the capital–labor ratio because returns to scale are constant. Since Q/K is the average product of capital (APK), equation (1.2) states that the marginal product of capital is a fraction ($\alpha$) of its average product. Since K/Q is the capital–output ratio (COR), equation (1.2) also states that MPK varies inversely with COR. Or, MPK varies inversely with the capital-intensity of output.

According to neoclassical economic theory, to which Wicksell subscribed, firms are hypothesized to maximize their profits by equating the marginal product of capital with its marginal cost, or the user cost of capital defined as $c = P_K(r + d)/P_Q$, where $P_K$ and $P_Q$ denote the prices of capital goods and output respectively, r denotes the real rate of interest paid by firms, and d denotes the rate of capital depreciation. Equation (1.2) implies:

$$K = L\left(\frac{c}{\alpha A}\right)^{\frac{1}{1-\alpha}} \tag{1.3}$$

Hence, the capital stock is proportionate to employment, varies inversely with the cost of capital, and varies directly with TFP.

Suppose that, because there is no inflation, the real rate of interest paid by firms is equal to the nominal rate of interest ($i_b$ in Chapter 2). Suppose further, for simplicity, that capital goods and output have the same prices, so equations (1.2) and (1.3) imply that $MPK - d = i_b$. According to Chapter 2, $i_b$ exceeds the rate of interest set by the central bank (i) by a risk premium. $MPK - d$ is Wicksell's natural rate of interest, which equals the money rate of interest plus the risk premium. This would be true if equation (1.3) held instantaneously. Since adjustment costs in capital prevent equation (1.3) from holding instantaneously, the money and natural rates of interest are generally unequal in the short run, as discussed in Chapter 2.

The important point here is that $MPK - d$ is conceptually the natural rate of interest, which, according to equation (2), may be measured using empirical data for capital (K) and output (Q) as well as estimates of $\alpha$ and d. If $\alpha$ and d are fixed, the natural rate of interest may be measured by:

$$r_n = \alpha APK - d \tag{1.4}$$

The Cobb-Douglas production function implies that the factorial distribution of income is constant. The labor share, the wage bill as a share of GDP, is $1 - \alpha$ and the share of capital, profits as a share of GDP, is $\alpha$. This property arises from the restriction that the elasticity of substitution between capital and labor (ES) is one. Hence, if output is unchanged, the percentage increase in capital equals the percentage decrease in labor. Since empirically these shares tend to vary over time, as shown below, either ES is not one, or the neoclassical theory is false.

The CES (constant ES) production function assumes that ES is constant but may take any value, including 1. Hence, Cobb-Douglas is a special case of CES. In a further generalization, the translog production function, ES varies.

The CES production function is:

$$Q = A[\alpha K^{\rho} + (1 - \alpha) L^{\rho}]^{\frac{rs}{\rho}} \qquad (1.5)$$

where rs denotes return to scale, which is set to 1, and ES = $1/(1-\rho)$. Note that when $\rho = 0$ ES = 1, ES exceeds 1 when $\rho$ is positive, and is less than 1 otherwise. Equation (1.2) becomes:

$$MPK = \alpha A^{\rho} \left(\frac{Q}{K}\right)^{1-\rho} \qquad (1.6)$$

Hence, MPK varies directly with APK, as before, if $\rho$ is positive, but varies inversely if ES is less than 1. Also, the factor share of capital in GDP (K.MPK/Q) is:

$$S_K = \alpha A^{\rho} \left(\frac{Q}{K}\right)^{-\rho} \qquad (1.7)$$

Equation (1.7) states that the profit share varies directly with the capital–output ratio if $\rho$ is positive, i.e., when ES exceeds 1, and varies inversely when ES is less than 1. When $\rho = 0$, equation (1.7) equals $\alpha$ because ES = 1 as in the Cobb–Douglas case. Notice also that, whereas in the Cobb-Douglas case factor shares do not depend on TFP, matters are different in the CES case.

The translog production function is:

$$lnQ = lnA + \alpha lnK + (1 - \alpha) lnL + \frac{1}{2}\gamma\alpha (1 - \alpha) (lnk)^2 \qquad (1.8)$$

Notice that when $\gamma = 0$, equation (1.8) reverts to the Cobb-Douglas case. The marginal product of capital is:

$$MPK = \alpha APK[1 + \gamma(1 - \alpha) lnk] \qquad (1.9)$$

As in equation (1.6), the marginal product of capital depends on APK and k. And the profit share is:

$$S_K = \alpha\left[1 + \gamma\left(1 - \alpha\right)lnk\right] \tag{1.10}$$

In equation (1.7), the relationship between the profit share and the capital–labor ratio depends on the sign of ρ. In equation (1.10), it depends on the sign of γ.

In summary, the average product of capital may be regarded as a sufficient statistic for the marginal product of capital in the Cobb-Douglas case. Matters are different in the CES and translog cases because MPK depends on the capital–labor ratio as well as the average product of capital.

Equations (1.2), (1.6), and (1.9) provide theory-based definitions of the marginal product of capital. The most direct measure of MPK would be, of course, to divide profits in the business sector by the business sector's capital stock, since the former are equal to KxMPK. By contrast, equations (1.2), (1.6), and (1.9) infer MPK indirectly from data on APK and k.

## From Theory to Data

Surprisingly, most national statistical authorities do not publish data for the return on capital. To my best knowledge there are only three exceptions. The Bureau of Economic Analysis in the US has regularly published data dating back to the beginning of the twentieth century, the Central Bureau of Statistics in Israel began publishing these data in 1980, and the Office for National Statistics in the UK began to publish these data in 1997. So meaningful official time series to follow secular trends are only available for the US and Israel. These statistical authorities also publish data on related phenomena, such as the factorial distribution of income (profit and wage shares) and capital–output ratios. So not only has the natural rate of interest as measured by the return on fixed assets been ignored by the DSGE movement, it has also been ignored by national statistical authorities. Perhaps this helps explain why the natural rate of interest has been overlooked or misunderstood by policy makers in most countries. However, this excuse does not apply in the US and Israel, where the relevant data should have appeared on the dashboards of their central banks.

## National Income Accounting

In this chapter we report official data for the return on fixed assets, the factorial distribution of income, and capital–output ratios for the US and Israel. As for other countries, we construct these data using data components from national sources.

National income accountants construct data for GDP, represented by Q in the previous discussion, as well as employment (L) and capital (K). They also construct data for the wage bill. Since the wage bill plus profits must equal GDP, it is tempting to define profits by GDP minus the wage bill. However, national income accountants refer to this residual euphemistically as the "gross operating surplus," or GOS. They do so because all the errors and omissions that accumulate in the construction of the national income accounts end up in GOS. Like all estimates in the national accounts, the operating surplus may be defined gross (GOS) or net of capital depreciation (NOS), and at factor cost (excluding indirect taxes) or at market prices (including indirect taxes).

A particularly troublesome item in the national accounts is the treatment of the self-employed. What part of their income is profit and what part is wages? For example, self-employed taxi drivers use their cars to earn income as well as for private purposes. They declare a wage income for tax purposes, which may be unrelated to the opportunity cost of their labor. How much should be regarded as profit earned from taxi services? National income accountants do their best to make some reasonable estimate, which they refer to as "mixed income." Below operating surpluses include mixed income. In summary, if operating surplus (OS) is used to represent profits, it undoubtedly contains measurement errors.

Since the marginal product of capital is represented by NOS/K we also require data for the capital stock. National income accountants have constructed various measures of K. Just as OS may be measured gross or net and at factor cost or at market prices, the same applies to K. The gross capital stock at constant prices is calculated by the perpetual inventory method, according to which $GK_t$ at the beginning of period t is a moving sum of gross domestic fixed capital formation over the previous n periods, where n denotes the lifetime of capital assets. This definition assumes that capital is scrapped after n periods.

The net capital stock at constant prices (K) at the beginning of period t is defined as the net capital stock in the previous period plus gross domestic fixed capital formation in the previous period minus capital depreciation in the previous period. Depreciation reduces the net capital stock. Scrapping reduces the gross capital stock. Whereas depreciation occurs over the lifetime of capital, scrapping is sudden death. The change in the net capital stock equals the change in the gross capital stock minus capital depreciation.

Since the return to capital is the ratio between operating surplus and the capital stock, the numerator and denominator do not have to be deflated to obtain the return to capital in real terms. Some statistical authorities, such as the Office for National Statistics (UK), report operating surpluses and capital stocks at current and constant prices. As we shall see, many statistical authorities report operating surpluses at current prices and capital stocks at constant prices, hence the need to adjust operating surpluses for inflation using the deflators for capital or fixed assets. These deflators are provided by some statistical authorities, such as in Germany, but they are mostly not provided. In such cases, operating surpluses are deflated by the implicit price deflator for gross domestic fixed capital investment. Some countries, such as Japan, report net capital stocks, while others, such as Germany, report both net and gross capital stocks.

The net return to (net) capital is NOS/K = MPK and the gross return to (gross) capital is GOS/GK = GMPK. The relation between the gross and net returns is:

$$GMPK = \frac{MPK + \delta}{1 + \frac{\Sigma dep - scrap}{k}} \tag{2.1}$$

where $\Sigma dep$ denotes cumulative capital depreciation, $\delta$ denotes the rate of depreciation and *scrap* is the current amount of capital scrapped. If cumulative depreciation equals scrap, the gross return to capital exceeds the net return by the rate of depreciation, as expected because gross and net capital are equal. If the capital stock is growing, cumulative depreciation naturally exceeds scrapped capital, in which event the gross return to capital decreases relative to the net return because the gross capital stock exceeds the net capital stock. In general, the gross return to capital may be larger or smaller than its net return. However, in the empirical examples below, gross MPK tends to be larger.

The terminology for gross and net capital is somewhat tendentious. The former is net of scrapping and the latter is net of depreciation. So they are both net measured in their own way; they are two legitimate measures of capital. It would be an empirical matter to determine which measure happened to explain gross domestic fixed capital formation. By contrast, NOS and GOS are conceptually different. Although the net return to capital is usually measured by the ratio of NOS to net capital, and the gross return to capital is usually measured by ratio of GOS to gross capital, it would be meaningful to measure the return to capital by the ratio of GOS to net capital, or NOS to gross capital. Indeed, for countries where there are data for gross and net capital, we follow the usual practice, but for countries where only net capital stocks are available, we express the gross return to capital by the ratio of GOS to net capital.

A further difficulty concerns indirect taxes on production and imports, which are reported by some statistical authorities but not others. For the former we may calculate NOS net of indirect taxes as well as gross of indirect taxes. Businesses care about NOS net of indirect taxes, which is conceptually equivalent to NOS at factor cost. Where it is not possible to calculate NOS at factor cost, it is measured at market prices by default. Businesses care even more about NOS net of all taxes, including direct (corporation) tax. However, national income accountants do not relate to corporation tax. What matters nationally is the return on capital at market prices gross of direct taxes, since indirect and direct taxes are transfers from the business sector to the public sector.

## Measurement Error

Net and gross definitions of MPK are subject to measurement error even if gross domestic fixed capital formation does not. Measurement error in net capital is induced by measurement error in depreciation, and in gross capital it is induced by measurement error in the longevity of capital (n) and its current cost of replacement. The estimate of the net return to capital is MPK = [NOS*(1 + $m_{os}$)]/[(K*(1 + $m_k$)], where asterisks denote true values and m denotes measurement error. Like most national income accounting data, real GDP, NOS, and K are difference stationary in logarithms, which implies that lnMPK = lnNOS* – lnK* + $m_{os}$ – $m_k$ is expected to be difference stationary (because the difference between difference stationary variables, such as lnNOS and lnK, is generally difference stationary except in the unlikely event that lnNOS and lnK happen to be cointegrated). If the measurement errors $m_{os}$ and $m_k$ are stationary as expected, time series for lnMPK are asymptotically independent of measurement error.

In summary, the concern that NOS in particular embodies measurement error is less serious than would be the case if the operating surplus and capital happened to be stationary. This implies that time series data for NOS and K may be used to estimate secular trends in the return to capital despite the fact that cyclical movements in the return to capital may be biased due to measurement error in NOS.

## Empirical Illustration

Table 4.1 illustrates these accounting issues for Israel. In 1995 the return to net capital in the business sector at market prices net of indirect taxes on production and imports was 16.9 percent per year. That is, the net operating surplus (net of indirect taxes on production and imports and depreciation) amounted to 16.9 percent of the net capital stock in the business sector at market prices. In the calculation of NOS, Israel's Central Bureau of Statistics (CBS) assumed that the wages of the self-employed were 10 percent of net output in the business sector. On this basis, the factor share of capital was 18 percent of net business output. The balance of 82 percent constituted the share of labor and indirect taxes. Since taxes on production and imports amounted to 21 percent of net business output and the capital–output ratio was 1.07, the rate of return on capital net of depreciation but gross of taxes on production and imports was 36.5 percent (=0.169 + 0.21/1.07). Note that minor discrepancies in Table 4.1 result from rounding.

Since the rate of capital depreciation in 1995 was 10.5 percent of net business output, the share of the gross operating surplus in gross output was 26 percent. The (net) capital–output ratio in terms of gross output was 0.97; hence the return

Table 4.1 The Return on Net Capital in Israel: Business Sector at Market Prices

| | 1995 | | 2018 | |
|---|---|---|---|---|
| | Net | Gross | Net | Gross |
| Taxes on production and imports | 21 | 19 | 17 | 15 |
| Compensation of employees | 51 | 46 | 51 | 46 |
| Wages of self-employed | 10 | 9 | 8 | 7 |
| Operating surplus | 18 | 26 | 23 | 32 |
| Return on capital: net of indirect taxes | 16.9 | 27 | 20.9 | 32.7 |
| Return on capital: gross of indirect taxes | 36.6 | 46 | 37.9 | 47 |
| Capital–output ratio | 1.07 | 0.97 | 1.11 | 1.0 |
| Depreciation | 10.5 | | 11.1 | |

*Source*: Central Bureau of Statistics (CBS), National Income Accounts 1995–2018 (February 2020). The data in rows 1–4 and in columns 1 and 3 and 2 and 4 refer to percentages of net and gross output respectively. Depreciation is expressed as a percentage of net output.

to net capital in terms of GOS was 27 percent net of indirect taxes and 46 percent gross of indirect taxes.

Between 1995 and 2018, the return to net capital increased from 16.9 percent to 20.9 percent net of indirect taxes, and from 36.5 percent to 37.9 percent gross of indirect taxes. Their gross output counterparts increased from 27 percent to 32.7 percent and from 46 percent to 47 percent. Businesses care about the increase from 16.9 percent to 20.9 percent. The government cares about the increase from 36.5 percent to 37.9 percent.

Another issue concerns the effect of historical cost accounting and current cost accounting on rates of return on capital. Since the net operating surplus is net of depreciation, the latter may be calculated according to the replacement cost of capital goods or according to its historical value. The same applies to the valuation of fixed assets by the statistical authorities. Most statistical authorities use current cost accounting rather than historical cost accounting.

Finally, the capital–output ratio in 1995 was 1.07; that is, the net capital stock divided by net output at market prices in the business sector was slightly more than 1. Table 4.1 shows that by 2018 the capital–output ratio had increased slightly to 1.1; the post-tax net return on capital had increased from 16.9 percent to 20.9 percent; the capital share in net output had increased from 18 percent to 23 percent; taxes on production and imports had decreased from 21 percent of net output to 17 percent; and the share of depreciation in gross output had increased slightly from 10.5 percent to 11.1 percent.

## Corporation Tax

The returns to capital in Table 4.1 are gross of corporate income tax. What matters for businesses are returns to capital net of corporate and indirect taxes. Table 4.2 reports the rates of corporation tax in countries in the study group. In 2020 these

Table 4.2  Corporate Tax Rates

|  | 1980 | 1985 | 1990 | 1995 | 2000 | 2005 | 2010 | 2015 | 2020 | Effective 2019 |
|---|---|---|---|---|---|---|---|---|---|---|
| Australia | 46 | 46 | 39 | 36 | 34 | 30 | 30 | 30 | 30 | 20.2 |
| Canada | 51 | 49 | 41 | 45 | 42 | 34 | 29 | 27 | 26 | 10.5 |
| Switzerland | 33 | 32 | 31 | 28 | 24 | 21 | 21 | 21 | 21 | 9.5 |
| Germany | 60 | 60 | 55 | 55 | 52 | 39 | 30 | 30 | 30 | 11.5 |
| Spain | 33 | 35 | 35 | 35 | 35 | 35 | 30 | 30 | 25 | 18.5 |
| France | 50 | 50 | 42 | 37 | 38 | 35 | 34 | 38 | 32 | 16.7 |
| UK | 52 | 40 | 34 | 33 | 30 | 30 | 28 | 20 | 19 | 13.6 |
| Israel | 61 | 65 | 44 | 37 | 36 | 34 | 25 | 26 | 23 | 13.9 |
| Italy | 36 | 46 | 46 | 53 | 41 | 37 | 31 | 31 | 28 | −56.3 |
| Japan | 50 | 50 | 50 | 50 | 41 | 39 | 39 | 32 | 30 | 8.7 |
| New Zealand | 45 | 45 | 33 | 33 | 33 | 33 | 30 | 28 | 28 | 18.3 |
| Sweden | 58 | 57 | 53 | 28 | 28 | 28 | 26 | 22 | 21 | 9.3 |
| US | 50 | 50 | 39 | 40 | 39 | 39 | 39 | 39 | 26 | 11.2 |

*Source*: Tax Foundation (July 2021). Effective marginal tax rate, OECD-Stats.

rates were roughly half of what they were in 1980. They were also more similar; there has been a process of convergence in corporate income tax rates. Since 2017 the OECD has calculated average and marginal effective tax rates for member counties. The former is the proportion corporations actually pay on average, which is less than the official rates in Table 4.2. The average effective tax rates are typically only about two percentage points below the official rates. On the other hand, the marginal effective tax rates are much smaller and are reported in Table 4.2. These differences stem from the nonlinearities in corporation taxation.

The UK had the lowest official tax rate in 2020, but six other countries had lower effective marginal tax rates. Japan had the highest official tax rates, but one of the lowest effective marginal tax rates. Only Italy had a lower effective marginal tax rate, which was −56.3 percent. Instead of paying corporation tax, Italian corporations received tax concessions at the margin.

In Table 4.1 the returns to capital net of indirect taxes but gross of corporation tax in 1995 and 2018 were 16.9 and 20.9 respectively. Using the official tax rates in Table 4.2, their counterparts net of corporation tax are 10.6 percent in 1995 and 16.1 percent in 2018. The return to capital net of all taxes is obviously lower, but the increase is larger because corporation tax rates decreased from 37 percent in 1995 to 23 percent in 2018.

Neoclassical economic theory predicts that, all else given, the reductions in corporation tax rates in Table 4.2 should have boosted business investment, lowered the return to capital, and increased capital–output ratios. In the following section, we follow these phenomena empirically in several countries that have adopted the New Abnormal.

## Marginal Products of Capital

The unimportance attached by statistical authorities to the return on capital is in itself a statement about the unimportance attributed to this macroeconomic variable. Whereas labor productivity and total factor productivity are widely studied, the productivity of capital has hardly attracted attention. Among policy makers, and especially at central banks, it seems to have attracted no attention at all. Whereas policy makers are naturally concerned with labor costs and labor productivity, the relation between capital costs and capital productivity has gone below their radar. Most probably, policy makers are unaware of what is happening to the return on capital, partly because their statistical authorities do not calculate it. And where they do, as in Israel, I am not sure that in the Bank of Israel they are aware that the return to business capital, net of indirect taxes, was 20.9 percent in 2018 (Table 4.1) despite the fact that the rate of interest was zero.

More importantly, we shall argue that in 2018 the Wicksell-Patinkin measure of the natural rate of interest was 20.9 percent (before corporation tax) in contrast to the Woodford measure of almost zero. Neo-Wicksellians have moved far from the original. At the very least, they haven't asked themselves why such an enormous gap has opened up between the cost of capital and its return. In what follows, we review these developments for as long as data make this possible.

The online databank of the OECD includes data on operating surpluses and capital stocks for a number of member countries. These data were used in its *Economic Outlook* (OECD 2018) to calculate net rates of return on capital since 1996 for several countries. In what follows we have chosen to rely on national sources, partly because they contain longer time series. For example, data for France go back to 1978 and data for the US and Australia go back to 1960. Although there are similarities between the calculation below and the OECD's, there are also some significant differences. However, the general picture is similar; rates of return to capital have not decreased under the New Abnormal, according to OECD (2018).

## United States

We begin with the US, for which the data date back to 1960. Figure 4.1 plots the net return to fixed assets of non-financial corporations before and after tax in the US. Note that here and elsewhere these returns exclude private dwellings from fixed assets, as well as the fixed assets of financial corporations.

Perhaps this is the point to mention that international comparisons of returns to capital are invidious because the definitions of capital, operating surplus, depreciation, imputed wages of the self-employed etc. vary between statistical authorities. Whereas various UN institutions, such as the International Labor

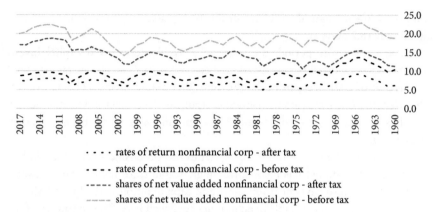

**Fig. 4.1.**  The Return to Fixed Assets and Factor Shares in the United States
*Source*: Bureau of Economic Analysis (January 2020) Private communication.

Organization (ILO), have striven for statistical consistency between countries in employment data, and Standardized National Accounting (SNA) standards have enhanced international comparability in national income accounting standards, there is no agreed method for calculating returns to fixed assets. Therefore, we focus on trends within countries rather than comparisons between them. In particular, we focus on the gap between the cost of capital, as influenced by central banks, and the return to capital, as influenced by business investment.

Figure 4.1 shows that during the 1960s and 1970s the pre-tax return to fixed assets decreased from a high of 13.6 percent in 1965–6 to a range of 7 percent to 9.5 percent during the next four decades. In 2001 the return to capital attained its lowest- ever level (6.9 percent) and in 2006 it peaked at 10 percent. Since 1980, the return to capital has been remarkably stable, trend-free, and pro-cyclical.

The gap between pre- and post-tax returns varies directly with corporate tax rates, which were particularly high during the 1960s. Subsequently, this gap has narrowed to about 2 percentage points. The post-tax return on capital peaked at 9.2 percent in 1966 and its next highest peak occurred in the wake of the Subprime Crisis in 2013 at 8 percent. The smallest return to capital was 5 percent in 1980.

The profit share in value added (pre-tax) fell during the 1960s from a high of 22.9 percent in 1965 to about 17 percent during 1970–2004, reaching a low point of 14.1 percent in 2001. Subsequently, the profit share increased, peaking at 22.3 percent during 2012–13. The decline in the profit share during the 1960s was accompanied by a decline in the return to capital. However, the increase in the profit share after 2004 was not accompanied by an increase in the return to capital. The post-tax profit was lowest in 1974 at 10.6 percent, in the wake of the increase in oil prices. Surprisingly, the post-tax profit share peaked after the Subprime Crisis in 2012 at 18.7 percent.

During the entire period, the share of gross domestic fixed capital investment (excluding dwellings) in GDP has been remarkably stable, averaging about 17 percent of GDP. Data from the Bureau of Economic Analysis (BEA) indicate that over the last 100 years the capital–output ratio has been stable at about 2.9 and has fluctuated between 2.6 and 3.3. Surprisingly, there has been no capital deepening.

In summary, the rate of return to capital in the US business sector (excluding financial corporations) has been surprisingly stable since records began over a century ago, and so have the profit share and capital–output ratio. Indeed, the US turns out to be the most stable of economies reviewed here. The constancy of the profit share and the return to capital is consistent with a Cobb-Douglas technology, since according to equation (1.2), MPK depends on the capital–output ratio, which has been stable.

## Japan

To calculate the rate of return on capital, data are required for the net operating surplus and the stock of fixed assets. The Japanese statistical authorities have systematically published the former since 1980, but only began to publish the latter in 1994 for the net capital stock. The Japanese statistical authorities do not publish data for gross capital stocks. However, they do publish data on indirect taxes on production and imports.

Chan-Lee and Sutch (1985) report that gross rates of return to capital in Japanese manufacturing were 33.3 percent in 1960, 32.4 percent in 1973 and 20.7 percent in 1982. These data are gross of indirect taxes and capital depreciation. Unfortunately, there are no data for the business sector as a whole. Nor are there data for net rates of return to capital, i.e. net of capital depreciation.

Table 4.3A reports rates of return on capital in the Japanese business sector since 1994. Since the data for operating surpluses are published in current prices, and the data for net capital stocks are published at constant (2011) prices, the former have been deflated using the GDP deflator. Between 1994 and 2018, the GDP deflator decreased by 15 percent. Table 4.3A indicates that in 1994 the return to net business capital net of indirect taxes (net of subsidies) and capital depreciation was 14.56 percent. That is, the net operating surplus net of taxes on production and imports was 14.56 percent of the net capital stock. When indirect taxes are included, the return to capital is obviously larger, at 19.39 percent. When the latter is expressed in terms of the GOS, the return to capital is obviously larger still, at 35.31 percent, reflecting the high rate of capital depreciation in Japan.

Table 4.3A  Rates of Return on Net Business Capital in Japan

|  | Net: net of indirect tax | Net: gross of indirect tax | Gross: gross of indirect tax |
|---|---|---|---|
| **1994** | 14.56 | 19.39 | 35.31 |
| **2000** | 14.53 | 19.81 | 35.91 |
| **2005** | 15.57 | 20.58 | 35.97 |
| **2010** | 14.61 | 20.04 | 38.01 |
| **2015** | 16.09 | 22.86 | 41.00 |
| **2018** | 14.38 | 21.12 | 39.25 |

Author calculations based on E-Stat database, June 2020.

Although the return to capital in column 1 remained stable, the return to capital in column 2 increased by 2 percentage points. This may be good news nationally, but not for Japanese businesses. On the other hand, corporation tax was reduced from 50 percent to 30 percent; hence, in 1994 the return to capital net of all taxes increased from 7.26 percent in 1994 to 10.4 percent in 2018 (not shown in Table 4.3A). In the final column of Table 4.3A, the return to capital increased by 5 percentage points. However, most of this increase arose from capital depreciation.

Table 4.3A implies, surprisingly, that despite Japan's so called "lost decades" (details in Chapter 8), the return on fixed assets was not only large, it even increased (gross of indirect taxes). This increase is consistent with a reduction in business investment, which increased the marginal productivity of capital. Despite the adoption of ZIP in 1996 by the Bank of Japan, the return to capital remained large and failed to decrease as it should have done according to theory. This measure of the natural rate of interest demonstrates that, in Japan, there was a disconnect between the money and natural rates of interest. Later, this interest rate gap is interpreted in terms of the growth of existential risk in Japan about the sustainability of its New Abnormal.

The return to capital in Japan appears to be much larger than in the US. However, we have already pointed out that international comparisons are problematic. What is more important is the fact that the return to capital did not decrease following the adoption of ZIP in 1996. It is as if the natural rate of interest in Japan, as measured by the net return to capital, was unaffected by the fact that the Bank of Japan had cut its rate of interest to zero since 1996.

The profit share in Japan (measured by NOS and net value added in column 1 and GOS and gross value added in column 2) has been remarkably stable (Table 4.3B). It increased slightly during 1994–2005 and has decreased slightly since 2015. During this period, the capital–output ratio remained steady at slightly

**Table 4.3B** Profit Shares and Capital–Output
Ratios: Japan

|      | Profit Share (%) | | Capital–output ratio |
| --- | --- | --- | --- |
|      | Net | Gross | Net |
| 1994 | 31.84 | 49.43 | 2.19 |
| 2000 | 33.17 | 51.53 | 2.28 |
| 2005 | 37.57 | 54.48 | 2.41 |
| 2010 | 34.28 | 54.48 | 2.34 |
| 2015 | 34.71 | 53.08 | 2.16 |
| 2018 | 30.78 | 50.33 | 2.09 |

Author calculations based on E-Stat database, June 2020.

more than 2. As in the US, the profit share, the natural rate of interest, and the capital–output ratio in Japan have remained stable despite the continuing economic crisis in Japan. The difference between the net and gross profit shares is induced by the high rates of capital consumption in Japanese national income accounts.

## Germany

There have been two attempts to estimate the return to capital in West Germany. Chan-Lee and Sutch (1985) report that the gross rate of return on gross capital in the West German business sector was 24.3 percent in 1960, 17.2 percent in 1973, and 14.5 percent in 1982. This secular decline concurs with Weiss (2015), who reports that between 1960 and 1990 the return to capital decreased from 58 percent to 30 percent. Because of the re-unification of Germany in 1991, it is problematic to compare Germany before and after 1990. Since 1991, the statistical authorities have reported data for net and gross capital stocks as well as indirect taxes on production and imports. Since the German statistical authorities do not publish data for the return on capital, we calculate it as for Japan. However, unlike Japan, where the data refer to the business sector, the return to capital in Germany is calculated for the economy as a whole, because the data for gross capital do not distinguish between the business and other sectors.

The secular decline in the rate of return on capital during 1960–1990 has continued since 1991. Column 1 in Table 4.4A refers to NOS gross of indirect taxes as a proportion of the net capital stock, which decreased from 9.91 percent in 1991 to 5.94 percent in 2019. Because the gross capital stock is considerably larger than the net capital stock, its counterpart to column 1 is smaller, decreasing from

**Table 4.4A**  Rates of Return to Capital in Germany

| | Net capital NOS gross of indirect tax | Net capital NOS net of indirect tax | Gross capital NOS gross of indirect tax | Gross capital GOS gross of indirect tax |
|---|---|---|---|---|
| 1991 | 9.91 | 6.79 | 6.28 | 12.01 |
| 1995 | 8.20 | 5.09 | 5.14 | 10.12 |
| 2000 | 7.21 | 4.14 | 4.42 | 8.72 |
| 2005 | 7.87 | 4.61 | 4.65 | 8.57 |
| 2010 | 6.83 | 3.55 | 3.92 | 7.35 |
| 2015 | 6.40 | 3.06 | 3.58 | 6.67 |
| 2019 | 5.94 | 2.41 | 3.18 | 6.41 |

Author calculations based on Genesis-online, July 2021.

**Table 4.4B**  Profit Shares and Capital–Output Ratios: Germany

| | Profit share percent | | Capital–output ratio | |
|---|---|---|---|---|
| | Net | Gross | Net | Gross |
| 1991 | 30.35 | 42.22 | 3.06 | 3.51 |
| 1995 | 29.61 | 42.23 | 3.59 | 4.18 |
| 2000 | 28.52 | 41.91 | 3.96 | 4.78 |
| 2005 | 31.88 | 44.82 | 4.05 | 5.23 |
| 2010 | 30.46 | 44.39 | 4.46 | 6.04 |
| 2015 | 28.65 | 42.80 | 4.48 | 6.41 |
| 2017 | 27.88 | 42.20 | 4.51 | 6.58 |
| 2018 | 26.75 | 41.90 | 4.26 | 5.75 |
| 2020 | | | | 6.14 |

Author calculations based on Genesis-online, July 2021. Profit shares: net
= NOS/ NVA, gross = GOS/GVA. Capital–output ratios: net = K/NVA, gross
= GK/GVA.

6.28 percent in 1991 to 3.18 percent in 2019 (column 3). Column 2 reports the
return to net capital net of taxes on production and imports. Finally, column 4
reports the return to gross capital in terms of GOS, which includes capital consumption, rather than NOS. These results conflict with Weiss (2015), who claims
that the returns to capital between 1991 and 2014 were stable.

Column 1 in Table 4.4B refers to NOS as a percentage of net output. Column 2
refers to GOS as a percentage of gross output. Column 3 refers to net output divided by net capital stock, and column 4 refers to gross output divided by gross
capital stock. The profit share was stable during the 1990s and the 2000s. It decreased slightly subsequently (Table 4.4B) in terms of net value added, but was
stable in terms of gross value added. The decrease in the return on capital is consistent with the increase in the capital–output ratio. Since unification, the German

economy has become increasingly capital-intensive, unlike in the US, Japan and Israel, where capital-intensity has remained stable.

As a member of the eurozone, Germany adopted ZIP in 2013 when the European Central Bank cut its rate of interest. Perhaps this contributed to the slight decrease in the net post-tax return to capital that occurred subsequently.

## United Kingdom

Chan-Lee and Sutch (1985) report that the gross rate of return on capital in the UK business sector was 13.3 percent in 1960, 13.6 percent in 1973, and 9.7 percent in 1982. The UK's Office for National Statistics calculates gross and net capital stocks and has published net and gross rates of return on capital systematically since 1997 for non-financial companies.

Column 1 of Table 4.5A reports NOS gross of taxes on production and imports as a percentage of the net capital stock, which decreased slightly between 1995 and 2018. Column 2 is the counterpart of column 1 net of taxes on production and imports. Columns 3 and 4 are the counterparts of columns 1 and 2 for gross capital. By implication, in contrast to Germany, where gross capital is larger than net capital, in the UK gross capital is less than net capital. Since 1995, all rates of return have decreased slightly. Since the UK adopted ZIP in 2009, this downward trend might have been expected to be steeper from 2010, but there is no evidence for this. Here too there appears to be a disconnect between the money and natural rates of interest.

The profit share in terms of net and gross output decreased in the 2000s (Table 4.5B) but the capital–output ratio remained stable. ZIP and reduced corporation tax (Table 4.2) might have been expected to increase the capital–output ratio and reduce the return to capital, but there is no evidence of either.

**Table 4.5A**  Rates of Return on Capital in UK Non-financial Corporations

|      | Net capital gross of indirect taxes | Net capital net of indirect taxes | Gross capital gross of indirect taxes | Gross capital net of indirect taxes |
|------|------|------|------|------|
| 1995 | 12.75 | 11.32 | 11.40 | 10.68 |
| 2000 | 12.08 | 10.54 | 11.23 | 10.42 |
| 2005 | 11.89 | 10.55 | 11.54 | 10.83 |
| 2010 | 11.30 | 9.90 | 10.76 | 10.02 |
| 2015 | 12.49 | 11.06 | 11.37 | 10.60 |
| 2018 | 11.20 | 9.92 | 10.88 | 10.19 |

Author calculations based on Office for National Statistics. Online data, June 2021. Non-financial corporations.

**Table 4.5B**  Profit Shares and Capital–Output Ratios: United Kingdom

| | Profit share percent | | Capital–output ratio | |
|---|---|---|---|---|
| | Net | Gross | Net | Gross |
| **1987** | 27.0 | 39.8 | | |
| **1990** | 26.5 | 38.7 | | |
| **1995** | 26.6 | 39.2 | 2.08 | 3.44 |
| **2000** | 23.4 | 34.9 | 1.93 | 3.11 |
| **2005** | 23.3 | 36.1 | 1.95 | 3.12 |
| **2010** | 22.7 | 34.7 | 2.01 | 3.22 |
| **2015** | 24.3 | 35.2 | 1.95 | 3.10 |
| **2018** | 22.7 | 33.8 | 2.03 | 3.11 |

Author calculations based on Office for National Statistics, June 2021. Non-financial corporations. See notes to Table 4.4B.

## France

Chan-Lee and Sutch (1985) report that the gross return to capital in the French business sector was 21.7 percent in 1960, 22.9 percent in 1973, and 19.3 percent in 1982. Since 1978, the French statistical authority (Insée) has published data on operating surpluses and capital stocks (gross and net). Column 1 in Table 4.6A refers to NOS net of indirect tax divided by net capital and column 2 refers to its counterpart gross of net indirect tax. The results reported in Table 4.6A are an order of magnitude smaller than those reported by Chan-Lee and Sutch, but are not dissimilar to the returns to capital reported so far.

Like the German and UK statistical authorities, the French statistical authorities report data on net and gross capital as well as NOS, GOS and taxes on production and imports. The return on capital (net of indirect tax) for non-financial corporations peaked at 10.66 percent in 1990 (Table 4.6A). Subsequently, it decreased in two steps: to 8.2 percent by 2005 and to 6.07 percent by 2010, after which it remained stable. The same applies to the return on capital gross of indirect tax (tax on production and imports). The difference between the two rates of return of about 1.5 percentage points reflects stability in the rate of indirect taxation of non-financial corporations in France. Since France, like Germany, is a member of the eurozone, it adopted ZIP in 2013. However, unlike in Germany, the rate of return to capital failed to decrease after 2013. Also, unlike in Germany, there has been no secular downward trend in the rate of return on capital.

Unlike in other countries reviewed so far, there seems to be no relation between the capital–output ratio and the return on capital (Table 4.6B). The capital–output ratio increased substantially between 1978 and 2018, but the returns to capital are similar in those years. The profit share in France recovered from a low level in 1978, peaked in 2000, and has remained stable subsequently.

**Table 4.6A** Rates of Return on Net Capital in French Non-financial Companies

|      | Net of indirect tax | Gross of indirect tax |
| ---- | ------------------- | --------------------- |
| 1979 | 6.26                | 8.15                  |
| 1980 | 5.42                | 7.36                  |
| 1985 | 6.73                | 8.47                  |
| 1990 | 10.66               | 12.83                 |
| 1995 | 9.01                | 10.72                 |
| 2000 | 9.20                | 11.55                 |
| 2005 | 8.20                | 10.31                 |
| 2010 | 6.07                | 7.72                  |
| 2015 | 6.21                | 8.32                  |
| 2019 | 6.59                | 8.56                  |

Author calculations based on on-line Insée database, June 2020.

**Table 4.6B** Profit Shares and Capital–Output Ratios: France

|      | Profit share percent | | Capital–output ratio | |
| ---- | ----- | ----- | ----- | ----- |
|      | Net   | Gross | Net   | Gross |
| 1978 | 2.30  | 8.86  | 4.31  | 5.47  |
| 1980 | 2.47  | 10.54 | 4.49  | 5.62  |
| 1985 | 5.16  | 16.82 | 5.01  | 6.15  |
| 1990 | 9.44  | 22.08 | 4.90  | 5.96  |
| 1995 | 9.74  | 22.87 | 5.30  | 6.34  |
| 2000 | 11.21 | 23.87 | 4.92  | 6.59  |
| 2005 | 10.62 | 26.16 | 5.15  | 6.12  |
| 2010 | 9.81  | 27.37 | 5.66  | 6.56  |
| 2015 | 10.96 | 28.68 | 5.81  | 6.72  |
| 2018 | 9.29  | 26.95 | 5.41  | 6.31  |

Author calculations based on online Insée database, June 2020. See notes to Table 4. 4B.

## Sweden

Chan-Lee and Sutch (1985) report that the gross rate of return on business capital in Sweden was 11.8 percent in 1960, 10.4 percent in 1973, and 8.3 percent in 1982. Like most statistical authorities, Sweden does not publish data on returns to capital. The Swedish statistical authorities (Statistics Sweden) have published data for net fixed assets dating back to 1993. Since these data include dwellings, we have removed them from the data. They publish data for operating surpluses (gross and net), including data for indirect taxes on production and imports of non-financial corporations.

The rate of return on capital peaked in 1995 and subsequently has tended to decrease, such that by 2018 the return to capital net of indirect tax was the lowest

**Table 4.7A** Rates of Return on Net Capital in Swedish Non-financial Corporations

|  | NOS: net of indirect tax | NOS: gross of indirect tax | GOS: gross of indirect tax |
|---|---|---|---|
| **1993** | 6.95 | 8.06 | 12.07 |
| **1995** | 10.47 | 12.00 | 15.75 |
| **2000** | 7.61 | 11.01 | 13.86 |
| **2005** | 7.03 | 10.16 | 13.01 |
| **2010** | 6.52 | 9.20 | 12.42 |
| **2015** | 6.38 | 9.19 | 12.36 |
| **2018** | 5.37 | 8.33 | 11.45 |

Author calculations based on online data of Statistics Sweden, June 2020.

**Table 4.7B** Profit Shares and Capital–Output Ratios: Sweden

|  | Profit share percent | | Capital–output ratio |
|---|---|---|---|
|  | Net | Gross | Net |
| **1993** | 11.02 | 17.70 | 1.59 |
| **1995** | 13.98 | 19.71 | 1.34 |
| **2000** | 10.02 | 16.83 | 1.32 |
| **2005** | 9.82 | 16.76 | 1.40 |
| **2010** | 9.90 | 17.31 | 1.52 |
| **2015** | 9.95 | 17.46 | 1.54 |
| **2018** | 8.08 | 15.79 | 1.50 |

Author calculations based on online data of Statistics Sweden, June 2020.

since 1993. The same applies to the two other measures of the return to net capital in Table 4.7A. Since Sweden adopted ZIP in 2009, and net returns to capital decreased subsequently, this might have been related to ZIP. On the other hand, the capital–output ratio remained unchanged instead of increasing (Table 4.7B). The capital–output ratio bottomed out in the mid-1990s and increased subsequently. Hence, the return on capital has been inversely related to the capital–output ratio, as expected. The profit share peaked in 1995 and decreased subsequently, suggesting that the elasticity of substitution between labor and capital is less than 1 in terms of equation (2.7).

## Australia

The statistical authority of Australia (Australian Bureau of Statistics) does not publish data on returns to capital. On the other hand, it publishes data on capital stocks (gross and net) and gross operating surpluses, which date back to 1960. We have constructed net operating surpluses by subtracting capital consumption

Table 4.8A  Rates of Return on Capital in Australian
Non-financial Companies

|      | Net capital | Gross capital |
|------|-------------|---------------|
| 1960 | 53.36 | 41.24 |
| 1970 | 37.82 | 30.26 |
| 1980 | 21.53 | 21.53 |
| 1985 | 24.75 | 19.57 |
| 1990 | 27.20 | 20.90 |
| 1995 | 27.76 | 20.73 |
| 2000 | 28.20 | 20.90 |
| 2005 | 30.02 | 21.86 |
| 2010 | 28.82 | 21.42 |
| 2015 | 22.84 | 18.16 |
| 2019 | 24.96 | 18.78 |

Author calculations based on online ABS data, June 2020.

Table 4.8B  Profit Shares and Capital–Output Ratios: Australia

|      | Profit share percent | | Capital–output ratio | |
|------|------|-------|------|-------|
|      | Net | Gross | Net | Gross |
| 1960 | 48.51 | 18.8 | 0.91 | 1.25 |
| 1970 | 45.55 | 21.8 | 1.2 | 1.64 |
| 1980 | 42.11 | 19.2 | 1.53 | 2.19 |
| 1985 | 42.35 | 22.2 | 1.71 | 2.43 |
| 1990 | 43.78 | 23.5 | 1.61 | 2.34 |
| 1995 | 43.76 | 25.3 | 1.58 | 2.38 |
| 2000 | 43.45 | 25.3 | 1.54 | 2.33 |
| 2005 | 40.00 | 25.6 | 1.36 | 2.26 |
| 2010 | 42.49 | 27.8 | 1.52 | 2.44 |
| 2015 | 45.07 | 25.6 | 1.77 | 2.87 |
| 2018 | 47.1 | 27.6 | 1.73 | 2.77 |

Author calculations based on online ABS data, June 2020. Gross profit share calculated by
NSA. See notes to Table 4.4B.

from gross operating surpluses. Returns to capital are reported in Table 4.8A. These
returns are gross of indirect taxes on production and imports, for which data are
unavailable.

The rates of return in Table 4.8A are very large, presumably reflecting ABS's
methods for calculating operating surpluses and capital. Also, Australia is unusual
in that the gross return to capital is smaller than the net return for reasons related
to equation (2.1). It is clear that in the 1960s the return to capital was large in Australia, but by 1980 the return on capital had fallen to 21.53 percent. Subsequently,
it peaked at 30.02 percent in 2005 before decreasing to about 25 percent in 2019.

The capital–output ratio was low in 1960 (Table 4.8B). It peaked in 1985 and peaked again in 2015. Broadly speaking, the return on capital is inversely related to the capital–output ratio. On the other hand, the profit share has hardly changed. The profit shares in net output in 1960 and 2019 were almost identical, although the profit share in gross output increased throughout the period.

Since Australia did not adopt ZIP until 2019, its returns to capital, profit shares and capital–output ratios were not affected by ZIP. In these respects, Australia serves as a comparator for other countries, which adopted ZIP beforehand.

## Israel

Israel is among the handful of countries for which the statistical authorities (Central Bureau of Statistics, CBS) have systematically published data for the return on capital. Indeed, since 1980 CBS has published annual data on the net return to capital, the profit share in net output, and the capital–output ratio in the business sector. In Tables 4.9A and 4.9B the data since 1995 in Table 4.1 have been updated (2020) and revised retrospectively by CBS. The data for 1980–90 have been chain-linked to the revised data.

In the aftermath of the Yom Kippur War of 1973, a debt-to-GDP ratio approaching 300 percent (Figure 5.16) resulting from double-digit fiscal deficits was about to erupt into triple-digit inflation (Ben Porath 1986). In 1985, a successful economic stabilization policy brought inflation under control and inaugurated an era of fiscal orthodoxy. At first, the exchange rate was pegged, but during the 1990s the shekel was floated. The fall of the Soviet Union triggered mass immigration from the former Union of Soviet Socialist Republics (USSR) to Israel. During the 1990s, Israel absorbed a million immigrants on a population base of only 4.5 million (Ben Bassat 2001). Since 2000, Israel has experienced steady economic growth and low inflation under a neoliberal political economy (Razin 2018, Zeira 2021).

The rate of return on capital (net) in 1980 was surprisingly high given the turbulent state of the economy at that time. Also, the profit share and capital–output ratio were large (Table 4.9B). A further surprise is that the return to capital and the profit share decreased despite mass immigration, which increased the supply of labor. During 1990–2005, the return to capital was stable at about 16 percent, but it has subsequently remained relatively high in a way that is consistent with Israel's growth performance.

The profit share has shadowed the return to capital, but the capital–output ratio has not. The capital–output ratio (net) decreased during the 1980s and 1990s, increased during 2000–5, and decreased once again subsequently. The gross

**Table 4.9A**  Rates of Return on Net Capital in Israel's Business Sector

|  | Net of indirect tax | Gross of indirect tax |
|---|---|---|
| **1980** | 24.0 | na |
| **1985** | 21.2 | na |
| **1990** | 16.2 | na |
| **1995** | 16.9 | 36.4 |
| **2000** | 16.9 | 32.7 |
| **2005** | 15.9 | 31.7 |
| **2010** | 21.0 | 38.3 |
| **2015** | 23.9 | 40.9 |
| **2018** | 20.9 | 36.0 |
| **2019** | 22.4 | 37.2 |

Source: *Statistical Yearbook*, CBS.

**Table 4.9B**  Profit Shares and Capital–Output Ratios in Israel's Business Sector

|  | Profit share percent | | Capital–output ratio | |
|---|---|---|---|---|
|  | **Net** | **Gross** | **Net** | **Gross** |
| **1980** | 32 | na | 1.35 | 1.88 |
| **1985** | 25 | na | 1.19 | 1.83 |
| **1990** | 18 | na | 1.10 | 1.56 |
| **1995** | 18 | 27 | 1.07 | 1.58 |
| **2000** | 19 | 29 | 1.13 | 1.58 |
| **2005** | 20 | 31 | 1.26 | 1.73 |
| **2010** | 22 | 31 | 1.07 | 1.59 |
| **2015** | 25 | 33 | 1.05 | 1.60 |
| **2018** | 23 | 32 | 1.11 | 1.60 |
| **2019** | 24.9 |  | 1.11 | 1.61 |

Source: CBS, private communication (January 2020).

capital–output ratio (gross capital stock/gross output) tells a similar story; it was relatively high in the 1980s, it peaked again in 2005, and has remained low subsequently. In contrast to other countries, the return to capital does not appear to be negatively correlated with the capital–output ratio.

## Overview

The main purpose of this chapter has been to measure rates of return on fixed assets for various countries for their own right and because they represent the natural rate of interest. We have also calculated the factorial distribution of income

Table 4.10 The Natural Rate of Interest before and after ZIP

|  | 1995 | ZIP |  | Latest |  |
|---|---|---|---|---|---|
| Israel | 36.4 | 2014 | 40.9 | 2019 | 37.2 |
| Australia | 27.8 | 2019 | 18.8 | 2019 | 18.8 |
| Sweden | 12.0 | 2009 | 9.2 | 2018 | 8.3 |
| France | 10.7 | 2013 | 8.0 | 2018 | 8.6 |
| UK | 12.7 | 2009 | 11.3 | 2019 | 11.2 |
| Germany | 8.2 | 2013 | 6.5 | 2019 | 5.9 |
| Japan | 19.4 | 1996 | 19.8 | 2018 | 21.2 |
| US | 9.1 | 2009 | 9.1 | 2017 | 8.7 |

with a particular focus on the profit share, as well as capital–output ratios. These data serve as inputs for our next task, which is to compare these estimates of the natural rate of interest with the "money" rates of interest for the countries included in the study. In the next chapter, the money rates of interest are the policy rates set by central banks. What matters for business investment is not the money rate of interest, but the real long-term cost of capital, which is influenced by the money rate of interest as well as quantitative easing. These and related issues are on the agenda for Chapter 5.

Since the main purpose was to generate estimates of the natural rate of interest as represented by the rate of return on fixed assets, we conclude by focusing on the returns to net capital stock gross of taxes on production and imports since 1995 (Table 4.10). Column 1 records the return to capital in 1995. Column 2 records the year in which ZIP was adopted and the contemporaneous return to capital. Column 3 records the latest year for which the return to capital was calculated. For example, in 1995 the return to net capital gross of indirect tax on production and imports in Israel was 36.4 percent. At the time the Bank of Israel adopted ZIP in 2014, the return to capital was 40.9 percent. According to latest data in 2019, the return to capital was 37.2 percent.

We repeat once again that, although comparisons between countries are inappropriate, matters are different for comparisons over time within countries. The key question is "did the returns to capital decrease after ZIP was adopted?" The answer appears to be "no."

## Synopsis

The natural rate of interest has attracted only minor empirical attention. The attention that it has attracted has been exclusively with Woodford's equilibrium rate of interest rather than with Wicksell's definition of the natural rate of interest as measured by the return on fixed capital assets.

The return to capital, the share of profits in GDP, and the capital–output ratio are related according to neoclassical economic theory. All else given, the return to capital and the capital–output ratio are expected to vary inversely with each other. For example, a reduction in the rate of interest is expected to increase business investment, which lowers the return to capital and increases the stock of capital. Because the capital stock is expected to increase by more than output, the capital–output ratio increases; output is more capital-intensive. Hence, the capital–output ratio increases and the return to capital decreases. By contrast, the relation between the return to capital and the profit share is ambiguous because it depends on the elasticity of substitution between labor and capital. In the well-known Cobb-Douglas case, the elasticity of substitution is 1, and there is no relation between the profit share and the return to capital.

Most of the chapter is devoted to calculating the return to capital for a number of OECD countries. The national income accounting theory behind these calculations is presented especially in relation to how national income accountants calculate net operating surpluses. Statistical offices in the US, the UK and Israel publish data for the return to capital. Data from the national statistical offices in several countries have been used to construct data on their returns to capital. These data show that, despite ZIP, which was expected to boost investment and reduce the return to capital, returns to capital have remained above double figures for most countries.

The return to capital for businesses should be net of the direct and indirect taxes that they pay. While most (but not all) statistical authorities report indirect taxes, none report direct taxes (corporation tax). Official corporate tax rates are used to infer returns to capital net of all taxes. Since 1980, corporate tax rates have been cut by half. Since the natural rate of interest is synonymous with the return to capital, and under the New Abnormal rates of interest have hovered around zero, there has emerged a major disconnect between the natural and money rates of interest. There is an elephant in the room, which Neo-Wicksellians have ironically failed to notice. As far as they are concerned, if inflation and output are on target under ZIP, the natural rate of interest must be zero or close to it.

# 5

# Descent into Zero Interest Policy and the New Abnormal

When the Bank of England was established in 1694, its policy rate was 6 percent before settling down at 5 percent until 1825 (Figure 5.1). Before the descent into ZIP in 2009, the Bank's previous lowest policy rate had been 2 percent (February 1868 and June 1932). Hence, the adoption of ZIP broke two precedents. Not only did it set a new historic minimum, it also chose this minimum to be (almost) zero. This is history in the making. Other lowest recorded policy rates (Figure 5.2) were 1.5 percent in Switzerland (November 1936) and New Zealand (July 1941). An exception is the Federal Reserve, which set its policy rate at 0.5 percent between November 1942 and April 1946, and the Bank of Japan, which set its policy rate at 0.9 percent between April 1936 and October 1946. Apart from the exigencies of war, central bank interest rates had never approached zero throughout the long and varied history of central banking. Hence, the adoption of ZIP in 1996 by the Bank of Japan, and its adoption by the Federal Reserve, the Bank of England and the Bank of Sweden in 2009, and the European Central Bank (ECB) in 2013, were unique events in financial history.

Figures 5.1 and 5.2 highlight graphically the sharp break with history in the New Abnormal. In adopting ZIP, the countries concerned entered uncharted macroeconomic waters. Table 5.1 shows that, although the number of central banks that have adopted ZIP has increased dramatically since 2008, this increase has not been continuous. After initially peaking at eight in 2009, the number of central banks that adopted ZIP decreased in 2010. The number peaked again in 2015, but began to decrease subsequently. During the Covid-19 epidemic, almost half the members of the Bank for International Settlements (BIS) had adopted ZIP. Table 5.1 conceals transitions into and out of ZIP, as discussed further below.

Some central banks adopted negative policy rates, including Denmark (2014), Switzerland (2015), Japan (2016), and Sweden (2019). These central banks paid banks to borrow from them, and penalized banks for holding reserves with them. In principle, there is no reason why central banks cannot pay banks to borrow from them instead of the other way around. The practical question is if banks are not prepared to borrow reserves from central banks when the rate of interest is zero,

*Zero Interest Policy and the New Abnormal*. Michael Beenstock, Oxford University Press. © Michael Beenstock (2022).
DOI: 10.1093/oso/9780192849663.003.0005

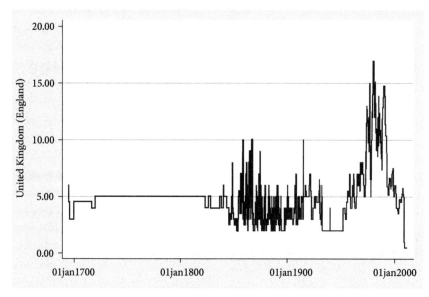

**Fig. 5.1** Three Centuries of Bank Rate
*Source:* Bank of England.

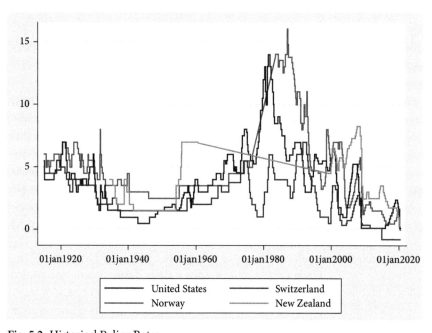

**Fig. 5.2** Historical Policy Rates
*Source:* Center for Financial Stability (Yale), updated and corrected.

**Table 5.1** Number of Members of BIS with Policy
Rates at Most 0.75 Percent

| End of year | Number |
|---|---|
| **2007** | 1 |
| **2008** | 4 |
| **2009** | 8 |
| **2010** | 5 |
| **2011** | 7 |
| **2012** | 9 |
| **2013** | 10 |
| **2014** | 10 |
| **2015** | 13 |
| **2016** | 12 |
| **2017** | 10 |
| **2018** | 8 |
| **2019** | 9 |
| **2020 (May)** | 19 |

*Source:* Bank for International Settlements. BIS has
40 members.

how likely is it that they will be prepared to borrow reserves if the rate of interest
is negative? If, for example, the rate of interest is −1 percent, there is nothing to
stop banks borrowing reserves from the central bank and holding them as vault
cash, which would provide riskless profits for the banks, but would be pointless
macroeconomically. The problem is that vault cash does not bear interest. Matters
would be different if fintech developments enabled cash to bear negative interest
rates too. Perhaps, this explains why so few central banks have adopted negative
policy rates.

Table 5.2 reports policy rates before and after the outbreak of the Covid-19 epidemic. With the exception of Iceland, Hungary, and Poland, the central banks in
Table 5.2 had adopted ZIP by May 2020. Some central banks, such as in Canada
and the US, had re-adopted ZIP, while other central banks, such as in Peru and
New Zealand, had adopted ZIP for the first time. The 20 BIS members not featured
in Table 5.2 had never adopted ZIP.

Since they no longer could cut interest rates under ZIP, central banks have engaged instead in quantitative easing (QE). The Bank of Japan was the first to adopt
ZIP in 1996, and it was the first to engage in QE shortly afterwards (Figure 5.12).
Among western central banks, the Federal Reserve pioneered QE in 2009 in the
wake of the Subprime Crisis by purchasing zombie assets from the banking system.
This desperate measure was undertaken to prevent a collapse in the banking system. However, the Federal Reserve subsequently adopted QE as an instrument of
monetary policy, since under ZIP it had forsaken conventional monetary policy.

Table 5.2  Policy Rates of Selected BIS Members

| | December 31 2019 | May 31 2020 |
|---|---|---|
| Australia | 0.75 | 0.25 |
| Canada | 1.75 | 0.25 |
| Croatia | 0.3 | 0.1 |
| Czech Republic | 2 | 0.25 |
| Denmark | −0.75 | −0.6 |
| ECB | 0 | 0 |
| Hong Kong | 2.48 | 0.62 |
| Hungary | 0.9 | 0.9 |
| Iceland | 3 | 1 |
| Israel | 0.25 | 0.1 |
| Japan | −0.1 | −0.1 |
| Korea | 1.25 | 0.5 |
| Norway | 1.5 | 0 |
| New Zealand | 1 | 0.25 |
| Peru | 2.25 | 0.25 |
| Poland | 1.5 | 1 |
| Sweden | −0.25 | 0 |
| Switzerland | −0.75 | −0.75 |
| United Kingdom | 0.75 | 0.1 |
| United States | 1.625 | 0.125 |

*Source:* Bank for International Settlements.

In Chapter 2, we discussed that QE might have some macroeconomic purpose when ZIP is expected to be temporary, but not when it is expected to be a permanent feature of the New Abnormal. Just as ZIP has its own epidemiology, so has QE turned out to be contagious. Adopted subsequently by the Bank of England, the ECB, and the Bank of Israel, QE has spread to most central banks. Initially QE involved central bank purchases of treasury bonds, but the Federal Reserve broke the taboo of financial distancing by purchasing commercial bonds. More recently, central banks in the US, Japan, Israel and the UK have extended QE to equity capital.

The consequence of ZIP and QE has been uninhibited growth in base money because banks can borrow unlimited reserves from the central bank at no cost, and because QE is funded by the issue of base money. In Chapter 2 we noted that, as the rate of interest tends to zero, so does the velocity of circulation of money because the demand for money becomes infinitely interest-elastic. Velocities of circulation may not be zero, but they have decreased substantially almost everywhere. For example, between 1960 and 2008, velocity ($M_1$) increased in the US from 3.8 to 10.8. After the Federal Reserve temporally ended ZIP between 2016 – 2020 (see below) velocity decreased to 5.2 by 2020.

In Chapter 2 we pointed out that under ZIP the decrease in velocity is not inflationary and is, indeed, of no immediate macroeconomic importance. The monetary overhang would only have macroeconomic relevance if the rate of interest became positive. We shall return to this issue in Chapter 10. In the meanwhile, in the present chapter we infer from empirical data for velocity the "kinetic inflation" that would be released once interest rates are eventually normalized.

Before the advent of ZIP, governments attached importance to fiscal orthodoxy, as enshrined in the Maastricht principles of 1992, according to which fiscal deficits should not exceed 3 percent of GDP and debt-to-GDP ratios should not exceed 60 percent, as discussed in Chapter 2. These guidelines reflected economic growth rates at the time. Because of lower economic growth, these guidelines would be more conservative today. After Japan adopted ZIP in 1996, it abandoned fiscal orthodoxy so that by 2020 its debt-to-GDP ratio approached 250 percent. The same occurred after other countries adopted ZIP, with some rare exceptions. In Chapter 2 we pointed out that ZIP creates a moral hazard issue for governments because they are tempted to borrow more. Even before the Covid-19 crisis, many governments had become heavily indebted. For example, it took the US government 50 years to pay off the debt it accumulated during World War Two. By 2020, the US debt-to-GDP ratio surpassed what it was in 1946.

Our purpose in this chapter is to chronicle the descent into ZIP and the New Abnormal and to investigate its epidemiology for outcomes, including interest rate policy, the structure of interest rates, quantitative easing, money supply, debt-to-GDP ratios, and fiscal deficits. These outcomes have become highly abnormal, if not extraordinary.

## Central Bank Policy Rates

Since Japan was the first country to descend into ZIP and the New Abnormal, we devote special attention to it in Chapter 8. Briefly, the Japanese economic miracle after World War Two came to an end in the late 1980s, despite the fact that Japan avoided worldwide stagflation during the 1970s. Japan's "lost decade" began towards the end of the 1980s. The Bank of Japan began to cut its policy rate during the first half of the 1990s to 2.5 percent in February 1993 and to 1.75 percent in September. In 1995 it reduced its interest rate to 1 percent in April and to 0.5 percent in September. Hence, Japan has been ZIPped since that time. Further cuts in interest rates to 0.1 percent occurred in 2001. The lost decade turned into the lost decade and a half, and by 2021 it had extended into the lost three decades.

Policy rates elsewhere were normal during the 2000s. Policy rates peaked at 5.75 percent in the UK (September 2007), 5.25 percent in the US (September 2007) and the ECB at 4.25 percent (October 2008). Hence, prior to ZIP, interest rates were entirely normal. The Japanese precedent had not spread. There were no signs of what was about to happen. It is important to mention this because, as noted in

Chapter 4, Neo-Wicksellians believe that ZIP was the consequence of a sudden global decrease in the natural rate of interest. By January 2008 the Federal Reserve had cut its interest rate to 3 percent in five steps. By December 2008 it had cut its interest rate to 0–0.25 percent in another five steps. By November 2008 Switzerland was ZIPped, as was the Bank of England in March 2009.

One does not have to look very far for the root cause of ZIP. The trigger was clearly the Subprime Crisis, which broke out in the US in August 2007. Since Swiss and UK banks had bought securitized US mortgages, their banking systems were directly affected. It is no coincidence that the UK and Switzerland were the first countries to follow the US into ZIP. Table 5.3 shows that central banks fall into three groups. The first, which includes the Bank of England and the Swiss National Bank, remained ZIPped from the start. They seem to have joined the Bank of Japan as central banks unable to extricate themselves from ZIP. The second group, which includes the Federal Reserve, the Bank of Canada, and the Bank of Israel have had more than one episode of ZIP; they extricated themselves, but subsequently returned to ZIP. The third group, which includes Denmark and ECB, did not adopt ZIP in the first wave, while the central banks of Norway, Australia, and New Zealand managed to resist ZIP for longer. But for the Covid-19 crisis in 2020, the central banks of New Zealand and South Korea, and some other countries featured in Table 5.2, might have resisted for longer, or even avoided ZIP completely.

Table 5.3 raises a number of questions. Why did some central banks manage to extricate themselves from ZIP while others failed? Why did some central banks manage to resist ZIP for so long? These questions are, of course, concerned with the epidemiology of ZIP. The adoption or re-adoption of ZIP during the Covid-19 crisis might seem obvious; lockdown policy in 2020 caused severe financial distress for business, which central banks wished to relieve. But why adopt ZIP instead of merely cutting interest rates, as in the US and Hong Kong (Table 5.2)? Most probably the answer to this question is that by 2020 ZIP had become the norm. Also, the central banks of the US and Hong Kong had managed to extricate themselves from ZIP once and felt confident that they could do so again.

Some central banks, such the Bank of England, could not extricate themselves from ZIP for country-specific reasons, and especially following the Brexit referendum in 2016. The same applies to the ECB, which adopted ZIP after the Greek debt crisis and found it difficult to extricate itself from ZIP following the Brexit referendum. As for the other central banks, there is a common theme to their epidemiology, which was discussed in Chapter 2. The adoption of ZIP elsewhere meant that the exchange rates of small open economies were expected by central bankers to appreciate according to absolute interest parity theory. For example, the re-adoption of ZIP by the Bank of Israel in 2014 was explicitly justified on these grounds. Governor Fischer temporarily adopted ZIP in 2009 on precautionary grounds, despite the fact that Israel was not directly or indirectly affected

Table 5.3  Episodes of ZIP

|  | First | Second | Third |
|---|---|---|---|
| **Australia** | October 2019 | | |
| **Canada** | March 2009 – July 2010 | July 2015 – July 2017 | March 2020 |
| **Czech Republic** | May 2012 | | |
| **Denmark** | December 2011 | | |
| **ECB** | May 2013 | | |
| **Israel** | March 2009 – August 2009 | July 2014 | |
| **Hong Kong** | December 2008 – December 2015 | May 2020 | |
| **Japan** | September 1995 | | |
| **New Zealand** | March 2020 | | |
| **Norway** | February 2016 – August 2018 | March 2020 | |
| **S. Korea** | May 2020 | | |
| **Sweden** | April 2009 – August 2010 | July 2014 | |
| **Switzerland** | December 2008 | | |
| **United Kingdom** | March 2009 | | |
| **United States** | December 2008 – December 2016 | March 2020 | |

*Source:* Bank for International Settlements.

by the Subprime Crisis. However, Governor Flug (November 2013 to November 2018), concerned by the strengthening of the shekel, intervened heavily in the forex market to weaken the shekel and adopted ZIP for the same reasons. Whenever the Bank of Israel intervened or reduced the policy rate, the exchange rate would weaken temporarily, as predicted by relative IPT, before returning to its previous level. In this way the Bank of Israel kept cutting interest rates until they could be cut no more. The ratcheted descent into ZIP was based on a flawed understanding about macroeconomic theory in general and exchange rate theory in particular.

This misunderstanding was common in other central banks where the DSGE movement had taken hold, and in which absolute IPT was axiomatic. It is likely that the adoption of ZIP by central banks in the Czech Republic, Sweden, Denmark, and Australia was similarly motivated. Since it is impractical to review the descent into ZIP for all countries, we focus here by way of illustration on Israel. No doubt the descent into ZIP varied in detail between countries. Nevertheless, the misunderstanding about the difference between relative and absolute IPT was most probably common to them all.

## Israel

My focus on Israel is for obvious reasons. However, it serves as a case study to show how a country that had no objective reason for adopting ZIP nevertheless ended up by getting ZIPped. It is a case study in the global epidemiology of ZIP, which is based on exchange rate targeting. Perhaps this case study will sound familiar in other small open economies that got ZIPped despite no apparent reason for their central banks to do so.

Between 1999 and 2007, the shekel floated cleanly. The Bank of Israel was ideologically against intervening in the foreign exchange market. This policy changed after Stanley Fischer was appointed as Governor in 2005. From early 2008 through mid-2011, the Bank of Israel intervened heavily in the foreign exchange market, and its foreign exchange reserves tripled. At the time it was argued with some justification that Israel needed more reserves because the economy had grown substantially. In the event of a foreign exchange crisis, Israel would need more reserves than it had needed during crises in the 1990s. Indeed, the ratio of reserves to GDP, which was less than 20 percent in early 2008, increased to just over 30 percent by mid-2011. Until Fischer ended his term of office in June 2013, the shekel floated freely once more.

During the transition between one governor and the next (Deputy Governor Karnit Flug eventually succeeded Fischer), massive one-way forex intervention was resumed so that by the end of Flug's appointment in November 2018 the reserves hd doubled to $115 billion. During this period, the forex intervention was expressly motivated to weaken the exchange rate rather than to stockpile reserves, in the belief that the shekel was "too strong." Flug believed that a "strong" exchange rate was bad for jobs and economic growth, despite the fact that Israel experienced rapid economic growth, growing labor market participation, and low rates of unemployment. Her neo-mercantilism induced her to protect exporters and to deny the public at large the benefits of a strong shekel. It became clear that Flug was targeting the exchange rate not only in terms of her forex policy but also in terms of her interest rate policy. She continued to cut interest rates until, by July 2014, she could cut them no further. Israel had descended into ZIP.

Figures 5.3 and 5.4 testify to the strength of the shekel in real as well as nominal terms. Ironically, the shekel weakened when the exchange rate floated freely during the early 2000s, and it weakened again when the exchange rate floated freely from mid-2011 to early 2013. By the time Bank of Israel began to intervene in 2008, the real exchange rate had already weakened, and it fluctuated about a stable level until 2013. Subsequently, after forex intervention was renewed in 2013 the shekel continued to strengthen.

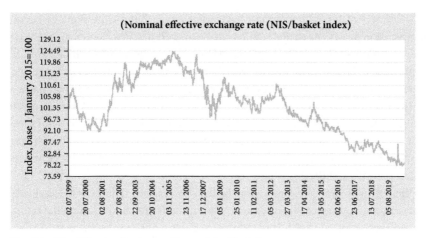

**Fig. 5.3** The Effective Exchange Rate of the Shekel
*Source:* Bank of Israel database.

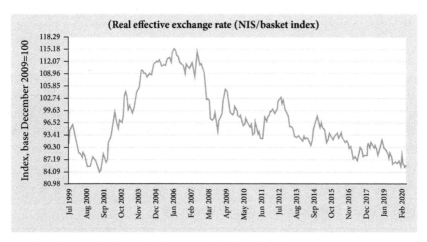

**Fig. 5.4** The Real Effective Exchange Rate of the Shekel
*Source:* Bank of Israel database.

Not only did this intervention fail to weaken the shekel, the interest rates cuts that led to ZIP in 2014 did not do so either. A temporary effect might be discernible in Figures 5.3 and 5.4, which ended once the rate of interest reached zero. As predicted by the exchange rate theory in Chapter 2, based on relative rather than absolute interest parity theory, interest rate cuts and forex intervention are expected to have only a temporary effect on the exchange rate. Thus did the Bank of Israel squander interest rate policy in Israel; its monetary policy committee did not understand the difference between relative and absolute interest parity.

Defenders of forex intervention have argued that, but for the Bank of Israel's intervention policy, the shekel would have been even stronger. Soreczky (2013) explored this possibility, estimating a Bayesian vector autoregression (BVAR) model during 2008–12, in which the state variables included inflation, the exchange rate, expected inflation, and forex intervention. He concluded that forex intervention weakened the shekel. However, he did not mention that forex intervention was not statistically significant in the model. Consequently, his research does not show that the exchange rate would have been stronger but for the intervention by the Bank of Israel. Rather, it establishes the opposite because forex intervention was not statistically significant.

Not only was forex intervention ineffective, it was costly. The Bank of Israel publishes annual reports on the reserves and their management, including the return on reserves reported in the third column of Table 5.4. However, these returns are measured in foreign exchange instead of in shekels. For example, in 2010 the return in foreign exchange was 1.7 percent, but the return in shekels was −2.59 percent due to the appreciation of the shekel. As a result, the Bank of Israel made a loss of $1.55 billion. Just as investors measure returns in their home currency, so should the Bank of Israel. Table 5.4 shows, not surprisingly, that the Bank of Israel made systematic losses because the shekel was strengthening throughout the period. In some years, such as 2013 and 2017, these losses were massive. In eight years out of eleven the Bank of Israel made losses. During these years it lost $6.4 billion. To put these losses into perspective, US economic and military assistance to Israel is $3.8 billion per year. It is as if in some years the Bank of Israel squandered this assistance on its foreign exchange speculations against the shekel.

Table 5.4  Israel's Forex Reserves and their Return

|      | Reserves $b | Return in forex % pa | Return in shekels % pa | Profit $b |
|------|-------------|----------------------|------------------------|-----------|
| 2010 | 64.94       | 1.7                  | −2.59                  | −1.55     |
| 2011 | 78.0        | 1.3                  | −0.15                  | −0.098    |
| 2012 | 76.0        | 1.6                  | 5.76                   | 4.49      |
| 2013 | 80.0        | 0.9                  | −5.45                  | −4.142    |
| 2014 | 81.0        | 1.3                  | −1.6                   | −1.28     |
| 2015 | 83.0        | 0.6                  | −1.32                  | −1.069    |
| 2016 | 90.0        | 1.6                  | −2.1                   | −1.743    |
| 2017 | 98.0        | 3.0                  | −3.33                  | −2.997    |
| 2018 | 115.3       | 0.2                  | 0.44                   | 0.431     |
| 2019 | 126.0       | 6.1                  | 2.0                    | 2.300     |
| 2020 | 173.3       | 4.0                  | −0.6                   | −0.750    |

*Source:* Annual Reports on Reserves, Bank of Israel. Columns 4 and 5 author calculations.

The rationale for foreign exchange rate intervention by central banks should be to smooth the foreign exchange market by buying foreign exchange when it is underpriced and selling it when it is over-priced. The litmus test for successful forex policy is that it should be profitable and two-way. The Bank of Israel's forex policy has failed on both counts; it has been loss making and one-way. Moreover, although the present Governor (Amir Yaron) took office in 2018 with the intention of reversing the Bank of Israel's forex policy, the reserves have continued to increase (Table 5.4) as a result of continued massive forex intervention.

Perhaps it is easy to understand the psychology behind continued forex intervention despite its inefficacy and cost. It is the same psychology that lies behind QE, which in theory and in practice makes no difference to economic activity. Having squandered their main operating instrument through ZIP, in frustration central bankers look to other activities, such as exchange rate intervention and QE, in the vain hope that they might be of some purpose.

## The Effect of Zero Interest Policy on Long-term Interest Rates

Since gross fixed investment involves assets of long-term duration, what matters to business investors is not the policy rate set by central banks, which under the Old Normal was subject to alteration from one month to the next, but long-term rates of interest, and especially gross redemption yields on commercial bonds. More generally, what matters is the weighted average cost of capital (WACC), which for firm i weights the cost of debt ($R_d$) and the cost of equity ($R_e$):

$$WACC_i = w_i R_{di} + (1 - w_i) R_{ei} \qquad (1.1)$$

where w denotes the share of debt in the value of the firm, and:

$$R_{ei} = R_f + \beta_i (R_m - R_f) \qquad (1.2)$$

$$R_{di} = R^* + \eta_i \qquad (1.3)$$

$$R^* = R_f + \phi + \tau \qquad (1.4)$$

Equation (1.2) is based on the capital asset pricing model (CAPM), where $R_m$ denotes the return on the market portfolio, $R_f$ is the risk-free policy rate of interest, and $\beta_i$ is the time series regression coefficient of $R_e$ on $R_m$. In equation (1.3), $R^*$ denotes the yield to maturity on default-free treasury bonds; hence, the slope of the yield curve is $R^* - R_f$, and $\eta$ denotes a default risk premium. Finally, the slope of the yield curve is determined in equation (1.4) where $\phi$ is positive if the policy rate is expected to increase in the future and is negative if it is expected to decrease, and $\tau$ denotes a term premium. Even if $\phi = 0$ the future policy rate is uncertain; hence $\tau$ is expected to be positive, and varies directly with the uncertainty of monetary policy in the future. The slope of the default-free yield curve varies directly with the term premium and $\phi$.

It may be shown that $\tau$ varies directly with the term to maturity but at a decreasing rate (Cochrane 2005, Duffie 1996, Singleton 2006). This happens because, although it is more difficult to predict more distant events, the marginal difficulty decreases with distance under mean reversion. It may be twice as difficult to predict four years ahead than one year ahead, but it is less than twice as difficult to predict eight years ahead than two years ahead. This explains why yield curves tend to slope upwards even when short rates are expected to remain unchanged, and why they tend to flatten out.

Substituting equations (1.2) and (1.3) into equation (1.1) and averaging across firms implies that the average WACC is:

$$WACC = R_f + w\left(\varphi + \tau + \eta\right) + \left(1 - w\right)\beta\left(R_m - R_f\right) \qquad (1.5)$$

where, for example, w is the average of $w_i$. The first term refers to the direct effect of interest rate policy on the cost of capital. The second term refers to the contribution of the slope of the yield curve and corporate default risk. The third term expresses the contribution of market risk to the aggregate weighted average cost of capital. In the absence of market risk and default risk, and if the policy rate remained fixed, equation (1.5) states that the weighted average cost of capital would equal the policy rate, as expected.

If the policy rate is zero under ZIP, and is expected to remain so with absolute certainty, the WACC would be $w\eta + \left(1 - w\right)\beta R_m$, i.e. it depends solely on default risk and market risk. Existential risk regarding the future of the New Abnormal would manifest itself in several ways. First, as the commitment to ZIP weakens, $\phi$ and $\tau$ cease to be zero and turn positive. Second, corporate default risk is likely to increase, hence $\eta$ increases. Third, for related reasons the market risk premium increases. For all of these reasons WACC is expected to vary directly with existential risk.

## United States

Under the Old Normal, yield curves had their classical shape; they were convex and sloped upwards. However, prior to the outbreak of the Subprime Crisis, the US yield curve was inverted. For example, on January 1 2007, short-term interest rates exceeded long-term rates (Table 5.5), suggesting that when the Federal Reserve

Table 5.5  Yields on US Treasury Bonds

|  | 3 months | 3 years | 5 years | 10 years | 30 years |
|---|---|---|---|---|---|
| 1 Jan 2007 | 5.07 | 4.71 | 4.61 | 4.08 | 4.79 |
| 31 Dec 2007 | 3.36 | 3.07 | 3.45 | 4.04 | 4.45 |
| 12 Nov 2008 | 0.18 | 1.6 | 2.37 | 3.75 | 4.17 |
| 31 Dec 2009 | 0.06 | 1.7 | 2.69 | 3.85 | 4.63 |
| 31 Dec 2011 | 0.02 | 0.36 | 0.83 | 1.89 | 2.89 |
| 31 Dec 2013 | 0.07 | 0.78 | 1.75 | 3.04 | 3.96 |
| 29 Dec 2017 | 1.39 | 1.98 | 2.2 | 2.4 | 2.74 |
| 31 Dec 2019 | 1.55 | 1.62 | 1.69 | 1.92 | 2.39 |
| 24 Feb 2020 | 1.53 | 1.35 | 1.21 | 1.38 | 1.84 |
| 25 March 2020 | 0 | 0.19 | 0.41 | 0.88 | 1.45 |
| 1 July 2020 | 0.14 | 0.19 | 0.31 | 0.69 | 1.43 |
| 8 July 2020 | 0.15 | 0.19 | 0.30 | 0.67 | 1.39 |
| June 2021 |  |  |  | 2.03 | 2.1 |

*Source:* Federal Reserve Bank of St Louis (FRED).

began the descent into ZIP some six months later, this did not come as a complete surprise. Indeed, by a year later the yield curve was no longer inverted. During the course of 2008 and 2009 the yield curve steepened because, despite ZIP, long-term rates remained stable.

Subsequently, Table 5.5 shows that long-term rates began to decrease because the public understood that ZIP was unlikely to be temporary. After Chairperson Yellen began to raise interest rates in 2016, long-term rates remained low. For example, on December 29 2017, the yield to maturity on ten-year bonds was only 2.4 percent, suggesting that a complete return to the Old Normal was in doubt. These doubts were confirmed in 2019 when the Federal Reserve resumed its descent into ZIP under Chairperson Powell. By July 2020 the yield curve had flattened, and ten-year rates reached an all-time low.

Overall, ZIP pulled down the yields to maturity on long-term treasury bonds. During 2020 they fell to below 1 percent for the first time in history. Figure 5.5 plots the difference over the last forty years between the yield to maturity on ten-year and three-month US Treasury bonds. As expected, the difference is positive because the yield curve generally slopes upwards, but the slope may be steeper and flatter. On four occasions the yield curve was inverted because short rates (three-month) exceeded ten-year rates. Interestingly, and as noted in Table 5.5, in the run-up to the Subprime Crisis the yield curve began to flatten and became inverted, suggesting that the public was anticipating a reduction in interest rates.

Figure 5.6 plots the ten-year forward rates, which show that during this period these expectations decreased by more than a percentage point (from almost 7

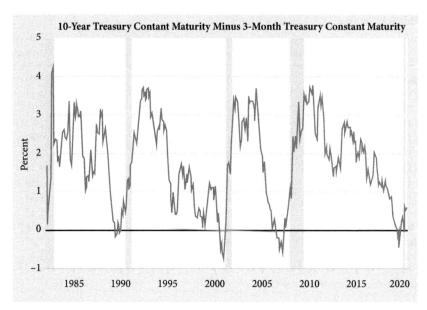

**Fig. 5.5** Difference between Yields to Maturity on Ten-Year and Three-Month US Treasury Bonds

*Source:* Federal Reserve Bank of St Louis (FRED).

percent to almost 6 percent). Figure 5.5 shows that when the Federal Reserve began to cut its policy rate in 2007 in response to the Subprime Crisis, the yield curve steepened because at first the public expected this policy to be temporary. Indeed, the ten-year forward rate even increased (Figure 5.6). By 2010–11 the forward rate began to decrease because the public understood that ZIP was not temporary. Following the policy of raising interest rates in 2016, the ten-year forward rate began to recover before reaching a historic low in 2020. However, the latter suggested that eventually the Federal Reserve would raise interest rates; otherwise the forward rate should have been almost zero too.

So did the financial futures market signal that Federal Reserve would raise interest rates. Futures rates differ from forward rates because the former are explicitly priced in financial futures markets, whereas the latter are implicitly priced through spot bond markets. This is why forward rates refer to longer horizons than futures prices. Also, futures contracts are marked-to-market and therefore generate cash flows through margin payments until they mature, whereas forward contracts do not (Duffie 1996 Chapter 8). Nevertheless, expectations of interest rates implicit in forward rates and futures are likely to be highly correlated.

Figure 5.7 plots the futures prices for thirty-day federal funds. To convert futures prices (P) into annualized interest rates, calculate $12[(100/P)^{1/12} - 1]$. For

**Fig. 5.6** Forward Rates Ten Years Hence
*Source:* Federal Reserve Bank of St Louis (FRED).

example, when P = 90, as in 1989, the federal funds rate thirty days hence is expected to be 10.58 percent. When P is almost 100, as in 2015 and 2020, the federal funds rate is expected to be almost zero. In summary, the higher the futures price, the smaller is the expected federal funds rate thirty days hence. The upward trend in the futures price in Figure 5.7 reflects the downward trend in the federal funds rate. The volatility in the futures price reflects the volatility in the federal funds rate.

Figure 5.7 suggests that the scale of interest rate cuts in 2007–8 took the market by surprise. Indeed, it wasn't until late 2009 that the market realized that ZIP was here to stay. On the other hand, the markets anticipated Yellen's policy to normalize interest rate in 2016. The flatness in the futures price at almost 100 during 2008–15 results from ZIP. These anticipations were reversed in 2019 until ZIP was re-adopted in 2020.

Figure 5.8 summarizes the term structures of market expectations of the federal funds rate derived from futures prices between January 2008 and June 2019. In contrast to Figure 5.7, which referred only to thirty-day federal funds forward rates, Figure 5.8 refers to the term structure going beyond thirty days to two years hence. At first, the policy rate was expected to be 3 percent two years ahead. By 2009–10 the policy rate was expected to be between 2 to 2.5 percent two years ahead, despite the fact that by this time ZIP had been adopted. Subsequently, the policy rate was expected to increase but to a lower level. By 2014 the interest rate

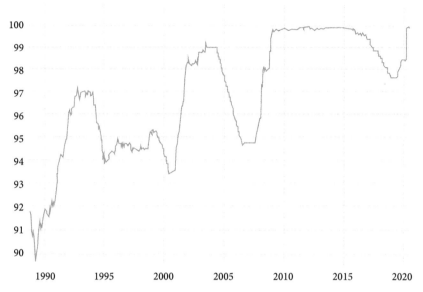

**Fig. 5.7** Prices of Federal Funds Futures −30 Days
*Source*: Federal Reserve Bank of St Louis (FRED).

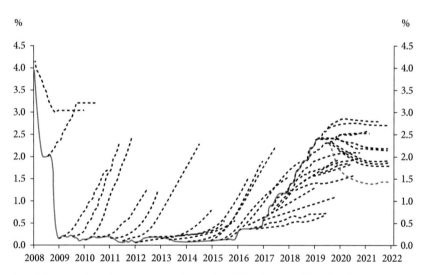

**Fig. 5.8** Term Structures of Expected Federal Funds Rates Based on Futures
*Source*: Torsten Stok, Deutsche Bank Research, June 2019.

futures market suggested that ZIP was expected to end. These expectations were eventually fulfilled after Yellen took over from Bernanke in 2014.

A striking feature in Figure 5.8 is that the term structure of policy rate expectations tends to slope upwards, suggesting that ZIP was expected to be temporary. In 2009–10 the Federal Reserve was expected to have increased its policy rate to about 2.5 percent two years hence. By 2011–12 these expectations were revised downwards to slightly more than 1 percent. Just before Yellen took office they were revised upward to 2 percent, which turned out to be correct.

When the Federal Reserve began to raise interest rates in 2016, the term structure of expected interest rates became flatter, suggesting that the exit from ZIP was expected to be temporary. Just as the Federal Reserve surprised the market by its persistence with ZIP until 2015, so did it surprise the market by its determination to normalize interest rates after 2015. By June 2019, when Figure 5.8 ends, the term structure of expectations for the federal funds rate slopes downwards instead of upwards. Shortly afterwards, in September 2019 the Federal Reserve began to cut its interest rate. Of course, in September 2019 nobody foresaw the Covid-19 epidemic, nor could they have known that ZIP would be reinstated, accompanied by massive quantitative easing.

In summary, because at first ZIP was expected to be temporary, it did not have much of an effect on expectations of long-term interest rates in the US. Matters changed when it was realized that ZIP was here to stay. But even then, the long-term forward rate remained above 3 percent, suggesting that ZIP was expected to end within the next ten years. Also, the interest rate futures market suggested that ZIP was unlikely to last beyond a year or two. Despite the fact that bond markets underestimated the scale of interest rate cuts and increases by the Federal Reserve, they got the direction right so that on average long-term bonds yield responded to ZIP when it was imposed in 2008 and 2020 and when it was lifted in 2016. Indeed, yields in 2020 had never been so low.

## Japan

Yield curve data for Japan demonstrate the relative rigidity of long-term interest rates with respect to ZIP (Table 5.6). Although the descent into ZIP began in September 1995, it took almost twenty years for the yield curve to flatten. In 2010, ten-year rates were still greater than 1 percent despite the fact that ZIP had been in force since 1996. By 2015 the ten-year rate had succumbed to ZIP, and by 2020 it had collapsed completely.

**Table 5.6** The Yield Curve in Japan

|          | 2 years | 5 years | 10 years | 20 years |
|----------|---------|---------|----------|----------|
| Dec 1991 | 5.103   | 5.604   | 5.575    | 6.031    |
| Dec 1997 | 0.652   | 1.298   | 1.934    | 2.572    |
| Dec 2003 | 0.11    | 0.6     | 1.363    | 1.862    |
| Dec 2005 | 0.281   | 0.854   | 1.473    | 1.989    |
| Dec 2010 | 0.167   | 0.399   | 1.127    | 1.881    |
| Dec 2015 | −0.033  | 0.032   | 0.267    | 0.997    |
| June 2020 | −0.14  | −0.102  | 0.042    | 0.417    |
| July 2021 | −0.116 | −0.117  | 0.045    | 0.42     |

*Source:* Ministry of Finance, Japan

## Countries with Index-linked Bond Markets

Wicksellian theory predicts that in the long run the natural and money rates of interest should converge. In an economy with inflation, this convergence is expected to apply in real terms. Representing the natural rate of interest by the return on fixed assets, which by definition is a real return, and the money rate of interest by the yield to maturity on ten-year bonds, the former is expected to converge with the latter when the yield to maturity on ten-year bonds is expressed in real terms. This means deducting expected inflation over the next ten years from the yield to maturity. A common practice is to use the current rate of inflation for these purposes, which means that investors expect inflation to remain at its current level over the next decade. If inflation happens to be a random walk, this practice would be plausible. However, inflation is typically autoregressive and has step-like properties, especially over long periods. In any case, yields on index-linked bonds differ greatly from their nominal counterparts minus measures of expected inflation.

In the absence of proxies for long-term expected inflation, it is therefore difficult to compare natural and money rates of interest in real terms, except in capital markets in which index-linked bonds happen to be traded. In such capital markets the yield to maturity on ten-year bonds indexed to the price level (typically the consumer price index) is real by definition. It embodies the term structure of expected inflation, as well as the term structure of expected spot interest rates. Such bonds are traded in the US and the UK, but they are relatively unimportant. By contrast, various types of indexed bonds have been traded in Israel for several decades. These include bonds linked to the consumer price index as well as bonds indexed to exchange rates. During the last twenty years they have also included commercial bonds in addition to treasury bonds. Trade in indexed bonds was obviously important when inflation was high, but it has continued to be important in the era of low inflation.

## United States

**Fig. 5.9**  Yield to Maturity on 10 Year Index Bonds (US)
*Sources*: (Federal Reserve Bank of St Louis (FRED))

The yield to maturity on ten-year indexed bonds in the US fell substantially under ZIP (Figure 5.9). Indeed, it was negative during 2012–13 and turned negative again in 2020. This decrease was not reflected, however, in the natural rate of interest. Comparing Figure 5.9 with the natural rate of interest as represented by the return on fixed assets in the US (Figure 5.1 in Chapter 4) suggests that the natural rate of interest did not decrease under ZIP. Instead, it suggests that the risk premium on fixed assets as measured by the difference between the return on fixed assets and the yield to maturity on index-linked bonds has increased from about 7 percent in the early 2000s to close to 10 percent since the Subprime Crisis.

## United Kingdom

Figure 5.10A is the counterpart to Figure 5.9 for the yield to maturity on index-linked gilts (gilt-edged treasury bonds in the UK). Index-linked gilts were introduced in 1980 by Mrs Thatcher to signal that she intended to fight inflation, which

Real 10yr spot yield

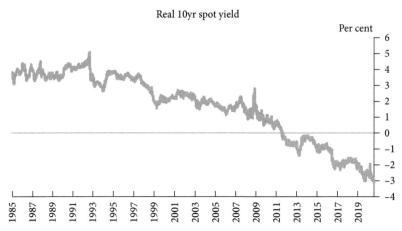

**Fig. 5.10A** Yields to Maturity on Ten-Year Index-linked Gilts
*Source:* Bank of England (personal communication).

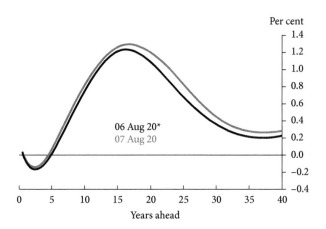

**Fig. 5.10B** Nominal Forward Rates Implied by the
Gilt-edged Market
*Source:* Bank of England.

was almost 20 percent. Hence the UK has a much longer history than the US with
index-linked bonds.

After being stable in the 1980s, the yield to maturity on ten-year indexed gilts
began to decrease. However, the rate of decrease accelerated after the Bank of
England adopted ZIP in 2009. Since 2011, the yield to maturity has been negative,
falling to −3.3 percent in July 2021.

Figure 5.10B plots the term structure of nominal forward rates implied by the
yield curves for gilt-edged securities (UK gilts) in early August 2020 calculated by
the Bank of England. Short or spot rates were expected to be negative over the

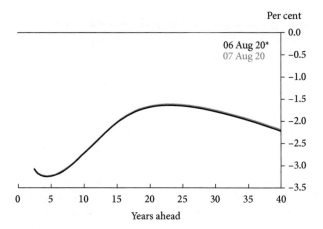

**Fig. 5.10C** Real Forward Rates Implied by the
Index-linked Gilt-edged Market
*Source*: Bank of England.

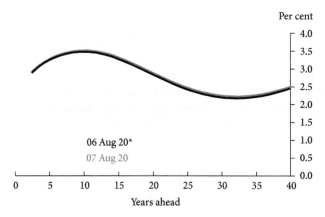

**Fig. 5.10D** The Term Structure of Expected Inflation
*Source*: Bank of England.

next five years, but were expected to be positive subsequently. They were expected
to peak at slightly over 1 percent by 2035. According to this interpretation, ZIP is
expected to remain in the UK until after 2025, and when it ends interest rates are
expected to be historically low.

Figure 5.10C is the counterpart to Figure 5.10A in the index-linked gilt-edged
market. It is the term structure of real forward rates. It implies that real spot rates
are expected to remain negative forever (at least until 2060)! Moreover, these negative rates of interest are large in absolute terms, ranging between minus 2 and
minus 3 percent. Such interest rates might have been expected to promote business investment and a decrease in the natural rate of interest as measured by the

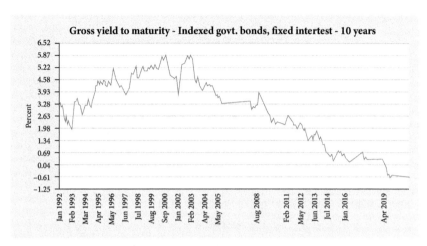

**Fig. 5.11** Yield to Maturity on Index Bonds: Israel
*Source:* Bank of Israel database.

return on fixed assets. However, neither of these expectations have been fulfilled (Table 5.5 in Chapter 4), Instead, as in the US, the risk premium on business investment appears to have increased.

The term structure of expected inflation is generated by the difference between the nominal and real forward rates (Figure 5.10D). Inflation was expected to increase until 2030 and to decrease thereafter.

## Israel

Yields to maturity on ten-year index-linked treasury bonds in Israel have behaved differently to their counterparts in the US and the UK. During the 1980s (not shown in Figure 5.11), the yield to maturity increased from 2 percent, and peaked at almost 5 percent in 1985 before gradually decreasing towards the levels in Figure 5.11. It peaked once again in the early 2000s at over 5 percent before gradually declining towards negative levels in 2020.

Recall that ZIP did not operate in Israel until 2014. This might have been responsible for the step-like decrease towards zero in the yield to maturity thereafter. The final drop into negative rates was most probably related to massive QE in early 2020 (see below). It is no coincidence that in Israel, as in the US and UK, yields to maturity on ten-year index-linked bonds have been negative since early 2020. The Covid-19 crisis dampened demand, increasing yields to maturity, but central banks more than offset market forces through massive QE.

The return on fixed assets in Israel (Figure 4.8A in Chapter 4) seems to be inversely related to the yield to maturity on index-linked bonds. Instead of increasing during the 1990s when the yield to maturity increased, the return on fixed assets decreased, and when the yield to maturity decreased, the return on assets tended to increase. Since 2014 when Israel adopted ZIP, the implicit risk premium on business investment increased because the return on fixed assets increased despite the decrease in the real long-term cost of capital, measured here by the yield to maturity on ten-year index-linked bonds.

In the absence of index-linked bonds, we might have represented the real long-term cost of capital by the nominal yield to maturity on ordinary ten-year bonds minus the current rate of inflation. Had we done so we would have found a rather different picture to Figure 5.11. In 2005, the real yield would have been 2.98 percent, having decreased from 6.84 percent in 2000. Subsequently, the real yield remained constant during 2005–18. In the case of Israel, we would have found that the real yield bore some similarity to Figure 5.11. It was 2 percent in 1980, increasing to 5 percent in 1985. The yield peaked again in 2000 at 5.5 percent and was mainly negative after 2010. These results suggest that deducting current inflation from nominal yields to maturity may be a misleading way to measure real yields to maturity.

## Countries without Index-linked Bond Markets

Since the countries in Table 5.7 do not have index-linked bonds, we construct the real long-term rate of interest by subtracting the rate of inflation (based on the GDP deflator) from the nominal yield to maturity on ten-year treasury bonds. Much of the short-term variability in Table 5.7 is induced by inflation rather than yields to maturity. On the whole, real yields are lower after 2010 and mostly become negative from 2015. Recall that Japan adopted ZIP in 1996, Sweden in 2009, and Australia in late 2019 (Table 5.3). Germany adopted ZIP as a member of the eurozone.

Because inflation in Japan was negative during 1995–2010, the real yields in Table 5.7 are larger than their nominal counterparts. This explains why real yields remained high despite the fact that nominal yields were low. In 2015, the nominal yield to maturity was only 0.35 percent, and in 2019 it was negative (−0.11 percent). On the whole, the flatness in the return on capital in Japan (Table 4.2A in Chapter 4) is associated with the flatness in the real cost of capital in Table 5.7. Since 2015, however, there is no evidence that the return on fixed assets decreased in line with the lower real cost of long-term capital. This also applies to Germany and Sweden. Perhaps for Germany the slight decrease in the return on fixed assets after 2010 is associated with the lower cost of capital since 2005. The final column in Table 5.7 refers to a weighted average of 19 OECD countries, which is broadly

Table 5.7  Real Yields to Maturity on Ten-Year Treasury Bonds

|  | Australia | Japan | Germany | Sweden | France | OECD[b] |
|---|---|---|---|---|---|---|
| **1980** | 1.64 | 2.34 | 3.02 |  | 2.09 |  |
| **1985** | 9.32 | 0.77 | 4.04 | 6.96[a] | 6.22 | 5.6 |
| **1990** | 7.71 | 4.39 | 5.3 | 3.69 | 7.27 | 5.7 |
| **1995** | 4.32 | 3.97 | 4.86 | 6.43 | 5.98 | 6.0 |
| **2000** | 5.26 | 3.12 | 5.73 | 3.86 | 3.84 | 3.7 |
| **2005** | 0.49 | 2.39 | 2.96 | 2.49 | 1.47 | 2.0 |
| **2010** | 4.20 | 3.05 | 2.09 | 1.94 | 2.11 | 3.7 |
| **2015** | 2.68 | −1.79 | −1.24 | −1.4 | −0.9 | 1.8 |
| **2019** | −1.55 | −1.62 | −1.76 | −2.71 | −0.17 | 0[c] |
| **2021[d]** | 0.41 | 0.04 | −2.79 | −1.38 | −1.19 | na |

*Sources:* Yields to maturity OECD.stats. Inflation (gdp-deflator) World Bank database. a: 1987. b: Bismut and Ramajo (2019), c 2017. d: June, OECD stats—CPI.

Table 5.8  Return on Fixed Assets minus Real Cost of Capital

|  | France | Australia | Japan | Germany | Sweden | US | UK | Israel |
|---|---|---|---|---|---|---|---|---|
| **1980** | 5.27 | 19.89 |  |  |  |  |  |  |
| **1985** | 2.25 | 15.43 |  |  |  |  |  |  |
| **1990** | 5.58 | 19.49 |  | 4.61a |  |  |  |  |
| **1995** | 4.74 | 23.4 | 15.42c | 3.34 | 5.57 |  | 9.85 | 32.47 |
| **2000** | 7.71 | 22.94 | 16.69 | 1.48 | 7.15 |  | 9.98 | 27.49 |
| **2005** | 8.84 | 30.69 | 17.46 | 4.91 | 7.67 | 7.7 | 9.99 | 28.42 |
| **2010** | 5.61 | 24.62 | 17.65 | 4.74 | 7.26 | 7.4 | 10.3 | 36.3 |
| **2015** | 9.22 | 20.18 | 21.65 | 7.64 | 10.58 | 8.8 | 13.49 | 40.2 |
| **2018** | 9.56 | 26.51 | 23.12 | 7.7 | 9.71 | 8.7b | 12.7 | 36.9 |

Author calculations. a 1991. b 2017. c 1994.

consistent with the picture that real long-term interest rates have decreased since the 1980s and 1990s, but have become particularly small under the New Abnormal.

In Table 5.8 the real cost of long-term (ten-year) capital in Figures 5.9, 5.10A and 5.11, and in Table 5.7, is subtracted from the rates of return on fixed assets that were reported in Chapter 4, Table 4.10 (return gross of indirect taxes on production and imports relative to net capital). Recall that the latter represent the natural rate of interest and the former represents the long-term money rate of interest minus expected inflation. In theory, as explained in Chapter 2, the differences reported in Table 5.8 should tend to zero over time. In practice, they tend to be positive because of risk premia, which reflect the fact that, whereas the cost of capital is certain, the return on fixed assets is not, and they reflect differences in national income accounting procedures. Also, whereas real capital costs are broadly comparable between countries in principle, the same does not apply to international comparisons of rates of return on fixed assets, which, as pointed out in Chapter 4, depend on national income accounting practices in different countries. Therefore, we do not make comparisons between countries, and focus instead on comparisons within countries. Specifically, according to existential risk theory we expect that the numbers in Table 5.8 should have increased under ZIP and the New Abnormal.

In the cases of France, Germany, Sweden, US, UK, and Israel, the last two rows of Table 5.8 tend to be larger by several percentage points after they adopted ZIP and the New Abnormal, consistent with existential risk theory. Since Australia adopted ZIP in 2019, existential risk theory should have been irrelevant, as it is in Table 5.8. In the case of Japan, which adopted ZIP and the New Abnormal in 1996, it is more difficult to judge because it has not been possible to estimate the return to capital prior to 1994. Miyagawa et al (2018) estimate that the gross return to capital peaked at 21 percent during 1985–1991, decreased to 17 percent by 1998 and fluctuated thereafter (until 2012) about this level. Unfortunately, these estimates cannot be compared with those reported in Table 4.4A in Chapter 4 because the latter refer to net capital. Nevertheless, they suggest that prior to 1994 the return to capital had been declining.

The data in Table 5.7 show that during the 1990s the real yield to maturity on ten-year treasury bonds decreased by a percentage point. Hence, prior to 1994 the difference between the rate of return on fixed assets and the cost of capital had been decreasing. Since 1994 this difference has increased (Table 5.8), especially after 2010. These developments are consistent with existential risk theory. What matters in Table 5.8 is within-country comparisons over time rather than between-country comparisons.

In almost all countries in Table 5.8 the gap between the return on fixed assets and long-term bond yields has widened during the New Abnormal instead of narrowing, as expected. For example, in Sweden this gap has doubled since 2009. Signally, the only exception is Australia, where the gap narrowed. However, Australia did not adopt ZIP until 2019. Later, these gaps are explained in terms of existential risk; instead of ZIP reducing the return on fixed assets, they either remained unchanged or even increased.

## Quantitative Easing

The Bank of Japan was the first central bank to undertake QE because it was the first to descend into ZIP, in September 1996. However, it took the Bank of Japan a few years to begin to undertake QE in earnest. Figure 5.12 shows the assets of the Bank of Japan in billions of yen that were acquired through QE. After 2006 the Bank of Japan began to undertake negative QE by selling off assets acquired

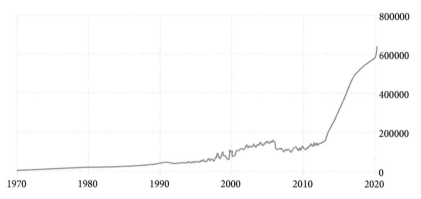

**Fig. 5.12** Quantitative Easing in Japan: Assets (Yen billions)
*Source:* Bank of Japan

previously in the belief that Japan was at last coming out of its twenty-year-long recession (see Chapter 8). As indicated by Figure 5.12, QE resumed in 2012, such that by early 2020 the assets of the Bank of Japan had more than tripled. On April 27 2020, the Bank of Japan announced that it would undertake unlimited QE in the future. This meant that in theory all financial assets were money-like or monetized.

From the outset, the Bank of Japan bought corporate debt as well as government bonds. However, this infringement of financial distancing was not new to Japan because the central bank had been intimately involved with the private sector since World War Two, as discussed in Chapter 8.

QE in other countries is generally limited in quantity and time so that the central bank plans to buy a pre-announced amount of assets within a certain time period. Table 5.9 reports the assets accumulated through QE by the Federal Reserve, the Bank of England and the ECB. QE by the Federal Reserve and the Bank of England involved the purchase of commercial debt, and subsequently equity. By contrast, ECB is the only major central bank to maintain financial distancing by limiting its purchases to governments securities. QE began during 2007 in the US with the outbreak of the Subprime Crisis and a year later in the UK and the Eurozone. Notice that the ECB undertook QE despite the fact that it did not adopt ZIP until 2013. Subsequently, all three central banks have had a similar QE profile as the Bank of Japan; central bank assets have roughly tripled in money terms since 2009. However, because inflation was negative in Japan, the increase in real terms was especially large.

Figure 5.13 shows that QE was proportionately much more salient in Japan than in the US and UK; by 2019, its assets were equivalent to 100 percent of GDP. By contrast, elsewhere this proportion was "only" between 20 and 40 percent of GDP. Whereas nominal GDP increased in the US, EU, and the UK, it decreased in Japan partly because inflation there was negative, as discussed in Chapter 8.

Table 5.9  Quantitative Easing by Major Central Banks: Assets

| | Federal Reserve $ trillions | Bank of England £ trillions | ECB € trillions |
|---|---|---|---|
| **July 2007** | 0.87 | 0.10 | 1.8 |
| **November 2009** | 2.21 | 0.2 | 1.8 |
| **July 2012** | 2.85 | 0.375 | 3.05 |
| **August 2016** | 4.48 | 0.435 | 3.10 |
| **June 2020** | 7.08 | 0.745 | 4.70 |
| **June 2021** | 8.08 | 0.947 | 7.74 |

*Source:* Balance sheets of central banks.

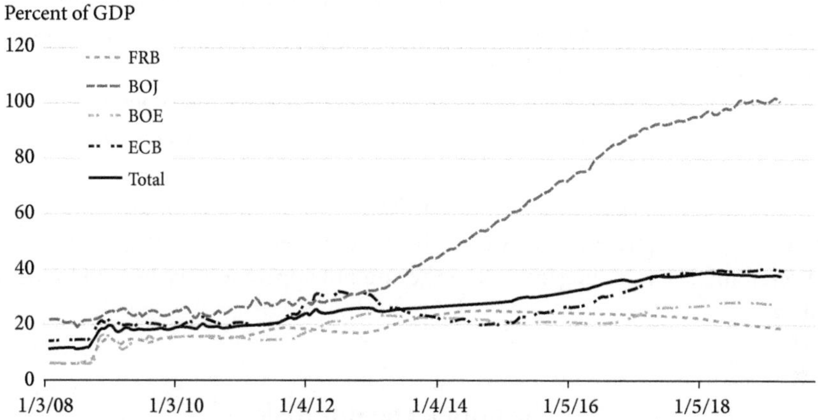

**Fig. 5.13** Central Bank Assets Acquired through QE as a Percentage of GDP
*Source:* Indicated below Figure.

Smaller central banks also engaged in QE. For example, in Israel QE was used in a minor way until 2018, by which time (January) QE had increased the assets of the Bank of Israel to 0.278 billion shekels. A year later these assets had increased to 4.39 billion shekels and by April 2020 to 15.64 billion shekels. QE in Israel was limited to government debt, but since July 2020 the Bank of Israel has begun to buy commercial debt. Signally, although nearly all central banks were using QE, the central banks that were last in line to adopt ZIP, the Reserve Bank of Australia and the Bank of New Zealand, resisted QE until the Covid-19 crisis in early 2020.

Our purpose in this chapter is simply to chronicle the descent into ZIP and the New Abnormal. In Chapter 2 we explained why QE is "full gas in neutral" for economies caught in the liquidity trap. It has no effect on economic activity and should be seen as the response of frustrated central bankers to their self-imposed policy impotence due to ZIP. It makes them feel as though they are conducting monetary policy by other means in the social interest. It does at least provide an agenda for monetary policy committees, for otherwise there would be no point in meeting.

There is, however, a possibility that there might be some purpose to QE. According to the neoclassical theory of the terms structure in equations (1.1 to 1.5), the shape of the yield curve is driven by expectations of interest rate policy ($\phi$) and term premia ($\tau$). It implies that transactions at different maturities cannot affect the shape of the yield curve. An alternative "preferred habitat" theory was proposed by Modigliani and Sutch (1966), according to which the shape of the yield curve could be "twisted" because individuals have different maturity preferences. For example, if "widows and orphans" invest for the long term and "speculators" invest for the short term, lengthening the maturity structure of government debt should increase the yield to maturity on long-term debt relative to short-term debt, i.e. the yield curve gets steeper. It should be said that Modigliani and Sutch claimed that "operation twist" in the US failed to twist the yield curve.

So might the massive $700 billion of QE undertaken by the Federal Reserve in March to April 2020 be expected to twist the yield curve. In late February the yield gap between long rates (ten years) and short rates was close to zero (Table 5.5). By March 25, this gap had widened to 0.88 percent but narrowed to about 0.5 percent by early July. The renewal of ZIP and the intensification of QE might have lowered interest rates in general, but they do not appear to have twisted the yield curve.

## Corporate Default Risk

Corporate default risk premia ($\eta$) may be represented by the difference between yields to maturity on corporate and treasury bonds with the same maturity. Figures 5.14 plot these differences for corporate bonds in the US (Baa and Aaa-rated corporate bonds). These premia are naturally smaller for the latter, but are highly correlated. Since the Subprime Crisis, these premia have been relatively large. For Aaa-rated as well as Baa-rated bonds, they have been a percentage point larger. For Baa-rated bonds, spreads have ranged between 0.3 and 6 percentage points. For Aaa-rated bonds, spreads have ranged between −0.35 to 2.5 percent.

Since 2010, credit risk spreads have been fairly stable, except for in 2017–19, when the spread decreased. Consequently, the risk premium in the return on fixed assets should not have been affected by credit risk during this period.

Spreads in the UK peaked at 5.5 percent during 2009 and peaked again in 2012 at 3.2 percent. Since 2014, however, they have been stable at about 1.75 percent.

In summary, what matters for business investment is the real rate of interest on long-term commercial bonds rather than the policy rate of the central bank.

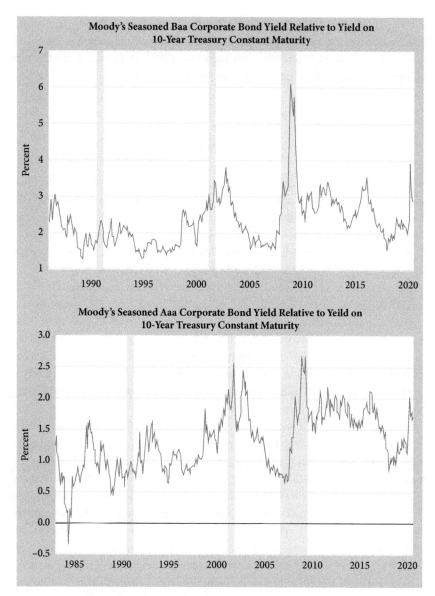

**Fig. 5.14** Credit Risk Spreads in the US Commercial Bond Market
*Source:* Federal Reserve Bank of St Louis (FRED)

With the onset of ZIP, real commercial bond rates hardly decreased because ZIP was perceived to be temporary. With the passage of time, gross redemption yields on treasury bonds began to decrease, but they remained positive, suggesting that ZIP is expected to end sooner or later. These decreases reduced the long-term cost of capital to businesses. Corporate default risk premia typically range between 1 and 3 percent, and although they are autocorrelated, they tend to be trend-free. Massive quantitative easing might have twisted treasury yield curves temporarily, but failed to do so permanently. This leaves expectations of future interest rate policy as the main determinant of the long-term real cost of capital to businesses.

## Fiscal Policy

Whereas ZIP, QE and foreign exchange intervention involve central banks, fiscal policy involves ministries of finance. Just as central bank policy has entered unchartered territory under the New Abnormal, so has fiscal policy been deviant. However, there is a difference in that fiscal policy had been out of control in the past and, though deviant, it was not abnormal or unique. In contrast, central banking was completely abnormal, and crossed several red lines.

Fiscal deficits have been too large, with the result that in most countries debt-to-GDP ratios have been spiraling out of control. In Chapter 2 it was suggested that ZIP creates an incentive for governments to engage in deficit finance because the cost of debt service becomes negligible. A further synergy between ZIP and fiscal policy is that, when the rate of interest is zero, money-financed deficits are not inflationary. If this issue was ever in doubt, the massive monetization of government debt through QE without any inflationary consequences (see below) during the Covid-19 pandemic proves the point.

We recall some of the conclusions reached in Chapter 2 regarding the relation between the growth in debt-to-GDP ratios (d), fiscal deficits as a percentage of GDP (def), interest rates (i), and the rate of growth of nominal GDP (g). The growth rate of the debt-to-GDP ratio equals the fiscal deficit as a percentage of GDP divided by the debt-to-GDP ratio minus the rate of growth of nominal GDP. This means that, all else given, debt-to-GDP ratios grow more rapidly in countries with smaller debt-to-GDP ratios. This perhaps counter-intuitive result may be understood by its parallel with overeating. If a slim person and a fat person over-eat by 1000 calories per day, the slim person will put on weight more rapidly than the fat person. Hence the effect of a given fiscal deficit as a percentage of GDP on its rate of growth of debt-to-GDP will be smaller in heavily indebted countries such as Japan and larger in countries such as Germany where debt-to-GDP ratios are small.

Since in the 1980s debt-to-GDP ratios were on the whole small, this meant that imprudent fiscal policy induced debt-to-GDP ratios to grow relatively rapidly. Also, nominal GDP growth decreased over time because not only did inflation decline, so did real economic growth. Slower nominal GDP growth increased the growth rate of debt-to-GDP ratios. In summary, debt-to-GDP ratios grew because of the widening gap between two blades of scissors.

In 1980, the debt-to-GDP ratio in Japan was about 50 percent, which was close to the average across OECD countries. By 1990, the debt-to-GDP ratio had increased by 10 percentage points, and by 2000 it was 130 percent. In 2020 the debt-to-GDP ratio was almost 250 percent (Figure 5.15). During the 1980s and 1990s, Japan ran fiscal deficits that reached 9 percent of GDP (Figure 5.16). This coincided with slower nominal GDP growth because the Japanese economy ceased to grow in real terms and because of deflation (Figure 5.17). Nominal GDP grew by 15 percent per year during 1956–80, and by only 5 percent per year during 1980–95. Nominal GDP peaked in 1998 and began to decrease because inflation was negative and economic growth was either almost zero or negative.

Towards the end of the 2000s, nominal GDP began to decrease rapidly. So even if the fiscal deficit was zero, the debt-to-GDP ratio was bound to increase. For reasons discussed in more detail in Chapter 8, nominal GDP began to grow again after 2013. Since Japan's budget was more balanced during this period (Figure 5.16), its debt-to-GDP ratio stabilized at a historically high level.

The decrease in nominal GDP in Japan was the exception rather than the rule (Figure 5.17). Elsewhere, although economic growth was sluggish, inflation tended

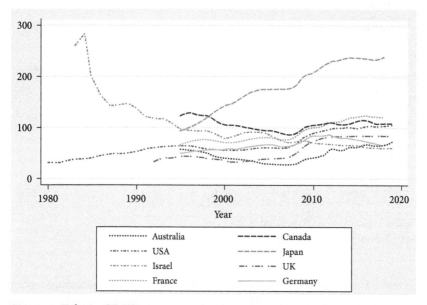

**Fig. 5.15** Debt-to-GDP Ratios

*Source:* National statistical offices and author calculations

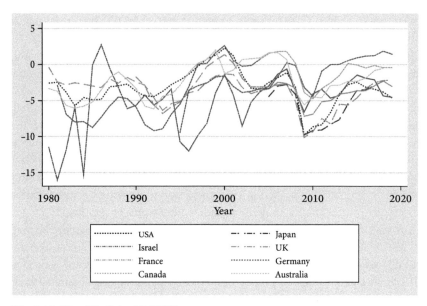

**Fig. 5.16** Fiscal Deficits (% GDP)

*Sources:* US, UK, and Israel from national statistical offices. Other countries from OECD-stat.

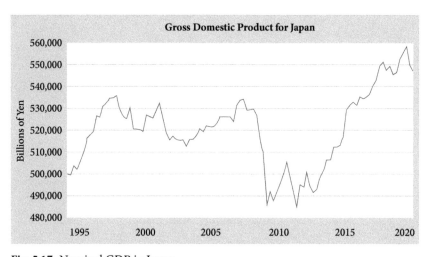

**Fig. 5.17** Nominal GDP in Japan

*Source:* Federal Reserve Bank of St Louis (FRED).

to be small and positive. For these countries the increase in their indebtedness cannot be blamed on negative growth in nominal GDP. Instead, larger fiscal deficits
were to blame. Under the New Deal and during World War Two, the US government ran large budget deficits such that by 1944 the debt-to-GDP ratio had
peaked at 100 percent. Over the next 40 years the debt-to-GDP ratio was gradually

reduced to 30 percent through a combination of fiscal restraint, economic growth and inflation. For example, in 1980 the debt-to-GDP ratio in the US was historically low (about 30 percent, Figure 5.15). By the mid-1990s this ratio had doubled and by 2013 it had already passed what it was in 1944, and it continued to grow subsequently.

Had economic growth been stronger, indebtedness would have grown more slowly. It would also have grown more slowly if fiscal deficits had been smaller. However, fiscal deficits were increased in the wake of the Subprime Crisis to almost 10 percent of GDP (Figure 5.16) and continued to be high for the rest of the decade.

Other OECD countries became indebted to various degrees for reasons broadly similar to the US because they ran larger fiscal deficits and experienced slower nominal GDP growth. However, Figures 5.15 and 5.16 highlight Israel as a double exception; it once had the largest debt-to-GDP and by 2020 had among the smallest. Following the Yom Kippur War in 1973, Israel's fiscal deficit reached 33 percent of GDP, largely as a result of the massive defense budget. This explains why in Figure 5.16 in the early 1980s the debt-to-GDP ratio was even higher than in Japan today. During the first half of the 1980s, the economy became hyperinflationary until a stabilization policy involving massive budgetary cuts reduced inflation from 400 percent to about 15 percent. Figure 5.16 shows that, during 1980–4, the budget deficit was double-digit but by 1986 there was a budget surplus.

Subsequently, a combination of fiscal restraint and rapid economic growth, driven by immigration in the 1990s and by high tech subsequently, reduced the debt-to-GDP ratio to less than 100 percent by 2000, and to 60 percent by 2019. Although Israel descended into ZIP in 2014, it has continued to respect fiscal orthodoxy by reducing its debt-to-GDP ratio. Indeed, successive Israeli governments have consciously adopted the Maastricht norm of 60 percent for Israel's debt-to-GDP ratio. They seem to be the exception that does not prove the rule.

## Kinetic Inflation

Kinetic energy is the potential energy in, for example, dammed water. Undamming the water turns kinetic energy into actual energy. Kinetic inflation is the potential inflation induced by ZIP. ZIP, as we have explained, makes inflation kinetic because the demand for money becomes infinitely elastic. This inflation is released when ZIP ends and the demand for money ceases to be infinitely elastic.

We add nominal GDP ($Y = QP$) to the specification of the demand for money in equation (4.3) in Chapter 2:

$$lnM = \alpha + lnY + \frac{\beta}{i} \qquad (2.1)$$

Equation (2.1) implies that the velocity of circulation of money is:

$$V = \exp\left[-\alpha - \frac{i}{\beta}\right] \tag{2.2}$$

Hence, velocity varies inversely with the rate of interest, and tends to a maximum of $V_{max} = e^{-\alpha}$ under ZIP. Since $\alpha$ varies inversely with fintech improvements, the latter are expected to increase the velocity of circulation. Kinetic inflation is defined by the ratio of $V_{normal}$ to $V_{max}$, where the former is the velocity of circulation when the rate of interest is positive and normal.

Figure 5.18 plots the income velocity of circulation of money (M1) in the US. Velocity has grown thanks to fintech, which has enabled individuals and businesses to manage their transactions with less inventories of money. During the 1980s, velocity stabilized before growing once more until it peaked with the outbreak of the Subprime Crisis. Its annual growth rate averaged 4 percent. By 2020, velocity decreased to where it was in 1970.

Velocity decreased because under ZIP the demand for money becomes perfectly elastic, and through its quantitative easing the Federal Reserve increased the supply of money massively. Notice that the decline in velocity ceased temporarily in 2016 when the Federal Reserve began to raise interest rates. However, velocity continued to decrease when the Federal Reserve reversed this policy and renewed

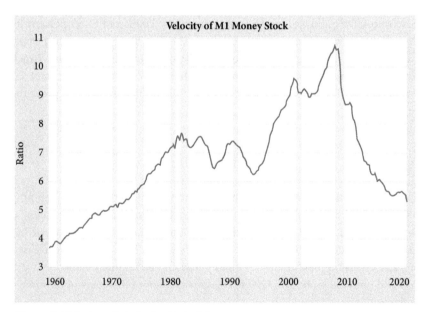

**Fig. 5.18** Velocity of M1 in the United States
*Source:* Federal Reserve Bank of St Louis (FRED).

ZIP in March 2020. Assuming that fintech, represented by α, would have continued to increase velocity by 4 percent per year, velocity would have been about 16 by 2020 instead of 5.25. Had nominal GDP been 304 percent larger in 2020, velocity would have been 16 instead of 5.25, and the demand for M1 would have equaled its supply. This implies that kinetic inflation is about 304 percent, i.e. if the general price level in the US in 2020 was 304 percent larger, velocity would have been 16 instead of 5.25. The same would apply if real GDP was 304 percent larger. However, it is unlikely that the massive expansion of money supply would induce real economic growth instead of inflation. A more conservative estimate of kinetic inflation is obtained by using velocity at the time of the Subprime Crisis as a reference point (10.7 in Figure 5.18), according to which kinetic inflation would be 194 percent.

This estimate of kinetic inflation is obviously crude, since a more precise estimate depends on α and β in equations (2.1) and (2.2). Nevertheless, it suggests an order of magnitude, which, because of its size, is sufficient for our present purposes. Kinetic inflation would still be very large if our crude estimate was "only" 100 percent instead of three times as much.

Kinetic inflation of 304 percent does not mean that as soon as ZIP ends the general price level would immediately increase by 304 percent. Rather it means that over some period of adjustment the general level of prices would eventually increase by this amount. For example, if the adjustment process was ten years, the average rate of inflation would be 11 percent per year.

If ZIP ended, the Federal Reserve would most probably take action to mitigate kinetic inflation. For example, it could undertake negative QE by selling the assets it had bought through QE. Nevertheless, our purpose here is to provide a metric for the abnormality of monetary policy, and kinetic inflation is an intuitive metric for present purposes.

Figures 5.19A – 5.19C plot M1 velocity for other countries. Whereas the trend for velocity in the US is positive, the opposite applies in most other countries. For example, velocity in Japan decreased during the 1970s and 1980s against a background of lower nominal interest rates. In 1996 the Bank of Japan adopted ZIP and velocity subsequently decreased by about 50 percent, suggesting that kinetic inflation was approximately 100 percent. Since the other countries in Figure 5.19A had not adopted ZIP by 2018, kinetic inflation does not apply to them.

There is no evidence that ZIP induced kinetic inflation in Denmark, Sweden, and the UK (Figure 5.19B), since there are no negative discontinuities in velocity in 2001, 2009, and 2014 respectively. The discrete decrease in velocity in Norway coincides with ZIP during 2016–18 (Table 5.3), which implies kinetic inflation of about 100 percent.

If there was any doubt about the matter, Figure 5.19C testifies to the empirical sensitivity of velocity to the nominal rate of interest. As mentioned, during 1980–5, Israel experienced triple-digit inflation, as a result of which the Bank of Israel

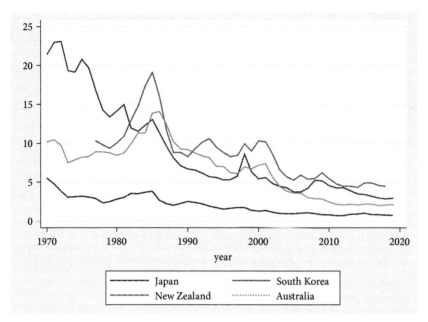

**Fig. 5.19A** Velocity of M1 in Australasia
*Source:* OECD – Stat.

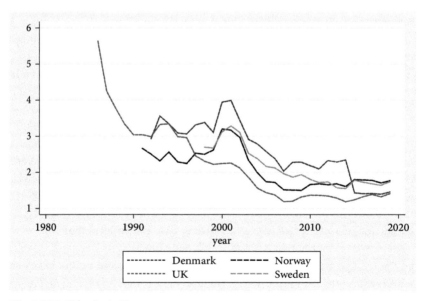

**Fig. 5.19B** Velocity in Europe
*Source:* OECD-Stat.

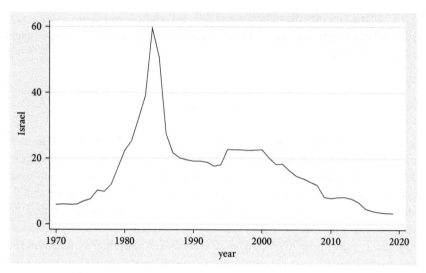

**Fig. 5.19C**  Velocity in Israel
*Source:* Bank of Israel.

raised its policy rate into triple digits. The demand for money decreased, as predicted by theory, as a result of which velocity increased more than tenfold. After the successful stabilization policy in 1985–6, velocity stabilized, but inflation remained between 10 and 20 percent. Tighter monetary policy at the turn of the millennium temporarily increased velocity, until during the 2000s inflation fell from 5 percent to almost zero. Against this background it is rather difficult to detect the effect of ZIP, adopted in 2014, on velocity. However, it may be discerned in the final step down in Figure 5.19C, which implies that kinetic inflation is of the order of 90 percent.

Table 5.10 summarizes kinetic inflation in the study group of countries, induced by ZIP and quantitative easing as of the end of 2019. They represent estimates of the pent-up price increase that would equate the demand for money with its current supply under normal interest rates. Under ZIP, inflation remains pent up

**Table 5.10**  Kinetic Inflation (percent)

| | |
|---|---|
| US | 304 |
| Japan | 100 |
| Norway | 100 |
| Israel | 90 |
| Sweden | 0 |
| Denmark | 0 |
| UK | 0 |

*Source:* Author estimates.

because of the liquidity trap. However, if ZIP ends and interest rates return to normal, this inflationary pressure is released because the economy ceases to be caught in the liquidity trap.

## Synopsis

This chapter completes a saga that started in Chapter 2 with a critique of contemporary Neo-Wicksellian macroeconomic theory, which focused on its inadequate attention to Wicksell's natural rate of interest, and even conceptual confusion about it. Drawing on Patinkin's interpretation of Wicksell, we maintained that the natural rate of interest is represented by the return on fixed assets and that, because it is costly for firms to adjust their capital stocks, the natural rate of interest, unlike the natural rate of unemployment, is not an equilibrium phenomenon. Perhaps the critique in Chapter 2 would not have been important but for the fact that central bankers (such as Janet Yellen) and many economists persuaded themselves that ZIP is justified because the natural rate of interest, as they (mis)understood it, had decreased and was either zero or close to zero. In other words, they believe that they are behaving like good Wicksellians. But for this belief, the critique in Chapter 2 might have been just another arcane academic argument about capital theory.

Chapter 2 introduced the concept of existential risk. This kind of risk arises when a form of political economy, such as the New Abnormal, is expected to end sooner or later. Matters would be different if ZIP lasted forever, but because the New Abnormal is incentive-incompatible, it must eventually come to an end. Since exiting the New Abnormal is unlikely to be easy, business investors act with caution to protect themselves from exposure to existential risk.

In Chapter 2, Keynes' liquidity trap theory is recalled to explain why there has been no inflation under the New Abnormal. Had the New Abnormal induced rising inflation, it is doubtful that it would have persisted. The absence of inflation has led many, including Federal Reserve chairman Powell and Treasury Secretary Yellen, to believe that all is well under the New Abnormal, and that inflation has ceased to be an issue. In a sense, this is true. Liquidity trap theory implies that ZIP generates kinetic inflation rather than actual inflation. However, when ZIP ends the same theory predicts that kinetic inflation is released into actual inflation.

Whereas Chapter 2 is a critique of macroeconomic theory, Chapter 3 is a critique of empirical methodology in macroeconomics. Normally, bad theory gets rejected through empirical testing. Economists have developed econometric theory to test empirically hypotheses in all fields of economics. Chapter 3 relates how classical or frequentist econometric theory has been abandoned by many macroeconomists, who have turned to postmodern methodologies in which it is assumed that the model is "true" but its parameters are unknown. This postmodern invasion means that bad theory can never be empirically rejected because the model is always "true." The highly influential DSGE movement in macroeconomics has devised its own unorthodox postmodern empirical methods to justify almost everything, to the point that rival DSGE models are believed by their proprietors to be "true."

As in Chapter 2, this postmodern invasion might not have been so important had the DSGE movement not infiltrated central banks. But for this, the methodological critique in Chapter 3 might have been just another arcane academic argument about hypothesis testing. Moreover, there is a negative synergy between the critiques in Chapters 2 and 3. When a postmodern result implies that some DSGE model failed to explain, for example, the Subprime Crisis, the model is patched up or fixed by some ad hoc theoretical device. After a number of such failures, DSGE models accumulate ad hoc patches, so these patchwork models continue to be "true."

Chapter 3 relates how classical econometric methods have recently been developed to carry out modernist tests on postmodern DSGE models. These "indirect inference" tests show that some canonical DSGE models are massively rejected by the data. However, the DSGE movement has gathered so much momentum that it is difficult to stop the juggernaut by confusing its members with facts.

So, what have the facts to say about the natural rate of interest? This is the focus in Chapter 4, where the return on fixed assets is measured for several OECD countries. The first thing to note is that this measure of the natural rate of interest is large and positive. Second, ZIP should have lowered the natural rate of interest because the return on capital is expected to follow the cost of capital. This did not happen. If anything, the natural rate of interest even increased. Hence, the third thing to note, is that the increasing gap between the return on capital and its cost is consistent with the theory of existential risk proposed in Chapter 2. These facts should have rung alarm bells among central bankers that something had gone wrong. Their blinkered preoccupation with the inflation and output gaps to the exclusion of the interest rate gap, measured by the difference between the return to capital and its cost, led them down a blind alley into ZIP, from which it is hard to escape.

Finally, Chapter 5 chronicled the descent into ZIP and the New Abnormal by various OECD countries, starting with Japan in 1996 and ending with New Zealand in 2020. Importantly, what matters for business investment is not the policy rate of interest set by central banks but the long-term cost of capital. Much of Chapter 5 is devoted to documenting the response of the latter to the former, and the role of quantitative easing in this process.

In summary, Chapters 2–5 are a *postmortem*. They are an attempt to explain how the New Abnormal, which might have been limited to Japan, turned global after the Subprime Crisis. The epidemiology of the New Abnormal is theorized in Chapter 2 and documented in Chapter 5. The next natural step is to consider the future of the New Abnormal. Does it have a future? Is there a prospect of it coming to an end? What will happen if it does? What can be done to limit the damage when it ends? How can a soft exit be engineered? These major prospective issues are addressed in the final chapter.

In the meantime, it is necessary to make the case that the New Abnormal incurs considerable economic and social costs, otherwise there might not be much point to the final chapter. These social costs are considered in Chapters 6 and 7, covering such issues as fertility, inequality, pensions, insurance, and intergeneration equity. They are also considered in Chapter 8, which is entirely devoted to Japan, which might serve as a crystal ball for other countries as the longest survivor under the New Abnormal.

Chapter 9 refers to the intensification of the New Abnormal since the outbreak of the Covid-19 pandemic at the beginning of 2020. Not only have countries such as New Zealand joined ZIP, and others, such as the US, rejoined ZIP, but most governments have increased their fiscal deficits and expanded their quantitative easing to a degree well beyond what they might have done before the New Abnormal. Furthermore, whereas in the past governments did not seek to fight pandemics with lockdown policy, matters were different in the case of Covid-19. Indeed, we show that the economic cost per life year saved by mitigation policy greatly exceeded its implicit value expressed in the investment of health infrastructure. Perhaps this too should be seen a phenomenon of the New Abnormal.

# 6

# Fertility Decline in the New Abnormal?

We argued in Chapter 4 that business investors have been frightened by existential risk induced by the New Abnormal. They cut back on investment because they are scared about the future. In this chapter we ask whether the decline in fertility observed in most advanced economies is related to the same phenomenon. Are couples having fewer children because they too are fearful about the future? They don't want to bring children into an unstable world. For example, fertility in Japan is almost half of what it was during the Japanese "economic miracle" of the 1960s and 1970s (Figure 6.1). Can this be related to the fact that the Japanese economy weakened during the 1980s, descended into ZIP in 1996 and became entangled in the New Abnormal subsequently?

Since the fertility rate that ensures population replacement is 2.1, Figure 6.1 implies that for more than half a century the Japanese have failed to replace themselves. The only reason why the population did not begin the decrease until after 2005 was because of the extraordinary increase in Japanese longevity.

Table 6.1 places Japan in an international perspective. Total fertility has declined in all the countries featured in Table 6.1. Whereas in 1960 total fertility exceeded replacement (2.1) in all countries, by 1980 matters had changed radically; all but two countries' fertility was below replacement. Japanese fertility was not large to begin with, and it has remained relatively small. The greatest proportionate decreases in total fertility occurred in Italy and Spain, which joined Japan at the bottom of the international league table for fertility. Israel has remained clearly at the top of this league table, and the decrease in fertility has been relatively small. Among OECD countries, South Korea has seen the greatest decline in total fertility, from 3.9 in 1970 to 0.9 in 2019.

The key question here is whether fertility decline is associated with the New Abnormal and its duration. In this context the most important country is Japan because the New Abnormal has existed in Japan since the 1990s. It is probably too soon to learn from other countries. On the other hand, these countries may serve as comparators for Japan. Since 1980 fertility remained stable at a lower level in Australia, France, Italy, Germany, Sweden, and the US and UK. In Italy and Spain, fertility decreased step-like in 1980 and 1990. Israel and Japan are unusual insofar as fertility remained high in the former and fell in two steps in the latter. The first

*Zero Interest Policy and the New Abnormal.* Michael Beenstock, Oxford University Press. © Michael Beenstock (2022).
DOI: 10.1093/oso/9780192849663.003.0006

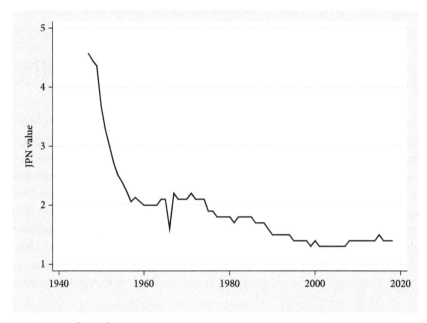

**Fig. 6.1** Total Fertility in Japan
*Source*: 1947–1959 Human Fertility Project. 1960–2018 e-Stat.

**Table 6.1** Total Fertility

|      | Australia | France | Italy | Germany | Spain | Japan | US | UK | Israel | Sweden |
|------|-----------|--------|-------|---------|-------|-------|-----|-----|--------|--------|
| 1960 | 3.45 | 2.85 | 2.37 | 2.37 | 2.86 | 2.00 | 3.65 | 2.69 | 3.87 | 2.17 |
| 1970 | 2.86 | 2.55 | 2.38 | 2.03 | 2.84 | 2.13 | 2.48 | 2.44 | 3.79 | 1.92 |
| 1980 | 1.89 | 1.85 | 1.64 | 1.44 | 2.22 | 1.75 | 1.84 | 1.90 | 3.24 | 1.66 |
| 1990 | 1.90 | 1.77 | 1.33 | 1.45 | 1.36 | 1.54 | 2.08 | 1.79 | 2.89 | 1.91 |
| 2000 | 1.76 | 1.89 | 1.26 | 1.38 | 1.22 | 1.36 | 2.06 | 1.64 | 2.95 | 1.56 |
| 2005 | 1.81 | 1.94 | 1.34 | 1.34 | 1.33 | 1.26 | 2.06 | 1.76 | 2.94 | 1.77 |
| 2010 | 1.93 | 2.03 | 1.46 | 1.39 | 1.37 | 1.39 | 1.93 | 1.92 | 3.03 | 1.98 |
| 2015 | 1.81 | 1.96 | 1.35 | 1.50 | 1.33 | 1.45 | 1.84 | 1.80 | 3.09 | 1.85 |
| 2019 | 1.66 | 1.83+ | 1.27 | 1.54 | 1.23 | 1.36 | 1,71 | 1.63 | 3.01 | 1.70 |
| 2020 |  | 1.80 |  |  |  |  |  |  |  | 1.66 |

*Source*: OECD-Stat. Japan: e-Stat. June 2021

step occurred in 1980–90 and the second has occurred since 2000. Can this second step be attributed to the New Abnormal?

These steps are also discernible in crude birth rates (Table 6.2). After 2000, Japan's crude birth rate became single digit and dropped to 7.4 by 2018. Spain and Italy are more similar to Japan in Table 6.2 than in Table 6.1. Their crude birth rates decreased into single digits in 2000, together with that of Germany. However,

Table 6.2  Crude Birth Rates (per 1000)

|       | Australia | France | Italy | Germany | Spain | Japan | US | UK | Israel | Sweden |
|-------|-----------|--------|-------|---------|-------|-------|------|------|--------|--------|
| **1960** | 22.4 | 18.7 | 18.1 | 17.3 | 21.7 | 17.3 | 23.7 | 17.5 | 26.9 | 13.7 |
| **1970** | 20.6 | 17.0 | 16.7 | 13.4 | 19.5 | 18.7 | 18.4 | 16.2 | 26.1 | 13.7 |
| **1980** | 15.7 | 14.2 | 11.3 | 11.1 | 15.2 | 13.5 | 15.9 | 13.4 | 24.3 | 11.7 |
| **1990** | 14.9 | 13.2 | 10.0 | 11.4 | 10.3 | 10.0 | 16.7 | 13.9 | 22.2 | 14.5 |
| **2000** | 12.7 | 13.1 | 9.5 | 9.3 | 9.8 | 9.4 | 14.0 | 11.5 | 21.7 | 10.2 |
| **2005** | 12.9 | 13.1 | 9.6 | 8.3 | 10.6 | 8.4 | 14.3 | 12.0 | 20.8 | 11.2 |
| **2010** | 13.6 | 12.7 | 9.6 | 8.3 | 10.4 | 8.5 | 13.0 | 12.9 | 21.8 | 12.3 |
| **2015** | 12.9 | 11.8 | 8.0 | 9.0 | 9.0 | 7.8 | 12.4 | 11.9 | 21.3 | 11.7 |
| **2018** | 12.6 | 11.0 | 7.3 | 9.5 | 7.9 | 7.4 | 11.6 | 11.0 | 20.8 | 11.4 |

*Source*: World Bank, July 2020.

Table 6.3  Completed Fertility

| Birth cohort | Australia | France | Italy | Germany | Spain | Japan | US | UK | Israel | Sweden |
|------|-----------|--------|-------|---------|-------|-------|------|------|--------|--------|
| **1925** | 2.8 | | | | | | | | na | |
| **1930** | | 2.63 | | | | | | 2.25 | | |
| **1935** | 3.0 | | | | | | | | | |
| **1932** | | | | | | 2.06 | 3.25 | | | |
| **1940** | | 2.41 | | 1.92 | | 2.05 | 2.79 | 2.39 | | |
| **1945** | 2.5 | | | | | | | | | |
| **1950** | | 2.11 | 1.97 | 1.96 | 2.13 | 1.97 | 2.08 | 2.10 | | 2.00 |
| **1955** | 2.2 | | | | | | | | | |
| **1960** | | 2.12 | 1.79 | 1.81 | 1.97 | 1.86 | 2.02 | 1.95 | | 2.05 |
| **1965** | 2.1 | | | | | 1.60 | | | | |
| **1968** | | | | | | | | 1.9 | | |
| **1970** | | 2.00 | 1.58 | 1.60 | 1.43 | 1.50 | 2.00 | | | 2.10 |

*Source*: Human Fertility Project. France, Insee. Australia, Australia National Statistics. UK, Office for National Statistics. July 2020.

Germany's crude birth rate recovered in 2015, reflecting the recovery in fertility, while the crude birth rates in Spain and Italy continued to plummet.

The measures of natality in Tables 6.1 and 6.2 are imperfect for different reasons. The ideal measure is "completed fertility," which is only ascertained after women have ceased to be able to bear children. For example, according to data from the Human Fertility Project (Table 6.3), the average completed fertility for Japanese women born in 1970 was 1.5 children. These women completed their fertility in 2019 and they had contributed to total fertility in Table 6.1 since 1985. The women in the earliest birth cohorts (1932) contributed to total fertility during 1947–81.

## The Relation between Total and Completed Fertility

To elucidate the difference between total fertility and completed fertility, suppose women may bear children in two periods. The completed fertility (CF) of women of cohort b is the sum of the children (F) that they have on average in period 1 and period 2:

$$CF_b = F_{b1} + F_{b2} \qquad (1.1)$$

Completed fertility for women in the next cohort is:

$$CF_{b+1} = F_{(b+1)2} + F_{(b+1)3} \qquad (1.2)$$

Let $\tau$ denote the proportion born during the first period of fertility, i.e. it is a birth timing parameter. Women who postpone fertility have smaller $\tau$.

Total fertility (TF) during period 2 is defined as the number of children born to the two cohorts of women in period 2:

$$TF_2 = F_{b2} + F_{(b+1)2} \qquad (1.3)$$

This implicitly assumes that $F_{b1} = F_{(b+1)2}$, or the fertility of cohort b when they are younger equals the fertility of cohort b + 1 when they are younger. Substituting equations (1.1) and (1.2) into equation (1.3) implies the following relation between total fertility in period 2, completed fertility and birth timing:

$$TF_2 = \left(1 - \tau_b\right) CF_b + \tau_{b+1} CF_{b+1} \qquad (1.4)$$

If fertility is equally spaced ($\tau = 0.5$) and completed fertility does not change between cohorts ($CF_b = CF_{b+1} = CF$), then equation (1.4) implies that total fertility equals completed fertility, as expected. Suppose instead that the women in cohort b decide to have all their children when they are young, so that $\tau_b = 1$ and the women in cohort b + 1 postpone their fertility so that $\tau_{b+1} = 0$. Total fertility would be zero! It is obvious that total fertility in general misrepresents completed fertility depending on birth spacing and changes in completed fertility. Also, because total fertility depends on birth timing, whereas completed fertility does not, the variance of total fertility tends to be larger than for completed fertility.

Table 6.4 provides some illustrative examples, where row 1 serves as the baseline in which total fertility equals completed fertility (2.5). In row 2, completed fertility for cohort b + 1 is reduced from 2.5 to 2. Total fertility continues to equal average completed fertility because births are equally distributed between the two periods. Row 3 shows that, when birth spacing is the same between cohorts and completed fertility is the same, total fertility continues to equal completed

**Table 6.4** Total and Completed Fertility in the two—Period Overlapping Cohort Model

| $CF_b$ | $CF_{b+1}$ | $\tau_b$ | $\tau_{b+1}$ | $TF_2$ |
|---|---|---|---|---|
| 2.5 | 2.5 | 0.5 | 0.5 | 2.5 |
| 2.5 | 2.0 | 0.5 | 0.5 | 2.25 |
| 2.5 | 2.5 | 0.25 | 0.25 | 2.5 |
| 2.5 | 2.5 | 0.25 | 0.5 | 3.125 |
| 2 | 2 | 0.25 | 0.75 | 3.0 |
| 2.5 | 1.5 | 0.25 | 0.75 | 2.95 |

fertility. If completed fertility is the same but birth spacing is different because cohort b postpones fertility, row 4 shows that total fertility overestimates completed fertility. The same happens in row 5; despite the fact that completed fertility decreases in both cohorts, total fertility increases. In the final row, completed fertility decreases in cohort b + 1; cohort b postpones fertility, while cohort b + 1 does the opposite. Although average completed fertility decreases to 2 from 2.5, total fertility increases from 2.5 to 2.95.

The calculations in Table 6.4 underestimate the degree to which total fertility may differ from completed fertility because, for simplicity, they assume that there are only two birth cohorts. The more cohorts and periods there are, the greater is the degree to which fertility timing may increase the difference between total and completed fertility. In practice, total fertility refers to women in seven quinquennial age groups aged 15–19 up to aged 45–49 and cohorts are defined by year of birth. Hence total fertility in 2000 is based on the average number of children born in 2000 to women who were born between 1952 and 1985. The completed fertility of the women born in 1952 became known in 2000 because this is the last year in which they can bear children. The completed fertility of the women born in 1952 was known by 2001, and so on until the completed fertility of the women born in 1985 will be known in 2034.

Total fertility in Japan during 1947–9 exceeded 4. The women contributing to this estimate were born between 1902 and 1935. The completed fertility of women born in 1932 was 2.02 (Table 6.3). Unfortunately, data are not available for completed fertility in Japan for women born between 1902 and 1931. They imply that completed fertility must have been high for these women. More probably, they imply that during 1947–9 there was a postwar baby boom. Completed fertility began to decrease for women born after 1960 (Table 6.3), so that completed fertility for women born in 1970 was only 1.5. The decrease in completed fertility contributed to the decrease in total fertility. Since total fertility in 2018 was 1.42, completed fertility for women born after 1970 will most probably turn out to be less than 1.4. Time will tell.

Since in the nature of things completed fertility data are only observed with a long delay, while total fertility may be calculated in real time, the popularity of the latter is self-explanatory. However, total fertility will tend to overstate true fertility if women are reducing their fertility relative to their predecessors, and if older women are postponing their fertility relative to younger women. It will take up to four decades to know what really happened.

Crude birth rates (CBR) may also misrepresent fertility, because they do not take account of the demographic composition of the population. CBR is expected to be greater in populations in which women of child bearing age are over-represented. CBR is expected to be smaller in elderly populations such as in Japan, which is an ageing society. Total fertility may be a superior measure than CBR because it refers to women of child bearing age. Ideally, however, completed fertility and birth spacing provide a complete picture of fertility.

Chapter 8 is devoted to Japan as the first country to adopt ZIP in 1996. We shall discuss Japanese demography in greater detail, including declining rates of marriage as well as the trend to marrying later. Our purpose here is more general, and is concerned with investigating economic rather than sociological and cultural change in Japan. Specifically, we draw on the economics of the family in general, and quantity–quality theory in particular (Becker 1992), to investigate whether the decrease in fertility that occurred in Japan after 2000 had anything to do with the New Abnormal.

## Demographic Theory

In their study of global fertility decline, Winter and Teitelbaum (2013) acknowledge the importance of quantity–quality theory (Becker 1992, henceforth QQT), but as demographers, they emphasize instead sociological explanations of fertility decline. Specifically, they argue that since World War Two there have been several major changes in society that paved the way to fertility decline. First, the traditional family has ceased to serve as the sole institution for raising children. Single parent families have become a common social feature. Second, cohabitation has rivaled marriage as a way for people of the opposite sex to live together. Third, divorce has become an accepted practice. Fourth, birth control and abortion have given women greater control over their fertility. Fifth, feminism has made women more aware of alternatives to motherhood. Sixth, the spread of education has enhanced the desire of both sexes to take charge of their destinies.

Whereas most of these developments reduced fertility, the first may have increased it. Women who might not have married and had children in the past may do so today as single parents. Also, fertility treatment that was not available in the past has enabled many women to have children today. On balance, however, the other developments mentioned were most probably dominant.

While the options for young men and women were limited prior to World War Two, not just with respect to fertility but also with respect to careers and self-fulfillment, young men and women have become increasingly liberated. The life prospects of Generation X and Millennials greatly exceed those of their grand-parents. Also, the prospect of divorce might have induced couples, and especially women, to reduce their fertility for fear of becoming unplanned single parents.

These developments suggest that fertility was expected to decline, especially in developed countries. However, in some countries, such as Italy and Spain, fertility decreased by more than in others, such as Australia and Sweden. Moreover, this decline is expected to be permanent. These developments should apply to all the countries in Table 6.1, since they were all exposed to them. They may explain why fertility declined in general, but they cannot explain why fertility in Japan continued its decline after 2000. Had fertility in Japan stabilized at its level in 1990, matters might have been different. What has to be explained is why fertility continued to decrease in Japan after 2000, and why it stabilized in 2015.

## Quality–Quantity Theory

The QQT of fertility developed by Becker (1992) has been influential across all the social sciences. Here we explain its main features as far as the New Abnormal is concerned. Specifically, we focus on the effect of the rate of interest and ZIP on fertility, and the effect of existential risk.

### Basic Model

The basic idea behind QQT is depicted in Figure 6.2 where the vertical axis measures human capital investment per child denoted by Q (for quality) and the number of children is denoted by N (for quantity). Parents face a trade-off between having more children and investing less in each child, and investing more in each child but having fewer children. Parents are assumed to value having more children (quantity), but they also value quality, as measured by the human capital they can invest in their children. The indifference curves in Figure 6.3 express parents' preferences between quality and quantity.

Because the number of children is discrete, these curves should be step-like, but they are drawn continuously for simplicity. The budget line is initially schedule $ab$; parents can afford to have $a$ children if they do not invest in them, or they can have one child only in whom they invest $b$ human capital. They may choose any integer combination of quantity and quality along the budget line. Given their preferences, parents maximize utility where indifference curve $U_0$ is tangential to the budget line. They have $N_0$ children and invest $Q_0$ human capital in each child.

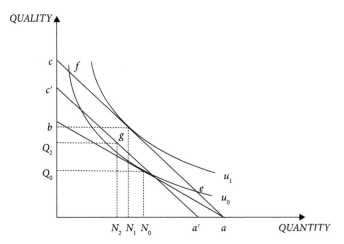

**Fig. 6.2** ZIP and Fertility

The slope of the budget line depends on the price of human capital relative to the direct cost of child rearing. The cheaper the relative price of human capital, the steeper is the budget line, as in schedule $ac$. The new parental choice must be on segment $ef$ of the new budget line. If quality and quantity are normal goods, their choice will be determined where indifference curve $U_1$ is tangential to the budget line so that they have fewer children ($N_1$) but invest more in them ($Q_1$).

Since human capital takes time to realize, the slope of the budget line depends on the rate of interest, because parents may borrow to pay for the education of their children. In Figure 6.2, we assume that loans are available for schooling, but not for current spending in raising children. Suppose the budget line is $ab$ when the rate of interest is positive, and is $ac$ when it is zero, i.e. they can afford to invest in more human capital because they can afford to borrow more. Therefore, under ZIP they will reduce their fertility but invest more in each child. However, if ZIP induces existential risk, the budget line $ac$ will contract towards the origin, e.g. to $a'c'$, because parents' permanent income is smaller. As a result, they will cut back on quality and quantity, but especially the latter. Hence, fertility decreases because of ZIP and existential risk, whereas investment in quality decreases because of existential risk, but increases because of ZIP.

## Parents as Stakeholders

This version of QQT may be too simple because it assumes that parents don't care about themselves; they only live for their children. Indeed, the consumption of parents is implicitly treated as a residual equal to their income minus the cost of raising and educating their children. It also assumes either that siblings are of equal ability or, if they are not, that their parents do not discriminate between them. For example, they do not compensate less able siblings by investing more in them, nor do they invest more in more able siblings whose return is higher. Nevertheless, Figure 6.2 captures the basic mechanism through which ZIP and fertility are related.

The version of QQT that we present below assumes that parents like having children but they also care about themselves. They are indirectly concerned about quality because parents expect that they will share in the income of their children when they (the parents) are old. They might be directly concerned about quality as in Figure 6.2, but in the interest of simplicity, this direct concern is ignored.

Individuals have three stages in their life cycle. They start out life as children, during which time their parents invest human capital in them. In stage 2 they use their human capital to earn a living, have children, educate them and transfer income to their parents. Parents are egalitarian towards their children, so they invest in them equally. In any case, their children are assumed to have the same return to human capital. In stage 3, as pensioners, they live off their savings (S) and transfers from their children (T). Since they leave no bequests, consumption in stage 3 is $C_3 = S(1 + r) + T$, where r denotes the rate of interest. Their budget line in stage 2 is $Y_p = C_2 + NP_N + NQP_Q + S$, where Yp is parents' permanent income in stage 2 net of transfers to their parents, $P_N$ is the unit cost of child rearing, and $P_Q$ is the unit cost of human capital. Transfers from children to parents in stage 3 are $T = \theta NY_c$, where $Y_c = \phi Q^\gamma$ denotes the earnings of children, $\theta$ is the transfer rate, and the return to human capital is $\gamma/Q$, where $\gamma$ is a positive fraction. Finally, parents' utility function in stage 2 is $U = C_2^\alpha C_3^{1-\alpha-\beta} N^\beta$, where $\alpha$ and $\beta$ are positive fractions.

The first-order conditions are:

$$\frac{\partial U}{\partial N} = -\alpha \frac{C_3}{C_2}(P_N + QP_Q) + (1 - \alpha - \beta)\phi\theta Q^\gamma + \beta\frac{C_3}{N} = 0 \qquad (2.1)$$

$$\frac{\partial U}{\partial Q} = -\alpha P_Q \frac{C_3}{C_2} + \phi\theta(1 - \alpha - \beta)Q^\gamma = 0 \qquad (2.2)$$

$$\frac{\partial U}{\partial S} = -\alpha \frac{C_3}{C_2} + (1 - \alpha - \beta)(1 + r) = 0 \qquad (2.3)$$

which, together with the intertemporal budget constraint, solve for consumption in stages 2 and 3, family size (N), investment in human capital per child (Q), and savings. Equations (2.1–2.3) have a convenient recursive structure. Equation (2.3) solves for $C_3/C_2$, which solves for Q when it is substituted into equation (2.2):

$$Q = \left[ \frac{\phi\theta\gamma}{P_Q(1+r)} \right]^{\frac{1}{1-\gamma}} \tag{2.4}$$

Equation (2.4) states that human capital per child varies inversely with its cost ($P_Q$) and the rate of interest, and it varies directly with its return ($\gamma$) and the transfer rate ($\theta$) from adult children to their elderly parents. Parents invest more in their children's human capital if they expect to benefit from its return through transfers. It also varies directly with $\phi$, which reflects parents' expectations in stage 2 of their children's earnings in stage 3. If parents are more optimistic about their children's economic prospects, $\phi$ will be larger. If parents are pessimistic about these prospects, $\phi$ will be smaller. Notice that Q does not depend on parents' income because they can borrow in stage 2 and redeem their debt in stage 3. Matters would be different if they were credit constrained.

Equation (2.1) solves for the number of children:

$$N = \frac{1}{\Omega}Y_p \tag{2.5}$$

$$\Omega = \frac{1}{\beta}\left[ P_N + QP_Q - \frac{\phi\theta Q^\gamma}{1+r} \right] = \frac{1}{\beta}\left[ P_N + \left(1 - \frac{1}{\gamma}\right) P_Q^{\frac{\gamma}{\gamma-1}} \left( \frac{\phi\theta\gamma}{1+r} \right)^{\frac{1}{1-\gamma}} \right]$$

where $\Omega$ is the inverse of the marginal propensity to have children, which must be positive. Since $\Omega$ varies directly with $P_N$, equation (2.5) implies that fertility varies inversely with the cost of rearing children. Since $\gamma$ is a positive fraction, $\Omega$ varies directly with $P_Q$, implying that, when educating children becomes more expensive, fertility decreases. The same applies when the rate of interest increases. $\Omega$ varies inversely with $\theta$, implying that fertility varies directly with the transfer rate.

When the rate of interest increases, parents reduce their investment in quality and they also reduce quantity. Quality and quantity are gross complements because parents do not invest in their children's human capital for itself, but for the economic security that it gives them. If $\theta$ was zero, they would not invest in them at all. Instead of rearing children and educating them, they would consume more over their life cycle. The present value of their consumption in stages 2 and 3 is:

$$PV(C) = \Theta Y_p \tag{2.6}$$

$$\Theta = 1 - \frac{1}{\Omega}\left[ P_N + QP_Q + \frac{\phi\theta}{1+r}Q^\gamma \right]$$

In summary, self-interested parents invest in quality because, like any other investment, they stand to benefit from it. When the rate of interest decreases under ZIP, they increase their current consumption, invest more in quality, and reduce their fertility. Therefore, despite its simplicity, Figure 6.2 is useful in summarizing the effect of ZIP on fertility through the slope of the budget line and the effect of existential risk through parallel contractions of the budget line.

In summary, QQT predicts that ZIP and existential risk reduce fertility. Since the adoption of ZIP precedes existential risk, the former is expected to occur before the latter.

## Population Ageing

This stakeholder version of QQT predicts that fertility will decline through population ageing, which increases the dependency ratio (pensioners divided by the working population). Chapter 8 records how, for example, life expectancy for men aged 70 increased from 7.93 years to 15.73 years in Japan between 1947 and 2017, and for women it increased from 9.41 to 20.3 years. If fertility is constant, this increase in longevity directly raises the numerator of the dependency ratio. The tax burden on the working population varies directly with the dependency ratio in social democracies because of the cost of state pensions and other age-related social security payments and benefits, as well as the cost of health and medical services, which increases with advanced age.

The basic QQT model predicts that, if the higher tax burden falls on the current generation of parents, the budget line in Figure 6.2 will contract, in which case fertility and quality will decrease. If it falls on the next generation, the stakeholder model predicts that the current generation of parents will have fewer children, who will have less human capital invested in them. Either way, an increase in longevity is expected to reduce fertility, which induces a further increase in the dependency ratio. Hence, longevity increases the dependency ratio directly, as well as indirectly, because it reduces fertility.

For expositional simplicity, in Figure 6.3 we ignore the dynamics induced by the fact that current parents eventually become senior citizens. Schedule A plots the inverse relation between the dependency ratio and fertility. It is convex to the origin because the dependency ratio is the ratio of senior citizens to the working population, or current parents. As fertility tends to zero, the dependency ratio naturally tends to infinity. Schedule A is drawn for given longevity of senior citizens. If their longevity increases, schedule A shifts to the right. Schedule B plots the inverse relation between fertility and the dependency ratio, predicted by QQT. It is drawn under the assumption that it is flatter than schedule A so that it intersects schedule A from below. The location of schedule B depends on the parameters of

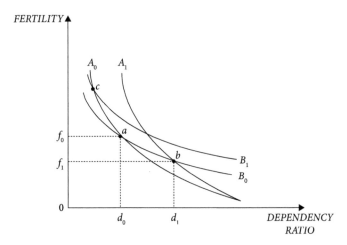

**Fig. 6.3** Fertility and Dependency in Transitional Equilibrium

QQT, including income, the cost of raising children and the rate of interest. For example, an increase in permanent income would raise schedule B.

Fertility and the dependency ratio are jointly determined at point $a$ where schedules $A_0$ and $B_0$ intersect. An autonomous increase in longevity shifts schedule A to $A_1$. The new equilibrium is at point $b$, at which fertility decreases and the dependency ratio increases. An autonomous increase in permanent income shifts schedule $B_0$ to $B_1$. The new equilibrium is at point $c$, at which fertility increases and the dependency ratio decreases. Had schedule A been flatter than schedule B, an increase in longevity would have increased fertility and reduced the dependency ratio, and an increase in permanent income would have reduced fertility and increased the dependency ratio. This is a theoretical possibility, which cannot be ruled out. Another theoretical possibility is that there are multiple equilibria because schedules A and B intersect more than once.

The equilibria in Figure 6.3 are inherently transitional. For example, the equilibrium at point $b$ lasts for up to two generations. Current parents have fewer children at point $b$. By the time these children become senior citizens, the dependency ratio decreases. However, schedule $A_0$ is not restored because in the new steady state the longevity of senior citizens is greater than it was at point $a$. Hence, after the transition is completed, fertility in the steady state will be less than $f_0$ (but greater than $f_1$) and the dependency ratio will be greater than $d_0$ (but less than $d_1$). Since the transition is spread over two generations, Figure 6.3 is useful for analyzing, for example, developments in countries such as Japan where the increase in longevity among senior citizens has been particularly pronounced.

## Empirical Analysis

On the face of it, the international decline in fertility (Table 6.1) is consistent with QQT because real interest rates have been decreasing (Chapter 5), human capital

**Table 6.5** Mean Years of Schooling

| | Australia | France | Germany | Italy | Japan | US | UK | Spain | Sweden | Israel |
|---|---|---|---|---|---|---|---|---|---|---|
| **1970–1** | 9.73 | | | 5.32 | 9.64 | 11.18 | | 4.71 | 6.53 | 7.43 |
| **1980–1** | | | | 5.36 | 10.6 | 12.5 | | 4.93 | | 9.11 |
| **1990–1** | 10.80 | 7.57 | 8.80 | 7.30 | 9.60 | 12.68 | 7.90 | 6.00 | 10.50 | 10.80 |
| **1995** | | | | | | 12.89 | | | 11.42 | |
| **2000** | 11.9 | 9.80 | 11.20 | 8.60 | 10.70 | 12.70 | 11.70 | 9.80 | 11.44 | 12.00 |
| **2005** | 11.86 | 12.59 | 13.6 | 9.19 | | 13.05 | | 8.97 | 12.42 | 10.82 |
| **2010** | 12.60 | 13.76 | 13.85 | 9.72 | 11.5 | 13.20 | 13.20 | 10.90 | 12.30 | 12.60 |
| **2014–5** | 12.28 | 13.9 | 14.08 | 10.19 | | 13.41 | 12.94 | 9.97 | 12.43 | 13.04 |
| **2017–8** | 12.70 | 14.05 | 14.03 | 10.20 | 12.80 | 13.40 | 13.40 | 11.40 | 12.40 | 13.00 |

*Source*: UNESCO database (October 2020). Human Development Reports (UNDP).

has been increasing (Tables 6.5, 6.6A, and 6.6B), and dependency ratios have been increasing (Table 6.7). The decrease in the cost of capital induced parents to have fewer children, and to increase investment in their human capital, i.e. less quantity and more quality. This would only have a causal interpretation if the decrease in real interest rates was independent of fertility.

Table 6.5 reports mean years of schooling for the OECD countries, which were the focus of attention in Chapters 4 and 5. Recall that high school completion is equivalent to 12 years of schooling, and first degree completion is equivalent to 15 years of schooling. Mean years of schooling have doubled since 1970 in Italy, Spain, Sweden, and Israel and have also doubled in France since 1990, suggesting that this measure of quality is beta-convergent. By 2018, mean years of schooling were broadly similar between countries, although Spain and Italy continue to lag behind.

In 2000, mean years of schooling ranged between 8.97 years in Spain and 13.05 years in the US. All countries increased their mean years of schooling after 2000. Mean years of schooling increased by 2.1 years in Japan. Only France and Germany registered a greater increase.

Table 6.6A reports an alternative measure of quality in terms of the proportion of young people who have completed higher education. The proportion increased in all countries, doubling from a low base since 1990 in the US and UK, Australia, France, Germany, and Sweden, and tripling from a lower base in Italy and Spain. In Israel and Japan, the base was high to begin with. However, since 2000 the proportion in Israel has increased by 6 percentage points, whereas in Japan it has increased by twice as much.

A similar story is told in Table 6.6B, which refers to older workers with tertiary education. The proportions in Table 6.6B are naturally smaller than in Table 6.6A because the former belong to earlier birth cohorts. For example, in 1981, rates of tertiary education among younger people in the US were twice as large as for their older counterparts. However, by 2019, older workers had closed much of the gap

Table 6.6A  Aged 25–34 with Tertiary Education (Percent)

|        | Australia | France | Germany | Italy | Japan | US | UK | Spain | Sweden | Israel |
|--------|-----------|--------|---------|-------|-------|------|------|-------|--------|--------|
| **1981**   |        | 15.12 |        |      |       | 23.28 |      | 9.84  | 23.56 |       |
| **1990–1** | 34.14  | 20.08 | 18.37  | 6.60 |       | 23.76 |      | 16.35 | 25.73 |       |
| **1995**   | 22.84  | 25.4  | 21.27  | 8.22 | 45.74 | 33.60 | 24.68 | 26.61 | 28.59 |       |
| **2000**   | 31.37  | 31.38 | 22.25  | 10.43 | 47.87 | 38.08 | 28.90 | 33.98 | 33.64 | 40.75 |
| **2005**   | 36.32  | 39.78 | 22.49  | 16.11 | 53.19 | 39.36 | 35.35 | 40.70 | 37.29 | 42.93 |
| **2010**   | 44.37  | 42.87 | 26.13  | 20.72 | 56.71 | 42.31 | 46.05 | 40.31 | 42.23 | 44.22 |
| **2015**   | 48.47  | 44.69 | 29.59  | 25.15 | 59.65 | 46.52 | 49.94 | 40.96 | 46.41 | 45.90 |
| **2019**   | 52.48  | 48.9  | 33.26  | 27.74 | 61.51 | 50.38 | 51.81 | 47.04 | 48.37 | 47.04 |

*Source*: OECD-Stat. July 2020

Table 6.6B  Aged 55–64 with Tertiary Education (Percent)

|        | Australia | France | Germany | Italy | Japan | US | UK | Spain | Sweden | Israel |
|--------|-----------|--------|---------|-------|-------|------|------|-------|--------|--------|
| **1981**   |        | 5.81  |        |      |       | 12.12 |      | 3.04  | 8.33  |       |
| **1990–1** | 20.45  | 7.52  | 11.78  | 3.21 |       | 17.05 |      | 4.21  | 15.48 |       |
| **1995**   | 17.19  | 8.87  | 17.62  | 4.43 | 13.70 | 24.75 | 16.11 | 6.04  | 20.74 |       |
| **2000**   | 19.08  | 12.90 | 20.19  | 5.53 | 15.14 | 29.66 | 18.85 | 9.80  | 22.96 | 41.81 |
| **2005**   | 23.85  | 16.12 | 22.92  | 8.02 | 21.73 | 36.95 | 23.86 | 14.47 | 24.95 | 42.47 |
| **2010**   | 29.63  | 18.28 | 25.35  | 10.67 | 28.97 | 40.96 | 29.96 | 17.65 | 27.23 | 44.58 |
| **2015**   | 33.93  | 22.13 | 25.61  | 12.25 | 38.18 | 41.44 | 36.35 | 22.81 | 29.89 | 47.23 |
| **2019**   | 34.94  | 24.42 | 26.92  | 12.8 | 44.49 | 43.37 | 38.66 | 26.66 | 32.13 | 46.87 |

*Source*: OECD-Stat. July 2020.

with respect to their younger counterparts through acquiring adult education. An unusual exception is Israel, where tertiary rates of education among older people are only slightly smaller than for younger people.

In Table 6.6B, Spain and Italy continue to stand out in tripling the proportions with tertiary education. However, in contrast to Table 6.6A, this proportion also increased in Japan, suggesting that, since 2000, older workers in Japan invested in tertiary education more than their counterparts in Germany, Australia etc. Consequently, older Japanese workers closed much of the tertiary education gap from 32 percentage points in 1995 to 17 percentage points in 2019.

Unlike other indicators considered here, dependency ratios have not increased steadily. The dependency ratio in Japan decreased between 1970 and 2000 before increasing strongly subsequently. In terms of Figure 6.3, the increase in longevity might have shifted schedule B to the right, inducing a decrease in fertility. Had there instead been an autonomous decrease in fertility, schedule A would have shifted downwards, inducing a decrease in fertility as well as the dependency ratio. Since 2000, dependency ratios have tended to increase in all the countries in

**Table 6.7** Dependency Ratios (Population aged 65+ percent of population of working age)

|  | Australia | France | Germany | Italy | Japan | US | UK | Spain | Sweden | Israel |
|---|---|---|---|---|---|---|---|---|---|---|
| **1960** | 63.38 | 63.38 | 49.04 | 52.89 | 55.97 | 66.13 | 53.66 | 55.22 | 51.96 | 69.87 |
| **1970** | 59.74 | 60.44 | 58.55 | 55.71 | 44.91 | 61.68 | 59.23 | 60.64 | 52.76 | 64.62 |
| **1980** | 53.67 | 57.07 | 52.09 | 54.64 | 48.14 | 52.06 | 56.17 | 58.82 | 56.03 | 71.48 |
| **1990** | 49.58 | 51.78 | 44.62 | 45.66 | 43.56 | 52.20 | 53.17 | 50.11 | 55.63 | 67.17 |
| **2000** | 49.71 | 53.76 | 47.41 | 48.39 | 46.55 | 51.60 | 53.67 | 45.78 | 55.58 | 61.57 |
| **2010** | 47.95 | 54.63 | 51.79 | 52.68 | 55.89 | 49.67 | 51.66 | 46.73 | 53.20 | 60.54 |
| **2015** | 50.92 | 59.32 | 52.52 | 55.43 | 63.96 | 51,21 | 55.11 | 50.50 | 58.49 | 64.17 |
| **2019** | 54.31 | 61.79 | 54.71 | 56.69 | 68.28 | 53.28 | 56.75 | 52.03 | 60.83 | 66.93 |

*Source*: World Bank. July 2020.

Table 6.7. However, in half of them, dependency ratios in 2019 were lower than in 1960. What stands out is the increase in the dependency ratio in Japan, and the consistently high dependency ratio in Israel.

Thus far, it appears that human capital grew differentially in Japan after 2000 with respect to other countries. It also appears that fertility decreased differentially in Japan. If so, it is arguable that, because Japan descended into ZIP in 1996, which was 13 years ahead of other countries, the lower cost of capital induced Japanese parents to invest more in quality at the expense of quantity. If this is true, we might reasonably expect fertility rates to decline in other countries that adopted ZIP. In countries such as the US, UK, and Sweden, which adopted ZIP in 2008–9, the decrease in fertility might be expected soon. Indeed, perhaps Table 6.1 hints at the start of this development in 2018.

If quality and quantity are normal goods, QQT predicts that, given the cost of raising children and the cost of educating them, fertility and schooling should vary directly with income. Hence, in better-off countries schooling and fertility should be greater than in less well-off countries. Since GDP per head in Table 6.8 is adjusted for cost-of-living differentials, Americans have been best-off since 1950, whereas Germans and Japanese, who were understandably among the worst-off in 1950, were among the best-off in 2018.

Since 1980, GDP per head has grown between 1.66 percent per annum in Australia and 2.46 percent in Germany. In Japan, GDP per head has grown by only 0.9 percent per annum since 2000 and by 0.95 percent in Italy. Since 2010, GDP per head decreased in Australia, and only Germany (2.44 percent) and Israel (3.4 percent) maintained their historical rates of growth.

What matters for fertility according to QQT is not only income per head, but also the affordability of children defined as permanent income relative to the cost of raising children. If the cost of raising children varies proportionately with permanent income, the affordability of children will remain unchanged. The US

**Table 6.8** GDP per Head (PPP adjusted at 2011 US Dollars)

|  | Australia | France | Germany | Italy | Japan | US | UK | Spain | Sweden | Israel |
|---|---|---|---|---|---|---|---|---|---|---|
| **1950** | 12,282 | 6849 | 4643 | 4076 | 2530 | 14,569 | 9354 | 3432 | 9136 | 5140 |
| **1960** | 14,223 | 10,020 | 9937 | 6844 | 4945 | 17,463 | 11,910 | 5677 | 11,766 | 8205 |
| **1970** | 19,375 | 15,714 | 14,044 | 11,783 | 11,876 | 23,285 | 15,025 | 10,556 | 17,288 | 13,215 |
| **1980** | 22,172 | 22,410 | 19,533 | 19,802 | 18,930 | 29,155 | 19,840 | 14,372 | 19,754 | 16,560 |
| **1990** | 26,560 | 24,327 | 24,941 | 24,393 | 26,780 | 36,222 | 22,563 | 16,604 | 26,491 | 20,892 |
| **2000** | 35,218 | 31,161 | 33,330 | 32,352 | 34,570 | 45,859 | 31,526 | 25,247 | 34,393 | 31,340 |
| **2010** | 44,854 | 35,786 | 40,627 | 34,727 | 36,595 | 49,501 | 34,810 | 31,610 | 40,422 | 28,639 |
| **2017** | 43,376 | 39,461 | 48,107 | 38,000 | 40,374 | 54,795 | 39,128 | 35,696 | 43,376 | 36,186 |

*Source*: Penn World Tables 9.1. July 2020.

Department of Agriculture (USDA) has been calculating the cost of raising children in the US since 1960 by state and income group. For example, in 1960 the average cost of raising a child up to age 18 for parents on middle incomes was estimated at $202,020 in constant 2015 prices. Note that this excludes college education. By 2015, USDA estimated this cost at $233,610, or a modest increase of 15.6 percent over 55 years. During the same period, GDP per capita increased by more than 200 percent (6.8) in the US. Hence, according to USDA, raising a child in the US became increasingly affordable.

In 2016, the cost of raising a child in the UK was estimated to be £231,843, which is obviously greater than the USDA estimate. Despite the fact that GDP per head is much greater in the US than in the UK, the cost of raising a child in the UK is much greater than in the US, partly because the cost of housing is greater, and also because the cost of living is higher. In 2001, the cost of raising a child in Japan was estimated at $238,350at current prices. Table 6.9 summarizes what little is known about the cost of child rearing. Whereas for the US estimates are available for different years, the estimates reported in Table 6.9 for other countries are only available for single years, which means that it is not possible to calculate the affordability of children over time within countries, apart from the US.

Although the estimates in Table 6.9 are rough, they suggest that it is cheapest to raise children in New Zealand and Germany and it is most expensive in Japan and the UK. These cross-section data do not suggest that the cost of child rearing is necessarily more expensive in richer countries. This suggestion is consistent with USDA's time series data for the US.

Ogawa, Matsukura and Lee (2016) studied the relationship between the affordability of children and total fertility in Japan and several other countries in South East Asia by pooling time series data for these countries. They found that fertility is inversely related to affordability.

Table 6.9  The Cost of Rearing a Child in 2015

|  | $ at 2015 prices |
| --- | --- |
| US | 233,610 |
| UK | 313,593 |
| Canada | 259,591 |
| Australia | 223,200 |
| Germany | 154,015 |
| New Zealand | 175,723 |
| Japan | 238,350 (2001) |

*Source*: US: US Department of Agriculture (USDA). UK: Child Poverty Action Group. Canada: MoneySense. Australia and New Zealand: Kendig, McDonald and Piggot (2016). Japan: Ogawa, Matsukura and Lee (2016).

## Discussion

This chapter is particularly speculative. We ask whether fertility decline in Japan is a consequence of the New Abnormal. If the answer is positive, this would constitute a major extension of the central thesis in this book. It would mean that, just as business investors invest less because they are fearful of existential risk, so do potential parents curtail their fertility out of fear for their future and their children's future. If, on the other hand, the answer is negative, it would not detract from the central thesis; it would simply mean that fertility behaves differently from investment.

The focus on Japan stems from the fact that it adopted ZIP and the New Abnormal 25 years ago. Trends in demographic phenomena, such as fertility, are slower to emerge than trends in economic phenomena such as investment. Consequently, there is little if anything to be learnt from countries such as the UK, which entered the New Abnormal a decade ago, and even less from Italy and Spain, which joined the New Abnormal less than a decade ago. If the New Abnormal lasts another decade, it will eventually be possible to study the relation between fertility and the New Abnormal in other countries. Meanwhile, we are left with Japan to carry out our investigation. This means that, even if fertility decline in Japan happens to be related to the New Abnormal, it might not apply more generally. Ideally, to corroborate a hypothesis, data are required for other countries apart from Japan.

There is, on the other hand, a strong theoretical prediction that the New Abnormal should induce fertility decline. According to quality–quantity theory, fertility is expected to decrease for a number of reasons. First, ZIP reduces the relative price of quality to quantity because it makes schooling cheaper without changing the cost of child rearing. Parents have an incentive to have fewer children and to invest more in their schooling. Second, existential risk adversely affects parents' demand for quality and quantity because they expect economic disruption to break out when ZIP and the New Abnormal break down. Third, if aged parents benefit from income transfers from their adult children, parents have a further incentive to curtail quality and quantity. Hence, there are three reasons why the New Abnormal is expected to decrease fertility, whereas its effect on quality is ambiguous; there are two reasons why quality should decrease and one reason why it should increase.

On the whole, the global trend in fertility reduction is consistent with quality–quantity theory. Skill-biased technical progress has increased the return to human capital both directly and indirectly through increased life expectancy. The latter has the same effect on investment in human capital that longer life times of physical capital have on investment in plant and especially machinery. If the cost of rearing children remains unchanged, quality–quantity theory predicts that parents will have fewer children and invest more in their human capital. In the specific case of Japan, fertility has been in secular decline since 1950. Fertility continued its decline with the adoption of ZIP and the New Abnormal, but stabilized after 2015. The latter appears to conflict with our theory. On the other hand, it is arguable that fertility stabilized because it hit a natural lower limit; it could no longer continue to decrease. Just as interest rates have zero lower bounds, so do fertility rates.

If indeed the New Abnormal encourages fertility decline, the prospects for economic growth are doubly bleak. Not only will existential risk continue to undermine business investment, it will eventually adversely affect labor supply. On the other hand, the labor force will be more educated because ZIP lowers the cost of investment in human capital. Perhaps the latter will promote technical progress during the 21$^{st}$ century.

The potential parents who have been the focus in this chapter are Generation X and Millennials. The life cycles of their baby boomer antecedents were lived out under the Old Normal, which was characterized by relative prosperity. They raised families and invested in careers with confidence. Generation X and Millennials have come of age under the New Abnormal, which is characterized by slower economic growth and a future shrouded by existential risk. They are struggling. They look forward with trepidation; they are not confident. To a large extent, the rise of the New Abnormal has contributed to the so-called war between the generations.

In summary, the data are not inconsistent with the hypothesis that the decline in Japanese fertility is related to the adoption of ZIP and the New Abnormal. Fertility would have had to fall to less than one (as in South Korea) to be more confident about the adverse effect of ZIP and the New Abnormal on fertility.

## Synopsis

During the last 40 years fertility has been decreasing among OECD countries. This trend was established well ahead of the New Abnormal. However, fertility decline intensified in Japan since ZIP was adopted in 1996. We ask whether this could have anything to do with the New Abnormal. Just as business investment suffered during the New Abnormal, despite the fact that ZIP should have encouraged investment, perhaps parents, like investors, are fearful of the future and are reluctant to have children.

An important difference between investment and having children is that, whereas ZIP was expected to encourage investment, it is expected to reduce fertility according to the influential quality–quantity theory of fertility because it is cheaper to finance the schooling of children. This creates an incentive to invest in quality at the expense of quality.

Since changes in fertility are slow to occur, Japan provides the main opportunity to study the relationship between fertility and the New Abnormal because twenty-five years have passed since it adopted ZIP. By contrast, it is most probably too early to investigate the relation between fertility and the New Abnormal in countries that adopted the New Abnormal more recently. This, no doubt, is yet another reason why investment and having children are inherently different.

Matters are complicated by the fact that fertility has been declining globally. Hence, the main issue is, did it decline more rapidly in Japan? Since fertility decline was particularly pronounced in Italy, Spain and South Korea (where fertility is less than 1!), it is difficult to reach clear conclusions about the relation between fertility decline and the New Abnormal. At the very least, it cannot be ruled out that the steep decline in fertility in Japan is unrelated to its deep involvement in the New Abnormal.

# 7

# Socioeconomic Consequences of the New Abnormal

Apart from the potential implications of the New Abnormal for fertility (Chapter 6), in this chapter we focus on a number of other socioeconomic consequences. The first concerns the pensions of Generation X and Millennials. If ZIP continues, these cohorts will be worse off when they retire than when their boomer antecedents retired, because the risk-free rate of interest for the former will continue to be zero, whereas the latter benefited from positive rates of interest during their working lives. Hence, future pensioners will be less well off than current pensioners. This issue is quite separate from the large public sector debt that Generation X and Millennials will inherit (Chapters 5 and 10), and their future tax burden generated by increasing dependency ratios (Chapter 6). There is a rational basis to the intergenerational discontent expressed by Millennials and Generation X. The New Abnormal is impoverishing them. We shall return to this intergenerational inequity in Chapter 10. For the moment, our focus is on the implications of ZIP for future pensioners.

The second concern is with intragenerational inequality rather than intergenerational inequity. This concern has attracted much media attention as well as academic attention. Whereas, according to the former, ZIP has increased economic inequality, results from academic studies are mixed. In their review of twenty-two studies of the effect of unorthodox monetary policy on economic inequality, Colciago, Samarina, and de Haan (2019) report that eight studies concluded that inequality increased, eight studies concluded that inequality was either not affected or negligibly affected, and six studies concluded that unorthodox monetary policy reduced inequality. The direct effects of ZIP are more obvious than their indirect effects. ZIP directly benefits net debtors and harms net creditors because the former pay less debt interest and the latter receive less interest. If ZIP inflates the price of capital assets (Chapter 2), asset holders benefit from capital gains. Mortgagees benefit twice because their mortgages are less expensive and their houses are worth more. If indeed ZIP prevented economic depression in the wake of the Subprime Crisis, workers would have been less likely to become unemployed. It is hardly surprising that academic results are so diverse; the indirect effects are difficult to quantify and are sensitive to how models are parametrized.

*Zero Interest Policy and the New Abnormal.* Michael Beenstock, Oxford University Press. © Michael Beenstock (2022).
DOI: 10.1093/oso/9780192849663.003.0007

Some of these results are based on DSGE models that were heavily criticized in Chapter 3. These models are "patched-up" in the sense of Chapter 3 to calibrate the effect of ZIP and quantitative easing on personal inequality. In Chapter 4 we focused on the implications of the New Abnormal for the factorial distribution of income in terms of neoclassical theory, according to which ZIP should have promoted investment and increased the capital–labor ratio. On the other hand, existential risk would have had the opposite effect because it reduces capital investment. In Chapter 4 we concluded that the capital–labor ratio, or the capital intensity of production, affects the factorial distribution depending on the technology of production as expressed by the elasticity of substitution between labor and capital.

In the present chapter we explore the implications of this neoclassical macroeconomic theory of the factorial distribution of income for the microeconomics of economic inequality. Specifically, we study the theoretical relation between profit shares and labor shares in national income for such popular measures of individual or household income inequality as the Gini coefficient. We also study the empirical relation over time between factor shares in national income and the Gini coefficient. In doing so, we may study the implications of the New Abnormal for personal inequality through its effect on the Gini coefficient.

Perhaps at this point it should be mentioned that the neoclassical theory of the factorial distribution of national income has important rivals, such as the "widow's cruse" theory (Kaldor 1956), in which workers and capitalists have different rates of saving, and Kalecki (1938), which involves monopolistic pricing by owners of capital. The nexus explored below between the factorial distribution, which is a macroeconomic phenomenon, and income inequality, which is a microeconomic phenomenon, is not dependent on the theory of the factorial distribution of income, neoclassical, Kaldorian, or whatever.

The third concern is with the price of housing. There is a consensus among economists that lower interest rates increase house prices. On the other hand, contracting populations decrease house prices, as do contractions in permanent income. If permanent income varies inversely with existential risk, and, as suggested in Chapter 6, fertility decline might be a feature of the New Abnormal, this implies that house prices should decrease. Hence, the implications of ZIP and the New Abnormal for house prices are ambiguous, especially in the longer term.

The fourth concern is insurance pricing. Since ZIP and quantitative easing reduce market rates of interest, it increases insurance premiums because insurance companies earn less on their premium income. This may be less of a social concern than fertility, pensions, inequality, and house prices. However, insurance seems to be the only service whose pricing may be directly affected by ZIP.

## Pensions

Due to compound interest, the value of pensions on retirement is very sensitive to the rates of return on the assets in which pensions funds are invested. On retirement, pension income varies directly with the value of pension funds and interest rates during the period of retirement. Consequently, ZIP is doubly important for pensioners, because it reduces the value of pension funds on retirement, and because it reduces the annuities that pensioners will be able to obtain as pension income. Baby boomers would have retired in or around 2010, having saved towards their pension since the late 1960s. During this period interest rates were relatively high (Chapter 5), so that by 2010 their pension fund was relatively valuable. Unfortunately, their retirement coincided with ZIP, so the pension income that they could buy with their pension fund was relatively low. At least they had a good run for their money until 2010.

The parents of baby boomers had a good run for their money before and also after retirement until they died. They would have retired in the late 1970s, having saved since the end of World War Two, and the annuity that their pension fund would have bought would have been relatively good because ZIP had not yet happened. Generation X and Millennials would have entered the labor force just as ZIP began. Thus far they will have seen little or no return on their savings. If ZIP continues into their retirement, they will have had a bad run for their money during their working lives and during their retirement. From this point of view, they will be twice cursed, just as their grandparents were twice blessed.

### Pension Income and Interest

Let S denote annual pension contributions paid at the beginning of the year during n years, and r denote the rate of interest. The value of the pension fund on retirement is:

$$V = S\frac{1+r}{r}\left[(1+r)^n - 1\right] \tag{1.1}$$

which is proportionate to S and varies directly with r and n. On retirement, V buys an annuity (A) paid at the beginning of the year during m years in retirement:

$$A = V\frac{r}{1+r}\frac{1}{1-(1+r)^{-m}} \tag{1.2}$$

which is proportionate to V, and varies directly with r and inversely with m. Substituting equation (1.1) into equation (1.2) implies that the annuity equals:

$$A = S \frac{(1+r)^n - 1}{1 - (1+r)^{-m}} \tag{1.3}$$

which is proportionate to S, varies directly with r and n and inversely with m.

In case 1 in Table 7.1, an individual contributes $300 per year during forty years to his or her pension fund when the annual rate of interest is 4 percent. The value of the pension fund on retirement is $29,647. If the rate of interest during retirement continues to be 4 percent, this fund will buy an annuity of $1,624 over twenty-five years. If instead the rate of interest is 2 percent (case 2), the pension fund is worth $18,483 on retirement, which will buy an annuity of $928. Notice that the ratio of case 1 to case 2 equals 2 for the rate of interest, 1.6 for the value of the pension fund and 1.75 for pension income. The former is induced by compound interest; hence, doubling the rate of interest does not double the value of the pension fund on retirement. The latter is due to the fact that working lives are longer than retirement.

Note that both the value of the pension fund and the annuity are proportionate to annual saving. Hence, to buy $1 of annuity in case 1, it is necessary to save $0.185 per year when the rate of interest is 4 percent. Under ZIP (case 3) it is necessary to save $0.625 per year.

In case 3 the rate of interest is zero (ZIP). Hence the pension fund is worth 40 x $300 on retirement and the annuity is $12,000. Annuities under ZIP (case 3) are approximately only 30 percent of their pre-ZIP counterparts (case 1). In case 4 the rate of interest is 4 percent on savings and zero during retirement. ZIP reduces annuities by 27 percent compared to case 1. In case 5 the rate of interest on savings is zero, but the rate of interest in retirement is 4 percent. Hence coming out of ZIP increases annuities by 54 percent compared to case 3.

Table 7.1  Pension and Interest

| Case | Interest rate | | Pension fund | Annuity |
|------|------|------|------|------|
| | Before retirement | After retirement | | |
| 1 | 4 | 4 | 29,647 | 1824 |
| 2 | 2 | 2 | 18,483 | 928 |
| 3 | 0 | 0 | 12,000 | 480 |
| 4 | 4 | 0 | 29,647 | 1186 |
| 5 | 0 | 4 | 12,000 | 739 |

Saving = 300 per year during n = 40 years. Pension (P) during m = 25 years.

Although these calculations are artificial, they nevertheless remind us of the powerful effect that interest rates have on pensions. They are artificial because interest rates and pension contributions do not remain constant. Nor does the onset of ZIP or its termination coincide with retirement. Implicitly in Table 7.1 the rates of interest are risk-free. In general, larger rates of return may be obtained by incurring risk. Furthermore, it is implicitly assumed in Table 7.1 that all individuals survive sixty-five years after entering the labor force. Perhaps this is an advantage because it unbundles life insurance, discussed below, from pension income, which is our present concern.

## Japan

It requires many decades of data to study the long-term effect of ZIP on pensions. Therefore, as in the case of fertility where the focus was on Japan (Chapter 6), we focus on Japan once more to study the relation between pensions and the New Abnormal. Ideally, we would wish to compare baby boomers with their parents, because the latter were not affected by ZIP whereas the former were affected by ZIP in their retirement. This comparison requires data for the pensions of baby boomers' parents, which are available in Household Income Surveys for the 1970s through the 1990s, but it also requires data for the pensions of baby boomers during the 2010s through the 2030s. For countries that adopted ZIP after 2010, the relevant period would be the 2020s through the 2040s. If ZIP continues into the 2040s, it will be feasible to carry out this comparison in twenty years' time, but not now.

An even better comparison would be between the parents of baby boomers and their grandchildren, because the latter would have spent their entire lives under ZIP, and not just their working lives. The data for this comparison will not be available until Generation X and Millennials eventually become pensioners. Therefore, this comparison is even less feasible than the previous one.

As discussed in Chapter 8, Japan has complicated arrangements for retirement (OECD 2019, Japanese National Pension Service http://www.nwnkin.go.jp/). First, there is a statutory age of retirement regarding entitlement to state pensions, which is currently 60 years, and is planned to be raised to 65 years for men by 2025 and for women by 2030. Currently state pensions may be deferred until 70 years in return for a larger pension. Eligibility for other social security benefits are also age-related to encourage workers to remain in the labor force for longer. Third, employers are entitled to set a mandatory age of retirement, which terminates lifetime employment contracts. Until recently, the mandatory age of retirement was 55 years. Since the statutory age of retirement was raised to 60 years, many workers have continued their employment with the same employer, but at a lower wage.

In Chapter 8 we review recent developments about the relation between mandatory and statutory ages of retirement.

Japan's pension system has three tiers (Watanabe 1996). First, adults of working age are required to contribute to the Government Pension Fund (GPF), which provides a basic flat pension for all. Second, they contribute to the GPF to obtain earnings-related supplements to their basic pension. Third, private pension plans, including Tax Qualified Pension Funds and Employee Pension Fund Plans, are available under the responsibility of the Pension Fund Association. These include occupational pensions provided by larger firms, as well as a range of defined-contribution and defined-benefit funds, which are funded and earnings-related. Beneficiaries contract out from the earnings-related component of their GPF pension. Whereas everybody is entitled to a basic state pension, only a large minority is entitled to occupational and private pensions.

The insured GPF population was stable at about 70 million from 1990 until 2010, after which it decreased to 67 million by 2018 in line with Japan's negative demographics. In 1991 there were 9.77 million subscribers to private Tax Qualified Pension Plans and 10.7 million subscribers to private Employee Pension Funds (EPF). During the 2000s most of the latter were replaced by Defined Benefit Plans (DBP) and Defined Contribution Plans (DCP). By 2013 there were only 4.08 million covered by EPFs, whereas DBPs and DCPs, which were zero in 2000, had grown to 7.88 million and 4.64 million respectively. However, the total number increased from 11 million in 2001 to 16.4 million subsequently. Since 2013 these trends have continued; the numbers covered by private pension plans have increased from about 30 percent of the GPF-insured population in the early 1990s, to 40 percent in 2013, increasing towards 50 percent by 2020.

Contributions to GPF are invested by the Government Pension Investment Fund (GPIF), which until recently was among the largest sovereign funds in the world. However, unlike private pensions, which are set according to economic and actuarial criteria, the government pension is decided politically. As we shall see in Chapter 8, a demographic timebomb is threatening the solvency of GPF, because the working population is decreasing while the population of pensioners is increasing.

Table 7.2 chronicles the assumed (by fund managers) and actual returns on the National Pension Fund. It makes clear that since 2000 the performance of the fund was both more volatile and returns were lower. It suggests that under the New Abnormal performance as a whole deteriorated. It also suggests that assumed rates of return are uncorrelated with actual rates of return. However, these discrepancies tend to balance each other out. The average assumed return was 3.21 percent and the average actual return was 3.56 percent.

Figure 7.1 chronicles the performance of the privately run EPF. Like Table 7.2 for the state-run fund, performance is more volatile and weaker after 2000. Indeed, matters begin to change with the onset of the "lost decade" (1990–2000). Despite

**Table 7.2** Investment Performance of the National Pension Fund

| Fiscal year | Assumed return | Return | Fiscal year | Assumed return | Return |
|---|---|---|---|---|---|
| 1991 | 5.50 | 4.91 | 2004 | 1.75 | 5.51 |
| 1992 | 5.50 | 5.58 | 2005 | 1.75 | 21.99 |
| 1993 | 5.50 | 4.05 | 2006 | 1.75 | 4.27 |
| 1994 | 5.50 | 0.93 | 2007 | 1.75 | −11.65 |
| 1995 | 4.75 | 10.00 | 2008 | 1.75 | −23.38 |
| 1996 | 4.75 | 2.22 | 2009 | 1.75 | 22.52 |
| 1997 | 4.75 | 5.59 | 2010 | 1.75 | −1.32 |
| 1998 | 4.75 | 1.82 | 2011 | 1.75 | 2.99 |
| 1999 | 4.75 | 12.98 | 2012 | 1.75 | 12.19 |
| 2000 | 4.00 | −11.23 | 2013 | 1.75 | 9.26 |
| 2001 | 4.00 | −4.75 | 2014 | 1.50 | 13.7 |
| 2002 | 3.00 | −13.35 | 2015 | 1.50 | −2.98 |
| 2003 | 3.00 | 17.63 | **Average** | 3.21 | 3.56 |

*Source:* Takayama (2016), The Annual Report of the NPF for Medical Doctors.

**Fig. 7.1** Investment Performance of Employees' Pension Fund
Source: Takayama (2016).

occasional large and positive returns during the New Abnormal, Figure 7.1 shows that returns were mainly negative. In these respects, the investment performance for the EPF was worse than its state-run counterpart in Table 7.2.

We use the Survey of Household Income and Expenditure (SHIE) for Japan undertaken by the Statistics Bureau of Japan to track pension income for successive retirement cohorts. These surveys are undertaken every five years, and started in 1994. Table 7.3 reports income from state pensions from 1994 and private pensions from 1999. The latter refer to occupational and private pensions. Since the data refer to age groups, each SHIE survey refers to a number of pension cohorts. For example, in 1994 the state pension income for couples without earned income aged 65 to 69 was ¥3.992 million per year, accounting for 87 percent of current income. Income from interest and dividends amounted to ¥0.171 million. In 1994, SHEI did not include data on private pensions. These

**Table 7.3** Pension Income in Japan (Yen 1000s per annum, 2015 prices)

| Age | Couple with earner | | | Couple with no earner | | |
|---|---|---|---|---|---|---|
| | 65–9 | 70–4 | 75+ | 65–9 | 70–4 | 75+ |
| **1994** | | | | | | |
| Current income | 6689 | 6387 | 5791 | 3992 | 3848 | 3576 |
| Public pension | 2538 | 2410 | 2324 | 3463 | 3463 | 3132 |
| Interest and dividends | 134 | 178 | 155 | 171 | 180 | 146 |
| Company and private pension | na | na | na | na | na | na |
| **1999** | | | | | | |
| Current income | 6248 | 6539 | 5851 | 3909 | 4040 | 3614 |
| Public pension | 2356 | 2739 | 2723 | 3282 | 3634 | 3242 |
| Interest and dividends | 56 | 53 | 58 | 46 | 48 | 64 |
| Company and private pension | 304 | 228 | 120 | 372 | 196 | 136 |
| **2004** | | | | | | |
| Current income | 6342 | 7664 | 7447 | 3875 | 3913 | 3913 |
| Public pension | 2244 | 2520 | 2815 | 3014 | 3299 | 3480 |
| Interest and dividends | 65 | 73 | 131 | 52 | 55 | 60 |
| Company and private pension | 429 | 340 | 261 | 564 | 334 | 262 |
| **2009** | | | | | | |
| Current income | 6349 | 6341 | 6104 | 3931 | 3856 | 3873 |
| Public pension | 2146 | 2514 | 2644 | 2837 | 3105 | 3294 |
| Interest and dividends | 64 | 67 | 95 | 92 | 78 | 82 |
| Company and private pension | 492 | 461 | 251 | 758 | 528 | 335 |
| **2014** | | | | | | |
| Current income | 5558 | 5618 | 6408 | 3629 | 3647 | 3401 |
| Public pension | 2193 | 2520 | 2418 | 2543 | 2803 | 2468 |
| Interest and dividends | 65 | 95 | 284 | 101 | 76 | 90 |
| Company and private pension | 520 | 572 | 381 | 664 | 544 | 335 |
| **2019** | | | | | | |
| Current income | 5062 | 5112 | 5167 | 3624 | 3519 | 3478 |
| Public pension | 2244 | 2423 | 2546 | 2638 | 2809 | 2890 |
| Interest and dividends | 59 | 51 | 46 | 64 | 60 | 52 |
| Company and private pension | 405 | 327 | 275 | 450 | 406 | 287 |

*Source:* Survey of Household Income and Expenditure; 1994: Table 413, 1999: Table 24, 2004: Table 25, 2009: Table 25, 2014 and 2019: Table 3.33 e-Stat.

pensioners would have retired in about 1990. Pensioners aged 75+ received less state pension and less interest and dividends. These pensioners would have retired in about 1980.

Table 7.3 shows that for households in which neither spouse works, current income decreased in real terms between 1994 and 2019 by about 7 percent after peaking in 1999. The Comprehensive Survey of Living Conditions (CSLC, Household Statistics Office) is an annual survey dating back to 1985, which includes the incomes of "aged households." It shows that between 1985 and 1998 their average income grew in real terms by 33 percent. Since 1998 their average income has decreased; by 2003 it had decreased by 9 percent from the peak in 1998. According to CSLC, between 1994 and 2019 average income decreased in real terms by about 5 percent after peaking in 1998. Hence, both surveys concur about the peak in the late 1990s but disagree to some extent about the depth of the subsequent decline.

Table 7.3 shows that public pension income decreased in real terms by about 18 percent between 1994 and 2019, with most of this decrease occurring after 2004. Income from interest and dividends was largest in 1994 and smallest in 2019, but this is only a minor source of income. Income from company and private pensions was smallest in 1999, peaked in 2009, and decreased subsequently. However, this income accounted for less than 20 percent of total income because most Japanese were not members of company and private pension schemes, although these schemes became increasingly important.

Since state pensions do not depend exclusively on interest rates and investment performance, whereas private pensions do, we are particularly interested in the latter. In 1999 pensioners who would have retired in about 1985 (aged 75+ in 1999) received on average ¥136,000 in private pensions, whereas their counterparts who would have retired about 1995 (aged 65–9 in 1999) received on average ¥372,000. This pattern is repeated across all surveys; private and corporate pension income varies inversely with age. If anything, the opposite might have been expected because older pensioners would have benefited more from the superior investment performance prior to ZIP. This consideration naturally becomes increasingly important with the passage of time. It is less forceful in 1999 because ZIP was only 3 years old. In 2019 it was 23 years old.

Also, private and corporate pension income appears to be a fraction of state pensions because, whereas all pensioners received state pensions, only some pensioners received private and corporate pensions. These two apparent anomalies are related to same cause; during this period the coverage of private and corporate pensions increased over time.

The distribution of private and corporate pensions has a large mass point at zero. What matters, of course, is the average private pension among retirees who received them. In 2019, roughly 75 percent of enterprises operated pension schemes with benefits equal to thirty-five to forty months' salary (website of Ministry of Health, Labour and Welfare). Presumably this proportion has increased over time. Ideally, we need data on the proportion of pensioners who did not receive corporate and private pensions. Unfortunately, these data are not available (according to the Pension Funds Association in Japan). However, according to the SHIE for 2004, recipients of private and corporate pensions constituted 29 percent of tabulated households. This proportion rose to 39.7 percent by 2009 and to 40.8 percent by 2014. (Data for 2019 are currently not publicly available.)

We have previously mentioned that in the early 1990s about 30 percent of employees were covered by private and corporate pension schemes, rising to 40 percent by 2013 and to 50 percent by 2020. These orders of magnitude are not out of line with the proportions for pensioners mentioned in the previous paragraph, especially when account is taken of the fact, for example, that pensioners in SHIE for 2004 would have been employees up to about 2000 in the case of those aged 65 to 69, and employees up to about 1990 for those aged 70 plus.

Backward extrapolation suggests that the proportion of pensioners receiving private and corporate pensions in 1999 might have been about 19 percent, and forward extrapolation suggests that the proportion for 2019 might have been about 43 percent. These assumptions, together with the data-driven proportions for 2004, 2009, and 2014, imply that the average corporate and private pensions for couples with no earners were ¥1,231,000 in 1999, ¥1,333,000 in 2004, ¥1,385,000 in 2009, ¥1,234,000 in 2014, and ¥902,000 in 2019.

In summary, corporate and private pension income was 27 percent less in real terms in 2019 than in 1999, and 33 percent less than in the 2000s. These calculations confirm the expectation from Figure 7.1 that, following the implementation of ZIP in 1996, pension income from private and corporate pensions decreased substantially after 2008. Pensioners were also worse off because the state pension decreased following the deterioration in the investment performance of the GPF (Figure 7.1).

## Economic Inequality

In Chapter 4 we presented the neoclassical theory of the factorial distribution of income, which measures how national income is distributed between the factors of production: labor and capital. We referred to the former by the "labor share" ($S_L$) and the latter by the "profit share" ($S_K$), which naturally sum to 1. We showed that these shares depend on the technology of production as well as on the capital–labor ratio. For example, equation (1.7) in Chapter 4 shows that if the elasticity of substitution between labor and capital exceeds 1, the profit share varies directly with the capital intensity of production. If instead the elasticity of substitution is less than 1, the profit share varies inversely with capital intensity. If the elasticity of substitution is 1, the profit share does not depend on capital intensity.

We also reported what happened to the factorial distribution of income over time in key OECD countries. The factorial distribution of income is a macroeconomic phenomenon, which is generally ignored in the microeconomic discussion of the personal distribution of income. This is surprising, because the incomes of individuals and households comprise wages, interest, and dividends, which in the aggregate depend on macroeconomic phenomena.

We begin by focusing on two sources of personal income: wages and profits. Income from interest is ignored, but it can be taken into consideration later. For further simplicity, we assume that profits are distributed as dividends; they are not retained. The population (excluding children) denoted by N consists of workers and pensioners. The number of workers is $L = (1-d)N$, where d denotes the dependency ratio expressed by the share of pensioners in the population. Workers receive wage income and dividends. Pensioners receive their pension and dividend income. Since pensions comprise transfers and annuities, they are ignored here because they are not factor payments or part of national income. Profits are not ignored because they are part of national income. National income $(Y)$ is the wage bill $(LW)$ plus profits $(P)$ where W is the average wage. Hence, $S_K = P/Y$ is the profit share and $LW/Y = S_L = 1 - S_K$ is the wage share.verage income from profits is $P/N$. For the moment, we assume that workers' share of profits equals their population share $(1 - d)$. Hence, the average dividend income of workers is $P_L = (1 - d)P/(1-d)N = S_K Y/N$, which equals the average dividend income of pensioners $(P_P = dS_K Y/dN = S_K Y/N)$.

In what follows, we focus on income inequality among workers using two measures of inequality, the variance and the Gini coefficient.

## Variance

The earnings of individual i is $L_i W_i$ where $L_i$ denotes inputs of labor of individual i and $W_i$ is the wage rate. The expected value of earnings is $E(LW) = E(L)E(W) + cov(L, W)$. If, for example, hourly wage rates and hours worked are positively correlated, the expected value of earnings exceeds the product of the expected values of hours worked and wages rates. The variance of earnings is $E(LW)^2 - [E(LW)]^2$, which measures inequality in earnings. Average earnings (AE) in the data are:

$$AE = \frac{\sum_{i=1}^{(1-d)N} (L_i W_i)}{(1 - d)N} = \frac{S_L Y}{(1 - d) N} = S_L y \qquad (2.1)$$

where y is GDP per worker. The numerator in equation (2.1) is the wage bill, which equals the labor share multiplied by GDP. The variance of earnings is defined as:

$$var(LW) = \frac{1}{(1 - d) POP} \sum_{i=1}^{(1-d)POP} (L_i W_i - S_L y)^2 \qquad (2.2)$$

Average dividend income of workers is $P_L = (1 - d)(1 - S_L)y'$, where $y'$ denotes GDP per capita. Hence, the variance of their dividend income is defined as:

$$var\left(P_L\right) = \frac{1}{(1-d)\,POP} \sum_{i=1}^{(1-d)POP} \left(P_i - (1-d)(1-S_L)y'\right)^2 \qquad (2.3)$$

The variance of total income is defined as:

$$var\left(Y_L\right) = var\left(LW\right) + var\left(P_L\right) + 2rsd\left(LW\right)sd\left(P_L\right) \qquad (2.4)$$

Where sd() are standard deviations and r denotes the correlation between earnings and dividend income. Var(Y) measures income inequality among the working population. As expected, income inequality as measured by the variance varies directly with inequality in earnings and dividend income, and it varies directly with the correlation between earnings and dividends. If, for example, higher earners have more assets, the correlation would be positive.

Differentiating equation (2.4) with respect to the labor share shows that the personal income distribution of workers does not depend upon the factorial distribution of income. This arises from the fact that the derivative of the variance with respect to the mean is identically zero. Therefore, inequality as measured by the variance or the standard deviation cannot depend on the factorial distribution of income by definition.

Matters, however, are different if inequality is measured by the coefficient of variation (the standard deviation as a percentage of the mean):

$$CV_L = \frac{sd\left(Y_L\right)}{\overline{Y}_L} \qquad (2.5)$$

where the mean income of workers is the sum of mean earnings and mean dividend income:

$$\overline{Y}_L = \left[\frac{S_L}{1-d} + (1-d)(1-S_L)\right]y' \qquad (2.6)$$

Since the numerator of equation (2.5) must be independent of the labor share, it is obvious that the coefficient of variation varies inversely with the denominator. Substituting equation (2.6) into equation (2.5) and differentiating the result with respect to the labor share implies that the elasticity of income inequality among workers with respect to the labor share is negative because d is a fraction:

$$\frac{\partial CV_L}{\partial S_L} \frac{S_L}{CV_L} = -\frac{d(2-d)}{d(2-d) + \frac{(1-d)^2}{S_L}} < 0 \tag{2.7}$$

Hence, if the labor share increases, income inequality among the working population must decrease. Notice that, as d tends to 0, so does equation (2.7), i.e. when there are no pensioners, personal income inequality no longer depends on the factorial distribution of income because everybody works.

Matters are simpler in the case of pensioners because they do not have earned income. The counterpart with respect to the capital share to equation (2.7) for pensioners is:

$$\frac{\partial CV_p}{\partial S_K} \frac{S_K}{CV_p} = -1 \tag{2.8}$$

The elasticity of inequality among pensioners as measured by the coefficient of variation with respect to the capital share is minus 1.

In summary, when personal income inequality is measured by the coefficient of variation, personal income inequality depends on the factorial distribution of income. If the labor share happens to increase, income inequality among the working population decreases and income inequality among pensioners increases. However, total income inequality cannot change, because the decrease in inequality among workers is offset by the increase in inequality among pensioners. This happens because the coefficient of variation across the population as a whole is the ratio of the standard deviation of income divided by average income. Since the denominator as well as the numerator cannot be affected by the factorial distribution of income, personal income inequality in the population as a whole is independent of the factorial distribution of income. On the other hand, it matters for subgroups of the population.

## Gini Inequality

Whereas variance-related measures of income inequality among the population as a whole are independent of the factorial distribution of income, matters are different if inequality is measured by the Gini coefficient. Therefore, in what follows we do not distinguish between workers and pensioners. All individuals receive earned income and dividend income even if for some these incomes may happen to be zero.

There are numerous ways of measuring inequality. The most popular measure is the Gini coefficient (G), for reasons that we shall not discuss here (Cowell 2011). Perhaps one of these reasons is that it is bounded between zero (complete equality) and 1 (complete inequality). The coefficient of variation is zero when there is complete equality but it tends to infinity with complete inequality. Also, the coefficient of variation penalizes inequality according squared differences from the mean, whereas G is concerned with absolute differences between incomes.

The Gini coefficient may be expressed (Yitzhaki and Shechtman 2013) as:

$$G = 2 \frac{cov\left(YR\right)}{\bar{Y}} \tag{3.1}$$

where the numerator denotes the covariance between incomes and their rank (R) in the distribution. Since incomes are ranked from the lowest to the highest, the numerator in equation (3.1) must be positive, and the mean of R is ½, at which Y is the median income. The mean income features in the denominator of equation (3.1). Differentiating equation (3.1) with respect to mean income implies:

$$\frac{\partial G}{\partial \bar{Y}} = \frac{-G}{\bar{Y}} \tag{3.2}$$

Hence, unlike the variance, the Gini coefficient varies inversely with the mean. This results from the fact that the variance is quadratic in deviations from the mean, whereas the Gini coefficient is based on absolute differences in income.

The Gini correlation between earnings ($Y_e$) and dividend income ($Y_p$) takes two values because unlike measures based on the analysis of variance (ANOVA), measures based on the analysis of Gini (ANOGI) depend on the direction of the correlation:

$$\Gamma_{ep} = \frac{cov\left(Y_e R_p\right)}{cov\left(Y_e R_e\right)} \tag{3.3}$$

$$\Gamma_{pe} = \frac{cov\left(Y_p R_e\right)}{cov\left(Y_p R_p\right)} \tag{3.4}$$

Unlike Pearson correlations, Gini correlations depend on direction, but like Pearson correlations, they are bounded between 1 and minus 1 and equal zero when earnings and dividend income are independent. If the joint distributions of earnings and dividend income happen to be exchangeable, Gini correlations do

not depend on their direction. This happens when earnings and profits are mono-
tonically related, or when their marginal distributions are identical. Earnings and
dividend income are unlikely to be exchangeable.

Since the sum of ranks minus the mean rank is zero, the covariances in equations
(3.3) and (3.4) are independent of of the means of $Y_e$ and $Y_p$. Hence:

$$\frac{\partial \Gamma_{ep}}{\partial \overline{Y}_e} = \frac{\partial \Gamma_{pe}}{\partial \overline{Y}_p} = 0 \tag{3.5}$$

The square of the Gini correlation for income as a whole has the following decomposition in terms of its components, earnings and profits (Yitzhaki and Shechtman
2013, p 56):

$$G^2 = G_e^2 + G_p^2 + \left(\Gamma_{ep} + \Gamma_{pe}\right) G_e G_p \tag{3.6}$$

Solving equation (3.6) for G and using the result to calculate its derivative with
respect to mean earnings implies:

$$\frac{\partial G}{\partial \overline{Y}_e} = -\frac{G_e}{G \overline{Y}_e} \left(G_e + 0.5 \left(\Gamma_{ep} + \Gamma_{pe}\right) G_p\right) \tag{3.7}$$

Equation (3.7) states that the overall Gini coefficient varies inversely with mean
earnings. The counterpart of Equation (3.7) for an increase in mean dividend income states that the overall Gini coefficient varies inversely with mean dividend
income:

$$\frac{\partial G}{\partial \overline{Y}_p} = -\frac{G_p}{G \overline{Y}_p} \left(G_p + 0.5 \left(\Gamma_{ep} + \Gamma_{pe}\right) G_e\right) \tag{3.8}$$

Using the fact that $\overline{Y}_e = S_L \overline{Y}$ and $\overline{Y}_p = (1 - S_L) \overline{Y}$ we conclude that the effect of an
increase in the labor share on the Gini coefficient for income as a whole is:

$$\frac{\partial G}{\partial S_L} = \frac{1}{G} \left\{ \frac{G_p}{1 - S_L} \left(G_p + 0.5 \left(\Gamma_{ep} + \Gamma_{pe}\right) G_e\right) - \frac{G_e}{S_L} \left(G_e + 0.5 \left(\Gamma_{ep} + \Gamma_{pe}\right) G_p\right) \right\} \tag{3.9}$$

The first term in curly brackets refers to the change in inequality resulting from
the decrease in mean dividend income, and the second term refers to the change
in inequality resulting from the increase in average earnings.

Table 7.4 reports some numerical illustrations for equation (3.9) in which the
baseline is row 1. We begin by assuming that earnings and dividends are uncorrelated. However, dividend income is less equally distributed than earned income.

**Table 7.4** The Relation between the Gini Coefficient and the Labor Share

| $\Gamma_{ep} + \Gamma_{pe}$ | $G_p$ | $G_e$ | $S_L$ | $G$ | Equation 3.9 |
|---|---|---|---|---|---|
| 0 | 0.5 | 0.3 | 0.75 | 0.583 | 0.0151 |
| 1 | 0.5 | 0.3 | 0.75 | 0.7 | 0.0240 |
| −1 | 0.5 | 0.3 | 0.75 | 0.436 | 0.0146 |
| 0 | 0.3 | 0.5 | 0.75 | 0.583 | −0.0133 |

The labor share is 0.75 in accordance with empirical data in Chapter 4. According to equation (3.6), the Gini coefficient is 0.583, i.e., total income is more unequal than its individual components. Substituting these values into equation (3.9) shows that it is positive; increasing the labor share by one percentage point from 75 percent to 76 percent increases income inequality as measured by the Gini coefficient by 0.0151 from 0.583 to 0.5981. The semi elasticity of the Gini coefficient with respect to the labor share is 2.57.

If earnings and dividends are perfectly positively correlated (row 2) the Gini coefficient is larger (0.7), as expected, and equation (3.9) increases to 0.024 from 0.015. Hence, an increase in the labor share increases inequality but by more. The semi elasticity is 3.43 instead of 2.57. If earnings and dividends are perfectly negatively correlated (row 3) the opposite happens; Gini is smaller (0.436), as expected, and the effect of the labor share on inequality is weaker (0.0146). However, the semi elasticity is 3.35 because the Gini coefficient is smaller.

For plausible values of the parameters in Table 7.4, it is difficult to find a combination in which an increase in the labor share induces a decrease in inequality. This is because the labor share tends to exceed 50 percent and dividends tend to be more unequally distributed than earnings. If in row 1 the Gini coefficients for earnings and dividends are exchanged, equation (3.9) is negative; an increase in the labor share of 1 percentage point reduces the Gini coefficient by 0.0133 or 2.28 percent (row 4).

Whereas the effect of the labor share on the Gini coefficient is positive for plausible values of the labor share and the Gini coefficients for earnings and dividends, the effect of capital intensity on the labor share is ambiguous, as noted. If ZIP increases capital intensity, as expected, the labor share decreases if the elasticity of substitution between labor and capital exceeds 1, and it increases if the elasticity of substitution is less than 1. In the former case ZIP would increase equality, as measured by the Gini coefficient, and in the latter case it would increase inequality.

Since the factorial distribution of income refers to labor and capital, ideally the Gini coefficient should refer to gross factor incomes for purposes of comparison, i.e. they should exclude transfer payments and include taxes. Typically, Gini coefficients are calculated for post-tax incomes inclusive of transfers, as in the World

Table 7.5  The Empirical Relation between the Gini Coefficient and the Labor Share

| | Israel | | Japan | | Germany | | UK | | France | | Sweden | | US | | Australia | |
|---|---|---|---|---|---|---|---|---|---|---|---|---|---|---|---|---|
| | $S_L$ | G | $S_L$ | G | $S_L$ | G | $S_L$ | G | $S_L$ | G | $S_L$ | G | $S_L$ | G | $S_L$ | G |
| 1960 | | | | 0.247 | | | | | | | | | 81.2 | 0.353 | 81.9 | |
| 1967 | | | | 0.236 | | | | | | | | 0.340 | | | | |
| 1970 | | | | | | | | 0.337 | | | | | | | 78.2 | |
| 1980 | | 0.434 | | 0.226 | | | | 0.284 | 89.4 | 0.352 | | 0.229 | 83.5 | 0.345 | 80.8 | 0.313 |
| 1985 | | 0.468 | | 0.231 | | | | 0.319 | 83.1 | 0.369 | | | | 0.374 | 77.8 | 0.325 |
| 1990 | | 0.480 | | 0.240 | 57.8 | 0.292 | | 0.359 | 77.9 | 0.322 | | 0.249 | 83.4 | 0.380 | 76.5 | 0.332 |
| 1995 | 73 | 0.497 | 50.6 | 0.244 | 57.8 | 0.289 | 76.9 | 0.363 | 77.1 | 0.323 | 80.3 | 0.252 | 81.9 | 0.400 | 74.7 | 0.326 |
| 2000 | 71 | 0.509 | 48.5 | 0.246 | 58.1 | 0.288 | 79.5 | 0.370 | 76.1 | 0.311 | 83.2 | 0.272 | 84.8 | 0.401 | 74.7 | 0.335 |
| 2005 | 69 | 0.526 | 45.4 | 0.259 | 55.2 | 0.321 | 80.3 | 0.343 | 73.8 | 0.298 | 83.2 | 0.268 | 78.7 | 0.403 | 74.4 | 0.331 |
| 2010 | 69 | 0.505 | 45.4 | 0.321 | 55.6 | 0.301 | 84.5 | 0.344 | 72.6 | 0.337 | 82.7 | 0.277 | 78.5 | 0.400 | 72.2 | 0.347 |
| 2015 | 67 | 0.472 | 46.9 | 0.329 | 57.2 | 0.317 | 80.6 | 0.332 | 71.3 | 0.327 | 82.5 | 0.292 | 78.5 | 0.411 | 74.4 | 0.344 |
| 2018 | 68 | 0.464 | 49.7 | | 57.8 | 0.274 | | 0.364 | 70.1 | 0.316 | 84.2 | 0.298 | 80.0 | | 72.4 | |

Notes: Data for gross labor shares ($S_L$) are extracted from Chapter 4. Israel: National Insurance Institute (2019) Gini coefficient for economic income. Data sources for Gini coefficients (G) for household incomes net of taxes including transfers Japan: Roser et al (2019), other countries: World Bank. Since data are not available quinquennially, in some cases data for nearest years are reported. For visual convenience, the data from Roser et al (2019) are plotted in Figure 7.2.

Bank data and Roser et al (2019). In Table 7.5 only the data for Israel refer to gross factor incomes. For comparison, their counterparts for net income (economic income plus transfers minus direct taxes) are 0.324 (1980), 0.326 (1990), 0.350 (2000), 0.384 (2010), and 0.356 (2018). The difference between these Gini coefficients increased after 1980 because policy became less redistributive, but by 2018 the difference was similar to what it was in 1980. Both measures of income inequality increased until 2005 and decreased subsequently.

In Table 7.5, the Gini coefficients increased in Australia, the US, Sweden, and Japan. In France, the Gini coefficient decreased until 2005 and increased subsequently. The Gini coefficients in Israel, Germany, and the UK tended to increase until 2000–5 and decreased subsequently (Figure 7.2).

We stress that Gini coefficients between countries are not comparable for a number of reasons. For example, the Gini coefficient tends to vary inversely with the length of the accounting period. Hence quarterly incomes tend to be more unequal than annual incomes because random elements in quarterly income tend to cancel out over time. Consequently, the Gini coefficient for annual incomes tends to be smaller than the average of the four quarterly Gini coefficients. Therefore, the Gini coefficients in Figure 7.2 do not necessarily mean that the countries with smaller Gini coefficients such as Germany have greater income equality than countries with larger Gini coefficients such as Japan. On the other hand, Gini coefficients within countries are comparable. Hence, in the US and Sweden income inequality increased, and in Israel it increased until 2005 before decreasing.

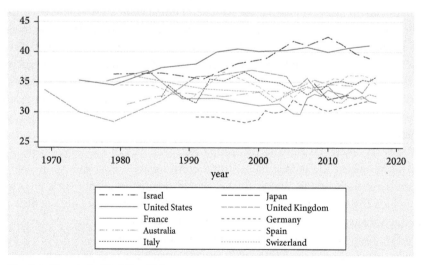

**Fig. 7.2** Trends in Gini Coefficients
*Source:* World Bank database. July 2020.

Yet more disconcerting is the uncomfortable fact that there are different estimates of Gini coefficients for the same country in the same year, using the same data by different agencies. For example, the World Bank reported a Gini coefficient of 0.348 for Japan in 2008 using the Household Income Survey. The OECD calculated the Gini coefficient at 0.336, and Roser et al (2019) report it at 0.254. It is puzzling that these organizations do not simply use Gini coefficients published by national statistical authorities, where they are available, as they do for GDP and numerous other variables. For example, the National Insurance Institute in Israel reported that the Gini coefficient for net income in 2015 was 0.366. The OECD estimate is very similar (0.36) but the World Bank estimate was higher (0.39 in 2016). Also, the Gini coefficient for Israel in Figure 7.2 (source World Bank) is only impressionistically related to the estimates of Israel's National Insurance Institute.

## Are Labor Shares and Income Inequality Correlated?

Since Gini coefficients between countries are not comparable, but are comparable within countries, we may only answer this question using time series data for labor shares and Gini coefficients within countries. Since there is no obvious reason why factor shares should depend on income inequality, whereas there is reason to suspect that income inequality depends upon factor shares, we focus on the latter. Recall from Table 7.4 that the correlation between labor shares and Gini coefficients may be positive or negative. For example, in Sweden and the UK, the labor shares and the Gini coefficients are positively correlated in Table 7.5, whereas the correlation tends to be negative in the US and Germany and perhaps Australia. In France the correlation is initially positive, but eventually the Gini coefficient increased despite the continued decrease in the labor share. In Israel the correlation is initially negative, but the Gini coefficient decreased after 2005 despite the fact that the labor share stabilized. Only in Japan does there appear to be no correlation between the labor share and the Gini coefficient, which continued to increase.

This casual empiricism suggests prima facie evidence that income inequality might be related to the factorial distribution of income, at least in some countries. To investigate this matter further would require an econometric analysis in which the time series relationship in a country between its Gini coefficient and labor share allows for third factors hypothesized to affect income inequality. For example, in Israel mass immigration from the former USSR during the 1990s increased the population by 20 percent, which partly explains why the labor share decreased (increase in labor supply) and income inequality increased, as predicted by immigrant assimilation theory. Since Gini coefficients and labor shares appear to be nonstationary time series, the null hypothesis would be that Gini coefficients are not cointegrated with labor shares and third variables. For these purposes, longer time series would be required, especially for countries such as Japan and Sweden for which data for labor shares are available from 1995 in Table 7.5.

Our casual empiricism suggests that this null hypothesis may be rejected. Suppose that Gini coefficients indeed depend on factor shares. The next question is, "Do factor shares depend on the capital intensity of output, measured by the capital–output ratio?" If the answer is positive, the final question would be, "Do capital output–ratios vary inversely with the cost of capital?" If the answer is positive, a causal nexus is established between ZIP and income inequality. It starts in stage 1 with ZIP aided by quantitative easing, which lowers the cost of capital. In stage 2 the latter increases the capital–output ratio, which, as discussed in Chapter 4, affects the factorial distribution of income. Finally, in stage 3 the latter affects income inequality as measured by the Gini coefficient.

For example, the capital–output ratio in Sweden has increased steadily (Chapter 4). So has the labor share (Table 7.5), suggesting that in Sweden the elasticity of substitution between labor and capital (ES) is less than one. As suggested by Table 7.4, the Gini coefficient in Sweden varies directly with its labor share. Sweden adopted ZIP in 2009 (Chapter 5), which increased income inequality in Sweden through this causal chain. In the UK the labor share, the Gini coefficient, and the capital–output ratio are approximately ∩-shaped, suggesting that ES is less than 1 and that ZIP increased income inequality, as in Sweden. In France the capital–output ratio increased over time and the labor share decreased, suggesting that ES exceeds 1. Hence, ZIP would have reduced the labor share, which should have affected income inequality. However, this last link in the causal chain is weak.

In Japan, the capital–output ratio is ∩-shaped (Chapter 4), whereas the labor share is U-shaped, suggesting that ES exceeds 1. ZIP would have reduced the labor share, which should have affected income inequality. As noted above, this link in the causal chain does not appear to apply in Japan. In Israel, the capital–output ratio and the labor share decreased over time (Chapter 4), suggesting that ES exceeds 1. Although the Gini coefficient is approximately ∩-shaped, it has increased over time, suggesting that, as in row 4 of Table 7.4, income inequality varies inversely with the labor share. Therefore, ZIP would have reduced income inequality.

In Germany, the capital–labor ratio increased over time, but the labor share was U-shaped. In the US and Australia, labor shares decreased over time, but capital–output ratios were flat. Although for these countries there are prima facie linkages between labor shares and income inequality, there are no prima facie linkages between labor shares and capital–output ratios. Hence, the effect of ZIP on income inequality is either zero or indeterminate.

In summary, ZIP and the New Abnormal are macroeconomic phenomena, whereas the distribution of personal income is a microeconomic phenomenon. It might seem, therefore, that economic inequality and the New Abnormal are unlikely to be related. If economic inequality is measured by the Gini coefficient, a link is established between the factorial distribution of income and economic inequality because the Gini coefficient varies inversely with mean income. Since, as we have seen, the factorial distribution of income depends on the New Abnormal, and the Gini coefficient depends on mean income, an indirect link is established between the New Abnormal and economic inequality.

The trouble is that this dependence is ambiguous because it depends on whether the elasticity of substitution between labor and capital is greater or less than unity. If the elasticity of substitution is unity, as it is if the technology or production is Cobb- Douglas, the factorial distribution of income is constant, in which event the link between economic inequality and the New Abnormal is severed. Since for most countries the elasticity of substitution is not unity, this link is established.

## House Prices

In the standard model of housing markets, which dates back to Smith (1969), the housing stock is fixed in the short run but flexible in the long run. The demand for housing services (measured in square meters) varies directly with the population (N) and permanent income $Y_p$ and inversely with the rental price of housing per square meter (R):

$$lnH^D = \alpha + lnN + \beta lnY_p - \gamma lnR \tag{5.1}$$

In equation (5.1) it is assumed that the demand for housing space is proportionate to the population. The return to housing as a capital asset is assumed to equal the rate of interest on treasury bonds (denoted by $r_b$ in Chapter 2) plus a risk premium (ρ):

$$\frac{R}{P} = r_b + \rho \tag{5.2}$$

where P denotes the price of housing per square meter. Since the housing stock is fixed in the short run, equations (5.1) and (5.2) solve for house prices:

$$lnP = \frac{1}{\gamma}\left[\alpha + \beta lnY_p - ln\left(\frac{H}{N}\right)\right] - ln\left(r_b + \rho\right) \tag{5.3}$$

Equation (5.3) states that house prices vary directly with permanent income and inversely with housing space per head and the rate of interest.

Finally, the change in the housing stock varies directly with housing construction (B) net of demolitions (D):

$$\Delta H = B - D \tag{5.4}$$

where construction varies directly with house prices and inversely with construction costs, and demolitions vary directly with age of the housing stock and inversely with house prices.

ZIP increases house prices directly through Equation (5.3). The increase in house prices increases the housing stock through equation (5.4), which subsequently lowers house prices. Hence, house prices overshoot their long-run equilibrium in which house prices are only slightly higher than they were prior to ZIP (Bar Nathan, Beenstock and Haitovsky 1998). Insofar as the New Abnormal reduces fertility and permanent income, the opposite happens. House prices decrease by more in the short run than in the long run. In the stationary state B = D so that in the very long run construction costs are the main driver of house prices.

In summary, ZIP raises house prices in the short run while the opposite happens if fertility and permanent income decrease. What happens to house prices subsequently depends on the balance between these countervailing forces and the speed of reaction of building contractors to increases in house prices, and associated gestation lags inherent in housing construction. Faster reactions mitigate the overshooting of house prices.

In the dynamic capital asset pricing model that has just been described, renting and owner occupation are regarded as perfect substitutes. In practice most of the frictions in housing supply arise (Beenstock and Felsenstein 2015) due to land zoning, planning permission delays and other regulatory practices, which have been ignored here. Nevertheless, this canonical model constitutes a good starting point for discussion.

Table 7.6 records real house prices for a number of countries where ZIP applies and which are entangled in the New Abnormal. With the exception of Japan, house prices have increased, especially in Sweden, Canada, and Australia. Note that in Japan the house price index in 1990 was 131, when house prices peaked following Big Bang style financial liberalization. Despite the adoption of ZIP in 1996, house prices decreased before stabilizing in the early 2000s at what they were in the 1970s. It is most probably no coincidence that this development coincided with the downturn in population as well as the decline in permanent income induced by the absence of economic growth.

Table 7.6 Real House Prices

|          | 2005 | 2010 | 2015 | 2020 |
|----------|------|------|------|------|
| Sweden   | 137  | 185  | 222  | 261  |
| Israel   | 89   | 113  | 137  | 162  |
| Germany  | 91   | 86   | 98   | 131  |
| US       | 152  | 109  | 119  | 150  |
| Japan    | 78   | 76   | 77   | 83   |
| France   | 170  | 184  | 171  | 196  |
| Australia| 149  | 174  | 208  | 219  |
| UK       | 170  | 159  | 173  | 194  |
| Canada   | 135  | 175  | 205  | 268  |
| Italy    | 141  | 139  | 109  | 107  |

Source: The Economist. 2000 Q1 = 100. Data refer to quarter 4.

Short of estimating separate econometric models for each country, it is difficult to decompose the data in Table 7.6 into factors such as ZIP that should have raised house prices and demographic factors that might have decreased them. Why were German house prices relatively stable from 2000 but increased sharply after 2015? Why did Italian house prices increase in the 2000s and decrease subsequently? Why did house prices generally increase in Sweden, Australia, and Canada? Whatever the answers may be, there is no obvious association with either ZIP or the New Abnormal.

This does not mean that ZIP does not matter. Assuming, for example, that the risk premium ($\rho$) in Equation (5.3) is 10 percent and equals the rate of interest on bonds ($r_b$), the direct effect of ZIP is a doubling of house prices. Even if this effect were smaller, it would still be large. Given the widespread empirical evidence of the effect of interest rates on house prices (Bar Nathan, Beenstock and Haitovsky 1998, Sutton, Mihaljek and Subelyte 2017), it is ironical that central bankers blame the increase in house prices on everyone except themselves.

Another misunderstanding is that house prices depend on ownership. In Israel, for example, stamp duty was raised for investors who bought housing for rental on the grounds that they were artificially raising the demand for housing. If renting and owner occupation are perfect substitutes, and as long as investors rent out their properties, the total supply of housing remains unchanged regardless of real estate ownership. Hence, house prices are not affected by investment in housing; ownership is irrelevant. Matters would be different if owner occupation and renting are not perfect substitutes. In this case investment in housing for rental would lower rents because it increases the supply of housing for rental, but it would increase the price of owner occupation. The implications for the average cost of housing services as a whole are ambiguous but minimal.

## Insurance

Insurance contracts share a common design. The insured pay premiums up front. The insurance company compensates the insured if the contingency occurs within a defined period of time. This means that insurance companies can invest their premium income until they have to pay compensation to the insured. Since insurance contracts tend to be for short periods, such as a year, insurance companies are interested in investing their premium income in liquid assets. It is easy to establish that the rate of interest that they earn on liquid assets reduces insurance premiums in equilibrium (Doherty and Garven 1995, Holsboer 2000). Therefore, ZIP should make insurance more expensive in equilibrium. It is difficult to think of other examples where ZIP is expected to raise the price of goods and services.

Consider the following insurance contract. The insurance company compensates customer j with $V_j$ if the contingency occurs during the contract period, which ends in period T. Customers pay a common premium P in period $t = 0$. The probability that customer j will submit a claim before period T is denoted by $\pi_j$. The contract is good for a single claim, which is paid in period T. For further simplicity, assume that there are no transaction costs. In competitive equilibrium with N customers the expected present value of claims must equal premium income. Hence:

$$P = \frac{E(\pi V)}{N(1+i)} = \frac{E(\pi)E(V) + r_{\pi V}sd(\pi)sd(V)}{N(1+i)} \tag{4.1}$$

where i denotes the rate of interest over period T, and $r_{\pi V}$ denotes the correlation between claims and their amount, which is positive if riskier customers claim more. Equation (4.1) states, as expected, that the equilibrium premium varies directly with the correlation between claims and their amounts, and if they are positively correlated it also varies directly with their standard deviations. It also varies inversely with the number of customers due to the law of large numbers in risk sharing, and, importantly in the present context, it varies inversely with the rate of interest.

Suppose that prior to ZIP the equilibrium premium happened to be $10 when the rate of interest was 4 percent. Equation (4.1) implies that under ZIP the equilibrium premium would increase to $10.4. This exaggerates the sensitivity of the premium to ZIP because we have assumed for simplicity that claims are paid in period T regardless of when they were made. This assumption makes the timing of payments independent of when the claims were submitted. If earlier claims are settled sooner than later claims, the equilibrium premium would increase by less under ZIP.

As indicated in Equation (4.1), insurance premia depend on several factors apart from the rate of interest. Our intention here is not to investigate these factors econometrically to test the hypothesis that ZIP increased insurance premia. Instead, a less formal approach is adopted in which we check whether insurance premia happened to increase abruptly with the adoption of ZIP. In what follows, data are used for the UK and US. Figures 7.3 and 7.4 show clearly how motor and home insurance premia in the UK increased with the adoption of ZIP in 2009. The positive trend in premia during the 1990s and 2000s exceeds the rate of inflation. Hence, the positive trend in real premia might be explained in terms of the downward trend in interest rates (Chapter 5) that led up to the adoption of ZIP.

Figure 7.3 shows that private auto insurance premia in the US were stable in the run up to the Subprime Crisis after having increased by 20 percent during 2000–5. After the adoption of ZIP in 2008, auto insurance premia had increased

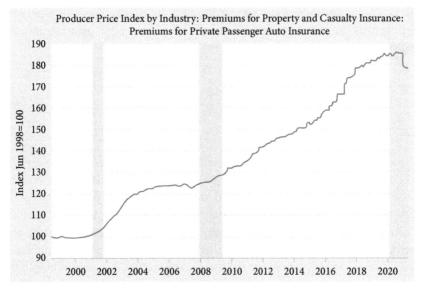

**Fig. 7.3** Private Auto Insurance Premia: United States 1998–2020

*Source:* Federal Reserve Bank of St Louis (FRED).

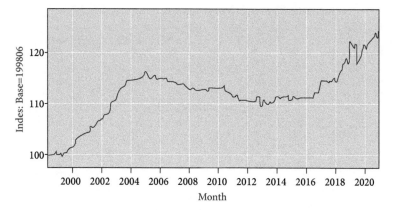

**Fig. 7.4** Commercial Auto Insurance Premia United States 1998–2020
*Source:* Bureau of Labor Statistics.

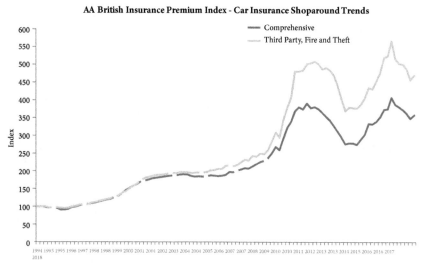

**Fig. 7.5** Car Insurance Premia: United Kingdom 1994–2018
*Source:* Automobile Association.

by almost 50 percent by 2020. Figure 7.4 shows that matters were similar in the case of commercial auto insurance, but the post-ZIP increase in premia took five years, and the increase was smaller. Also, a similar pattern is observable in the case of auto insurance premia in the UK (Figure 7.5) and house insurance premia (Figure 7.6). On the other hand, not all insurance premia increased in the aftermath of ZIP (Figure 7.7).

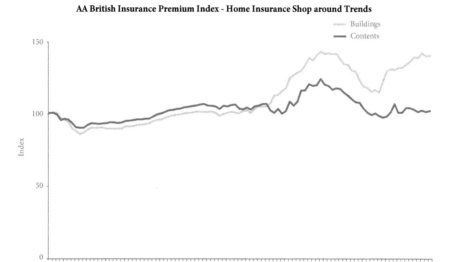

**Fig. 7.6**  House Insurance Premia: United Kingdom 1994–2018
*Source:* Automobile Association.

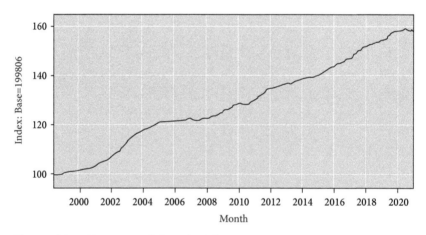

**Fig. 7.7**  Direct Property and Casualty US 1998–2020
*Source:* Bureau of Labor Statistics.

# Synopsis

The rate of interest has a major impact on the value of pensions, both during working lives and in retirement. If ZIP were to last indefinitely, Generation X and Millennials would be worse off in retirement than their parents because they will get no return on their funded pension contributions. Alternatively, they will have to expose themselves to more investment risk than their parents to get some return on their contributions. ZIP is bad news for pensioners.

Since Japan has the longest experience of ZIP, we use data from the Survey of Household Income and Expenditure in Japan to compare pensioners in the 1990s with pensioners 20 years later. Pensioners under the New Abnormal suffered twice. First, their state pension was cut in real terms following the poor investment performance of the Government Pension Fund. Second, private and corporate pensions were also cut following the poor investment performance of their fund managers under ZIP. Pensioners in 2019 had 20 percent less pension income than their counterparts in 1999. Public pension income fell by 18 percent and private and corporate pension income fell by 27 percent.

The New Abnormal is obviously inequitable from an intergenerational perspective because future generations will have to bear the burden of public debt that the current generation has imposed upon them. It is less clear whether the New Abnormal is inequitable from an intragenerational perspective. The personal distribution of income, measured by the Gini coefficient, is a microeconomic phenomenon, which is unlikely to depend on the macroeconomic issues discussed here. On the other hand, the neoclassical theory of the factorial distribution of income (Chapter 4) turns out to be related to the Gini coefficient because the latter varies inversely with mean income. Furthermore, the population comprises workers and pensioners. The income of pensioners varies directly with the profit share and the income of workers varies inversely with it.

It turns out that the theoretical channel between the factorial distribution of income and the personal distribution of income depends on the elasticity of substation between labor and capital, discussed in Chapter 4. If ZIP increases capital intensity, as expected, the labor share decreases if the elasticity of substitution between labor and capital exceeds 1, and it increases if the elasticity of substitution is less than 1. In the former case, ZIP would increase equality, as measured by the Gini coefficient, and in the latter case it would increase inequality.

The countries included in the study group are classified into those in which ZIP increased inequality, as measured by Gini, and those where inequality decreased. Of course, for some countries there is no connection between the factorial distribution of income and the personal distribution of income.

ZIP directly increases house prices because housing is a capital asset whose return is correlated with the yield to maturity on long-term bonds. Since these yields have decreased because of ZIP by about 3 percentage points in real terms, ZIP increased real house prices by about 25 percent. On the other hand, negative demographics induced by fertility reduction due to ZIP, and the adverse effect of the New Abnormal on permanent income, reduced house prices, especially in Japan and Italy. In most New Abnormal countries real house prices increased both before and after they adopted the New Abnormal.

Although it is of more limited social importance relative to fertility, pensions and inequality, we show that ZIP is expected to increase the price of insurance because insurance companies invest their premium income in liquid assets, which have little or no return. This phenomenon is documented with empirical examples from insurance markets in the US and the UK.

# 8

# The Japanese Crystal Ball?

Japan merits a chapter on its own because it was the first country to adopt ZIP in 1996, after which it quickly became embroiled in the New Abnormal. Japan serves as a crystal ball for what might happen elsewhere after a quarter of a century under the New Abnormal. I shall argue that Japan embraced the New Abnormal because it could not face up to carrying out deep structural reforms. These reforms would have cut too deeply into Japanese culture and the character of the Japanese themselves. The failure to reform was not the usual story of short-termism or the lack of political will. For the Japanese, the New Abnormal was a way of coping with problems that they could not solve. This remains so today. However, in addition to these deep-seated problems, the New Abnormal has left them with a further problem: a debt trap created by a debt-to-GDP ratio of 260 percent. This problem seems just as insolvable as all the others.

In Chapter 10, which discusses the future of the New Abnormal, I shall distinguish between countries like Japan, which have adopted the New Abnormal because, like the Japanese, they failed to carry out structural reforms, and countries that slid into the New Abnormal despite the fact that they were not in need of structural reform. The US is an example of the former and Israel and Australia are examples of the latter. Hence, Japan may serve as a crystal ball for the former but not the latter. However, the structural problems of the former are not as deep-seated as Japan's, and their descent into the New Abnormal has more to do with short-termism and political turpitude.

As is well known, after World War Two Japan experienced an "economic miracle," which ended in the late 1980s. Then came the "lost decade," which turned into the lost decade and a half and beyond. As we shall see, the economic miracle ended for the same reasons as it began. The Japanese way of doing business, or Japan Inc, was based on a "corporatist" form of political economy, which had outlived its time, in which leaders of business conglomerates or keiretsu, public administrators, and politicians were very much involved with one another. The public administrators included senior officials of the Ministry of Finance, the Ministry of International Trade and Industry (MITI), the Bank of Japan, and the Economic Planning Agency. The politicians belonged to the Liberal Democratic Party (LDP), which has governed Japan for almost the entire period since World War Two.

*Zero Interest Policy and the New Abnormal.* Michael Beenstock, Oxford University Press. © Michael Beenstock (2022).
DOI: 10.1093/oso/9780192849663.003.0008

During the early years of postwar reconstruction, corporatism may have suited Japan's economic needs, and paved the way to the Japanese economic miracle. However, eventually the overinvolvement of, and closeness between, keiretsu, officials and politicians turned the economic miracle into an economic disaster, involving restrictive practices, the cultivation of monopolies, the falsification of company accounts, misbehavior by regulators, zombie loans on bank balance sheets, scandals, and corruption. Japan failed to reform itself, and adopted the New Abnormal instead. During the entire period, debt service costs have been low thanks to ZIP. Also, economic growth has been lackluster. Japan continues to have the same structural problems it had in the lost decade.

The New Abnormal has made matters worse for Japan. Not only do Japan's structural problems remain, it has burdened future generations with public debt, made worse by the fact that Japanese fertility is far below replacement (Chapter 6). In fact, Millennials in Japan are thrice cursed. Baby boomers have indebted them, and subsequent birth cohorts are small due to falling fertility, so the debt burden per capita is larger. In addition, growing longevity has raised the economic burden on the working population through the increase in the dependency ratio. Young people in Japan today face a stark future.

For purposes of comparison, the postwar economic recovery in West Germany was "miraculous" too. West Germans might have been tempted by corporatism at first, but under Konrad Adenauer and Ludwig Erhard they adopted a liberal market-based political economy (Bark and Gress 1993, part II). They rejected corporatist solutions involving cooperation between trade unions, industry, and government. So, the Japanese economic miracle might have occurred despite corporatism rather than because of it. However, corporatism in Japan ended its economic miracle. By contrast, the absence of corporatism in West Germany and in Germany since reunification underpinned its sustained economic progress. Indeed, although Germany had ZIP forced upon it as member of the eurozone, it has otherwise avoided the New Abnormal.

The juxtaposition of the Japanese miracle and its demise is clearly visible in Figure 8.1. During the economic miracle, the rate of growth averaged 10 percent per year. However, the aftermath of the economic miracle has two sub-periods. The first was the so-called lost decade (which lasted 1½ decades), which ended in the late 1990s, during which the economy grew on average by 4 percent per year. The second subperiod refers to the first two decades of the twenty-first century, or the New Abnormal, during which the economy barely grew at 1 percent per year. We begin by discussing the first of these periods.

## The Japanese Economic Miracle

In 1854 Commander Perry of the US Navy arrived in Japan, spelling the beginning of the end of the feudal Edo Period (1603–1867) during which Japan was closed to the rest of the world. During the Meiji Period or Restoration (1868–1912), Japan

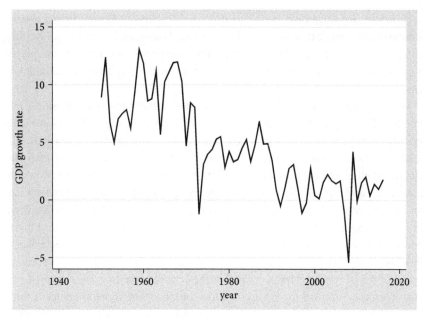

**Fig. 8.1** Japanese Economic Growth
*Source*: e-Stat.

modernized, industrialized, and became an integral part of the world economy. It also saw the development of the zaibatsu, which were family-owned conglomerates that were granted monopoly powers, and which embraced economic activities in industry, manufacturing, finance, and banking (Ohno 2017). The government also established the Bureau of Industrial Promotion to oversee statist economic development, which served as the prototype to the Ministry of International Trade and Industry (MITI) after World War Two. From the start, zaibatsu, such as Mitsubishi, Yasuda, and Mitsui, were heavily involved with public administrators in the Bureau and elsewhere and with politicians to their mutual advantage. This set the pattern for "Japan Inc," which was to continue through the twentieth century and into the twenty-first.

Like the industrial conglomerates in Nazi Germany, such as I.G. Farben and Theissen, which were broken up after World War Two, at first the all-powerful zaibatsu in Japan were broken up under the US occupation. They were seen to be an insidious influence, contributing to Japanese aggression starting with Mukden and Manchuria in the 1930s and the attack on Pearl Harbor in 1942. The difference is that, in Japan, the zaibatsu re-established themselves as keiretsu, which were no longer owned by families but were otherwise similar. General MacArthur as Supreme Commander of the Allied Powers in Japan decided not to impose American ways of doing business on the Japanese, and understood that the keiretsu were necessary for Japan's economic recovery. Horizontal keiretsu, such as Suntory, Mitsubishi, and Mitsui, are holding companies organized around a major bank. Vertical keiretsu, such as Toyota, Nissan and Toshiba, are holding companies covering an extensive range of business activities. The keiretsu played a major part in Japan's economic miracle; this was the way business was done in Japan.

We have remarked elsewhere that there are two main models of business and finance. The Anglo-Saxon model is devolved; firms raise capital from banks but mainly through financial markets such as stock exchanges and bond markets. The relation between banks and their commercial customers is characterized by financial distancing. Also, central banks maintain financial distancing with respect to businesses and individuals. The banking system intermediates between the latter and the central bank. The Japanese model is integrated rather than devolved. In its extreme form there is no financial distancing between banks, central banks and businesses. Whereas financial markets play a major role in the Anglo-Saxon models, they play a minor role in the Japanese model. The keiretsu have representation in the commercial banks as well as the central bank. In a less extreme form, West Germany adopted the Japanese model, but there was more financial distancing by the Bundesbank than by the Bank of Japan, but less than by the Bank of England.

During the economic miracle the share of investment in GDP exceeded 50 percent (Figure 8.2). Economic growth was achieved through the brute force of statist economic development, instigated by MITI in particular, but financed by the Bank of Japan and the Ministry of Finance. The economic miracle was not the result of growth in total factor productivity. Indeed, since the 1990s the share of investment in GDP continued to be high by international standards, but it failed to secure economic growth (Figure 8.2). There has been no shortage of investment in Japan; the problem is that its return has been disappointing.

The following account largely follows Katz (1998), whose main thesis is that the Japanese model might have been sustainable in the postwar recovery, but it was no longer suited to Japan's needs thereafter. Indeed, it proved to be deleterious. In the 1950s and 1960s, MITI, the Economic Planning Agency, the Ministry of Finance, and the Bank of Japan successfully oversaw the postwar reconstruction and set up numerous infant industries (Johnson 1982). The Bank of Japan provided credit to the Ministry of Finance to finance infant industries selected by MITI. These infant industries were heavily protected by commercial policy. Many of them were successful; they matured into adulthood and constituted the backbone of Japan's economic miracle. But many did not. Instead of letting the failures close down, MITI propped them up by intensifying the policy of protection and by cartelizing them.

Katz describes a two-tier economy in which the backward sector comprised services and failed infant industries that had been set up by MITI and a dynamic export-orientated manufacturing sector. MITI encouraged cartelization in the

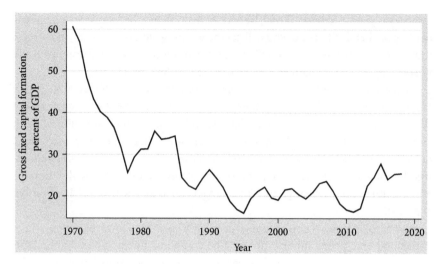

**Fig. 8.2** Gross Domestic Fixed Capital Formation
*Source*: e-Stat

backward sector and protected it by setting up tariff and non-tariff barriers. By contrast the dynamic sector was competitive.

"The greatest MITI failure, however, has been in the way it handled scale and entry into the petroleum refining industry. In order to reduce the large foreign share in Japanese oil refining, MITI promoted the entry – under pressure from a number of business groups each of which wanted a piece of the action – of a large number of too-small refining plants and companies with inadequate capacities to upgrade facilities to optimum scale ... These mistaken policies and programs have carried over into some petrochemical product as well." (Patrick 1986, p 22)

The infant aluminum industry turned out to be a major failure too. Japanese aluminum could not compete with imported aluminum. Instead of coming to terms with this failure, MITI continued to protect it and organized its aluminum producers into a cartel, which fixed prices and shared out the indigenous need for aluminum between members of the cartel. This policy stemmed from two sources. First, the keiretsu involved in these failures lobbied MITI directly, and indirectly by lobbying politicians who brought pressure to bear on MITI. Second, for cultural reasons Japanese mandarins found it particularly difficult to admit failure. As we shall see, this cultural phenomenon manifested itself in the misrepresentation of company accounts, the growth of zombie loans in bank balance sheets, and exaggerating the quality of industrial products. Katz provides examples other than aluminum, including textiles, resin, and numerous other failed industries.

MITI's failures were not limited to industries in which international competition was involved. They also included non-traded goods as well as services. For example, in the case of the construction industry, "Costs are so high because the industry is pervaded by an illegal, but protected system called *dango* in which bidders agree ahead of time on who will get the winning bid. As one of Japan's biggest industries – 10 percent of its GDP and of its work force – construction lies at the heart of Japan's daisy-chain of inefficiency." (Katz 1998, pp 14–15)

Furthermore, "While domestic rivalry is intense in every industry in which Japan is internationally successful, however, it is *all but absent in large sectors of the economy* [italics in original]. In fields such as construction, agriculture, food, paper, commodity chemicals, and fibers, there are cartels and other restrictions on competition, some sanctioned by the government ... Japan, then, is characterized by some of the fiercest domestic rivalry of any nation juxtaposed with large areas of little or no rivalry. [This is a] a danger signal for the future." (Porter 1990 a, p 414).

Pork barrel politics is not, of course, peculiarly Japanese. However, when Kakuei Tanaka became prime minister in 1972 he combined buying votes for the LDP with personal gain, "with Tanaka's personal take adding up to 3 percent of the gross amount on construction projects ... Little of Tanaka's grip was diluted either by his fall from power in 1974 over one bribery scandal or by his indictment and jailing (and eventual conviction) over another in 1985. For the next two decades, Tanaka was the kingmaker, the 'shadow shogun'. His faction remained the largest in the LDP, he and his cronies continued to extract payoffs, and he had a virtual veto over who would become next prime minister." (Katz 1998, p 99). Apart from Tanaka, three other prime ministers were to resign over corruption scandals.

MITI also cartelized services, which were not subject to international competition. The practice of lifetime employment meant that the keiretsu and employers in general were under pressure to preserve jobs. Employers that might have wished to trim their labor forces had to find other ways of coping; cartelization was a popular solution. Lifetime tenure might have saved Japanese workers from the "shame" of losing their job, but it generated a moral hazard problem in that the incentive to perform was reduced. In Chapter 7 we noted that the mandatory retirement age of 55 was to enable firms to terminate lifetime employment without incurring shame, Japanese style.

The keiretsu mitigated the burden of lifetime employment on employers because workers were mobile within keiretsu. So, an employee who had been laid off could be transferred to another job within the keiretsu. Indeed, the development of the keiretsu and the culture of lifetime employment might have been mutually suited to deeper aspects of Japanese culture. A related matter is the Japanese practice of pay according to seniority rather than productivity. Automating pay in this way avoided the embarrassment and shame involved in granting a pay increase to one worker but not to another.

Katz makes the case that by the 1970s the backward tier of the Japanese economy was turning into a millstone around the neck of the dynamic tier. For example, the car industry in the dynamic tier had to buy expensive components from the

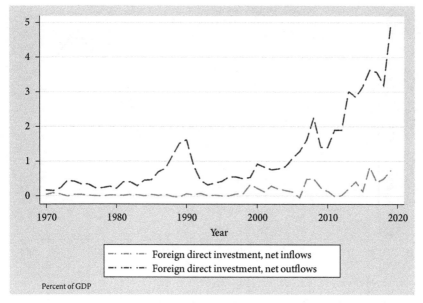

**Fig. 8.3** Foreign Direct Investment
*Source*: e-Stat

backward tier and to pay inflated labor costs. To survive, the car industry and other manufacturing industries switched their production from Japan to other Asian countries and then to the rest of the world, where they would not be committed to lifetime employment and where they could buy cheaper components. To observers outside Japan this looked as though Japan Inc was taking over the world, but it was in fact an act of desperation in the interest of survival.

Katz's thesis is supported by Figures 8.3 and 8.4, which plot foreign direct investment (FDI) as a percentage of GDP and the stock of outward FDI. Unfortunately, the latter data are only available from 1995. Katz was referring to the bulge on outward FDI that occurred around 1990. By contrast, inward FDI was minimal and remained so until 2000. During the lost decade and its New Abnormal aftermath, the share of outward direct investment in GDP continued to grow, reaching 5 percent of GDP by 2020. Whereas the share in GDP of gross domestic fixed capital formation remained flat (Figure 8.2), the share of gross national fixed capital formation continued to grow through outward direct investment. Indeed, by 2018 the stock of outward foreign direct investment had increased fourfold relative to what it was in the late 1990s (Figure 8.4).

The hollowing out of Japanese industry is also reflected in the ratio of gross national product (GNP) to GDP (Figure 8.5). The profits of Japanese companies abroad are part of GNP but not GDP. During the economic miracle GNP was smaller than GDP because there were foreign companies operating in Japan

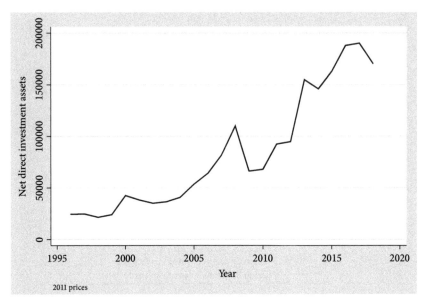

**Fig. 8.4** The Stock of Outward Foreign Direct Investment

*Source*: e-Stat

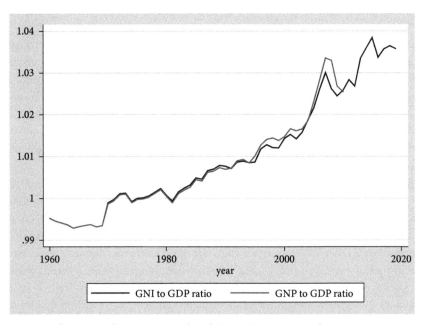

**Fig. 8.5** The Ratio of Gross National and Gross Domestic Product

*Source*: e-Stat

while there were almost no Japanese companies operating abroad. During the lost decade matters began to change; GNP exceeded GDP because Japanese companies began to produce abroad. The increase in GNP relative to GDP reflects the trend in outward FDI relative to inward FDI observed in Figure 8.3. By 2020 GNP was almost 4 percent larger than GDP thanks to the profits and dividends earned on Japanese assets abroad.

Goodhart and Pradhan (2020, Chapter 9) have drawn attention to the "safety valve" of outward direct investment for frustrated Japanese businesses, which established themselves abroad, for essentially the same reasons originally proposed by Katz. Indeed, they ask (without reference to Katz), "Why has outward foreign direct investment not received greater attention?" They also point out that these businesses were reluctant to repatriate their overseas profits due to the fact that they were not eligible for dividend tax exemption policy; hence, they do not fully appear as interest, profits, and dividends in the national income accounts.

By the 1980s the Japanese economy was turning into a rump dominated by the backward tier. The Japanese miracle had turned sour. It is ironical that leading economists such as Lawrence Summers (1989) and Lester Thurow (1992) should have praised the Japanese way of doing business just as it was about to collapse. Katz (1998) was skeptical about Japan's ability to undergo structural reforms in the short run. However, he was confident that matters would be different in the longer term. "While nothing dictates that reform will succeed; it's hard to imagine that a nation as intelligent and resourceful as Japan could let itself fail. At the same time, it's difficult to chart the path that will let Japan overcome its institutional roadblocks in the near future. In all likelihood, Japan will not reform within five years; within twenty, it almost certainly will." (Katz 1998, p 26). He was wrong.

## The Lost Decade and a Half

The OPEC oil price hikes initiated by the Gulf States following the outbreak of the Yom Kippur War in 1973 and by Iran following the Iranian Revolution in 1979 adversely affected economic growth across the world. They halved the rate of growth in Japan too (Figure 8.1). Nevertheless, in comparison with other OECD countries, the Japanese economy was perceived to be relatively immune to the economic damage wrought elsewhere. Indeed, during the 1980s the world looked upon Japan with envy, which explains why leading economists mentioned above and others continued to see in Japan an exemplar worth copying.

During the 1980s Japan sought to liberalize its financial markets "Big Bang" style (after the UK in 1979), which led to an asset price bubble that burst in 1991 and 1992. The confusion that this created obscured the deeper problems facing Japan. "The flawed financial liberalization process combined with a set of political institutions wedded to an old regime, turned Japan into an 'accident waiting to happen'" (Cargill and Sakamoto 2008, p 14). Cargill and Sakamoto refer to "old Japan," which they claim worked until 1980 in the same spirit as others refer to Japan Inc, or I refer to the Japanese model. They argued that the old regime was wedded to mutual support and was overconfident in its ability to manage. According to Weinstein, Kayshap, and Hamada (2011), until 1997 the lost decade seemed just like any other recession. However, they agree that after 1997 there seemed to be some kind of structural break.

As already noted, it was common practice for politicians to take bribes in return for favors. However, public administrators were believed to be beyond reproach. In 1998 two major financial scandals rocked Japan. In January two officials at the Ministry of Finance were accused of selling audit information to four banks under their regulatory supervision. They were also accused of warning banks in advance about spot checks and turning a blind eye to non-performing loans. In April a senior regulator at the Bank of Japan was accused of taking bribes; 98 officials were disciplined, the Governor of the Bank of Japan resigned, and an executive director committed suicide. He was the fifth official to commit suicide in 1998. Also, it was discovered that politicians had been accepting bribes from security firms in the form of "hot" stocks. These scandals turned out to be part of a trend that included the keiretsu as well as public officials and politicians. Also, the suicides were to continue.

Examples of scandals among the keiretsu include the Olympus scandal of 2011, in which $1.7 billion of losses were hidden over two decades; the Toshiba scandal of 2015, in which operating profits were overstated by $1.2 billion; and the Nissan scandal of 2018. These scandals sound as though they belong to a later period, but they do not, because it took many years before they were discovered. For example, the Olympus scandal started in 1991 during the lost decade. Japan is not of course unique in experiencing scandals; however, it may be unique in their longevity. The fact that scandals could last so long is indicative of a culture in which bad behavior is tolerated and blind eyes turned.

This bad behavior should be seen as an intrinsic aspect of the Japanese model. The cozy ethos of mutual backscratching between bankers, businessmen, administrators, central bankers, and politicians was unhealthy and blurred the line between the practical and the criminal.

During the economic miracle MITI reached the peak of its powers. One of the reasons behind its ascendancy stemmed from the Bretton Woods system, under which exchange rates were fixed against the US dollar; MITI was responsible for approving the use of foreign exchange. However, with the breakdown of the Bretton Woods system in 1971 and the transition from fixed to floating or managed exchange rate regimes in Japan and elsewhere, MITI lost some of its importance. In addition, as we have seen, it became an object of criticism, especially by foreign academics, as well as international organizations. As the lost decade dragged on,

MITI became increasingly marginalized until it was formally disbanded in 2001 when the Ministry of Economics and International Trade (METI) was established.

Formally, METI was formed out of MITI and the EPA (Economic Planning Agency). However, its agenda was more liberal and market-orientated than MITI's. METI's mission statement includes three components: promotion of economic vitality in private companies, advancement of external economic relationships, and to secure a stable and efficient supply of energy and raw materials. METI's main purpose was to spearhead structural economic reform. It was specifically instructed to stop undertaking MITI practices such as "pursuing measures to promote specific industries or redistribute income among industries, or to reduce such practices and shift to policies that reject market principles." Also, "The Fair Trade Commission will continue to be responsible for policy on competition that is centered on anti-trust policy, which will not be taken over by METI." Previously, MITI had successfully marginalized the Fair Trade Commission. In summary, METI was to spearhead policy on structural reform, adopt outward-orientated instead of inward-looking international trade policy, promote competition, and join the comity of nations in multilateral trade negotiations.

There is no doubt that the dismantling of MITI constituted a structural reform in its own right. "Nevertheless, in a number of areas, such as energy and chemicals, more traditional policies were still implemented, including tolerance of collusion to avoid excessive competition and restrain imports … the broad outline of policy change and continuity appeared to reflect a METI strategy to enhance its own bureaucratic status." (Elder 2015 p 162). Watanabe (2019, Chapter 4) too argues that in some respects the spirit of MITI lives on in METI, which rescued businesses in the electronics industry such as Renesas Electronics, Sharp, and Toshiba and blocked foreign takeovers. Also, METI continued to pick losers in nuclear power. "These projects led by METI have demonstrated the quintessential industrial policy based on economic nationalism of the Japanese developmental state, but all of them have ended in failure." (Watanabe 2019, p 73).

Prime minister Koizumi (2001–6) understood that Japan needed structural reforms. He opposed the "Old LDP" and its Tanaka faction, fought corruption, encouraged transparency in financial reporting by banks, but lost public support. He was criticized for going too fast. Nevertheless, Cargill and Sakamoto conclude, "A new Japan is emerging – one whose economy is more open and transparent and one whose political institutions are more competitive and responsive to the public … there is more reason to be optimistic than pessimistic about Japan's prospects … Hopefully, Japan will provide in the near future a case study of a country that successfully revitalized its economy from stagnation and adjusted to the economic challenges created by population ageing." (Cargill and Sakamoto 2008, p 298). It turned out to be a case study of failure rather than success.

Chapter 5 has already chronicled Japan's descent into the New Abnormal. It began with the cutting of interest rates by the Bank of Japan until it adopted

**Fig. 8.6** Fiscal Deficit (percent of GDP)
*Source*: Ministry of Finance

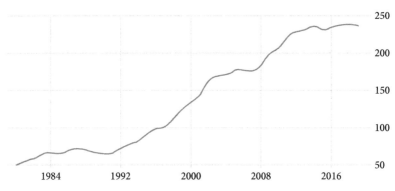

**Fig. 8.7** Public Debt-to-GDP Ratio (percent of GDP)
*Source*: Ministry of Finance

ZIP in 1996 (Table 5.5 in Chapter 5), which was followed by quantitative easing (Figure 5.13 in Chapter 5). Most important is what happened to fiscal policy.
During the economic miracle, Japan operated fiscal surpluses rather than fiscal
deficits (Figure 8.6) so that by 1980 it had reduced the indebtedness inherited
from World War Two to only 50 percent of GDP (Figure 8.7). The halving of
economic growth during the 1980s turned these surpluses into deficits, which
were temporary. During the 1990s Japan began to operate fiscal deficits The debt-
to-GDP ratio increased from about 60 percent to 180 percent! This massive
increase set the scene for what was to follow under the New Abnormal.

Under normal circumstances expansionary monetary and fiscal policy would
be inflationary, especially when Japan had no shortage of aggregate demand, but
a shortage of aggregate supply induced by the breakdown of Japan Inc and a labor
force that was contracting. Expansionary monetary policy had been inflationary
during the economic miracle, so why was it not inflationary during the lost decade?
The answer lies in the liquidity trap induced by ZIP (Chapter 2); the demand for
money became infinitely elastic as the rate of interest tended to zero. The velocity

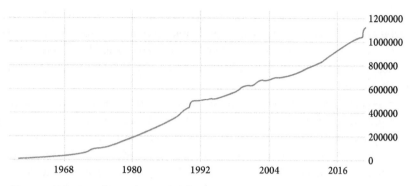

**Fig. 8.8** Velocity of Circulation (M2)
*Source*: Bank of Japan

of circulation of money had increased (Figure 8.8) for structural reasons since the 1960s, and especially because the income elasticity of demand for money in Japan is less than one. The dog-leg in Figure 8.8 coincides with the adoption of ZIP in the 1990s; as expected, velocity grew more slowly after ZIP than before. Velocity increased fivefold between 1960 and 1990, and it increased slightly more than twofold between 1990 and 2020. This difference was not induced by the end of the economic miracle, but by the adoption of ZIP.

In summary, during the lost decade and a half the government tried to spend its way out of recession by introducing aggressive Keynesian-type policies and by cutting the rate of interest to zero. This failed because the recession was not induced by a deficiency in aggregate demand, but by a deficiency in aggregate supply brought about by the breakdown in trust associated with the "Japanese syndrome." This syndrome is deeply rooted in Japanese culture. Because the rate of interest was zero this failure did not express itself in inflation, which remained kinetic.

Following the Koizumi reforms, many observers of the Japanese economy believed that it had turned a corner, and the two lost decades had finally come to an end. Cargill and Sakamoto (2008), mentioned above, were not alone in the optimistic prospects for Japan. "The lost decade is now a thing of the past." (Yoshikawa 2008, p 219). "The recovery in Japan is real, and the signs of an end to the fifteen-year recession are finally here." (Koo 2009, p 1). Finally, "We are confident that in due course the Japanese economy can and will rise again." (Ito, Patrick and Weinstein 2008, p 35). They were all wrong.

"The zero-interest rate may well be a consequence of an uncertainty trap ... a lack of demand creating innovation is a part of the explanation for the lost decade." (Yoshikawa 2008, p 219). According to Yoshikawa, and in reference to the asset pricing bubble induced by the Big Bang, "the instability of the financial system was the ultimate source of uncertainty." (p 240). In the uncertainty trap businesses were frightened of innovating and investing and consumers were scared of consuming. Koo (2009) has a similar theory. In the aftermath of the Big Bang and the credit crunch of 1997–8, corporate balance sheets were over-leveraged. To reduce their indebtedness, businesses cut back on profitable investments because they prioritized balance sheets over profits. By 2005 Japanese companies had adjusted their balance sheets and uncertainty had abated; hence, the lost decades were reputed to have ended.

These authors joined their predecessors such as Katz (1998) in underestimating the profundity of Japan's structural problems, economic, social, and political. A contemporary of these authors (Johnstone 1999) took a more upbeat view of where Japan was heading. According to Johnstone the role of MITI and the bureaucrats had been overestimated if not exaggerated. The Japanese business elite did not passively let the bureaucrats run their lives. On the contrary, the business elite had always been the engine of economic growth in Japan. As Japan entered the 21$^{st}$ century Johnstone expected this elite would lift the Japanese economy out of the doldrums by leveraging the digital revolution. However, the 21$^{st}$ century, to which we now turn, has continued to be disappointing thus far.

## The New Abnormal: Abenomics

Following Koizumu's failed attempt to carry out structural reforms, Japan entered into a mature phase of the New Abnormal, which commenced with the appointment of Shinzo Abe as prime minister in 2006. Abe served twice as prime minister, from September 2006 to September 2007 and from December 2012 to September 2020. In the interim, the LDP ceased to hold power. It was during the latter period that so-called "Abenomics" was conceived and implemented. Abenomics comprised three "arrows." The first consisted of expansionary monetary policy designed to end price deflation and to achieve an inflation target of 2 percent per year. The policy rate of the Bank of Japan was to remain zero, and QE was to be greatly extended in scale and in scope. The second arrow consisted of expansionary fiscal policy to support economic recovery. The third arrow was the most important (and if it was so important why was it not the first arrow?): structural reform. There were two key components to the latter: reforms to make the labor market more flexible, and reforms related to the demographic imbalance brought about by declining fertility (Chapter 6) and by increasing longevity (Table 8.1) among pensioners.

The main labor market reform was to enable a limited number of foreign workers to work in Japan to make up for the labor shortage brought about by the shrinkage in population (Figure 8.13). Structural reforms intended to change lifetime employment and pay according to seniority were not implemented in practice. The government also provided incentives to increase fertility by providing free preschool facilities and increasing the supply of subsidized child care. The reversal

**Table 8.1** Life Expectancy

|       | At birth | | At 70 | |
|-------|--------|--------|--------|--------|
|       | Men    | Women  | Men    | Women  |
| 1947  | 50.06  | 53.96  | 7.93   | 9.41   |
| 1975  | 71.73  | 76.89  | 10.53  | 12.78  |
| 1985  | 74.78  | 80.48  | 12.00  | 14.89  |
| 1995  | 76.38  | 82.85  | 12.97  | 16.76  |
| 2005  | 78.56  | 85.52  | 14.39  | 18.88  |
| 2010  | 79.55  | 86.3   | 14.96  | 19.43  |
| 2015  | 80.75  | 86.99  | 15.59  | 19.85  |
| 2017  | 81.09  | 87.26  | 15.73  | 20.03  |

*Source*: e-Stat

**Table 8.2** Fertility

|       | Total fertility | Net rate of reproduction | Crude birth rate |
|-------|-----------------|--------------------------|------------------|
| 1950  | 4.25            |                          | 28.69            |
| 1955  | 2.40            | 1.28                     | 20.17            |
| 1960  | 2.00            | 0.98                     | 17.41            |
| 1965  | 2.14            | 0.94                     | 17.58            |
| 1970  | 2.13            | 0.96                     | 18.73            |
| 1975  | 1.91            | 1.01                     | 17.27            |
| 1980  | 1.75            | 0.88                     | 13.84            |
| 1985  | 1.76            | 0.85                     | 11.87            |
| 1990  | 1.54            | 0.79                     | 10.35            |
| 1995  | 1.42            | 0.71                     | 9.57             |
| 2000  | 1.36            | 0.66                     | 9.14             |
| 2005  | 1.26            | 0.63                     | 8.77             |
| 2010  | 1.39            | 0.65                     | 8.59             |
| 2015  | 1.45            | 0.68                     | 7.96             |
| 2019  | 1.37            |                          | 7.31             |

*Source*: Total Fertility: e-Stat. Data for 1950 and 1955 Winter and Teitelbaum (2013, p 71), Net rate of reproduction (daughters per woman), Crude birth rate (per 1000), Koenka.

in the decline of total fertility (Chapter 6 and Table 8.2) and its subsequent minor recovery may be related to this policy.

Perhaps the most important structural reform concerned the fiscal burden induced by the coincidence of population ageing accompanied by low fertility (Chapter 7). The main impetus of policy was to encourage senior citizens to postpone their retirement and to abolish the practice of mandatory retirement operated by employers. Recall from Chapter 7 that there is a five-year difference

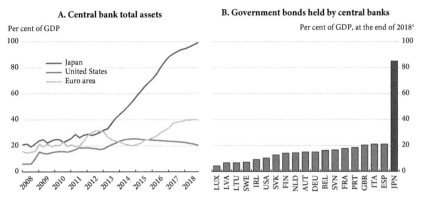

**Fig. 8.9** Ultra Quantitative Easing
*Source*: OECD (2019) p 33.

between the mandatory age of retirement and the age for pension eligibility. Employees who continued working lost their status as "regular" workers and took large pay cuts as a result (Figure 8.17). Many preferred to leave the labor force. To offset this disincentive to keep working, the government also provided incentives for senior citizens to postpone their retirement by enhancing their pension if they continued to work.

Figure 8.9 reinforces the conclusion in Chapter 5 that not only was the Bank of Japan a pioneer in QE, it has applied QE more aggressively by far than other central banks. At the end of 2018 the debt-to-GDP ratio stood at 240 percent (Figure 8.6), and the Bank of Japan owned 82 percent of public debt (Figure 8.9). This means that the net debt-to-GDP ratio was substantially smaller (about 160 percent) after consolidating the balance sheets of the Ministry of Finance and the Bank of Japan. At the end of 2018 the assets of the Bank of Japan amounted to almost 100 percent of GDP (Figure 8.9 panel A), of which 18 percent included ETFs (index funds of Japanese equity) and J-REITs (Japan Real Estate Investment Trusts). The Bank of Japan currently owns about 80 percent of the ETF market. The Bank of Japan had expanded the scope of QE to equity and real estate.

This policy was designed to flatten the yield curve, or in central bank parlance the Bank of Japan officially engaged in "QE with yield curve control" in September 2016. The effect of this policy is clearly apparent in Figure 8.10. Ultra-aggressive QE forced bond yields down into negative regions and the gap between long and short rates was halved.

Whereas between 1997 and 2012 GDP grew by 0.6 percent (Figure 8.1) and inflation was negative between 1997 and 2017 (Figure 8.11), GDP grew by 1.2 percent after 2015. Optimists began to feel that Abenomics had turned the tide on deflation. Moreover, employment, which had peaked in 1997 and decreased subsequently, increased after 2012, and passed its previous peak in 2017

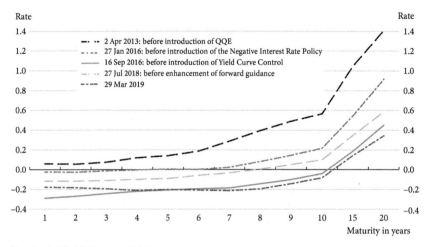

**Fig. 8.10** Yield Curves 2013–19
*Source*: OECD (2019) p 35.

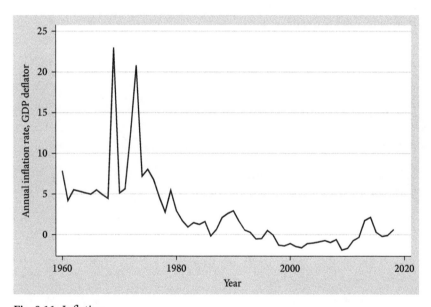

**Fig. 8.11** Inflation
*Source*: Author based on e-stat.

(Figure 8.14). The rate of unemployment decreased to its lowest level since the end of the economic miracle (Figure 8.12). The increase in employment was also enabled by an increase in the participation ratio after 2016, which had been in secular decline since 1960 (Figure 8.13). On the other hand, the growth in labor productivity, which had been 0.9 percent per year dropped to zero after 2012. Abenomics

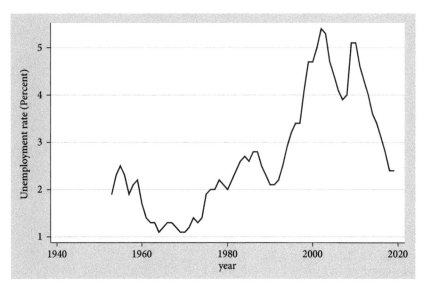

**Fig. 8.12**  The Rate of Unemployment
*Source*: Author based on e-stat.

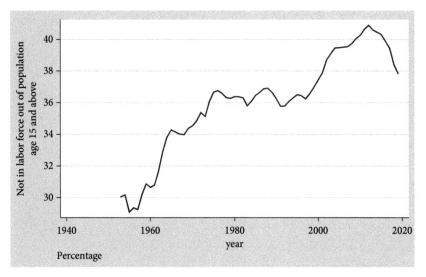

**Fig. 8.13**  Non-Participation in Labor Force
*Source*: Author based on e-stat.

had failed to increase labor productivity, whose lackluster performance had been the proximate cause of the lost decade and a half.

The third arrow of Abenomics involved structural reforms. Labor market reform was a key component of the third arrow of Abenomics. The population of

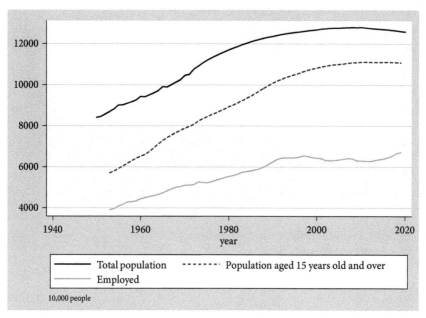

**Fig. 8.14** Demography and Employment
*Source*: Author based on e-stat.

Japan is among the most homogeneous in the world, and Japan has one of the smallest shares of foreign-born, most of whom are ethnic Japanese born in South Korea and Latin America (Figure 8.15). The government sees foreign workers as a solution to labor shortages created by population decline. Between 2013 and 2017 the number of foreign workers doubled to 1.3 million, most of whom were on five-year trainee visas. In 2018 a new residency status was created for trainees to remain for five additional years after completing their training, provided that they speak Japanese, among other criteria. These initiatives are far removed from foreign worker policies in other OECD countries. It is unlikely that Japan will allow its extreme ethnic homogeneity to be diluted.

When the pensionable age was 60 the mandatory retirement age was 55. With the raising of the pensionable age to 65 firms have raised the mandatory retirement age to 60. The Act for the Stabilization of Employment for Elderly Persons was revised to encourage forms to raise the mandatory age of retirement to at least 65, if not to abolish mandatory retirement altogether. In 2005 91 percent of firms practiced mandatory retirement at 60 (Figure 8.16). By 2010 this percentage decreased to 81 percent, but did not decrease further subsequently. Figure 8.16 also records rehiring rates among mandatory retirees, which rose towards 20 percent for retirees age 65 and over. Figure 8.16 shows that the mandatory retirement problem has hardly been mitigated and that firms continue to force workers into retirement after which they rehire them at a reduced wage.

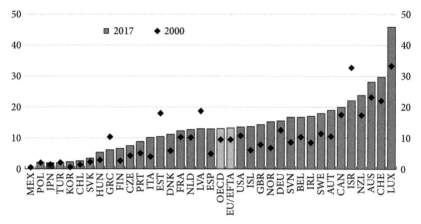

**Fig. 8.15** Population Shares for Foreign Born
*Source*: OECD (2019) p 107.

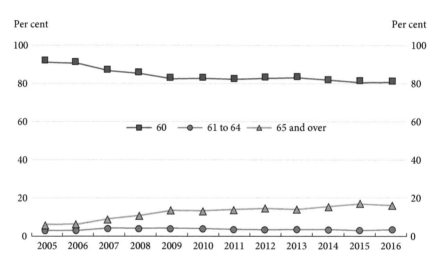

**Fig. 8.16** Mandatory Retirement

Figure 8.17 shows that raising the age of eligibility for pensions prolonged working lives. However, Table 8.1 shows that the life expectancy of senior citizens increased at approximately the same pace as the increase in pensionable age. Therefore, the need remains to increase the age of eligibility for pensions. However, there are currently no plans to raise pensionable age beyond 65. Meanwhile, longevity among senior citizens shows no sign of slowing down.

The culture of lifetime employment remains strong, but it has weakened slightly. In 2016, 46 percent of male employees in large manufacturing firms aged 50 to 59 had never changed employer. Lifetime employment is more prevalent in large firms, among graduates, and among men aged 40 and above in 2016. However,

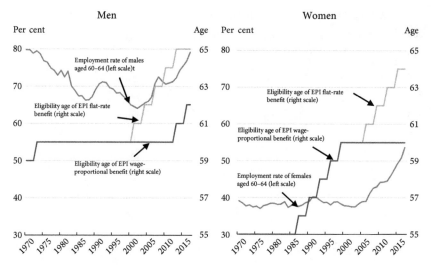

**Fig. 8.17** Pension Eligibility and Employment Rates
*Source*: OECD (2019) p 78.

**Table 8.3** Share of Lifetime Employees in Male Employees (%)

| Age | 2006 | 2016 |
|---|---|---|
| 5–29 | 43.2 | 46.7 |
| 30–39 | 31.2 | 23.5 |
| 40–49 | 29.4 | 24.3 |
| 50–59 | 22.7 | 23.8 |

Based on data in OECD (2019) pp 77 and 78.

lifetime employment was less prevalent in 2016 than in 2006 for employees aged 30 to 49 (Table 8.3).

The weakening of lifetime employment is reflected in a weakening in seniority-based pay (Figure 8.18). Regardless of firm size, the age–wage relation in 2016 was weaker than in 2006. For example, in medium sized firms, employees aged 55 to 59 in 2006 earned 255 percent more than employees aged 20 to 24, whereas in 2016 they earned 229 percent more. The sharp drop in relative pay for employees aged 60 to 64 is induced by the mandatory age of retirement at 60 years, as already mentioned. Notice that this effect was stronger in 2016 than in 2006.

The age–wage profiles in Figure 8.18 also apply in other countries in which pay is not based on seniority. According to human capital theory, pay varies directly with age-related experience, with a wide variance reflecting the unobserved ability of individual workers. Moreover, this variance tends to be proportionately greater

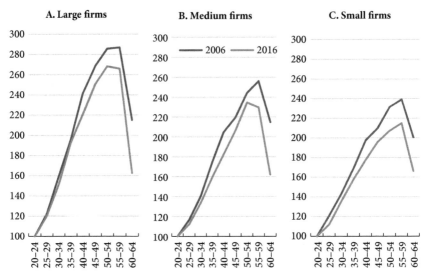

**Fig. 8.18**  Seniority-based Pay: 2006 and 2016

Note: Lifetime employees are all employees who were continuously employed by enterprises directly after leaving school or university. Large firms are those with more than a thousand employees and small firms are those with between ten and ninety-nine.
*Source*: OECD (2019) p 76.

among younger workers, whose ability is relatively less observable. In Japan the correlation coefficient between pay and age is much higher than elsewhere because ability and pay are less related in Japan than elsewhere.

As we have seen, the lack of corporate governance in Japan provided an environment in which corruption could thrive and agency problems became endemic. Agents such as senior management were not answerable to their principals; they struck deals with bureaucrats and politicians, and company directors were appointed in the interest of agents rather than principals. In 2017 the New Economic Policy Package called for improving corporate governance. This led to the Corporate Governance System Guideline in 2018, which embodied several significant changes. First, cross-shareholdings within holding companies were to be reviewed annually and disclosed. Recall that cross-shareholdings support the financial architecture of the keiretsu. Second, directors should be more diverse. The chairperson should be a non-executive director. This change is intended to give more power to directors in representing the interests of principals. Third, boards should appoint and dismiss CEOs transparently. Fourth, independent advisory committees should be appointed for remunerations and nominations.

It is too soon to evaluate whether corporate governance has improved. An encouraging sign is that, "The share of large firms with more than two independent directors increased from less than a half in 2015 to 91 percent in 2018." (OECD 2019, p 49).

In March 2011 the Fukushima nuclear disaster struck. Earthquakes and tsunamis had occurred before in the area, and in the tenth century the area experienced a tsunami on the scale that occurred in March 2011. In addition, there is a widespread view that the calamity was man-made rather than natural (Funabashi 2012). MITI and its successor (METI) had been responsible for nuclear energy development, which was badly planned. Risks were taken to cut costs, there was insufficient stress-testing, and warning signs had been ignored. The calamity had the hallmarks of another failure of Japan Inc. At the very least a public inquiry might have been expected. The government undertook administrative reforms to prevent further recurrences. No one took responsibility. Faces were saved.

In summary, the New Abnormal continued unabated under Abe (the New Abenormal?) The third arrow involving structural reform achieved very little. The labor market remained inflexible in terms of lifelong employment and seniority-based pay. The gradual increase in the retirement age to 65 did not take proper account of increasing longevity among senior citizens. Outward foreign direct investment by the dynamic tier continued apace (Figure 8.3), increasing to 5 percent of GDP by the time Abe resigned in 2020, and labor productivity continues to be static. Abe's resignation was officially for reasons of health. Associates of his had been involved in alleged scandals, including Tsukosa Akinoto, who was arrested in December 2019 on suspicion of taking bribes. In May 2020, 660 lawyers filed a criminal complaint against Abe and two of his aides over the "cherry blossom party" affair, in which public funds were allegedly use to pay for the party. Yoshihida Suga, who took over from Abe as prime minister, was one of these aides.

Unlike the authors mentioned at the end of the two previous subsections, Watanabe (2019) is more sanguine about Japan's economic plight. He identifies two structural issues. The first, which has been discussed at length above, is that the spirit of Japan Inc, or Old Japan, lives on. The triangle binding keiretsu, METI, and politics continues to be eternal, if less forceful. He refers to the second as the "Galopagos Syndrome," in which Japan's digital economy has developed separately from global developments and, consequently, less efficiently. He concludes, "The Japanese economy may not face immediate or rapid decline. However, its challenges need to be overcome. Although politics matters significantly in this respect, there is no guarantee that future Japanese leaders will be able to manage the economy and solve these challenges. Although Japan needs to rid itself of the legacy of the developmental state and reduce the influence of powerful interest groups in order to promote economic efficiency through digitalization, it would also eventually need to establish a more competitive democracy by overcoming the one-party dominance of the LDP and transform itself from a corporate-centered society to a consumer-orientated one." (p 166).

## The Future

The massive increase in the debt-to-GDP ratio resulted from ultra-expansionary fiscal policy in which Japan tried in vain to spend its way out of its lost decades. During this period, Japan's demographic imbalance, which increased social spending on senior citizens, contributed significantly to the increase in public indebtedness.

Between 1994 and 2016, the population share of senior citizens increased from 16 percent to 27 percent (Figure 8.19). Social benefits in cash and kind, including state pensions, increased from 15 percent of GDP to 25 percent of GDP. In the future, however, the demographic imbalance is projected to be more important, with fewer Japanese in employment having to support a growing number in retirement. In its most recent review of the Japanese economy, the OECD undertook an analysis of the implications of Japan's demographic imbalance for the fiscal solvency of Japan (OECD 2019).

Note, however, that even without its peculiar demographics Japan faces a solvency problem to which we shall return in Chapter 10. Since the current debt-to-GDP ratio is close to 250 percent, Japan is caught in a debt trap because ending ZIP would massively increase the cost of debt service, which thanks to ZIP is minimal. The increase in debt service would drive the primary deficit into a politically unfeasible surplus. Hence, the OECD study is largely concerned with maintaining the status quo, and preventing the debt-to-GDP ratio from reaching 600 percent by 2060.

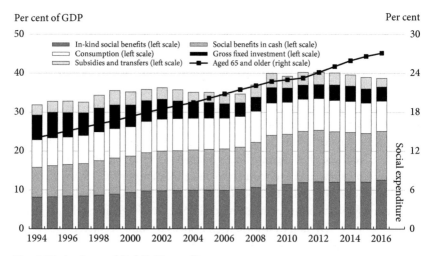

**Fig. 8.19** Ageing and Public Expenditure
*Source*: OECD (2019) p 124.

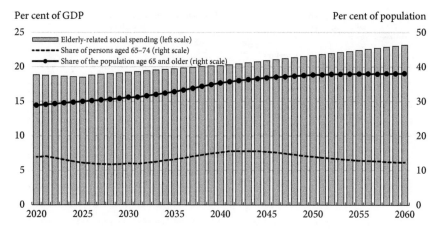

**Fig. 8.20** The Demographic Outlook
*Source*: OECD (2019) p 130.

In 2020, senior citizens (aged 65+) accounted for 28.9 percent of the population. Extrapolating current total fertility and trends in life expectancy among
senior citizens implies that their share in the population will increase towards
40 percent by 2060 (Figure 8.20). Age-related social spending, including state pensions and income support, accounted for 18.9 percent of GDP in 2020, which
is projected to grow to 23.2 percent of GDP by 2060 under current pension
and social security policy. Whereas the population share stabilizes, the social
spending share continues to increase because health care per head varies directly
with age.

Japan is an outlier in terms of its decrease in its population of working age during
2000 and 2018 (Figure 8.21 panel A). It is also an outlier in terms of its dependency
ratio, according to which in 2017 the average worker had half a senior citizen
dependent on him or her (Figure 8.21 panel B). By 2050. the dependency ratio
in Japan is expected to reach 80 percent. Dependency ratios are expected to increase elsewhere too, by 2050, the average dependency ratio for OECD countries
as a whole is projected to reach the current level in Japan (50 percent). Although
life expectancy in Japan is the highest among OECD countries, it is not particularly unusual (Figure 8.21 panel C). As noted in Chapter 6, total fertility in Japan
is unusually small, although Spain and Italy have experienced low total fertility,
but for less time than Japan. This explains why the population of working age in
Japan peaked in the early 1990s, about fifteen years ahead of the population as a
whole (Figure 8.20 panel D). By 2050, the population in Japan is projected to be
100 million or 22 percent smaller than at its peak. The growing dependency ratio
is reflected in the vertical distance between the two upper schedules in panel D.

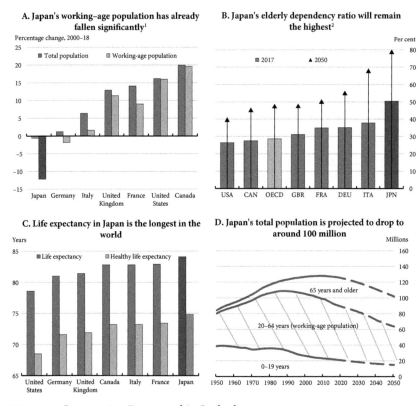

**Fig. 8.21** Comparative Demographic Outlook

The ageing of the population is reflected in the downward trend in the zero to nineteen age group.

To project Japan's debt-to-GDP ratio, the OECD study used fiscal arithmetic similar to what was presented in Chapter 2. Tables 8.4 record the macroeconomic and fiscal assumptions used in these projections. The population of working age is projected to decrease on average by 0.9 percent per year. However, labor input is projected to decrease by 0.3 percent per year thanks to an increase in participation, slightly offset by a decline in hours. Hence, over the period as a whole, the growth in labor productivity reaches 1.8 percent per year. Inflation is assumed to reach its target of 2 percent by 2028. Table 8.4A assumes that Japan ends ZIP and that the rate of interest is raised to 1.8 percent in the short run, and to 5 percent from 2028. The real rate of interest, which is currently negative, is assumed to be 3 percent from 2028.

The underlying government healthcare spending projections in Table 8.4B, column 5 are based on current per capita benefit levels by age, taking changes in demographic structure into account as a result of which healthcare spending

**Table 8.4A** Macroeconomic Assumptions in OECD
Study (% pa)

|        | Economic growth | Inflation | Interest rate |
|--------|-----------------|-----------|---------------|
| **2021–7** | 2.0 | 1.4 | 1.8 |
| **2028–60** | 1.4 | 2.0 | 5.0 |

**Table 8.4B** Spending and Revenue Assumptions (percent of GDP)

|        | Public pension | Social security | Other spending | Tax and social security | Health care |
|--------|----------------|-----------------|----------------|-------------------------|-------------|
| **2020** | 9.8 | 2.6 | 15.5 | 34.3 | 9.0 |
| **2025** | 9.1 | 2.7 | 15.5 | 34.3 | 9.4 |
| **2040** | 9.2 | 2.8 | 15.5 | 34.3 | 11.0 |
| **2060** | 9.5 | 2.8 | 15.5 | 34.3 | 13.7 |

increases from 9 percent of GDP to 13.7 percent due to population ageing. Social security spending (column 2) is projected to increase too, but more modestly. Tax and social security contributions and other public spending as a percentage of GDP are assumed to remain at their current levels.

These assumptions generate the baseline projection in Figure 8.22A (dark grey schedule), in which by 2060 the debt-to-GDP ratio reaches 560 percent of GDP. To gauge the impact of population ageing on the debt-to-GDP ratio, healthcare benefits and other social security benefits as percentages of GDP are assumed to remain at their current levels. In this scenario the debt-to-GDP ratio in 2060 is reduced to 455 percent of GDP (not shown in Figure 8.22A) from 560 percent. Hence, the fiscal implications of ageing are large, but in Japan they are dwarfed by deeper structural issues.

To quantify the scale of these structural issues, suppose that Japan ran a primary fiscal balance from 2025. Figure 8.22A (Medium grey schedule) shows that the debt-to-GDP ratio would reach 344 percent of GDP by 2060 instead of 560 percent of GDP. The debt-to-GDP ratio continues to increase because the fiscal deficit equals the interest cost of debt service if the primary deficit is zero. Given the initial conditions for the debt-to-GDP ratio and the assumptions about the rate of interest and the rate of growth of nominal GDP in Table 8.4A, the fiscal deficit continues to be large.

This demonstrates that Japan is caught in a debt trap; exiting ZIP and running a balanced primary budget is not feasible. If, in addition, between 2026 and 2035

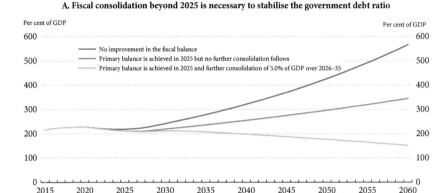

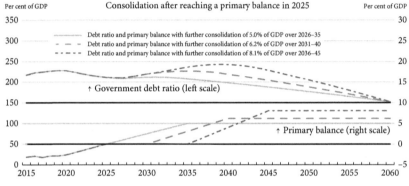

**Fig. 8.22** Fiscal Projections 2020–60
*Source*: OECD (2019) p 31.

it runs a primary surplus of 5 percent of GDP, the debt-to-GDP ratio is reduced to 152 percent of GDP by 2060 (light grey schedule). Panel B shows some other scenarios that would reduce the debt-to-GDP ratio in 2060 to somewhere in the region of 150 percent of GDP. The primary fiscal surpluses involved in these scenarios are most probably politically unfeasible. Even during the economic miracle when Japan ran fiscal surpluses, they never reached 5 percent of GDP, nor did they last for so long.

In summary, we agree with Baldwin and Allison (2015) that Japan's future is precarious. While Japan was hopeful that Abenomics might end its lost decades, in 2021 Japan's future looks more precarious than it did six years ago. Japan is trapped by its debt. If it raises interest rates even modestly it would have to operate large primary fiscal surpluses, which means either large cuts in public spending or higher taxation. As for the latter, the OECD study assumes optimistically that higher taxation will not adversely affect economic growth. The combination of population ageing and a severe decline in fertility make bad matters worse. Even without these demographic trends, Japan would have been stuck in a debt trap.

Japan's continued failure to undergo structural reforms to lift the economy out of its cumulation of lost decades raises the question of whether there is some deeper force at work, which accounts for this failure. The next section is concerned with this deeper force.

## 'Face' in Japan's Economic Architecture

Face-saving is a universal phenomenon, but it is particularly important among Asian peoples and societies (Kim and Nan 1998) and it assumes an extreme form in Japan (Matsumoto 1996, Lebra 1976). I shall argue that many of Japan's structural economic problems may have deep cultural foundations related to *mentsu* (face). For example, peculiarly Japanese practices such as lifelong employment and seniority-based wages are in fact face-saving arrangements, as were MITI's policies to protect and cartelize failed infant industries: to have let them close down would have been an admission of failure, leading to loss of face. The same applies to the embellishment of bank balance sheets by overlooking non-performing loans, and the overstatement of profits in corporate accounts. These and other practices share a common cultural denominator: they save face.

If this thesis is empirically valid it does not bode well for structural economic reform in Japan. Reform is rather like asking a leopard to change its spots. It also explains why Japan has failed to reform, and why what was initially a lost decade has turned into a lost thirty years. In time it will most probably turn into a lost half century. Whereas there is general agreement that face plays a key role in Japan's business organization (Kim and Nan 1998, Waugh 2005, Waugh and Watanabe 2009), the role of face in the Japanese economy and the design of economic policy has not been explored. Kim and Nan remark that western models of business organization are not relevant to Asia, and Waugh warns western business personnel about pitfalls in negotiating with their Japanese counterparts. A natural extension, therefore, is to explore the possible relation between face and Japan's economic architecture.

Whereas in western societies face is an individual phenomenon, in Japan it is also a collective or group phenomenon. The cultivation of social harmony runs deep in Japan (Lebra 1976). So, it is important for embarrassment among the group, through confrontational individual behavior, to be avoided. This is the opposite of the western model, in which justified confrontation is valued even if the group has to pay a price. Perhaps even more important than face-saving is face-giving to the group. Whereas face-saving is about avoiding embarrassment of the group, face-giving is concerned with making the group feel more harmonious. In summary, whereas the western model values the individual over the group, the Japanese model values the group over the individual.

Hierarchy, like face, is a universal phenomenon. However, hierarchy matters more in Asian than in western societies, and it is extremely important in Japan. Although Japan is not China, in Confucian culture senior personnel in the hierarchy expect more respect than they would in western organizations. Since the group is hierarchical, it is especially important to ensure harmony in its upper echelons. For example, senior managers lose face more easily than their junior counterparts. Therefore, individuals in the group face a double balancing act. Apart from maintaining harmony horizontally within their level in the hierarchy, they must also maintain harmony vertically throughout the hierarchical chain.

Criticism may upset the harmony of the group in its various aspects. Hence, in Japanese organizations it must be handled with extreme care, especially when more senior members of the hierarchy are involved. For criticism to be effective, it must emerge by consensus. Whereas in western organizations junior personnel might catch the ear of senior management to criticize intermediate management, this would not be acceptable in Japan. Argumentative personnel risk being ostracized. As a result, the concept of truth in Japanese organizations is relative rather than absolute. If telling the truth threatens the harmony of the group, it is better not to say it. Ways must be found to soften its edges so that especially senior personnel in the group are saved face. Loss of face among seniors will adversely affect the harmony of the group as a whole.

The institution of lifetime employment avoids the loss of face in laying off workers. It also maintains harmony among the work force as a group. At age 55 workers reach the age of mandatory retirement (not to be confused with retirement age, Chapter 7), which is the Japanese way of ending lifetime employment with minimal loss of face. It is better in terms of harmony if all workers are laid off as a group rather than some are laid off individually.

The same applies to pay according to seniority. If pay was by merit, workers who did not get an increase in pay would lose face, and workers who got a pay rise would be embarrassed. Also, harmony among workers as a group would be disturbed. Workers with more merit prefer to give face to workers with less merit.

If MITI had allowed failed infant industries to close, this would have involved loss of face, especially by senior personnel who initiated them. Also, personnel in the failed industries concerned would have suffered loss of face. By protecting and cartelizing these failed industries, MITI personnel saved face among their group and gave face to personnel in the industries concerned. This would not have made sense in the west, but it made sense in Japan. This syndrome also helps to rationalize the practice of avoiding loan loss provisions for non-performing loans in bank balance sheets. Face would be lost by the loan officers concerned as well as the debtors. The culture of zombie loans may be understood in terms of face-saving and giving. It might also help to understand the Olympus scandal of 2011, in which \$1.7 billion of losses were hidden over two decades,; the Toshiba scandal of 2015, in which operating profits were overstated by \$1.2 billion, and the Nissan scandal of 2018. Papering over the cracks preserves harmony. Facing the truth is disruptive.

This cultural or ethnographic theory for the lost decades implies that the Japanese almost have to change their DNA to overcome the structural economic problems that confront them. A similar point has been made by Katzner (2007), who argues that Anglo-Saxon cultural norms, which emphasize rationalism, liberty, individualism, and efficiency, do not go down well in Japan. Hence, reform in Japan is not a relatively simple matter of changing incentives and regulatory practices as it might be elsewhere. On the other hand, cultural norms are not necessarily cast in stone. For example, the prevalence of lifetime employment has weakened, although it remains widespread. Also, pay based on merit is becoming more common. In any case, societies do not have to adopt western cultural standards. The Japanese need to find their way of respecting their own culture.

Lebra (1976 p 257) herself was not optimistic about the ability of the Japanese to undergo cultural change. On the one hand, she noted, "the postwar generation compared with the prewar, parental generation, is weaker in social relativism, less socially sensitive, and has a stronger bias toward unilateral egoism ... Japan might be moving toward the Western model based on the complex of individuality, autonomy, equality, rationality, aggression, and self-assertion, and away from the traditional complex of collectivism, interdependence, super-ordination-coordination, empathy, sentimentality, introspection, and self-denial." On the other hand, "I have a hunch that any immediate changes will be constrained or contaminated by the traditional system." She was right.

## Personal Note

I joined HM Treasury in London as an economist in 1970 aged 23; it was my first job. Each economist was allocated a country to follow; mine was Japan. In 1972 it was the turn of the UK to chair the discussion at the OECD on its review of the Japanese economy. The Foreign Office asked the Treasury to assist; I was given the task. The Japanese delegation was large and included senior officials. There were delegates from many other countries in the main conference room. I was the sole UK delegate. The Foreign Office received a formal complaint from the Japanese that the UK delegate was too junior and that the delegation was too small.

In 1980 I was invited by the Economic Planning Agency as a consultant. My suitcase failed to turn up at the airport in Tokyo, where representatives of EPA met me. When they understood that I was without my suitcase, they became very worried. When we arrived at my hotel, an EPA official was waiting with several borrowed suits for me to try on. They were all too small. It was a Sunday and the shops were closed, so I could not buy a suit to fit. I was told that I was due to meet the Director of the EPA at 9 o'clock the following morning, which was why it was urgent to obtain a suit.

I was still in my jeans when I met the Director. He could not look at me; everyone was deeply embarrassed. My suitcase turned up three days later, but it took much longer for everyone to get over it.

## Suicide

Suicide runs deep in Japanese culture (Lebra 1976, Chapter 11), and *hara-kiri* (ritual suicide) has been ennobled in Japanese Samurai history and literature; it is better to kill oneself than to face the shame of defeat (as did Generals Ushijima and Saito after the defeat at Okinawa, General Anami after the Japanese surrender, and the attempted suicide of Tojo, who survived to be executed in 1948). Although Japan has the highest suicide rate among OECD countries, 29 countries have higher suicide rates, including Guyana and Lesotho with the highest. Otherwise, the suicide rate in Japan is not much higher than in Belgium and Sweden.

If a cultural phenomenon as deeply entrenched as suicide can be mitigated by policy reforms, then perhaps other cultural phenomena that underpin Japan's lost decades can be mitigated through reform. The leopard might be helped to change its spots, or at least, some of them.

The suicide rate in Japan was fairly stable between 1960 to 1990, at an average of 23 suicides per year per 100,000. Suicide rates vary directly with age (Figure 8.23). However, suicide rates among the population aged 70+ have converged from above on the suicide rates among people aged 50 to 69. After 1995 suicide rates began to increase and remained high until 2010. Yoshikawa (2008 p 220) attributes the increase in the suicide rate in the late 1990s to the continuation and prolongation of the lost decades, which inculcated a sense of hopelessness in the future. Perhaps this explains why suicide rates increased among the population of working age, but decreased among the retired population.

In 2009 the government launched a program to reduce suicides by providing SOS helplines, improving treatment for failed suicides and promoting publicity campaigns and educational programs to weaken the endemic suicide culture. During 2010–15 suicide rates decreased but stabilized subsequently. The age-standardized suicide rate after 2015 reverted to its level in the early 1990s. Just as it might have been precipitous of Yoshikawa to attribute the increase in the suicide rate to the depressed state of the economy, so might it be precipitous to attribute the subsequent decrease in the suicide rate to the success of government's program to cut the suicide rate. Had the suicide rate decreased relative to its level in the early 1990s, this might have suggested that the Japanese are capable of deep cultural change.

**Suicide death rate by age, Japan, 1990 to 2017**
Death rate from suicide measured per 100,000 individuals across various age categories. Also shown is the total death rate across all ages (not age-standardized) and the age-standardized death rate. Age-Standardization assumes a constant population age & structure to allow for comparisons between countries and with time without the effects of a changing age distribution within a population (e.g. aging).

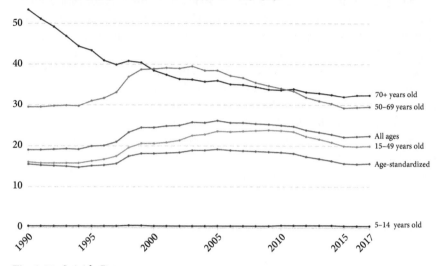

**Fig. 8.23**  Suicide Rates
*Source*: Global Burden of Disease (Our World in Data)

The cultures of face-saving and suicide are deeply embedded. The structural reforms required to put an end to the chain of lost decades share the common denominator of face-saving and face-giving. The prospects for structural reform are slim if not zero.

## Synopsis

Because Japan has been entangled in the New Abnormal since the 1990s, it may serve as a crystal ball for its long-term economic and social consequences. By contrast, other countries such as the US and UK are relative newcomers to the New Abnormal. Our thesis is that Japan became entangled because, for deeply cultural reasons, it was unable to carry out structural reforms that were necessary in the aftermath of its postwar economic miracle.

After the Meiji reforms in the late nineteenth century, Japan adopted a statist form of political economy in which bureaucrats directed credit to family-run industrial agglomerates (zaibatsu) and the favored received protection in terms of trade policy and cartelization. After World War Two, this political economy was re-established under the tutelage of the all-powerful Ministry of International Trade and Industry (MITI), the Bank of Japan, the Ministry of Finance, the Economic Planning Agency, the keiretsu (successors to the zaibatsu but no longer family-run) and the Liberal Democratic Party. Politicians, bureaucrats and businessmen combined forces to create the postwar economic miracle.

The economic miracle ended in the late 1980s. Not only did economic growth cease to be stellar, it vanished completely. The so-called lost decade failed to respond to expansionary fiscal and monetary policies, and turned into the lost decades. The cozy relations between politicians, bureaucrats, and businessmen fostered corruption and a wave of financial and economic scandals involving senior politicians, bureaucrats (including from the Bank of Japan), and businessmen. Public trust broke down. By 1996 the Bank of Japan had cut its rate of interest to almost zero, and it has remained there ever since.

After 2000 the Ministry of Finance ran large fiscal deficits, partly to pump-prime the economy out of recession and price deflation, and partly to pay for the cost of looking after the burgeoning population of pensioners. By 2021 the debt-to-GDP ratio reached 260 percent of GDP, and is still rising. Meanwhile, successive governments failed to undertake essential structural reforms in corporate governance, social spending, the labor market, and the capital market.

The repeated failure to undertake structural reforms does not result from short-termism in policy making; it results from deeply ingrained cultural reasons that are peculiar to Japan. The common denominator to many of Japan's structural problems is *mentsu* (face-saving). Since structural reform clashes with *mentsu*, it has not been implemented, and Japan has tried to paper over the cracks by implementing the New Abnormal instead.

A recent study by the OECD shows that Japan is caught in a debt trap. Even if it runs unprecedented primary fiscal surpluses, the debt-to-GDP ratio will continue to grow towards 400 percent in the next decades. Escape from the New Abnormal seems impossible.

# 9

# Covid-19 and the New Abnormal

The world has experienced pandemics in the past and will continue to experience them in the future. However, the policy response to the Covid-19 pandemic has been abnormal. Instead of passively waiting for the pandemic to run its course, as in the case of Spanish flu a century ago or swine flu in 2009, governments fought it by implementing mitigation policies at enormous economic and social cost. Moreover, these costs are out of all proportion to the social benefit of life years saved, or QALYS (quality-adjusted life years saved) as health economists refer to it.

Had the pandemic broken out prior to the New Abnormal it is doubtful that governments would have fought it; they most probably would have waited for the pandemic to run its course, as they did in the past. However, because the pandemic broke out in 2020 rather than 2000, or even 2010, their experience of the New Abnormal induced them to be active rather than passive. They figured that they could finance mitigation policy by running fiscal deficits at almost zero cost because, thanks to ZIP, the cost of debt service was small if not zero, and because, thanks to the liquidity trap, fiscal deficits and quantitative easing were not inflationary. They could not have got away with such mitigation policy in 2000 or even 2010, while the Washington Consensus prevailed. Hence, mitigation policy should be regarded as an expression of the New Abnormal; it was an abnormal response made possible by the New Abnormal.

In pre-modern times matters might have been different. Defoe (1722) describes how the Lord Mayor of London implemented very strict mitigation policy during the outbreak of bubonic plague in 1665. This policy involved the strict isolation of the sick in their homes, the closure of playhouses, social distancing, restrictions on employment, and quarantine of sailors. Defoe notes that some Londoners survived the plague but died of hunger because they could not work. Because Defoe was born in London in 1660, he could not have recalled the plague. However, social historians agree that his journal is realistic and accurate. It is an interesting question whether in pre-modern times mitigation policy was widespread, but fell into disuse after the Industrial Revolution.

As we shall see, mitigation policy deepened the grip of the New Abnormal on policy makers by greatly increasing their debt-to-GDP ratios as well as fueling kinetic inflation. If the prospects of escaping the New Abnormal were weak in 2019, they were much weaker after 2021. In this chapter we record the contribution of

*Zero Interest Policy and the New Abnormal.* Michael Beenstock, Oxford University Press. © Michael Beenstock (2022).
DOI: 10.1093/oso/9780192849663.003.0009

mitigation policy to the increase in debt-to-GDP ratios and kinetic inflation for various countries. Also, countries such as New Zealand that had managed to survive outside the New Abnormal before the pandemic adopted the New Abnormal in March 2020 with its outbreak. The US, which began to emerge from the New Abnormal in 2016 by ending ZIP, re-adopted the New Abnormal in March 2020.

To quantify the abnormality of mitigation policy, we calculate the cost per life year saved (LYS) by comparing estimates of the economic cost of mitigation policy with the number of LYS. We do not engage in quality adjustment on moral grounds, so each LYS is equally valuable regardless of age, gender, and ethnicity, hence our focus is on LYS rather than QALYS. Because conditional life expectancy varies inversely with age (80-year-olds have fewer years left to live than 40-year-olds), LYS naturally varies inversely with age. The cost per LYS greatly exceeds the planning prices used by ministries of health to determine their investment in public health. The difference between these costs per LYS and their planning prices measures the abnormality in mitigation policy.

Natural disasters such as epidemics, earthquakes, tsunamis, and floods raise questions of how to pay for the damage they cause. Local disasters can be insured through re-insurance markets such as Lloyds of London because they are uncorrelated with other risks. For example, earthquake risk is insurable because earthquakes are local and are uncorrelated with earthquakes elsewhere. Matters are different for pandemics because the risks are highly correlated; by definition pandemics are global rather than local. Hence, pandemic risk is non-insurable. This is true within generations, but if pandemics are sufficiently rare, they might be insurable between generations. In this case pandemic risk may be spread intergenerationally, even if it cannot be spread intragenerationally. Since future generations are currently unborn, intergenerational insurance schemes raise questions about intergenerational equity. Is it legitimate to lock down economies at the expense of future generations by bequeathing them public debt incurred by the present generation? An intergenerational application is proposed of Rawls' second principle of justice to justify intergenerational insurance of pandemic risk.

## Intergenerational Equity

Governments across the world have engaged in mitigation policy to fight the Covid-19 pandemic (Hale et al 2020). In doing so they lost tax income because mitigation policy induced economic recession, and for related reasons public expenditure on income support increased, thereby incurring massive increases in public sector debt as recorded below. These debts are on a scale not seen since World War Two. They are probably too large to be paid off by the current generation. The question arises, therefore, whether the current generation should have indebted future generations to pay for mitigation policy.

Questions of intergenerational equity have arisen recently regarding global warming, the discovery of natural resources, and the establishment of sovereign funds. The Intergovernmental Panel on Climate Change (IPCC) at the United Nations adopted the thesis (Stern 2006) that carbon abatement policy by the present generation is essential to protect the economic interests of future generations. Sovereign funds have been established by many governments, such as Norway and Saudi Arabia, to protect the economic interests of future generations. Revenues from oil production are invested by the sovereign funds for safekeeping on behalf of the unborn. If eventually the unborn behave like their predecessors by protecting the interest of generations subsequent to them, the original revenues from oil production will never be used. In these and other examples, the current generation imposes self-restraint to protect the interests of the unborn. By contrast, in the Covid-19 crisis the current generation seems to have acted against the interests of the unborn by bequests of public debt.

Since the Industrial Revolution successive generations have been economically better off than their predecessors, thanks to economic growth. The current generation is better off than their parents' generation and even more so than their grandparents' and great-grandparents'. Unless economic growth has come to an end, our grandchildren and great-grandchildren will be better off than us. Just as intragenerational equity involves transfers from the better off to the less well off, so might intergenerational equity have been expected to transfer resources from future generations, who will be better off than us, to the current generation, rather than the other way around.

Because the unborn are expected to be better off than us, the intergenerational discount rate tends to be low or even negative (Stern 2006, Chapter 9), which would justify the transfer of resources from the unborn to the born, as in the Covid-19 crisis. According to this perspective, the IPCC view and the existence of sovereign funds are unusual. There are ethical issues involved with this perspective because the unborn have no political representation; they are not here to object. Even if they will be better off than us, benefit from better healthcare, and enjoy a higher standard of living, this does not necessarily justify extraction of resources by the current generation at the expense of future generations.

Our purpose here is to suggest a completely different perspective on intergenerational equity that avoids ethical issues concerned with the inability of the unborn to represent themselves. According to this perspective, fiscal deficits induced by the Covid-19 pandemic are different to regular fiscal deficits and may therefore be justified in terms of Rawlsian distributive justice. Rawls' (1971) theory of justice has the following key components. He posits an "original position" in which there is a "veil of ignorance": "no-one knows his place in society, his class position or social status; nor does he know his fortune in the distribution of natural assets and abilities....More than this, I assume that the parties do not know the particular circumstances of their own society. That is, they do not know its economic or political situation, or the level of civilization and culture it has been able to achieve. The persons in the original position have no information to which generation they belong." (p 137). "It is taken for granted, however, that they know the general facts about human society. They understand political affairs and the principles of economic theory; they know the basis of social organization and the laws of human psychology." (p 137).

Rawls argues that, because people do not know their position in the distribution, they should agree voluntarily to a social contract in which "All social values – liberty and opportunity, income and wealth, and the bases for self-respect – are to be distributed equally unless an unequal distribution of any, or all, is to everyone's advantage." (p 62), Later, Rawls confines "to everyone's advantage" to "the advantage of the worst-off." The so-called maximin principle of justice permits inequalities provided that they are advantageous to the worst-off.

Rawls' social contract may be interpreted as a form of social insurance. Since we are born under a "veil of ignorance," we should agree to an insurance contract that makes the worst-off better-off because all of us face the risk of being worst-off. This second principle of distributive justice (the first being "each person is to have equal right to the most extensive basic liberty compatible with a similar liberty to others" (p 60)) lies at the heart of social insurance theory. Although this principle has been challenged, e.g. Nozick (1974), we accept it uncritically for the present.

By similar argument, unborn cohorts should agree to an insurance policy to cover themselves against natural disasters, such as the Covid-19 pandemic. Suppose generations are ordered from generation 1 to N and meet under a veil of ignorance before generation 1 is born. Generation 1 proposes to generation 2 a pandemic insurance policy in which generation 2 compensates generation 1 if a pandemic occurs during generation 1, and generation 3 compensates generation 2 if a pandemic occurs during generation 2. Generation 4 compensates generation 3 and so on. If pandemic risk is imperfectly correlated across generations, the proposal provides intergenerational insurance through spreading risk. It implements Rawls' second principle of justice intergenerationally rather than intragenerationally. If, however, pandemic risks are perfectly correlated between generations, intergenerational insurance is not feasible.

Viewed in this way, it is intergenerationally just to finance the current pandemic by increasing public debt, which will be paid off by future generations. In any case, provided economic growth continues, future generations will be better off than the current generation, and will be more able to afford the cost of the pandemic.

Rawls himself (pp 284–93) discusses the implications of his second principle of justice for intergenerational equity. Recall that under the "veil of ignorance" people in the original position do not even know to which generation they belong. So, generations should agree to a social contract in which intergenerational inequality is justly provided if it is to the advantage of the worst-off generation. So much for the principle. In practice, Rawls provides a critique of the neoclassical

growth model (Chapter 2) in which he considers how much the present generation should save according to the intergenerational maximin principle. In this
critique, "... persons in the original position have no pure rate of time preference."
(p 293).

To understand what he means, let $C_1$ denote consumption per head in the
current generation and $C_2$ denote consumption per head in the next generation. Suppose that each generation benefits from consumption in the same way;
$C^\beta$ where $\beta$ is a positive fraction so that the marginal utility from consumption
decreases. The intergenerational discount rate is:

$$r = \left(1 + rtp\right)\left(1 + g\right)^{1-\beta} - 1 \tag{1.1}$$

where rtp denotes the pure rate of time preference and g denotes the rate of growth
of consumption between generations. Positive rtp means that the welfare of generation 2 from consumption is valued less than the welfare of generation 1 simply
because it occurs later. Positive rtp implies that the intergenerational discount rate
would be positive even if the rate of growth is zero. Rawls was right to object that,
although rtp may be positive within generations, it is unjust to apply it between
generations because this comparison involves the unborn. If $g = 0$ and $rtp = 0$,
Rawls is suggesting that the intergenerational discount rate is zero according to
equation (1.1).

By assuming that there is no economic growth, Rawls seems to contradict his
assumption that in the initial position people "understand the principles of economic theory." Or he abstracted from economic growth for the sake of simplicity.
Either way, a Rawlsian case for sharing the cost of mitigation with future generations can be made. In this context Rawls was wrong to argue, "There is no way for
later generations to improve the situation of the least fortunate first generation."
(p 291). The first generation achieves this resource transfer by indebting future
generations, as in the Covid-19 pandemic.

## Mitigation Theory

### The SIR Model

The SIR model has framed epidemiological research into the spread of infectious
disease for almost a century (Kermack and McKendrick 1927). S refers to susceptibles (the population not yet been infected). I refers to infectives (the population
currently contagious). R refers to 'removals' (infectives who have recovered or
died). The SIR model consists of nonlinear differential equations, which do not

have analytical solutions (Daley and Gani 1999). This nonlinearity arises because the newly infected are assumed to depend on the product of S and I. Specifically:

$$\frac{dS(t)}{dt} = -aS(t)I(t) \tag{2.1}$$

In the early stages of epidemics S is naturally very large because the vast majority of the population are not yet infected. Hence, the percentage change in S is very small while the percentage change in I is very large. To simplify matters we assume here that S is approximately fixed. The differential equation for infectives is:

$$\frac{dI(t)}{dt} = \frac{S(t)}{dt} - (r+d)I(t) \tag{2.2}$$

where r denotes the rate of recovery and d denotes the rate of mortality among the infected. Substituting equation (2.1) into (2.2) assuming S(t) is fixed at S gives:

$$\frac{dI(t)}{dt} = (aS - r - d)I(t) \tag{2.3}$$

Multipying equation (2.3) by d turns it into a differential equation for mortality (Z):

$$\frac{dZ(t)}{dt} = \theta Z(t) \tag{2.4}$$

where $\theta = d(aS - r - d)$. The rate of reproduction ($R_0$) for mortality varies directly with $\theta$. $R_0$ exceeds 1 when $\theta$ is positive, $R_0 = 1$ when $\theta = 0$, and R is less than 1 when $\theta_0$ is negative.

## The Cost per Life Year Saved

Mitigation policy, denoted by M, incurs economic costs, denoted by C, and it reduces mortality. However, the effect of mitigation policy on mortality is not immediate; it takes time. Also, it takes time for the economy to recover after relaxing mitigation policy. To frame the discussion of the economic cost per LYS, a simple dynamic model is proposed in which mortality and the state of the economy depend on mitigation policy. Equation (2.4) is modified to:

$$\dot{Z} = \theta Z - g(M) \tag{2.5}$$

where $\dot{Z} = dZ/dt$. In the absence of mitigation policy (M = 0), mortality grows at the rate of $\theta$, which is assumed to be positive (otherwise mortality would tend to zero naturally). If stricter mitigation policy is more effective, then g'(M) > 0, where g' denotes a partial derivative. If M is positive (mitigation cannot be negative), mortality is reduced; as long as mitigation policy remains in force, cumulative mortality is less than what it otherwise would be. However, once mitigation policy is relaxed, mortality tends to revert to its natural growth rate of θ unless Z happens to be zero. Equation (2.5) implies that it takes time for mitigation policy to be effective through θ, and it takes time for mortality to recover after mitigation policy is relaxed.

If M is fixed the general solution to equation (2.5) is:

$$Z(t) = \left(Z_0 - \frac{1}{\theta}g(M)\right)e^{\theta t} + \frac{1}{\theta}g(M) \tag{2.6}$$

where $Z_0$ is the initial condition for mortality. According to equation (2.6) the marginal effect of mitigation on mortality is:

$$\frac{\partial Z(t)}{\partial M} = \frac{1}{\theta}g'(M)\left(1 - e^{\theta t}\right) < 0 \tag{2.7}$$

Since g'(M) is positive and the term in brackets is negative, mitigation policy reduced mortality by an amount that grows over time. Equation (2.6) also implies that cumulative lives saved (LS) by increasing mitigation from $M_0$ to $M_1$ during τ periods equals:

$$LS = -\frac{1}{\theta}\left[g(M_1) - g(M_0)\right]\left[\tau + \frac{1}{\theta}\left(1 - e^{\theta \tau}\right)\right] > 0 \tag{2.8}$$

An increase in mitigation from $M_0$ to $M_1$ initially makes no difference to lives saved (equation (2.8) is zero when τ = 0). Subsequently, lives saved increase by period τ according to equation (2.8).

Similar laws of motion apply to the economic cost of mitigation policy:

$$\dot{C} = -\phi C + f(M) \tag{2.9}$$

if M = 0 the economic cost of mitigation policy is zero by definition. If f"(M) > 0 mitigation is increasingly costly. Equation (2.9) states that it takes time through 0 < φ < 1 for economic costs to build up and it takes time for the economy to recover after mitigation policy is relaxed. The time taken varies directly with φ. For simplicity, equations (2.5) and (2.8) assume symmetry with respect to the imposition and relaxation of mitigation policy.

From equation (2.8), the counterpart to equation (2.6) is:

$$C(t) = \left[ C_0 + \frac{1}{\phi} f(M) \right] e^{-\phi t} + \frac{1}{\phi} f(M) \tag{2.10}$$

The economic cost varies directly with mitigation and inversely with $\phi$ and $t$. The counterpart to equation (2.8) is the undiscounted cumulative cost of mitigation policy:

$$J = \frac{1}{\phi} \left[ f(M_1) - f(M_0) \right] \left[ \tau + \frac{1}{\phi} \left( 1 - e^{-\phi \tau} \right) \right] \tag{2.11}$$

which varies directly with the duration of mitigation policy and its intensity. The average economic cost per life saved by increasing mitigation from $M_0$ to $M_1$ is J/LS. To turn this into the average economic cost per LYS it needs dividing by the average life year saved per person, which naturally varies inversely with their average age.

## Optimal Mitigation Policy

Thus far mitigation policy has been set arbitrarily at $M_1$. Perhaps policy makers behaved arbitrarily in practice. Sophisticated policy makers trade-off the cost of mitigation against the benefit of reduced mortality. We make the very strong assumption that they design this policy efficiently and rationally. In each time period the total cost is $y = \lambda Z + C$, where $\lambda$ is the shadow price or planning price of mortality applied by policy makers. Policy makers who value life more have higher $\lambda$. Policy makers juggle their mitigation policy to minimize $y$ over planning horizon T. Their objective function is:

$$Y = \int_0^T y e^{-\delta t} dt \tag{2.12}$$

which they wish to minimize, where $0 < \delta < 1$ is a policy discount rate. Policy makers who are more conservative have smaller $\delta$.

To obtain the optimal solution to the juggling problem, policy makers minimize the Hamiltonian:

$$H = y e^{-\delta t} + \mu \left( -\phi C + f(M) \right) + \eta \left( \theta Z - g(M) \right) \tag{2.13}$$

where $\mu$ and $\eta$ are costate variables. The first-order conditions are:

$$\frac{\partial H}{\partial M} = \mu f'(M) - \eta g'(M) = 0 \tag{2.13a}$$

$$\frac{\partial H}{\partial C} = -e^{-\delta t} - \phi\mu = -\dot{\mu} \tag{2.13b}$$

$$\frac{\partial H}{\partial Z} = -\lambda e^{-\delta t} + \theta\eta = -\dot{\eta} \tag{2.13c}$$

Equation (2.8) states that mitigation is optimal when its marginal socioeconomic cost equals its marginal benefit in terms of reduced mortality. Substituting equations (2.9) and (2.10) into (2.3) generates, as expected, a second order, homogeneous nonlinear differential equation in the optimal policy rule for mitigation:

$$-\delta f_M + \Omega g'_M + \Phi \dot{M} + \Psi \dot{M} = 0 \tag{2.14}$$

$$\Omega = \lambda (\delta + \phi) - \theta (\theta + \phi) Be^{-(\theta+\delta)t}$$

$$\Phi = \left(1 + \phi A e^{(\phi-\delta)t}\right) f''_M - \lambda g'_M + (\phi + \theta) Be^{(\theta+\delta)t} g''_M$$

$$\Psi = A e^{(\phi-\delta)t} f''_M - Be^{-(\theta+\delta)t} g'''_M$$

where A is the arbitrary constant in the solution for μ, and B denotes the arbitrary constant in the general solution for equation η, which is determined by the transversality condition for mortality (Z), i.e. $\eta(T) = Z(T) \partial y[(Z(T)]/\partial T$, and e.g. $g'''_M$ denotes the second-order partial derivative of g(M). Homogeneity in equation (2.14) implies that mitigation policy tends to zero; it is not possible to "flatten the curve" indefinitely.

If the roots of equation (2.14) are complex, mitigation policy is cyclical, generating "waves" of mortality and waves of mitigation. The two roots of equation (2.14) are expected to be negative, otherwise mitigation policy would tend to be explosive, i.e. M tends to infinity. Because Ω, Φ and Ψ depend on M and t, equation (2.14) does not have an analytical solution, but may be solved numerically.

This simple model captures the stylized facts of mitigation policy, which during 2020–1 expressed itself in waves. During the first wave in March 2020, mitigation policy was imposed to various degrees of severity as measured by the Oxford University mitigation policy tracker (see below), as a result of which morbidity and then mortality decreased. Mitigation policy was subsequently relaxed, but not reversed entirely. After some time, a second wave began and mitigation policy was re-imposed in September, as a result of which morbidity and mortality were reduced. A third wave occurred during the winter of 2020–1, coinciding with the beginning of mass vaccination.

Given the model and the data for mitigation and mortality, the shadow price of mortality ($\lambda$) may be obtained by reverse engineering of equation (2.14). More generally, the dynamic shadow price of mortality is represented by the costate variable $\eta(t)$, which may be obtained by substituting the solution for M from equation (2.14) into equation (2.11).

## Stochastic Mitigation Policy

The model just described is deterministic and implies unrealistically that the effect of mitigation policy on mortality is perfectly predictable. Nevertheless, it captures the essence of designing mitigation policy when its effect on mortality takes time, as do the adverse effects of mitigation policy on the economy. To make the model more realistic, equation (2.5) is expressed as a stochastic differential equation in which W denotes Brownian motion:

$$dZ = \left[\theta Z - g(M)\right] dt + \sigma dW \tag{2.15}$$

where the predictability of mortality varies inversely with $\sigma$. Stochastic calculus (Malliaris and Brock 1988, p 112) augments equation (2.13) to:

$$H = ye^{-\delta t} + \mu\left(-\phi C + f(M)\right) + \eta\left(\theta Z - g(M)\right) + \frac{1}{2}\sigma^2 \frac{\partial \eta}{\partial Z} \tag{2.16}$$

The augmented term in equation (2.16) is positive, since $\eta$ is the shadow cost of mortality, which varies directly with mortality. Hence, the first-order condition, equation (2.13a), is augmented to:

$$\frac{\partial H}{\partial M} = \mu f'(M) - \eta g'(M) + \frac{1}{2}\sigma^2 \frac{\partial^2 \eta}{\partial Z \partial M} = 0 \tag{2.17}$$

The augmented term in equation (2.17) expresses the idea that because mitigation policy has an uncertain effect on mortality, it is less attractive to risk-averse policy makers. Hence mitigation is expected to vary inversely with $\sigma$.

Equation (2.13c) is augmented to:

$$d\eta = -\frac{\partial H}{\partial Z} dt + \sigma \frac{\partial \eta}{\partial Z} dW \tag{2.18}$$

Equation (2.13b) remains unchanged because the economic cost of mitigation has been assumed to be deterministic. Notice that if $\sigma = 0$ the last two equations revert, as expected, to their determinsitic counterparts in equations (2.13a) and (2.13c).

We do not solve the counterpart to equation (2.14) for the stochastic case. However, it has the same structure and involves an extra parameter $\sigma$. As already mentioned in relation to equation (2.14), uncertainty penalizes mitigation policy, so policy makers mitigate less.

## Endogenous Contagion

The canonical SIR model is mechanical in the sense that a and $r + d$ in equations (2.1) and (2.2) are fixed parameters. The infection rate (a) does not vary inversely with social distancing, and the recovery and mortality rates (r and d) do not depend on investment in health services, which would reduce d and increase r. In summary, these parameters are exogenous in the original SIR model and largely remain so today. In this subsection we endogenize the infection rate under the assumption that the public engages in social distancing and related precautionary behavior when the risk of contagion is larger.

Since the individual risk of contagion varies directly with number of infectives it is assumed here that the infection rate (a) depends on the inverse of the number of infectives (I). Whereas the SIR model is not amenable to analytical solution, matters are different when the infection rate is assumed to be endogenous in this way. If $a = a_0/I$ the solution to equation (2.1) becomes:

$$S(t) = S_0 e^{-a_0 t} \qquad (2.19)$$

Unlike the basic SIR model, equation (2.19) implies that sooner or later everyone gets infected. This does not necessarily happen in the original SIR model because the number of infectives (I) may be zero before the number of susceptibles is zero. Solving for $\dot{S} = -a_0 S_0 e^{-a_0 t}$ from equation (2.19) and substituting the result into equation (2.2) provides the solution for the number of infectives:

$$I(t) = \frac{a_0 S_0}{r + d - a_0} \left( e^{-a_0 t} - e^{-(r+d)t} \right) + I_0 e^{-(r+d)t} \qquad (2.20)$$

Maximizing equation (2.20) with respect to t implies that the number of infectives peaks when:

$$t^* = \frac{1}{r + d - a_0} \ln \left[ \frac{r + d}{a_0} \left( 1 - \frac{(r + d) I_0}{a_0 S_0} \right) \right] \qquad (2.21)$$

The number of new cases diagnosed also peaks at $t^*$; it equals $a_0 I(t^*)$. Hence, until period $t^*$ the number of infectives increases and the infection rate decreases from its initial value $(a_0)$. Consequently, the reproductive factor $(R_0)$ decreases from its initial value of $a_0/(r + d)$ to $I_0 a_0/(r + d)I(t^*)$. After period $t^*$ the infection rate begins to increase because the number of infectives decreases and the reproductive factor increases. When the number of infectives decreases to $I_0$ the infection rate and the reproductive factor return to their initial value at the start of the epidemic. In the final stage of the epidemic a exceeds $a_0$ because the number of infectives is less than the initial number. The epidemic ends with a bang.

In summary, when the infection rate is endogenous the epidemic spreads more slowly than when the infection rate is exogenous. Also, the reproductive factor, which is constant when the infection rate is exogenous varies over the course of the epidemic when the infection rate is endogenous. It initially decreases before increasing after the number of infectives peaks. On average, however, the reproductive factor is smaller when the infection rate is endogenous.

As mentioned, the recovery and mortality rates are likely to be endogenous too. As the epidemic progresses and the treatment of the infected improves through experience, the recovery rate is expected to increase and the mortality rate is expected to decrease. Also, the more efficient isolation of the infected is expected to reduce the infection rate.

## Identifying the Causal Effect of Mitigation Policy

In the previous section the effect of mitigation policy on mortality, $g(M)$, was assumed to be known. When the pandemic first broke out, nothing was known about the effect of mitigation policy because there had been no previous experience with Covid-19. Beyond understanding that social distancing is likely to be important, policy makers were groping in the dark. As experience with Covid-19 accumulated, it began to be possible to learn from the different mitigation policies applied by different countries. The present section is concerned with making empirical inferences about the effect of mitigation policy; it is concerned with identifying $g(M)$.

## Covid-19 Equilibrium

According to the theory of mitigation, given everything else, mitigation policy is expected to be more intense when mortality is greater. Hence, in bringing theory to data, it is necessary to take account of reverse causality from mortality to mitigation policy (Beenstock and Xieer 2020). In other words, the causal effect of mitigation policy is not identified unless the feedback from mortality to mitigation policy is taken onto account. Indeed, if mitigation policy is more intense when mortality increases, naïve empirical investigators might reach the misleading conclusion that mitigation policy makes mortality worse instead of better. More generally, they will underestimate the efficacy, or treatment effect, of mitigation policy on mortality.

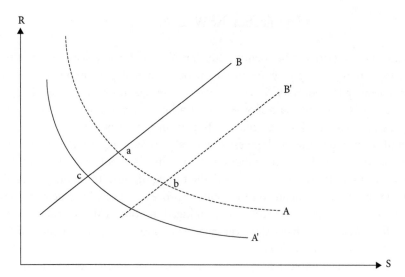

**Fig. 9.1**  Covid-19 Equilibrium

The identification problem is illustrated in Figure 9.1, where the reproduction rate for mortality (R) is measured on the vertical axis and the severity of mitigation policy (S, from the Oxford tracker representing M) on the horizontal. Schedule A plots the hypothesized negative causal effect of mitigation policy on R. The size of the treatment effect varies directly with its slope. Schedule B plots the policy response of mitigation to the rate of contagion. It expresses the idea that, if mortality is low, governments will mitigate less if at all. Governments more politically prone to mitigation will have flatter B schedules. The data for R and S (M) are jointly determined at point *a*, where schedules A and B intersect. We refer to this as the "Covid-19 equilibrium."

Since the treatment effect of mitigation is reflected in the slope of schedule A, we ideally wish to apply an autonomous increase in mitigation policy, such that schedule B shifts to the right to B', in which the new equilibrium would be at point *b*. For example, countries with weaker healthcare infrastructure may resort to more stringent mitigation, as in schedule B. The slope of schedule A between points *a* and *b* is the local average treatment effect.

Suppose the population in another country is less susceptible to Covid-19, e.g. because of indigenous social distancing as in schedule A', i.e. R is smaller given mitigation policy. The equilibrium will be determined at point *c* instead of point *a*, at which both R and S are smaller. The unwitting or naive might think that R is smaller because S is smaller, but this confuses cause and effect. The Covid-19 equilibrium in countries with low susceptibility (A') and strong healthcare infrastructures (B) mitigate less, or may not even mitigate at all.

## Identification by Weak Exogeneity

Figure 9.1 exaggerates the identification problem because it assumes that the effects of mitigation policy are instantaneous and that governments react instantaneously to mortality. Since the effect of mitigation policy takes time, as in equation (2.5), and the response of mitigation policy to mortality takes time too, as in equation (2.9), the causal effect of mitigation policy on mortality is identified provided the randomness in mortality (dW in equation (2.15)) is not cross-autocorrelated with the randomness in mitigation policy (not featured in the previous section). As we have seen, the timing of mitigation policy is highly random because it depends on the political process, especially in democracies. In the absence of cross-autocorrelation, mitigation policy (M) is weakly exogenous for g(M), in which event the causal effect of mitigation policy in mortality is identified as discussed below.

Consider, for example, a first-order, linear vector autoregression (VAR) model in mortality (Z) and mitigation policy (M):

$$Z_t = \delta + \alpha Z_{t-1} - \beta M_{t-1} + \varepsilon_t \tag{3.1}$$

$$M_t = \gamma M_{t-1} + \theta Z_{t-1} + e_t \tag{3.2}$$

where $\varepsilon$ and $e$ are normally distributed mean-zero innovations (shocks) in mortality and mitigation policy. Notice that it takes one period for mortality to begin to respond to mitigation policy, and it takes one period for mitigation policy to begin to respond to mortality. In the absence of mitigation policy ($M = 0$), equation (3.1) implies that mortality is expected to tend to $\tilde{o}/(1-\alpha)$ if $\alpha$ is a positive fraction, it tends to zero if $\alpha$ is a negative fraction and $\tilde{o} = 0$, and it tends to grow at the rate of $\alpha -1$ if $\alpha$ exceeds 1. In the former case the reproductive rate for mortality is $R = 1$, in the second case R is less than 1, and in the latter case R exceeds 1. In the second case mortality is stationary and in the first and third cases mortality is nonstationary. In the second case the government has no interest in mitigation policy because mortality tends to zero without mitigation. Matters are different if in the absence of mitigation policy R is at least 1, as in the first and third cases.

The two roots of equations (3.1) and (3.2) are:

$$\rho = \frac{\alpha + \gamma \pm \sqrt{(\alpha - \gamma)^2 - 4\beta\theta}}{2} \tag{3.3}$$

Equation (3.3) applies only when $\alpha$ is at least one, for otherwise there is no need for mitigation policy, in which event $\gamma = \theta = 0$. Table 9.1 reports settings for $\theta$ when $\gamma = 0.5$ which force the larger root to equal 1 for different values of $\alpha$ and $\beta$.

Table 9.1 Flattening the Curve

| α | β | θ |
|---|---|---|
| 1 | 0.2 | 0 |
| 1.2 | 0.2 | 0.5 |
| 1.3 | 0.2 | 0.75 |
| 1.2 | 0.3 | 0.33' |

These settings imply that R = 1 for mortality. If α = 1 the required setting for θ is, of course, zero (row 1 in Table 9.1) because R = 1 by definition in the absence of mitigation. Therefore, any setting for θ, which is fractionally greater than zero, forces the larger root to be smaller than 1, in which event R is less than 1.

Row 2 shows that the critical setting for θ is 0.5 if α = 1.2. This setting reduces R from 1.2 to 1. If R = 1.3 the critical setting for θ is larger (0.75), as expected; mitigation policy must be more intense to flatten the curve. Comparing row 4 with row 2 shows, as expected, that if mitigation policy is more effective (β = 0.3 instead of 0.2) the critical setting for θ is 0.33 instead of 0.5. The greater the efficacy of mitigation policy the less mitigation is required to flatten the curve. In summary, if θ is fractionally larger than the critical settings in Table 9.1, mitigation policy forces R to be less than 1, and mortality eventually tends to zero.

Substituting equation (3.2) into equation (3.1) generates the final form for mortality:

$$Z_t = \left(1 - \gamma\right)\delta + \left(\alpha + \gamma\right)Z_{t-1} - \left(\alpha\gamma + \beta\theta\right)Z_{t-2} + \varepsilon_t - \gamma\varepsilon_{t-1} - \beta e_{t-1} \qquad (3.4)$$

Equation (3.4) is an ARMA(2, 1) process, in which mortality depends on its first two lagged values, as well as on current and lagged mortality innovations, and lagged innovations for mitigation policy. Suppose that the roots of equation (3.4) are positive and real, and that they are also less than 1 because mitigation policy has set θ sufficiently high to more than flatten the curve. It is well known that in this case equation (3.4) generates cycles in mortality induced by the "Slutsky equation effect" through random shocks to ε and e (Hendry 1995). For similar reasons the counterpart of equation (3.4) for mitigation generates cycles in mitigation policy. These cycles are damped because θ is set sufficiently high so that the larger root is less than 1. If the setting of θ is insufficiently high and the larger root exceeds 1, the Covid-19 cycle will be explosive rather than damped so that successive rounds of Covid-19 involve higher peaks of morbidity.

The Wold representation (Sargent 1979, Chapter 9) expresses autoregressive processes such as equation (3.4) into infinite moving average processes in terms of ε and e. The Wold representation for equation (3.4) is:

$$Z_t = \frac{(1-\gamma)\,\delta}{(1-\rho_1)(1-\rho_2)} + \frac{1}{\rho_1 - \rho_2} \sum_{i=0}^{t-\tau} \left(\rho_1^{1+i} - \rho_2^{1+i}\right)\left(\varepsilon_{t-i} - \gamma\varepsilon_{t-1-i} - \beta e_{t-1-i}\right)$$

(3.5)

where τ denotes the time period when the pandemic started. The final term in equation (3.5) is a root-weighted average of the innovations that induce Covid-19 cycles with the passage of time (t).

If the square-rooted term in equation (3.3) is negative instead of positive, the roots are complex rather than real. In this case, De Moivre's theorem implies that the counterpart to equation (3.5) is (Sargent 1979, Chapter 9):

$$Z_t = \frac{(1-\gamma)\,\delta}{1 - \alpha(1-\gamma) + \gamma + \beta\theta} + \frac{1}{\sin\varphi} \sum_{i=0}^{t-\tau} r^i \sin\varphi\,(1+i)\left(\varepsilon_{t-i} - \gamma\varepsilon_{t-1} - \beta e_{t-1-i}\right)$$

(3.6)

where $r = \sqrt{\alpha + \theta\beta}$ and $\varphi = \cos^{-1}\frac{\alpha+\gamma}{2r}$. The weights on the lagged innovations in equation (3.6) are sinusoidal, in which event Covid-19 cycles are induced structurally and not just through Slutsky equation effects. These structural cycles are damped if r is less than 1.

In summary, mitigation policy induces Covid-19 cycles as well as cycles in mitigation policy. These cycles are damped if mitigation policy is sufficiently proactive so that it more than flattens the curve. These cycles are induced by Slutsky equation effects alone if the roots are real. If the roots are complex Covid-19 cycles are additionally induced for structural reasons.

If β is statistically significant, mitigation policy "Granger causes" mortality, and if θ is statistically significant, mortality "Granger causes" mitigation policy. Granger causality is concerned with predictability and sequencing; it is not concerned with genuine causality. If β is statistically significant, this does not mean that mitigation policy reduces mortality. It simply means that mitigation precedes mortality, just as, say, infection precedes hospitalization. To establish that β is a causal effect $M_{t-1}$ in equation (3.1) must be "weakly exogenous" for β (Hendry 1995). Weak exogeneity requires that $M_{t-1}$ must be independent of $\varepsilon_t$. If ε is autocorrelated, the parameter estimates of α and β are inconsistent, in which event the causal effect of mitigation policy is obviously not identified. Suppose that ε is not autocorrelated but it is contemporaneously correlated with $e_t$, and e is autocorrelated. In this case the estimates of α, β, γ and θ are not consistent; the inconsistency of equation (3.2) is contagious and transmits itself to equation (3.1). If ε and e are uncorrelated and they are not cross-autocorrelated (e.g. $\varepsilon_t$ and $e_{t-1}$ are independent), the inconsistency of equation (3.2) is not contagious for equation (3.1), in which event the causal effect of mitigation on mortality ($\beta$) is identified.

Note that $\beta$ is identified without recourse to instrumental variables. The sequencing of morbidity and mitigation policy enables the causal effect of $M_{t-1}$ on $Z_t$ to be identified through weak exogeneity.

## 2020

## Overview

The Oxford University Covid-19 mitigation policy tracker index, denoted by S (for stringency), is used to measure the stringency of mitigation policy to represent M. S is a score between zero and one hundred, which weights lockdown and other features of mitigation policy, including limitations on international travel etc. (Hale et al 2020). The global distribution of S during 2020 is shown in Figure 9.2, which shows that the stringency of mitigation policy varied widely. In the countries with darker shading (such as Austria and Israel), mitigation policy was particularly stringent. In the countries shaded white, there was no mitigation policy at all.

Figures 9.3 plot the stringency index (broken line on the right vertical) in five countries over time and mortality (in complete line on the left vertical). In these countries mitigation policy was implemented in steps during March–May 2020 and was maintained at this level into 2021. For example, in the UK the stringency score ranged between 60 and 70 except during early 2021 with the arrival of the

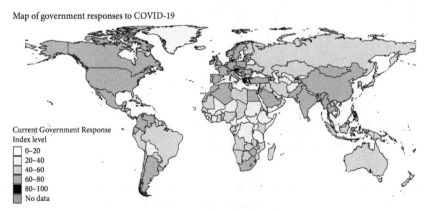

Map of government responses to COVID-19

Current Government Response
Index level
- 0–20
- 20–40
- 40–60
- 60–80
- 80–100
- No data

**Fig. 9.2**  The Global Distribution of Mitigation Policy
*Sources*: Oxford Covid-19 Government Response Tracker

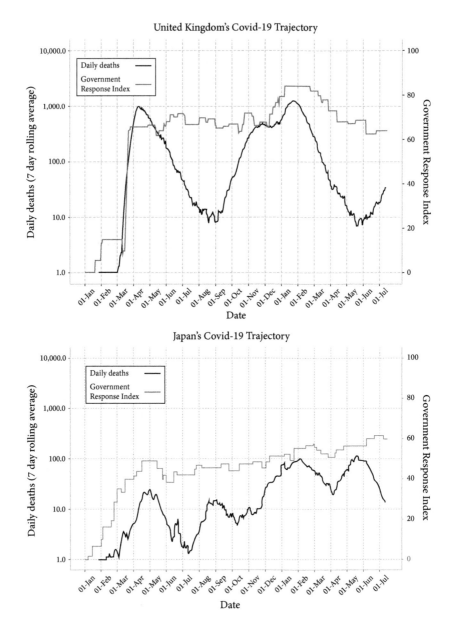

**Fig. 9.3a** Mortality and Mitigation Policy 2020–1
*Sources*: Oxford Covid-19 Government Response Tracker

British variant. By contrast, mortality remained stable but had a large wave-like variance. These waves did not, however, induce waves in stringency.

Whereas the stringency of mitigation policy was similar across countries, mortality was wave-like Two incomplete waves are discernible for the UK and Israel.

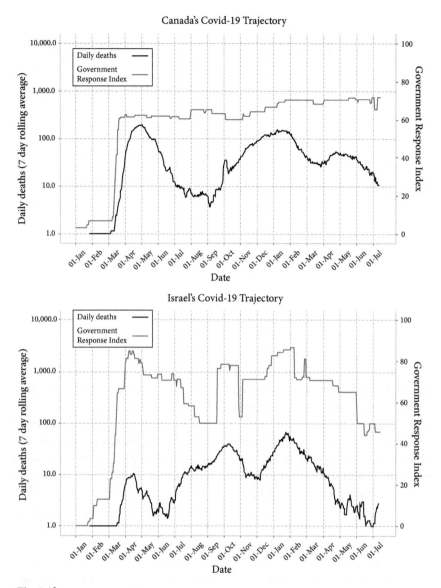

**Fig. 9.3b**

*Sources:* Oxford Covid-19 Government Response Tracker

Figures 9.3 do not suggest any clear statistical relation between mortality and mitigation policy. Mortality seemed to respond favorably to initial steps in mitigation policy, which was subsequently relaxed but not reversed.

This pattern was repeated in many countries, including Canada but not Japan, where mortality has been wave-like and increasing. The stringency score in Japan

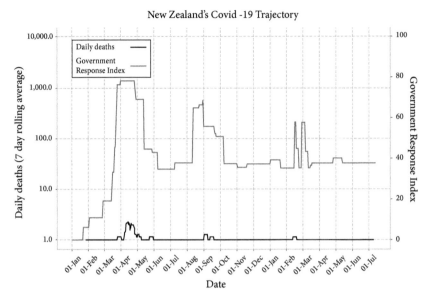

**Fig. 9.3c**

*Sources*: Oxford Covid-19 Government Response Tracker

was initially relatively low, but increased over time with the trend in mortality. Another exception is Israel, where mitigation policy as well as mortality was wave-like. The decrease in mortality towards zero since February 2021 is a result of the rapid vaccination roll-out during February and March (see below). This was followed by an almost complete reversal of mitigation policy and a reopening of the economy. However, the stringency index remained in the 40s because of severe restrictions on international travel.

An unusual case is New Zealand, which has experienced almost no mortality with relatively little mitigation. Spikes in contagion were accompanied by spikes in mitigation. The baseline level of mitigation (stringency score 40) reflects severe controls over international travel. Thus far, New Zealand has shown little interest in vaccination; New Zealanders appeared to have defeated Covid-19 without mass vaccination. By 2022 it became clear that this was a strategic error (repeated also be Australia). International travel bans are no substitute for mass vaccination.

There have been huge differences in morbidity and mortality rates by country (Table 9.2). During 2020 Belgians were on average 4.3 times more likely to die of Covid-19 than Israelis, who were 11 times more likely to die than Australians. Australians were 7 times more likely to die than New Zealanders. Taiwanese were least likely to die. These differences reflect morbidity rates and case fatality rates,

Table 9.2  Covid-19 Mortality Data for 2020

| Country | Morbidity per 100,000 | Mortality per 100,000 | Case mortality % | Dependency ratio |
|---|---|---|---|---|
| US | 6476.7 | 109.2 | 1.7 | 23.47 |
| UK | 4191.2 | 114.95 | 2.7 | 29.04 |
| Italy | 3641,8 | 126.3 | 3.5 | 36.28 |
| Belgium | 5657.9 | 173.59 | 3.0 | 28.87 |
| Spain | 4240.3 | 110.07 | 2.6 | 29.50 |
| France | 4089.6 | 99.15 | 2.4 | 31.70 |
| Germany | 2197.5 | 44.32 | 2.0 | 32.77 |
| Canada | 1673.1 | 43.86 | 2.6 | 25.35 |
| Israel | 5354.3 | 39.95 | 0.8 | 19.42 |
| Denmark | 3032.7 | 24.49 | 0.8 | 30.82 |
| Norway | 977.0 | 8.51 | 0.9 | 25.72 |
| Australia | 111.9 | 3.64 | 3.2 | 23.68 |
| New Zealand | 453.0 | 0.51 | 1.1 | 23.60 |
| Japan | 205.1 | 2.8 | 1.4 | 45.03 |
| S. Korea | 130.1 | 1.8 | 1.6 | 19.16 |
| China | 6.1 | 0.34 | 5.0 | 14.85 |
| Taiwan | 3.4 | 0.03 | 0.9 | |

*Source:* Our World in Data (January 6, 2021).

defined as the proportion of patients diagnosed with Covid-19 who subsequently died. 3 percent of Belgians diagnosed with Covid-19 died by January 6, 2021 whereas only 0.8 percent of Israelis died. Since the mortality rate among Belgians was 173.59 per 100,000, and the case fatality rate was 3 percent, the morbidity rate was 5.79 percent. Almost 6 percent of Belgians caught Covid-19 in 2020. Almost 5 percent of Israelis caught Covid-19 in 2020, so the reason why Belgians were 4 times more likely to die of Covid-19 than Israelis was not because the morbidity rate was much higher in Belgium, but because for some reason Belgians were more much more likely to die if they became ill. Either Belgians are less genetically fit than Israelis, or the Belgian virus was more lethal than the Israeli virus, or the Belgian health services were less efficient than the Israeli health services. A further possibility is that, because older people face higher risks of morbidity and case fatality (Omori, Matsuyama and Nakata 2020) and because Belgium has a larger proportion of senior citizens than Israel, as measured by the dependency ratio, given everything else Belgians are more likely to die than Israelis. On the other hand, Japan has the largest proportion of senior citizens in the world, yet it has one of the lowest mortality rates.

Table 9.2 suggests that morbidity and mortality are correlated at the bottom but not at the top. Countries such as Norway and South Korea have low rates of morbidity and mortality, whereas Israel and the US have high rates of morbidity, but they do not have particularly high rates of mortality. Table 9.2 also suggests that mortality rates and case fatality rates have little to do with the proportion of senior citizens, as measured by the dependency ratio, with the possible exception of Italy.

## Measuring Mortality for Covid-19

Measures of morbidity and mortality for Covid-19 are problematic for at least three reasons. First, asymptomatic morbidity is not measured at all, yet it is reckoned to be possibly larger than symptomatic morbidity. Second, not all symptomatic morbidity is diagnosed; an unknown proportion either believe that they are simply unwell or they do not bother their doctor and eventually recover. If, instead, they die, the cause of death may not be recorded as Covid-19. Hence, both morbidity and mortality related to Covid-19 are generally underestimated.

However, in the case of mortality there is a third reason, which is concerned with the official cause of death that is registered. In Israel only about one hundred people per year officially die of influenza, which suggests that it is among the least fatal diseases. In fact, in the cause of death statistics compiled by the Ministry of Health, the death rate per one hundred thousand is even too small to be measured. In an interview, the Deputy Director General of the Ministry of Health remarked that, for as many as seven hundred to one thousand people with background diseases who died after catching influenza, their official cause of death was registered as the background disease rather than influenza. The one hundred people who officially died of influenza had no background diseases.

The Deputy Director General further remarked that in the case of people who died of Covid-19 doctors typically attributed their cause of death to Covid-19 rather than to their background disease. If doctors applied this practice to influenza, the death rate from influenza would have been about ten times larger than the official death rate. Alternatively, if they recorded causes of death of patients with Covid-19 as they do for influenza, the death rate from Covid-19 would have been a fraction of the official statistics. According to Ministry of Health data, as of December 2020, 34 percent of Covid-19 patients who died had high blood pressure, 25 percent had diabetes, 27 percent had heart disease and altogether 90 percent had background diseases. These data suggest that death rates from Covid-19 may be overestimated by about a factor of 10.

In recognition of the risk of falsely attributing cause of death to Covid-19, and the risk of falsely attributing cause of death to another cause when the true cause is Covid-19, "excess mortality," popularized by *The Economist* magazine, is often considered to be a superior measure of Covid-19 mortality (Karlinsky and Kobak 2021). This measure compares total deaths in 2020 and 2021 with average deaths during 2015 - 2019. An obvious shortcoming of this measure is that it presumes that there is no trend in mortality. Ideally mortality in 2020 should be compared with its counterfactual in the absence of the pandemic. This counterfactual is unlikely to be average mortality in previous years. If there were fewer road deaths during 2020 because of lockdowns should this mean that mortality from Covid-19 is smaller? Or if more people died of heart disease because the treatment of Covid-19 patients crowded out other patients, should this mean that mortality from Covid-19 is larger? Suppose, however, that excess mortality truly measures mortality and that during 2020 mortality increased by 10 percent. Suppose further that half would have died in any case during 2021 from background morbidity. Had excess mortality been measured during 2020 and 2021 it would have been 5 percent rather than 1 percent. The mortality rate naturally varies inversely with the period over which it is measured.

If doctors elsewhere registered causes of death as they do in Israel, official death rates from Covid-19 would be vastly overestimated. Would governments have engaged in mitigation policy at enormous economic and social cost had the statistical authorities responsible for medical statistics measured mortality rates for Covid-19 as they do for influenza and other diseases? For example, would the Israeli government have locked down the country three times during 2020 had 350 officially died of Covid-19 instead of 3,500?

## Mortality and Age

As noted by Omori, Matsuyama, and Nakata (2020) mortality rates in Asia do not vary directly with age up to 60 years. Thereafter, they increase precipitously. The same applies in Europe (Table 9.3), which also shows that mortality rates for men are approximately double what they are for women. Table 9.3 shows that mortality rates in England and Wales are about ten times larger than their counterparts in Denmark and Spain. The relative risk of mortality for Danish men in their 70s relative to their 60s is 4.05 and for women it is 2.53. According to Danish life tables for 2019 the relative risks for the general population are 2.36 for men and 2.54 for women. The relative risks for Covid-19 for octogenarians relative to septuagenarians are 3.43 for men and 6.84 for women. Their counterparts in the general population are 4.12 and 4.8. In Denmark, the relative risks of mortality

**Table 9.3** Mortality Rates for Covid-19 by Gender and Age (per 100,000)

| Age | Denmark | | England and Wales | | Germany | | Spain | |
|-----|---------|-------|-------|-------|-------|-------|-------|-------|
|     | men | women | men | women | Men | women | Men | women |
| < 60 | 0.55 | 0.23 | 9.00 | 5.06 | 1.01 | 0.4 | 3.76 | 1.74 |
| 60–69 | 11.34 | 6.52 | 100.84 | 50.04 | 12.63 | 4.21 | 50.41 | 19.72 |
| 70–79 | 45.88 | 16.51 | 296.63 | 156.15 | 38.79 | 15.76 | 187.4 | 73.52 |
| 80+ | 157.62 | 112.92 | 1234.8 | 848.08 | 131.5 | 89.09 | 597.8 | 362.22 |

*Source*: Ahrenfeldt et al (2020).

from Covid-19 are not greatly higher than their counterparts in the general population. In other words, just as older people in the general population are more likely to die, the same applies to death from Covid-19.

Of course, the absolute mortality risk is larger due to Covid-19. Table 9.3 implies that for Danish men in their 60s mortality risk increased by 0.001134 from 0.01291 (1.291 percent) in the general population to 0.014044 (1.4044 percent), or 1.087 in terms of relative risk. For Danish men in their 70s mortality risk increased by 0.004588 from 0.030523 (3.0523 percent) to 0.035111 (3.5111 percent), or 1.15 in terms of relative risk. According to Danish life tables for 2019, the average remaining life expectancy for Danish men in their 60s is 20.27 years. Because Covid-19 increased their risk of mortality by 0.001134, the expected loss of life days per person is 8.39. For Danish men in their 70s, the expected loss of life days is 42.95. Table 9.3 implies that for Welshmen and Englishmen in their 60s the expected loss of life days is approximately 74.61, and for men in their 70s it is 277.69 days.

Note that the estimates of mortality risk due to Covid-19 in Table 9.3 would have been larger had Denmark and other countries not engaged in mitigation policy. To calculate the expected loss of life days per person that were saved as a result of mitigation policy, we need to know the counterfactual version of Table 9.3 that would have been observed in the absence of mitigation policy. These counterfactual mortality rates would obviously have been larger than those reported in Table 9.3.

The UK's National Institute for Health and Care Excellence (NICE) recommends that the value of a life year saved is £40,000. This planning price is used by the Department of Health to determine its investment in the National Health Service. According to the Department's Social Care Unit, the cost per life year saved during 2020 was £180,000, or 4.5 times greater than the planning price proposed by NICE (Wood 2020). In other words, the UK government behaved arbitrarily as if it valued death from Covid-19 4.5 times more than the Department of Health valued death from other causes. The lockdown policy was abnormal; it would have been more sensible had the government invested the forgone output due to lockdown on improving the National Health Service. Here, too, the crucial parameter is counterfactual mortality in the absence of mitigation policy. If counterfactual mortality was 4.5 times larger than assumed by the Social Care Unit, the cost per life year saved for Covid-19 would have been only £40,000, which would have been consistent with the planning price of NICE.


## The Cost per Life Year Saved in Israel

The cost per life year saved estimated by the UK's Social Care Unit suggests two aspects to the New Abnormal that are related to Covid-19. The first concerns the fact that in the UK as elsewhere governments engaged in mitigation policy almost without exception, even in Brazil. The second concerns the abnormally large value attributed to death from Covid-19 relative to death from other causes. In this section we show that in Israel too the government behaved as if it considered the value of death from Covid-19 to be many times greater than deaths from other causes. The basic methodological problem in these calculations is the estimate of counterfactual mortality in the absence of mitigation policy. The larger this counterfactual mortality, the lower the cost per life year saved.

To estimate counterfactual mortality, it is first necessary to identify the causal effect of mitigation policy on morbidity. The Social Care Unit's estimate of the cost per life year saved in the UK is as reliable as its estimate for this counterfactual. In the absence of details regarding the estimation of the counterfactual for the UK, in the present section a detailed discussion is presented of how the counterfactual was estimated for Israel.

This discussion has several steps, the first and easiest of which is to calculate the economic cost of mitigation. The other steps are concerned with estimating life years saved as a result of mitigation policy. The second step is concerned with identifying the causal treatment effect of mitigation policy on morbidity as measured by R. The third is concerned with converting the latter into mortality data. The next step is to convert the latter into life years saved. Finally, dividing the results from the first step by the results from the last step gives the average cost per life year saved. I apologize in advance if the penultimate step is rather tedious.


## The Cost of Mitigation Policy

During the late 2010s the Israeli economy grew at an annual rate of 3.5 percent. Prior to the outbreak of Covid-19 it was projected to grow at a similar rate. However, during 2020 the economy contracted by 2.5 percent because the government locked down the economy three times. Even in the absence of mitigation policy the tourist industry would have suffered because of the global collapse of tourism and the contraction of the global economy would have adversely affected exports. The cost of mitigation policy in terms of GDP works out at about 84 billion shekels (or about \$26 billion) in 2020, or 6 percent of GDP. Hence, J in equation (2.11) is 84 billion shekels.

## Estimating the Treatment Effect of Mitigation Policy

It is much easier to estimate J than it is to estimate lives saved, i.e. LS in equation (2.8). In Israel, 3600 died of Covid-19 during 2020. In the absence of mitiga-tion policy this number would have been larger. This counterfactual cannot be calculated without estimates of the treatment effect of mitigation policy on mor-tality. A large empirical literature on this issue has accumulated (IMF 2020), which indicates that prompt and stringent mitigation policy significantly reduced mor-bidity after two weeks and mortality subsequently. Unfortunately, much of this literature does not address the identification problem discussed above regarding "Covid-19 equilibrium".

Beenstock and Xieer (2020) estimated counterfactual mortality for Israel dur-ing the first wave of Covid-19 using a number of methodologies. First, they used a triple differences-in-differences (3DID) strategy (Berck and Villas-Boas 2016, Olden and Møen 2020) in which the first two differences refer to the changes in R before and after the change in mitigation policy, and the third difference consists of a comparison with R in a country that did not mitigate. For example, Italy adopted a stringent mitigation policy after which R decreased. But so did R decrease in Sweden, despite the fact that it refrained from serious mitigation. If, however, the decrease in R in Italy was greater than in Sweden, the difference may be attributed to the fact that Italy mitigated whereas Sweden did not.

The semi-elasticity model implies that the difference, post-mitigation, between the percentage change in R in Italy minus the percentage change in R in the com-parator country, Sweden, may be attributed to the change in the relative stringency of mitigation policy in Italy relative to Sweden:

$$\Delta lnR - \Delta lnR^* = -\gamma\Delta\frac{1 + S}{1 + S^*} \tag{4.1}$$

Suppose, as in Figures 9.3, that S is scaled between 0 (no mitigation) and 100, and Italy increases S from 0 to 70 whereas S* remains unchanged at 0 in Sweden. Equation (4.1) states that R in Italy will grow more slowly than in Sweden by $71\gamma$. This triple difference represents the treatment effect of mitigation policy upon R in Italy relative to the comparator, Sweden. Note that according to the Oxford Uni-versity Covid-19 policy tracker S* increased in Sweden but by considerably less than in Italy, which is taken into account in the specification of equation (4.1). Es-timates of $\gamma$ are reported in Table 9.4, which suggests that, during the first wave, mitigation policy had the greatest effect on morbidity in Denmark and the smallest effect in Switzerland.

**Table 9.4** 3DID Estimates of Treatment Effects for Mitigation Policy

| Country | Semi-elasticity ($\gamma$) |
|---|---|
| Austria | 1.20 |
| Denmark | 2.00 |
| France | 0.45 |
| Germany | 1.60 |
| Israel | 0.78 |
| Italy | 0.56 |
| Norway | 1.8 |
| Spain | 1.00 |
| Switzerland | 0.43 |

*Source:* Beenstock and Xieer (2020).

Equation (4.1) and the results in Table 9.4 imply that when Israel ramped up its mitigation policy in mid-March (depicted in Figure 9.3d), R subsequently decreased by 0.64.

Beenstock and Xieer (2020) also estimated a vector autoregression model (VAR) for Israel, as in equations (3.1) and (3.2), where Z is specified in terms of R for morbidity, M is represented by the Oxford University stringency index (depicted in Figure 9.3D), and the data are daily observations. Whereas in equations (3.1) and (3.2) the VAR order was 1 for purposes of exposition, the empirical VAR in equations (4.2) and (4.3) is third order, hence the number of roots is six rather than two.

$$R_t = \frac{0.410}{(2.56)} + \frac{0.998}{(20.44)} R_{t-1} - \frac{0.0047}{(-2.34)} S_{t-2} + \frac{0.0127}{(1.47)} \Delta S_{t-3} + r_t \qquad (4.2)$$

$$R^2 \, (adj) = 0.932 \; LM = 0.965 \; se = 0.196$$

$$S_t = \frac{11.654}{(4.49)} + \frac{0.883}{(32.03)} S_{t-1} + \frac{0.384}{(3.14)} \Delta S_{t-2} - \frac{4.659}{(-1.77)} \Delta R_{t-1} + \frac{2.032}{(1.44)} \Delta_3 R_t + s_t. \qquad (4.3)$$

$$R^2 \, (adj) = 0.973 \; LM = 11.1 \; se = 2.482$$

where t statistics are reported below their respective parameter estimates, r and s denote innovations, LM denotes the lagrange multiplier statistic for fourth-order autocorrelated residuals (not significant), and se denotes the standard error of estimate. R and S Granger-cause each other. As expected, S Granger-causes R negatively, but so does $\Delta R$ Granger-cause S negatively. Also, equation (4.2) contains a unit root and equation (4.3) contains a near-unit root. Since the LM test statistics for autocorrelation are not statistically significant, the lagged values of S in equation (4.2) are weakly exogeneous for the causal parameters of mitigation policy on R. The ten-day cumulative impulse response of R with respect to a temporary impulse in $s$ (equivalent to $\Delta S = 30$) reduces R by $-0.15$, which continues to intensify through the unit root in R. This means, for example, that if R for morbidity would have been 1.5 in the absence of lockdown, a lockdown with stringency 60 would reduce R to 1.3 after ten days and to below 1 after twenty days, which is what happened.

Whereas VAR and 3DID estimates of treatment effects for mitigation policy are conventional, Beenstock and Xieer suggested a third, unconventional, method, the "Chinese Crystal Ball model" (CCB). The intuition for CCB is to use morbidity in China as a leading indicator for morbidity elsewhere. By the time the epidemic broke out elsewhere in March 2020, China had accumulated three months' experience with the epidemic. In fact, by March R had peaked in China and by May it was close to zero. If elsewhere Chinese-style mitigation was adopted, it might be plausible to assume that the temporal diffusion profile of R might be similar to China's. If so, what happened to R in China might serve as a crystal ball, or lead indicator, for countries elsewhere. Since in most other countries mitigation policy was less stringent than in China, CCB needs to take account of differential mitigation policy.

To motivate CCB, we propose the following simple hypothesis in which relative contagion varies inversely with relative stringency, as in equation (4.4). Let subscripts i, c, and 0 refer respectively to country i, China and a baseline country that did not undertake mitigation. Hence, R in China relative to R in the baseline country is assumed to be:

$$\frac{R_c}{R_0} = \alpha_c - \beta_c \frac{S_c}{S_0} \qquad (4.4)$$

Normalizing $S_0 = 1$, equation (4.4) states that if China had not practiced mitigation, R in China would have been larger than in the baseline country if $\alpha_c - \beta_c$ exceeds 1. Importantly, the decrease in R in China has two components. The first results from maximal stringency. The second results from the decrease in R in the baseline. Similarly, R in country i relative to R in China is assumed to be:

$$\frac{R_i}{R_c} = \alpha_i - \beta_i \frac{S_i}{S_c} \qquad (4.5)$$

If $\alpha_i - \beta_i$ exceeds 1, R in country i would exceed R in China if it undertook Chinese mitigation policy. If it did not, $S_i/S_c$ is a fraction and R in country i may be larger or smaller than in China.

Equations (4.4) and (4.5) imply the following relation between R in country i and the baseline country:

$$R_i = R_0 \left( \alpha_i \alpha_c - \alpha_i \beta_c \frac{S_c}{S_0} - \alpha_c \beta_i \frac{S_i}{S_c} + \beta_i \beta_c \frac{S_i}{S_0} \right) \qquad (4.6)$$

According to equation (4.6), R in country i varies proportionately with R in the baseline country. If the term in brackets exceeds 1, R in country i is larger than in the baseline country. If mitigation policy in China and country i are proportionate, and $\alpha_i - \beta_i$ exceeds 1, R in country i varies inversely with stringency in China and country i. Matters are more complicated when mitigation policy is not proportionate because the partial derivatives with respect to stringency in China and country i have ambiguous signs. If mitigation policy is entirely reversed in China and country i, the term in brackets equals $(\alpha_i - \beta_i)(\alpha_c - \beta_c)$. Therefore, if mitigation is entirely reversed, R in country i may be greater or smaller than in the baseline country.

Representing country i by Israel, CCB predicts that R in Israel varies directly in Covid time (since the outbreak of the epidemic) with R in China, and it varies inversely with the stringency of mitigation policy in Israel. In principle, what matters is relative stringency, as in the triple difference method, but since stringency in China was maximal during this period, its effect is absorbed into $\beta_i$. Note that CCB does not imply that, had Israel mitigated maximally as in China, R in Israel would have been the same as R in China. It means, instead, that R in China serves as a lead indicator for R in Israel. Moreover, the relation between R in Israel and R in China is not instantaneous. Instead, it is dynamically related.

We report the following result (estimated with data as of April 23, 2020) for Hubei and Zhejiang provinces, where t refers to Covid time in Israel with respect to Hubei and Zhejiang. Note that in terms of calendar time Hubei is fifty-three days ahead of Israel and ten days ahead of Zhejiang.

$$\ln R_t = \frac{0.338}{(3.02)} \ln R_{t-1} + \frac{0.626}{(4.85)} D\ln R_{t-1} + \frac{0.443}{(3.69)} \ln(1 + Z_{t-1})$$

$$- \frac{0.089}{(-2.03)} D\ln(1 + Z_{t-1}) + \frac{1.128}{(2.23)} \ln(1 + H_{t-1}) - \frac{0.528}{(-4.37)} D\ln(1 + H_{t-1})$$

$$- \frac{0.0018}{(-3.30)} S_{t-2}H_{t-1} - \frac{0.0079}{(-7.10)} S_{t-2} \qquad (4.7)$$

R(adj) = 0.9821 LM = 5.16 se = 0.073

In equation (4.7) H and Z denote R in Hubei and Zhejiang, and D is a dummy variable, which is 1 until R peaked in Israel on March 21, 2020 and is zero afterwards. The LM statistic means that the residuals are not autocorrelated. Equation (4.7) implies that the weights on R in Hubei and Zhejiang were larger after R peaked in Israel, but the autoregressive coefficient was smaller (0.338). It also implies that mitigation policy in Israel reduces R but this effect varies inversely with R in Hubei. Equation (4.7) implies, for example, that after R peaked in Israel, the long run elasticity of R in Israel with respect to its counterpart in Zhejiang is $0.669\frac{Z}{1+Z}$, which tends to zero as Z tends to zero. The semi-elasticity with respect to stringency is $-(0.0119 + 0.0027H)$, hence the mitigation effect increases with R in Hubei.

To estimate the effect of mitigation policy in Israel on R for morbidity during the first wave of the epidemic, we switch off mitigation policy in equation (4.7) by setting S = 1. The results are plotted in Figure 9.4 in which the broken line represents the data for R, the intermittent broken line represents the prediction of R according to CCB (equation (4.7)), and the dotted line represents the counterfactual: what would have happened to R according to CCB in the absence of mitigation policy. Note that CCB tracks that data well; the history of R in Hubei and Zhejiang serves as a lead indicator for R in Israel. CCB predicted that R should have peaked on March 21 at 2.8 before gradually decreasing to less than 1 by April 20, which is what happened.

The vertical difference between the dotted and intermittent broken lines measures the difference in R that may be attributed to mitigation policy. In the absence of mitigation policy, R would have reached double figures before peaking on March 21, after which it would have decreased towards 1 by April 20. Notice that, even in the absence of mitigation policy, R would have decreased by itself as the public learns to engage in social distancing. However, Figure 9.4 suggests that without mitigation policy R would have grown more rapidly than it did. In Figure 9.4 the level of R appears to be very large. In the initial stages of wave one, R exceeded 5 in some countries (Beenstock and Xieer 2020) before decreasing towards 1 after several months.

In summary, three different methodologies suggest that mitigation policy had a beneficial causal effect in reducing R for morbidity in Israel during the first wave.

## The "Overlapping Generations" Method

What we have done so far is to estimate the reduction in R for morbidity that may be attributed to mitigation policy during wave one in Israel. To estimate LS in equation (2.8) it is necessary to convert R for morbidity into units of mortality. This turns out to be a tedious calculation for which I apologize in advance. It involves the following steps. First, R for morbidity is converted into the number of people diagnosed with Covid-19. Second, the case fatality rate is used to convert morbidity into mortality. Finally, the age structure of the dead is used to calculate life years lost due to premature death from Covid-19 using life tables for remaining life expectancy at age of death.

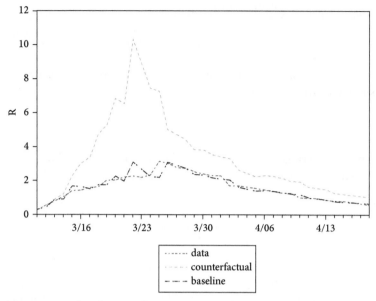

**Fig. 9.4** R in the Absence of Lockdown: Israel Wave 1
*Source*: Beenstock and Xieer (2020)

Let $n_t$ denote the number of newly infected during period t, $y_t$ the number of infectives at the end of period t, and $Y_t$ the number of ever-infected at the end of period t. Assume that infectives remain contagious on average for $\tau$ periods so that each infective infects an average of $R/\tau$ people per period. The number of newly infected during period t is the contagion rate per period multiplied by infectives at the beginning of period t:

$$n_t = \frac{R}{\tau} y_{t-1} \tag{4.8}$$

The number of infectives at the beginning of period t (at the end of period t–1) is the sum of newly infected over the previous $\tau$ periods:

$$y_{t-1} = \sum_{i=1}^{\tau+1} n_{t-i} \tag{4.9}$$

The upper limit for i = $\tau$ + 1 is induced by the fact that the infected cease to be contagious after $\tau$ periods. The number of ever-infected at the end of period t is the sum of all newly infected since the outbreak of the epidemic in period s < t:

$$Y_t = \sum_{i=0}^{s} n_{t-i} \tag{4.10}$$

According to equation (4.9) the change in the number of infectives is:

$$\Delta y_t = n_t - n_{t-\tau-1} = \Delta_{\tau+1} n_t \tag{4.11}$$

Substituting equation (4.8) into equation (4.11) expresses the change in the number of infectives as:

$$\Delta y_t = \frac{R}{\tau} \Delta_{\tau+1} y_{t-1} \tag{4.12}$$

By reverse engineering, equation (4.12) implies that R equals the short difference in y divided by the average of its lagged long difference:

$$R_t = \tau \frac{\Delta y_t}{\Delta_{\tau+1} y_{t-1}} \tag{4.13}$$

Equation (4.13) allows for the fact that R may change over time. It is also the "overlapping generations" method (OLG) for calculating R in real time (Beenstock and Xieer 2020), so-called because each cohort of infectives survives for $\tau$ periods after which it ceases to be contagious. R = 1 when the short difference equals the average long difference, and it exceeds 1 when the short difference exceeds the average long difference. R tends to zero as the short difference decreases relative to the average long difference. R was calculated in this way in the three empirical applications above.

Equation (4.12) is $\tau$ + 2 order difference equation with $\tau$ + 2 roots illustrated in Table 9.5 for different values of R. Two of the roots are real and 14 roots are complex. All the complex roots are stable. One of the real roots is 1. The other real root exceeds 1 if R is greater than about 0.9, otherwise it is less than 1. Notice that a unit root is induced by the fact that infectives cease to be contagious after $\tau$ periods, as in the last row in Table 9.5. The other root increases with R as expected.

Table 9.5 Roots of Equation (4.12)

| R | Real | | Complex: stable |
|---|---|---|---|
| 2 | 1 | 1.11491 | 14 |
| 1.3 | 1 | 1.00875 | 14 |
| 1 | 1 | 1.00875 | 14 |
| 0.7 | 1 | 0.966 | 14 |
| 0.2 | 1 | 0.84996 | 14 |
| 0 | 1 | - | - |

Notes: $\tau$ = 14 days.

Thus far equation (4.13) converts R into infectives. The next step is convert infectives into mortality. Denote the case mortality rate by $\delta$, which in Israel was 0.8 percent (Table 9.2). The case mortality rate is defined as cumulative mortality ($Z_T$) divided by cumulative morbidity ($Y_T$) over T periods, hence $\delta = Z_T/Y_T$. OLG implies that $\tau$ periods into the epidemic $Y_\tau = y_s(1 + R/\tau)^\tau$ where $y_s$ is the initial number of infectives. This "compound interest" formula cannot be applied beyond period $\tau$ because the initial cohort ceases to be contagious. For example, $Y_{\tau+1} = y_s[(1 + R/\tau)^{\tau+1}-1]$. The OLG version of the compound interest formula is:

$$Y_T = y_s\left[\left(1 + \frac{R}{\tau}\right)^T - \left(1 + \frac{R}{\tau}\right)^{T-\tau-1}\right] \tag{4.14}$$

$$T = g\tau + j \tag{4.15}$$

where $j = 0, 1, ..., \tau-1$ indexes periods within cohorts or generations of infectives and $g = 1, 2, ...$ indexes generations. For example, Figure 9.4 covers a period of forty days, hence T = 40. Using $\tau = 14$, g = 2 and j = 12, i.e. $2\tau$ +12 = 40. Observation 40 refers to the twelfth period into the third generation of infectives. If R = 2 and $y_s$ = 10, equations (4.14) and (4.15) imply that ever-infected after 40 periods is $Y_T$ = 1806. If $\delta$ = 0.008 (0.8 percent) then mortality would be 14.45. If mitigation policy would have reduced to R to 1.2, the number of ever-infected would have been 190.16, and mortality 1.52.

If R is variable rather than fixed, as in equation (4.14), the counterpart to equation (4.14) is:

$$Y_T = y_s\left[\prod_{t=1}^{T}\left(1 + \frac{R_t}{\tau}\right) - \prod_{t=1}^{T-\tau-1}\left(1 + \frac{R_t}{\tau}\right)\right] \tag{4.16}$$

where $R_t$ denotes R for the cohort, which ceases to be contagious in period t.

## Counterfactual Saving of Life

Let $Y_B$ denote the value of $Y_T$ according to equation (4.16) using the values of R from the intermittent broken line in Figure 9.4 and let $Y_G$ denote its counterpart using the from the dotted line values of R in Figure 9.4. Then $Q = \delta(Y_G-Y_B)$ is the number of lives saved, and the cost per life saved is J/Q.

During the first wave the case mortality rate in Israel was 1.61 percent, which was double the case mortality rate for 2020 as a whole (Table 9.2). The health services learnt to cope with hospitalized patients, and by September the case mortality rate stabilized at 0.8 percent. By May 15, 260 people had died out of 16,101 ever-diagnosed by May 1. During the period covered by Figure 9.4 (extended by ten days until the end of April), R averaged 1.8. In the absence of mitigation policy, it would have averaged 5 until the end of March and 2.3 subsequently. In the absence of mitigation there would have been 1,024,980 ever-infected instead of 16,101 and there would have been 16,503 deaths instead of 260.

Assuming that a third of the annual lockdown cost of 88 billion shekels is attributed to the first wave (out of three waves in 2020), the cost per life saved works out at about 1.81 million shekels per life ($517,000). As suggested by Table 9.2, senior citizens are overrepresented in Covid-19-related mortality (as they are in mortality for the general population). During wave one, 92 percent of deaths from Covid-19 were of people over the age of 60. Using the latest life tables provided by the Central Bureau of Statistics the deceased would have lived, on average, another 11.24 years had they not succumbed to Covid-19. Therefore, the cost per life year saved works out at about 161,000 shekels ($46,000).

This estimate of the cost per life year saved for Israel is considerably less than the cost of £180,000 in the UK reported by Wood (2020). The difference depends on numerous factors, including the economic cost of mitigation policy, the effect of mitigation policy on R, the efficiency of the health services, the fitness of populations, and possible differences in strains of virus.

## Reservations and Limitations

The estimated cost for Israel is at best a rough approximation because it is based on equation (4.14), in which R changes periodically, instead of equation (4.16), in which R changes continuously as in Figure 9.4. Also, margins of error have not been calculated, which would have taken into account that equation (4.7), upon which Figure 9.4 is based, is stochastic, with standard error of 7.3 percent. Despite the fact that Figure 9.4 suggests that mitigation policy had a large effect on morbidity, the cost per life year saved turns out to be large. Just as in the UK, where the cost per life year saved greatly exceeds the shadow cost used by the Department of Health, so in Israel 161,000 shekels per life year is larger than the shadow cost used by the Ministry of Health. These estimates of the cost per life year saved provide quantitative expressions of the abnormal attention paid to mortality from Covid-19 relative to mortality in general.

These cost estimates solely reflect economic costs and exclude the social costs of lockdowns. They ignore the stress of confinement to home, the disruption to children because of school closures, the loneliness of senior citizens, and fears of bankruptcy. Therefore, the cost estimates that are reported should serve as lower bounds; the total socioeconomic cost exceeds 161,000 shekels, which adds to the abnormality of lockdown.

The cost per life year saved for Covid-19 in Israel refers to the first wave in the absence of estimates of the treatment effect of mitigation policy for subsequent waves. Figure 9.3 seems to suggest a positive trend to mortality, despite the fact that the stringency of mitigation policy is trend-free. After mortality peaks, most countries relax their mitigation policy, but do not reverse it completely, after which a new wave starts and mitigation policy is reimposed. However, in the new wave, mitigation policy seems to be less effective than in the previous one, even before the "British variant" of the virus struck Israel in January 2021 and the "Delta variant" struck in September 2021.

My purpose is not to pass judgment on whether it was worth spending 161,000 shekels on saving a life year in Israel or spending £180,000 in the UK. Just because in previous epidemics, such as Spanish flu a century ago and Swine flu in 2009, governments did not engage in lockdown policy and instead let people die as the epidemic ran its course, does not mean that it was wrong to act differently in the case of Covid-19. Nevertheless, it is fair to point out that the New Abnormal policy response to Covid-19 implies valuations of death from Covid-19 that seem to be an order of magnitude greater than valuations of deaths from other causes.

## 2021

The race to develop a vaccine against Covid-19 ended in a photo-finish in December 2020. By early 2021 several vaccines were available. Israel got off to a head start in rolling out the vaccine. The author received two shots of the Pfizer vaccine by early February, a third shot in August and a fourth in December. By April, 90 percent of the population (excluding children up to 16 years) had been vaccinated. The advent of the vaccine coincided with the arrival of the British variant, which was more contagious than the original. During January and February, morbidity increased alarmingly, but by March the beneficial effect of the vaccine dominated the harmful effect of the British variant. By March 15, mitigation policy was almost completely scaled back.

The vaccination rollout rates reported in Table 9.6 convey the enormous differences in vaccination campaigns. However, they provide an incomplete picture because they are defined in terms of the total population, including children aged 16 and under, who were not eligible for vaccination as of early June 2021. For example, the roll-out rates (at least one shot) for the UK and Israel appear to be similar (60 percent). However, the dependency ratio (Table 9.2) is considerably greater in the UK (29.04) than in Israel (19.42). Hence, apart from the fact that almost all Israelis had two shots, a larger percentage of the population at risk is

**Table 9.6** Rollout Rates for Vaccination, Stringency, Morbidity, and Mortality: June 6, 2021

| | 2 shots percent | 1 shot percent | Stringency 1–100 | Morbidity per million | Mortality per million |
|---|---|---|---|---|---|
| Israel | 59 | 3.7 | 29.63 | 29.11 | 1.62 |
| UK | 41 | 19 | 62.5 | 801.52 | 1.77 |
| Chile | 48 | 11 | 80.09 | 5128.53 | 74.23 |
| US | 42 | 9.5 | 52.31 | 729.43 | 22.86 |
| Denmark | 23 | 17 | 55.56 | 2256.65 | 1.73 |
| Switzerland | 22 | 15 | 48.15 | 1148.4 | 6.47 |
| Spain | 22 | 19 | 61.57 | 1315.97 | 12.32 |
| France | 19 | 23 | 54.63 | 1617.3 | 20.77 |
| Germany | 21 | 25 | 75 | 611.52 | 21.72 |
| Italy | 22 | 22 | 62.09 | 665.63 | 21.47 |
| Belgium | 22 | 22 | 50.93 | 1891.43 | 16.48 |
| Canada | 7.5 | 54 | 73.61 | 890.73 | 12.93 |
| S. Korea | 4.45 | 10.37 | 50 | 159.35 | 0.78 |
| Australia | 5 | 15 | 74.54 | 6.75 | 0 |
| Japan | 3.4 | 6.8 | 49.07 | 340.42 | 10.1 |
| New Zealand | 4.9 | 4.1 | 22.22 | 2.9 | 0 |

*Source:* Our World in Data. Vaccination: percent of population. Morbidity and mortality: biweekly.

covered in Israel than in the UK. This explains why Israel has a stringency index for mitigation of 29.63, whereas for the UK this index was 62.5 on June 6, 2021.

Table 9.6 shows that there are countries, such as Australia and New Zealand, that have not invested in vaccination because they have managed to achieve low rates of morbidity and mortality by other means. The same is true of China and Taiwan (not included in Table 9.6). Nor has South Korea invested in vaccination roll-out. However, it has succeeded in reducing mortality, enabling it to reduce the mitigation stringency index to 50, although it has been less successful in reducing morbidity. A further suggestion is that the "one shot first" policy to cover more of the population with one shot (as in the UK and Canada) might have been a mistake, instead of the "two shot first" alternative to fully immunize less of the population (as in Israel). It takes two shots to develop the necessary antibodies. Although as many as 54 percent of Canadians had received one shot by June 6, 2021 they were still exposed to risk of contagion, as reflected in their morbidity and mortality rates.

By October 16, 2021 the countries in Table 9.6 had caught up and even surpassed Israel. The leading countries with two shots were Denmark (76 percent), Chile (75 percent) and Canada and Belgium (73 percent), while the laggards were New

Zealand (44 percent), Australia (55) percent, and the US (56 percent). These numbers include 12- to 16-year-olds, who began to be vaccinated in the summer. For example, by October 16, 44.4 percent of 12- to 16-year-olds in Israel had received two shots and 11.3 percent had received one shot.

## Macroeconomic Developments

Almost all governments responded to the pandemic by engaging in various forms of mitigation policy, including restrictions on international travel and lockdowns to enforce social distancing. Because of the contraction in international trade, the whole was more than the sum of its parts; each country's economic contraction was all the greater because of economic contractions among trading partners. On the other hand, the price of oil remained weak throughout 2020; clouds have silver linings. Also, some sectors of the economy benefited, especially online communications (such as Zoom).

Table 9.7 measures the economic cost of lockdown in terms of the growth in GDP during 2020 minus its growth rate in previous years. For example, in Israel GDP grew by 3.4 percent in 2019 but contracted by 2.53 percent in 2020, hence lost output in 2020 due to Covid-19 amounted to 5.93 percent of GDP. However, had Israel not locked down its economy, there would have been slower growth in 2020 because of lockdowns elsewhere. Spain suffered the worst output loss (12.79 percent of GDP), followed by the UK (10.28 percent of GDP). South Korea suffered the smallest loss (2.95 percent of GDP), followed by Japan and Australia. Most economies suffered output losses of more than 6 percent of GDP.

Some of the countries that suffered most economically also suffered most from Covid-19. Comparing Tables 9.7 and 9.2 shows, for example, that the UK, Spain, and Italy suffered most on both accounts, whereas Japan and South Korea suffered least. Bad news brings bad news.

Just as there was enormous diversity in the economic cost of Covid-19, so was there enormous diversity in the response of fiscal policy. Several countries increased their fiscal deficit by more than 10 percent of GDP, including Canada, the UK, and the US, whereas in Sweden and South Korea fiscal deficits increased by less than 4 percent of GDP. Because in all countries fiscal deficits increased as a percentage of GDP, so did their debt-to-GDP ratios. The smallest increases occurred in Sweden and South Korea, as expected, and the largest increases (in terms of percentage points) occurred in Canada and the US, as well as in Japan. Recall that even had fiscal deficits been zero (balanced budgets), debt-to-GDP ratios would have risen because GDP decreased everywhere.

Finally, Table 9.7 shows that QE increased massively in key central banks. Note that QE does not apply within the eurozone. However, for countries such as Australia a program of QE was launched in 2020, and in Israel QE was massively

**Table 9.7** Macroeconomic Developments

| | Economic growth | | Fiscal deficit % of GDP | | Debt % of GDP | | Quantitative easing USD trillion | |
|---|---|---|---|---|---|---|---|---|
| | 2019 | 2020 | 2019 | 2020 | 2019 | 2020 | 2019 | 2020 |
| Australia | 1.94 | −2.51 | 0 | 4.3 | 19.2 | 24.8 | | |
| Belgium | 1.78 | −6.28 | 1.9 | 9.4 | 98.1 | 114.1 | | |
| Canada | 1.86 | −6.03 | 1.7 | 16.1 | 65.2 | 91.6 | | |
| Denmark | 2.85 | −2.73 | −3.8 | 1.1 | 33.3 | 42.2 | | |
| France | 1.49 | −8.16 | 3.1 | 9.2 | 97.6 | 115.7 | | |
| Germany | 0.59 | −5.13 | −1.5 | 4.2 | 59.7 | 69.8 | | |
| Israel | 3.4 | −2.53 | 3.7 | 11.7 | 60.0 | 73.1 | 1.985* | 50.349* |
| Italy | 0.28 | −8.93 | 1.6 | 9.5 | 134.6 | 155.8 | | |
| Japan | 0.01 | −4.71 | 3.1 | 10.3 | 238.0 | 266.2 | 5.3 | 6.6 |
| South Korea | 2.04 | −0.91 | 2.6 | 6.1 | 36.4 | 42.6 | | |
| New Zealand | 3.0 | −3.75 | −2.4 | 7.5 | 19.0 | 27.0 | | |
| Spain | 1.95 | −10.84 | 2.9 | 11.0 | 95.5 | 120.0 | | |
| Sweden | 1.41 | −2.99 | −0.6 | 3.1 | 35.0 | 39.9 | | |
| UK | 1.43 | −9.85 | 2.5 | 14.3 | 84.0 | 97.0 | 0.8 | 1.1 |
| US | 2.46 | −3.49 | 4.6 | 14.9 | 106.7 | 129.1 | 4.2 | 7.3 |
| ECB | | | | | | | 5.2 | 8.1 |

*Sources*: National statistical offices. Note that the data in columns 2 and 3 often differ from those published in *World Economic Outlook* (IMF, April 2021), *Economic Outlook* (OECD, May 2021) and *World Bank DataBank* (June 2021). * billions of shekels.

expanded in 2020 and continued to expand in 2021, such that by the end of April financial assets purchased under QE stood at almost 60 billion shekels.

## Economic Recovery in 2021

GDP peaked in most countries in the last quarter of 2019, which in Table 9.8 is used as a benchmark for comparisons of economic activity during 2020 and 2021. Also, GDP troughed in most countries during the second quarter of 2020. For example, in the first quarter of 2020 GDP was 10.1 percent smaller than in the last quarter of 2019 in the US, and 21.8 percent smaller in the UK. Notice that these differences cannot be compared with the cost of mitigation; they were based on the difference between economic growth in 2019 relative to 2020, and in Israel this was almost 6 percent of GDP (Table 9.7) and 10.3 percent in Table 9.8.

Table 9.8 shows that with the exception of Japan economic activity, as measured by GDP, had almost recovered in most economies to what it was before the pandemic by the third quarter of 2021. The US and Israel passed this milestone in

**Table 9.8**  Economic Recovery in 2021

|         | 2019 Q4 | 2020 Q2 | 2021 Q2 | 2021 Q3 | 2021 Q4 |
|---------|---------|---------|---------|---------|---------|
| US      | 100     | 89.9    | 100.9   | 101.4   | 103.2   |
| UK      | 100     | 78.2    | 95.6    | 97.9    | 99.9    |
| France  | 100     | 81.6    | 97.0    | 99.8    | 101.1   |
| Germany | 100     | 88.5    | 95.3    | 96.9    | 96.2    |
| Italy   | 100     | 82.2    | 96.4    | 98.9    | 99.5    |
| Canada  | 100     | 86.9    | 98.0    | 98.3    | 100.1   |
| Japan   | 100     | 87.5    | 94.3    | 93.6    | 96.9    |
| Israel  | 100     | 89.7    | 102.7   | 105.1   | 109.1   |

Based on national income estimates (seasonally adjusted at constant prices) by national statistical offices (April 2022).

the second quarter of 2021 and continued to recover at a slower rate in the third quarter. The strongest recovery occurred in the UK, where the output loss in 2020 was the largest. During the third quarter, the recovery weakened in the US and Canada, while the economy of Japan contracted.

The pre-pandemic baseline (fourth quarter of 2019) is arbitrary. It is obviously harder to surpass this baseline for countries such as Italy and Japan, which have low rates of economic growth, than it is for countries such as Israel, where the rate of economic growth is relatively high. For example, by the third quarter of 2021 GDP in Israel should have been about 4.8 percent larger than the baseline because the annual growth rate is of the order of 3 percent, whereas GDP in Japan should have been similar to the baseline. Table 9.8 shows that Israel exceeded this dynamic baseline by 0.3 percent; it has made up for its lost economic growth. Indeed, in the final quarter of 2021 GDP was 9.1 percent greater than what it was in the final quarter of 2019

Most governments (Austria excluded) have sensibly abandoned nationwide lockdown to combat Covid-19. They have decided that life must go on as normal and be lived alongside the pandemic. Mass vaccination has replaced lockdown as the main instrument of policy. Hence, in the absence of new Covid-19 variants that are immune to current vaccination technology, economic recovery is likely to continue. With the exception of Japan, the countries in Table 9.8 will probably exceed their baselines during the first half of 2022, establishing that economic recovery from natural disasters, including pandemics, is more rapid (see chapter 10) than economic recovery from man-made disasters, such as the Subprime Crisis of 2008.

## Synopsis

It was not obvious that governments would decide to "flatten the curve" through mitigation policy. After all, they had not behaved this way in previous pandemics.

The New Abnormal set the scene for activist mitigation policy because its key features, cheap money and loose fiscal policy, were naturally extended during the Covid-19 crisis. Had the Covid-19 pandemic occurred before the New Abnormal, governments' responses might have been less activist, as in the case of SARS and Swine flu.

A Rawlsian case is made for justifying the deficit financing of Covid-19 mitigation policy. Pandemics cannot be insured within generations, but they may be insured between generations provided they do not occur in every generation. Hence, future generations have an interest in sharing the risk of pandemics with other generations born before and after them. Future generations compensate current generations by the latter bequeathing Covid-19-related public debt.

Just as the principle of mitigation policy should be seen historically as an abnormality induced by the New Abnormal, so has the practice of mitigation policy been abnormal. Specifically, governments have incurred enormous economic costs to keep people alive one extra year from Covid-19, which stand out of all proportion to their willingness to pay to prolong life from other diseases. Governments have acted as if dying from Covid-19 is inherently worse than dying from something else. To conduct such an audit, it is first necessary to calculate what morbidity would have been counterfactually in the absence of mitigation policy.

A case study is presented for Israel during the first wave of Covid-19 in which the counterfactual is solved using different econometrics methods. The average cost per life year saved is 161,000 shekels ($46,000), which is cheaper than a comparable estimate for the UK (£180,000). These estimates are vastly larger than health economists' estimates of the value of life. It is perfectly normal to mitigate, but this evidence suggests that the economic cost of mitigation has been out of all proportion to the benefit in terms of life years saved. Perhaps this explains why policy makers are abandoning lockdown as a policy option and have increasingly turned to "living alongside Covid-19" as a more sensible policy.

Just as there is enormous variety in morbidity and mortality rates for Covid-19 across countries, there is enormous variety in its economic cost in terms of lost GDP, as well as enormous variety in macroeconomic policy in general and fiscal policy in particular. On the whole, however, countries that suffered most economically also suffered more in terms of mortality and had the largest fiscal deficits. Trouble chases trouble.

The macroeconomic responses to the pandemic intensified the New Abnormal. The prospects of ending the New Abnormal after 2021 were much worse than they were in 2019.

# 10

# The Return to Normality: Ending the New Abnormal

## The Unsustainability of The New Abnormal

Can the New Abnormal last forever, as perhaps suggested by the experience of Japan? Our answer is no, because the New Abnormal sows the seeds of its own destruction. This is a case of Herbert Stein's Law, according to which "if something cannot go on forever, it will stop." In Chapter 2 we noted that according to macroeconomic theory (Patinkin 1966) the central bank must eventually acquire all the economy's financial assets for ZIP to last forever, and in the process money supply tends to infinity through increasingly aggressive QE. As the central bank becomes the sole owner of everything, private enterprise, as we know it, cannot survive. In this process, financial distancing breaks down because the central bank is directly involved in financing the non-bank private sector. Also, the public is prepared to accumulate money balances forever because the opportunity cost of liquidity is zero when the rate of interest is zero. The central bank eventually owns all the assets, and in return the public becomes paper millionaires. At some point the public will increase its spending, and kinetic inflation will break out. This theoretical solution is a politically impossible backstop in democratic societies.

Central banks such as the Federal Reserve have crossed a new red line in extending QE to equity capital. It is a realistic prospect that in their urge to flatten rates of return on all financial assets, other central banks will extend QE to equity capital, and perhaps to other private assets too. This apocalyptic prospect would concentrate power in central banks in a way that is incompatible with democracy. Because central banks are supposed to be constitutionally independent, they are exempt from democratic control. Presumably central banks would forfeit their independence if they became major owners of equity capital and corporate debt.

Apart from the above, the social implications of ZIP for pensions and social insurance (Chapter 7) are most probably politically unsustainable. The current generation of Millennials (and Generations X) will realize that their pensions will have little value. If the New Abnormal persists, future pensioners will be twice cursed. Their pensions will not be worth much because of ZIP, and they will inherit the public debt bequeathed by their parents' generation. Social commentators

*Zero Interest Policy and the New Abnormal*. Michael Beenstock, Oxford University Press. © Michael Beenstock (2022).
DOI: 10.1093/oso/9780192849663.003.0010

(Taylor 2014, Filipovic 2020) are already speaking about intergenerational conflict between boomers on the one hand, and Generation X and Millennials on the other. Intergenerational inequity induced by the New Abnormal aggravates this conflict. For all of these reasons, the New Abnormal is not a sustainable form of political economy. It is storing up trouble.

On the other hand, the New Abnormal may last a long time, during which existential risk increases. The unsustainability of the New Abnormal is characterized in Figure 10.1, where existential risk is measured on the vertical and duration of the New Abnormal is measured on the horizontal. Schedule $R_0$ plots the relation between existential risk and the duration of the New Abnormal at the onset of the New Abnormal. Notice that existential risk is initially zero or negligible, but with the passage of time $(t_0)$ it becomes positive. Initially, the New Abnormal is expected to end in period $T_0$, either because the political economy constraint described in the previous paragraph is binding, or for other reasons.

By time $t_1$ existential risk is positive, as a result of which investment decreases (Chapter 2). Because output is lower, debt-to-GDP ratios, kinetic inflation etc. increase so that schedule $R_0$ tilts leftwards to schedule $R_1$, and the New Abnormal is expected to break down earlier, in period $T_1$. This logic implies that, over time, schedule $R_1$ continues leftwards until the New Abnormal eventually breaks down in e.g. period $t_2 = T_2$. In the nature of things, towards the end the negative feedback of existential risk on schedule R becomes ever stronger. By contrast, in its initial stages, there is no feedback at all from existential risk on to schedule R. If agents are forward-looking, schedule $R^*$ implies that from the start the New Abnormal is expected to end in period $T_2$. If in the interim there are negative shocks, e.g. Covid-19, schedule $R^*$ will contract and the New Abnormal will end sooner than initially expected. Positive shocks will have the opposite effect.

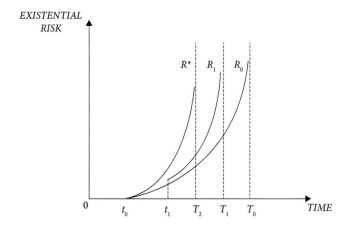

**Fig. 10.1** Survival Analysis for the New Abnormal

In summary, the New Abnormal cannot last in democracies because central banks cannot become major holders of corporate debt and equity and remain independent. In addition, existential risk induced by spiraling debt-to-GDP ratios and the build up of kinetic inflation damage business investment and economic growth and undermine confidence in fiat money. The first sign of collapse will most probably be the release of kinetic inflation, which will force central banks to end ZIP. The increase in interest rates will increase fiscal deficits through the cost of debt service. This chain reaction rapidly spirals out of control. Just as the Bretton Woods system seemed safe until it collapsed, so will the New Abnormal.

## Ricardian Unequivalence

Another preliminary issue concerns the economic status of public sector debt that has accumulated under the New Abnormal. The common view is that this debt will eventually have to be redeemed at the expense of the public. According to Ricardian equivalence theory, the public regards government debt as a future tax liability, which affects current spending and not merely future spending. This implies that deficit-financed government spending has little or no effect on current aggregate spending; it is equivalent to tax-financed government spending. It also means that public debt does not matter per se because the public is indifferent between a "haircut," which would reduce their future tax liability, and an increase in taxation to reduce public debt. Ricardian equivalence implies that public debt is not an issue in itself; the real issue is government spending, which the public must pay for through current taxation or future taxation.

The theoretical mainstay behind Ricardian equivalence is the permanent income hypothesis. Although there is much empirical evidence in favor of the role of permanent income in the determination of current consumption, there is a consensus that consumption also depends on transitory income for a variety of reasons (Romer 2019, pp 671–2). These include imperfect access to credit markets by consumers, the fact that many consumers have no wealth, and the fact that consumers save for precautionary reasons. Therefore, in what follows, we do not think that public debt is of no consequence because of Ricardian equivalence. We are in good company because nor did Ricardo (O'Driscoll 1977).

## Three Aspects of Normalization

There are three interrelated theoretical issues involved in the return to normality in the aftermath of the New Abnormal (after $T_2$ in Figure 10.1). We saw in Chapter 2 that when the rate of interest is zero, liquidity trap theory suspends the unpleasant monetary arithmetic (UMA) because the demand for money becomes infinitely elastic. For the same reason expansion of the money supply as a result of QE is not inflationary. When ZIP ends, the economy will emerge from the liquidity trap, UMA will no longer be suspended, and kinetic inflation induced by QE will be activated. Of course, this is what makes the New Abnormal so attractive to policy makers in the first place. If only it could last forever, but alas it cannot.

The first theoretical issue concerns, therefore, the exit from the liquidity trap. The second concerns policies to mitigate the effects of kinetic inflation. The third concerns the unsustainability of fiscal policy; when interest rates are positive the cost of debt service will drive primary fiscal deficits to zero, implying either massive cuts in public expenditure or increases in taxation. To make things simple, we begin by focusing on the first issue. Thereafter, we extend the discussion to the second issue, ignoring the third. Finally, we consider all three issues together.

## Escaping the Liquidity Trap

### Krugman's Model

The academic literature on ZIP and the liquidity trap has been narrowly concerned with attempts to establish that monetary policy may nevertheless not be entirely impotent. Indeed, these attempts have justified QE as an effective instrument of monetary policy (Romer 2019, section 12.7). This literature appears to suggest that ZIP and QE may be viable even in the long term. This literature is not concerned with ending ZIP and the return to normality. In many respects it is an apologetic for unorthodox monetary policy under the New Abnormal. Interestingly, this literature seems to be unaware of Patinkin's critique (Patinkin 1966) and the adverse political economy implications of QE.

We begin with a discussion of Krugman (1998), which was introduced in Chapter 2 and was originally concerned with Japan. Krugman ignored public debt and QE because they were not relevant to Japan twenty-five years ago, and he presumably did not imagine in 1998 that Japan would still operate ZIP in 2021. Nor did he take into consideration how and why Japan fell into the liquidity trap in the first place. It just so happened that Japan fell into the liquidity trap, as if through bad luck rather for structural reasons. On the other hand, Krugman's model might be relevant for economies that are not heavily indebted and that adopted ZIP relatively recently (such as Israel, Australia, and New Zealand).

Krugman assumed that infinitely-lived households maximize utility:

$$U = \sum_{t=0}^{\infty} \rho^t b_t ln C_t \tag{1.1}$$

where $0 < \rho < 1$ denotes an intertemporal discount rate, C denotes household consumption and $b > 0$ is a demand shifter discussed later. Households are endowed with y goods per period and are subject to a cash-in-advance constraint, so they cannot sell their endowment in period t to buy goods in period t. Households start period t with holdings of bonds $(B_{t-1})$ and money $(M_{t-1})$, which they acquired during period t-1. P denotes the general price level for y. During period t the authorities set $M_t$ and $B_t$ so that consumption during period t, if the rate of interest (i) is positive, is:

$$C_t = \frac{M_t}{P_t} \tag{1.2}$$

and is:

$$C_t \leq \frac{M_t}{P_t} \tag{1.3}$$

if the rate of interest is zero. Equation (1.2) is an equality because households hold minimal money balances when the opportunity cost of money is positive. Equation (1.3) is an inequality because the opportunity cost of money is zero.

The Euler equation for household intertemporal utility maximization implies:

$$1 + i_t = \frac{P_{t+1}}{P_t} \frac{b_t}{b_{t+1}} \frac{1}{\rho} \tag{1.4}$$

After consuming, households receive interest payment $i_t B_t$ on their bonds, and the government sets transfers and taxes.

Notice that equation (1.4) implies that the real rate of interest (r) varies over time if b is not constant:

$$1 + r_t = \frac{b_t}{\rho b_{t+1}} \tag{1.5}$$

If b is constant, equation (1.5) implies, as expected, that the real rate of interest equals the rate of time preference $(1/\rho - 1)$. Equation (1.4) also implies that:

$$\frac{\partial i_t}{\partial P_t} = -\frac{1 + i_t}{P_t} \tag{1.6}$$

In Figure 10.2 (based on Figure 12.5 in Romer 2019), schedule CC plots equation (1.6), whose location varies directly with $P_{t+1} b_t / b_{t+1}$. This schedule embodies current combinations of P and i, which equate the supply of goods (y) with demand. Schedule $MM_0$ represents equations (1.2) and (1.3) when C = y and the money stock is $M_0$.

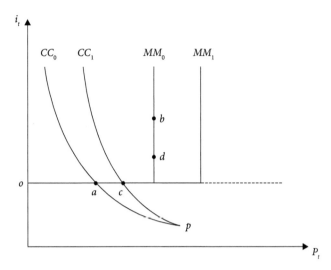

**Fig. 10.2** Krugman's Liquidity Trap Model

If schedule $CC_0$ intersected schedule $MM_0$ on its vertical segment, such as point *b*, the rate of interest would be positive in equilibrium. If, instead, the intersection is on its horizontal segment at point *a* as drawn ($CC_0$), the rate of interest is zero, i.e. ZIP. In this case an increase in money supply simply moves the vertical segment to the right ($MM_1$), in which event the intersection remains unchanged at point *a*. Hence, under ZIP conventional monetary policy is impotent as we saw in Chapter 2. So far, no surprises.

However, this does not mean that other forms of monetary policy are impotent. Suppose, for example, that in period t the central bank announces a price level target for the next period ($P_{t+1}$) that is greater than expected. This would tilt schedule $CC_0$ to the right from its pivot at point *p* to schedule $CC_1$. If schedule $CC_1$ intersects schedule $MM_0$ at *c* (as drawn), the price level increases despite the fact that the rate of interest is still zero. This happens because the decrease in the real rate of interest raises the demand for consumption. Since aggregate supply is fixed, the price level increases. This establishes that under ZIP a credible price level target increases aggregate demand. Alternatively, if at time t the central bank announces that it intends to undertake QE in time t +1 and beyond, the public will raise their expectation of the future price level ($P_{t+1}$), which will tilt schedule CC to the right as in Figure 10.2.

However, in reality price level targets are unlikely to be credible, especially because they might be time-inconsistent. How can central banks manipulate future price expectations, especially when their operating instrument is their policy rate rather than the quantity of money? Through forward guidance central banks may commit to maintaining low interest rates once they have escaped the liquidity trap. Since ZIP induced the liquidity trap in the first place, commitment to low interest rates is unlikely to persuade. Indeed, forward guidance may even be counterproductive (Romer 2019, p 626).

Tilting schedule CC may be induced by increasing $b_t$, which serves as a demand shifter. If QE reduces parallel interest rates (other than i) they may increase aggregate demand ($b_t$ increases) such that schedule $CC_0$ steepens to $CC_1$. However, according to equation (1.4) this would only work if $b_{t+1}$ did not increase too. Hence QE only increases aggregate demand if its scale and scope get ever-larger, contrary to expectations.

In summary, Krugman's model does not provide convincing theoretical justifications for unorthodox monetary policy under ZIP. Tilting schedule CC does not seem to be feasible. On the contrary, the traditional liquidity trap case concerning the impotence of monetary policy under ZIP comes out more convincing than ever.

Nevertheless, Krugman's model sheds light on how to exit ZIP and return to normality. If schedule $CC_1$ intersected schedule $MM_0$ at point $d$ instead of point $c$ in Figure 10.2, the economy would exit ZIP into normality at positive interest rates. To achieve this, the public needs to be persuaded that inflation is about to increase. This becomes a self-fulfilling expectation, since at point $d$ the price level is greater than at point $a$. If the economy descended into ZIP recently, i.e. it had been at point $a$ for a short period of time (as was the case in Japan when Krugman wrote his paper) so that inflation had not been zero for long, it might be easier to persuade the public that inflation was about to recur than if ZIP was well established, and perceived by the public to be a permanent feature of the economic landscape. For countries that recently adopted ZIP, such as New Zealand, this may be a practical option, but not for the vast majority of countries that have adopted ZIP since the precedent of Japan in 1996, during which time they have also accumulated large debt-to-GDP ratios, which were ignored by Krugman. Krugman's model might have been relevant in 1998, but not in 2021.

## Ending Zero Interest Policy Directly

In Krugman's model there is a single rate of interest, which is endogenous. Implicitly, the Bank of Japan set its policy rate at zero in 1996 because the natural rate of interest in Japan just happened to be zero. In Chapter 5 we noted that many economists think that ZIP came about because natural rates of interest just happened to tend to zero across the world. Central banks passively adapted themselves to the dictates of the natural rate of interest. We strongly rejected this interpretation of events. On the contrary, the causality runs in the opposite direction. By committing themselves to ZIP, central banks forced market interest rates down to zero despite the fact that natural rates of interest were positive. In doing so, they artificially distorted rates of interest across the world. In the specific case of Japan, we showed in Chapter 8 that the Bank of Japan adopted ZIP in 1996 in a desperate attempt to end the "lost decade and a half." It had nothing to do with Japan's natural rate of interest, which at the time was clearly positive (Chapter 4).

We therefore introduce a second interest rate into the analysis so that there is a market rate of interest (i), which is endogenous, and a policy rate ($i_{CB}$), which is exogenous, as in Figures 10.3 and 10.4 in Chapter 2. In this model ZIP is ended directly by increasing the policy rate from zero to some normal number. We do not impose cash-in-advance restrictions, which are not essential, and assume that the demand for money is expressed by equation (5.3) in Chapter 2, which is repeated here for convenience:

$$lnM = lnQ + lnP + \frac{\beta}{i}$$ (2.1)

where $\alpha$ in equation (5.3) equals the logarithm of nominal GDP. Equation (2.1) implies that schedule MM in Figure 10.2 is no longer reverse L-shaped. Instead, its slope is:

$$\frac{di}{dP} = \frac{i^2}{\beta P}$$ (2.2)

which is zero under ZIP (because i = 0), is positive otherwise, and schedule MM is convex, as drawn in Figure 10.3. Schedule MM shifts rightwards when the quantity of money is larger and when aggregate supply (Q) is smaller. Schedule CC is the same as in Figure 10.2.

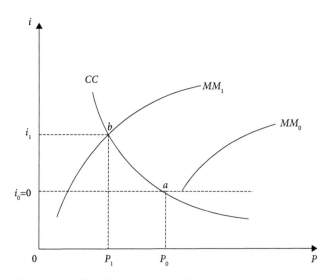

**Fig. 10.3** Ending ZIP: Interest and Prices

Under ZIP the equilibrium is determined where schedules CC and $MM_0$ intersect at point $a$, which is in the liquidity trap. Point a in Figure 10.3 corresponds to point a in Figure 10.4, which is based on Figure 10.3 in Chapter 2. The demand for money, represented by schedule $D_0$, is perfectly elastic at point $a$, and the supply of money, represented by schedule $S_0$ is also very elastic.

Recall from equation (5.2) in Chapter 2 that the supply schedule for money varies directly with the market rate of interest and inversely with the policy rate of the central bank through its effect on the money multiplier (m):

$$m = \frac{1 + c_p}{c_p + \rho + f} \tag{2.3}$$

where $c_p$ denotes the cash ratio, $\rho$ the required reserves ratio (if any) and $f(i, i_{CB})$ denotes the "free reserves" ratio, which varies inversely with the market rate of interest and directly with the cost of borrowed reserves from the central bank ($i_{CB}$). The slope of schedule S in terms of its semi-elasticity is:

$$\frac{\partial lnm}{\partial i} = \frac{1}{c_p + \rho + f}\frac{\partial f}{\partial i} > 0 \tag{2.4}$$

and is convex if $f()$ is convex. Hence, as expected, schedule S has a positive slope, and its semi-elasticity varies inversely with the rate of interest. Hence, at point $a$ in Figure 10.3 schedule $S_0$ has finite elasticity.

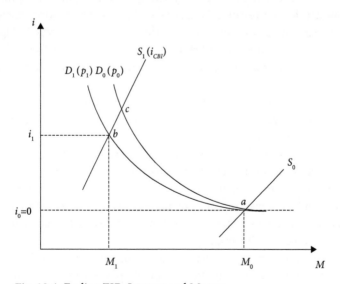

**Fig. 10.4** Ending ZIP: Interest and Money

The counterpart to equation (2.4) for the policy rate is:

$$\frac{\partial lnm}{\partial i_{CB}} = \frac{1}{c_p + \rho + f} \frac{\partial f}{\partial i_{CB}} < 0 \tag{2.5}$$

Hence the location of schedule S varies inversely with the policy rate, and its semi-elasticity varies inversely (less negative) with the policy rate.

Schedule $D_0$ in Figure 10.4 is drawn for the price level $P_0$ in Figure 10.3, and schedule $MM_0$ in Figure 10.3 is drawn for the stock of money under ZIP, which in Figure 10.4 is $M_0$. Figure 10.4 is drawn under the realistic assumption that the market rate of interest is zero or close to zero at point $a$.

Suppose that the central bank terminates ZIP by raising its policy rate, so that in Figure 10.4 the supply schedule for money shifts leftwards to $S_1$ from $S_0$. In partial equilibrium it is clear that the market rate of interest will be positive at point $c$ in Figure 10.4. In general equilibrium, however, the price level decreases to $P_1$ in Figure 10.3 where schedules CC and $MM_1$ intersect at point $b$. Schedule $MM_1$ is drawn for the equilibrium money stock ($M_1$) in Figure 10.4. Hence the market rate of interest is $i_1$ instead of $i_0 = 0$. In the nature of things, $i_1$ is expected to be greater than the policy rate ($i_{CB1} > 0$) because the latter is risk-free whereas the former is not, and because banks require positive margins of intermediation. Because P decreases, the demand for money shifts leftwards in Figure 10.4 to schedule $D_1$, which is drawn for price level $P_1$. Hence points $b$ in Figures 10.3 and 10.4 correspond with each other.

When the central bank exits ZIP by setting a normal policy rate, the money stock contracts for two reasons. First, because the cost of borrowing reserves from the central bank increases, banks cut back their borrowed reserves. In Figure 10.4 this is represented by the leftward shift in the supply of money from schedule $S_0$ to $S_1$. Second, price deflation induces a movement down schedule $S_1$ from point $c$ in Figure 10.4 to point $b$.

In summary, ending ZIP is deflationary. This is not surprising because monetary policy under ZIP is expansionary, in which case normalizing interest rate policy must be contractionary.

These theoretical results are very different to Krugman's. In our analysis, ending ZIP is straightforward. The central bank simply raises its policy rate, which is deflationary. In Krugman's model, the central bank does not have an independent policy rate, and it controls the stock of money directly. Consequently, the central bank has to persuade the public to expect inflation despite the fact that there was no inflation in the liquidity trap.

At this point, we wish to emphasize that we have so far focused on the single issue of the escape from ZIP and the liquidity trap. We have ignored the fact that under the New Abnormal debt-to-GDP ratios have spiraled, and QE has increased massively the stock of base money, and has turned central banks into major economic stakeholders. Under such circumstances the transition from point *a* to point *b* in Figures 10.3 and 10.4 seems a relatively simple matter.

Matters would be simpler if wages and prices were perfectly flexible, but this is unlikely. Giving advance warning about the exit from ZIP may provide the public with an opportunity to adjust more easily. Certainly, exiting ZIP unannounced is not advisable. Also, a gradual exit is most probably more advisable than a sudden and immediate normalization of interest rate policy. The credibility of forward guidance on this matter is likely to vary inversely with the duration of ZIP. It is easier to convince the public that interest rates will be raised for countries such as New Zealand, where ZIP is recent, than it is for countries such as Japan. Once again, if ZIP were the only feature of the New Abnormal matters would be simpler. However, we leave the issue of coordination with respect to other features of the New Abnormal, such as high debt-to-GDP ratios and kinetic inflation, until later.

In 2016 the Federal Reserve exited ZIP. By January 2019 the policy rate reached 2.5 percent. On the whole, this transition turned out to be uneventful and painless.

## Public Debt Overhang

In this discussion we ignore ZIP and QE and focus solely on coping with large public sector debts. However, we assume that interest rates are normalized. As noted in Chapter 2 the main issue here is that normalizing interest rates increases the cost of debt service. As long as the cost of debt service remained low or zero, debt did not really matter. Investors provided governments with an infinitely elastic supply of funding at almost zero cost. Indeed, in the liquidity trap bond-financed and money-financed fiscal deficits are equivalent because bonds bear zero interest like money. This happy situation ends as soon as the cost of debt service becomes positive post-ZIP.

For convenience we repeat equation (6.5) in Chapter 2:

$$d(t) = d_0 e^{-(q-r)t} + \left(1 - e^{-(q-r)t}\right) \frac{defp - \mu}{q - r} \tag{3.1}$$

where d denotes the debt-to-GDP ratio with initial value $d_0$, q denotes the real rate of economic growth, $r = i - \pi$ denotes the real rate of interest on public debt where $\pi$ denotes inflation, defp denotes the primary fiscal deficit as a percentage of GDP, and $\mu$ denotes the "monetization ratio" defined as seigniorage as a percent of GDP. Equation (3.1) takes account of the fact that inflation erodes the real value of public debt (unless it is indexed to inflation) and the government receives seigniorage through inflation tax. According to equation (3.1), if the real rate of interest exceeds the rate of economic growth, there is no steady state debt-to-GDP ratio, in which event d is explosive.

In Chapter 2 we assumed for convenience that $\mu$ is fixed. However, it varies directly with inflation ($\pi$) and economic growth (q). We use the following identity (based on the fact that $M_0/Y = e^{\beta/i}/m$) to solve for the dynamics of the inverse velocity of base money to solve for $\mu$:

$$\frac{d\left(\frac{M_0}{Y}\right)}{dt} = -\frac{e^{\beta/i}}{m}\left(\frac{\beta^2}{i^2}\frac{di}{dt} + \frac{\dot{m}}{m}\right) = \mu - \frac{M_0}{Y}g \qquad (3.2)$$

When the rate of interest is constant at e.g. point b in Figure 10.3 the middle term in equation (3.2) is zero, in which case $\mu$ equals the seigniorage tax base ($M_0/Y$) multiplied by the rate of growth of nominal GDP (g). During the transition between points a and b in Figure 10.3, the middle term in equation (3.2) is no longer zero because it depends on the relative reductions in the money stock and its base. It is:

$$-\frac{e^{\beta/i}}{m}\left(\frac{\beta^2}{i^2} - \frac{1}{c_p + p + f\,di}\frac{\partial f}{di}\right)\frac{di}{dt} \qquad (3.3)$$

The term in brackets is negative if base money contracts relatively rapidly, in which event the middle term in equation (3.2) is positive during the transition. Hence, during the transition, $\mu$ would be larger. If, instead, base money contracts relatively slowly, the converse would apply.

In summary, equation (3.2) implies that $\mu = gM_0/Y$ in equilibrium.

Table 10.1 reports simulated values for the long-term debt-to-GDP ratio (d*) and overall fiscal deficit as a percentage of GDP for different assumptions regarding the first four columns of Table 10.1. Notice that Table 10.1 does not feature inflation and real economic growth separately, because these variables do not have independent roles in equation (3.1). The first row serves as a base case in which the primary deficit is 2 percent of GDP, nominal GDP growth is 5 percent per year,

**Table 10.1** Stationary State Debt-to-GDP Ratios

| defp | g | i | $M_0/Y$ | d* | def |
|------|------|------|---------|--------|--------|
| 0.02 | 0.05 | 0.03 | 0.2 | 0.5 | 0.035 |
| 0.04 | 0.05 | 0.03 | 0.2 | 1.5 | 0.085 |
| 0.02 | 0.04 | 0.03 | 0.2 | 1.2 | 0.0536 |
| 0.02 | 0.05 | 0.02 | 0.2 | 0.33' | 0.0207 |
| 0.02 | 0.05 | 0.03 | 0.3 | 0.166' | 0.025 |

Based on equation (3.1) at t = ∞. In row 4 $M_0/Y$ is expected to change through equation (3.4).

the rate of interest is 3 percent, and base money velocity is 5 (hence $M_0/Y = 0.2$).
The baseline long-term debt-to-GDP ratio is 50 percent of annual GDP ($d^* = 0.5$)
and the overall deficit is 3.5 percent of GDP. Table 10.1 shows that minor change
in these parameters can make major changes to the long-term debt-to-GDP ratio.
For example, doubling the primary fiscal deficit triples the debt-to-GDP ratio (row
2). Reducing nominal income growth (row 3) more than doubles the debt-to-GDP
ratio because nominal GDP grows more slowly and seigniorage decreases. Reducing the rate of interest from 3 percent to 2 percent (row 4) cuts the debt-to-GDP
ratio from 50 percent of GDP to 33 percent. Finally, reducing velocity from 5 to
3.33' (row 5) cuts the debt-to-GDP ratio to 16.7 percent of GDP. The latter demonstrates the role of seigniorage, which tends to be overlooked in the arithmetic of
public debt.

Notice that equation (3.1) is specified in terms of the primary fiscal deficit rather
than the overall fiscal deficit (def) because we are concerned for the present with
the implications of terminating ZIP for the burden of government on the economy,
which is measured by defp. Under ZIP the nominal rate of interest is zero, hence
$r = -\pi$. Equations (2.1) and (2.3) imply:

$$\frac{M_0}{Y} = e^{\beta/i} \frac{c_p + p + f}{1 + c_p} \tag{3.4}$$

Under ZIP f = f(0, 0), which is the free-reserves ratio in the liquidity trap, when
policy and market rates of interest are zero. Since the market rate of interest is
zero and the cost of borrowed reserves is zero, banks have no incentive to borrow;
hence, f is expected to be zero. However, the dominant component in equation
(3.4) is the exponential term, which tends to infinity as i tends to zero. This means
that μ tends to infinity because the demand for money is infinitely elastic in the
liquidity trap. It also means that the inflation tax base is infinite and seigniorage is
potentially infinite. In principle, therefore, the government can finance its deficit
through monetization without issuing public debt. In fact, debt and money tend
to be perfect substitutes under ZIP, in which case, in theory, d tends to zero as
equation (3.4) tends to infinity.

In practice, both d and $M_0/Y$ have increased (Chapter 5) under ZIP. This might
have happened for a number of reasons. First, even though policy rates are zero
under ZIP, market interest rates were nevertheless small but positive, although
during 2020 they too have been driven down to zero through QE. Second, policy makers in central banks and finance ministries may have failed to understand
that monetizing fiscal deficits is not inflationary in the liquidity trap. So they increased public debt through bond-financing without realizing that, as far as the
public is concerned, bonds and money are perfect substitutes in the liquidity trap.
Therefore, in what follows, we set an upper limit to $M_0/Y$ under ZIP denoted by
$M_{0z}/Y$.

Under ZIP equation (3.1) becomes:

$$d(t) = d_0 e^{-gt} + \left(1 - e^{-gt}\right)\left(\frac{defp}{g} - \frac{M_{0z}}{Y}\right) \tag{3.5}$$

An important difference between equations (3.1) and (3.5) is that, whereas in the former the debt-to-GDP ratio explodes if the real rate of growth (q) is less than the real rate of interest (or the nominal rate of growth (g) is less than the market rate of interest i), in the latter the debt-to-GDP ratio cannot explode, unless nominal income growth happens to be negative (as threatened in Japan, Chapter 8).

The steady state debt-to-GDP ratio under ZIP is:

$$d^* = \frac{defp}{g} - \frac{M_{0z}}{Y} \tag{3.6}$$

which is positive provided, as seems plausible, that seigniorage is insufficient to finance the primary deficit. The steady state debt-to-GDP ratio is finite and varies inversely with the rate of nominal economic growth.

Ending ZIP means that equation (3.1) applies instead of equation (3.6). The difference between them is:

$$\Delta_t = e^{-gt}\left\{ d_0\left(e^{it} - 1\right) + \left[\frac{1 - i/g - e^{it}}{g - i} defp + g\left(\frac{e^{it}}{V'_0} \frac{1}{V_{0z}}\right)\right]\right\}$$
$$+ \left[\frac{idefp}{(g-i)g} + g\left(\frac{1}{V'_0} - \frac{1}{V_{0z}}\right)\right] \tag{3.7}$$

where $\Delta$ denotes the difference between d post-ZIP, $g = q + \pi > i$ denotes the rate of growth of nominal GDP, $V_{0z}$ is base money velocity under ZIP, and $V'_0 > V_{0z}$ is its post-ZIP counterpart. Seigniorage is smaller post-ZIP because tighter monetary policy increases base money velocity. The first term in curly brackets is positive. The last term is also positive, provided the loss of seigniorage is not massive. The second term in curly brackets is ambiguous. However, overall, the debt-to-GDP ratio increases post-ZIP for the simple reason that the cost of debt service ceases to be zero.

The long-term increase in the debt-to-GDP ratio is represented by the final term in equation (3.7). If, for example the post-ZIP rate of interest is 3 percent, nominal GDP grows at 5 percent per year, the primary deficit is 2 percent of GDP, and base money velocity is 5 (as in Table 10.1, row 1), the debt-to-GDP ratio tends to 50 percent of GDP. By contrast, according to equation (3.6) the debt-to-GDP ratio cannot exceed 40 percent when seigniorage is ignored, and is even smaller when seigniorage is taken into consideration. Therefore, under ZIP, debt-to-GDP ratios tend to be substantially smaller than their post-ZIP counterparts

In summary, if the primary deficit as a percentage of GDP remains unchanged after terminating ZIP, either the stationary-state debt-to-GDP ratio increases at best, or at worst it has no stationary state and is explosive. In the latter case the primary deficit must be reduced because it is not sustainable. If the real rate of interest exceeds the rate of economic growth ($r > q$) and the target debt-to-GDP ratio cannot exceed $d^*$, equation (3.1) implies that the primary fiscal deficit must be cut. For example, if $r - q = 0.02$ ($= i - g$), $d_0 = 0.4$, $d^* = 0.6$, $V'_0 = 0.2$ and $g = 0.05$ it takes 6.9 years for the debt-to-GDP ratio to reach the cap of 0.6 if the primary deficit is 3 percent of GDP. Thereafter, the primary deficit must be reduced to $-0.2$ percent of GDP to remain within the cap for $d^*$. In other words, the government must turn the primary fiscal deficit into a primary fiscal surplus, as in the OECD study for Japan described in Chapter 8.

If nominal GDP grows more slowly, the cap is reached more rapidly, and the cut in the primary deficit must be larger. For example, if nominal GDP grows at 4 percent instead of 5 percent, the cap is reached after 6.25 years instead of 6.9 years, and the primary fiscal surplus must be increased to 0.4 percent of GDP instead of to 0.2 percent. Finally, if the rate of interest increases by a percentage point, it takes 5.73 years to reach the cap and the primary fiscal surplus must be increased to 0.8 percent of GDP.

These simulations suggest that normalizing interest rates will be politically in-feasible, especially if nominal GDP growth is less than the normalized (post-ZIP) rate of interest ($g < i$), and debt-to-GDP ratios under ZIP are large. The cost of debt service will be so great that governments must run primary fiscal surpluses, either by raising tax rates, or by cutting government consumption. If, instead, nominal GDP growth exceeds the normalized rate of interest ($g > i$), the simulations in Table 10.1 show that even in highly indebted economies (large $d_0$) primary fiscal deficits are feasible, although in some cases (rows 3 and 4) debt-to-GDP ratios may exceed 100 percent. Although such large debt-to-GDP ratios might be technically sustainable, they might not be politically feasible.

During the New Abnormal there has been a false honeymoon between central banks and finance ministries, which under the Old Normal made a quarrelsome couple. Finance ministries benefited from ZIP because it kept the cost of debt ser-vice down. This honeymoon is of course an aspect of the New Abnormal, which will break down after ZIP is terminated.

In summary, nominal GDP growth is the great healer. Since real economic growth ($q$) is less easy to manipulate than inflation ($\pi$), governments may escape the debt trap by inducing inflation. This has been the panacea throughout the ages. It is how governments make "haircuts" without recourse to scissors. However, as noted in Figures 10.3 and 10.4, ending ZIP is inherently deflationary during the transition, because monetary policy is inevitably tighter when it normalizes its policy rate. Before we can resolve this contradiction, however, we have to discuss kinetic inflation.

## Kinetic Inflation

Thus far we have ignored kinetic inflation induced by QE. In Figure 10.4 the relative locations of money supply schedules $S_1$ and $S_0$ depended solely on the central bank raising its policy rate from zero to some positive number. In Chapter 2 we showed that the location of the money supply schedule depends also on non-borrowed reserves, or base money ($M_0$). Since central banks finance their QE with base money, it shifts schedule S to the right. Figure 10.4 is drawn under the assumption that base money is the same in schedules $S_1$ and $S_0$.

Equation (4.1) recalls equation (5.6) in Chapter 2, according to which an increase in base money as a result of QE reduces the market rate of interest:

$$\frac{\partial i}{\partial M_0} = -\frac{1}{M_0} \left[ \frac{1}{\frac{\beta}{i^2} - \frac{1}{c_p + \rho + f} \frac{\partial f}{\partial i}} \right] \leq 0 \qquad (4.1)$$

Equation (4.1) is zero in the liquidity trap because i = 0, hence QE cannot affect aggregate demand or the price level since:

$$\frac{dP}{dM_0} = \frac{\partial P}{\partial i} \frac{\partial i}{\partial M_0} \qquad (4.2)$$

where $\partial P/\partial i < 0$ as in schedule CC in Figure 10.2.

Suppose at point a in Figure 10.4 QE increases base money. Its effect on the price level is zero because point a is in the liquidity trap. The effect on the price level of QE at point b, which is outside the liquidity trap, is positive because equation (4.1) is negative instead of zero. Substituting equations (1.6) and (4.1) into equation (4.2) and multiplying by the real money base ($M_0/P$) gives the elasticity of the price level with respect to base money ($\varepsilon$):

$$\varepsilon = \frac{i^2}{1 + i} \frac{1 + c_p}{\beta(1 + c_p) - i^2 m \frac{\partial f}{\partial i}} > 0 \qquad (4.3)$$

Equation (4.3) expresses kinetic inflation; it is the increase in the price level induced by QE when the economy escapes the liquidity trap after exiting ZIP. Recall that, because f varies inversely with the rate of interest, equation (4.3) is positive as expected. Also, because it is the product of two fractions, it implies that the elasticity ($\varepsilon$) is positive and less than 1. When QE increases the money base, the reduction in the market rate of interest mitigates its influence on the price level, which is why the elasticity is less than 1.

Table 5.9 in Chapter 5 reports QE for various countries. For example, since the Subprime Crisis, cumulative QE by the Federal Reserve amounted to $17.5 trillion.

During the same period, base money in the US increased from \$0.9 trillion in September 2008 to \$5.15 trillion in May 2020. Base money increased by less than QE because it depends on other factors discussed in Chapter 2. Assuming, for example, that $\varepsilon = 0.8$, a fivefold increase in base money implies that kinetic inflation in the US is of the order of 266 percent, i.e. during the transition from point a to point b in Figure 10.4 the price level would increase by 266 percent. During the same period, there was a sixfold increase in base money in Japan, which implies that kinetic inflation is about 300 percent.

## Exit Strategy from New Abnormal: Theory

In the last three sections we have dealt separately with three different aspects of ending the New Abnormal. First, we considered what might happen if the central bank ended ZIP by normalizing its rate of interest, abstracting from the debt trap and kinetic inflation. Next, we considered the implications for the debt trap of an increase in the cost of debt service, in abstraction from kinetic inflation. Finally, we considered the implications for kinetic inflation in abstraction from the debt trap. In this section, we attempt to integrate these issues in the design of exit strategies from the New Abnormal.

Perhaps we should begin by remarking that policy makers in central banks and finance ministries have a mutual interest in perpetuating the New Abnormal because it enables them to have their cake and eat it. They can finance fiscal deficits by costless bond finance or simply through monetization without any fear of inflation. Also, they have no fear of the "unpleasant monetary arithmetic" discussed in Chapter 2. It is as if all the nasty laws of macroeconomics have been suspended. Ending the New Abnormal must seem to them like paradise lost and a descent into hell. Current policy makers are naturally concerned about the short term. They don't want to rock the boat. Better the devil you know. Future policy makers will be left to clear up the mess.

As pointed out by Goodhart and Pradhan (2020), central banks and finance ministries have a mutual interest in ZIP. Under normal circumstances there tends to be tension when central banks tighten monetary policy because ministers of finance have a political interest in promoting the real economy, whereas central banks are the guardians of inflation. Under ZIP there is no such tension. When the Federal Reserve raised interest rates during 2016 to 2019 this tension re-emerged rapidly, but disappeared as soon the Federal Reserve headed back into ZIP in the second half of 2019. Exiting ZIP means returning to conflicts of interest between central banks and finance ministries.

Or, it may be the case that current policy makers truly believe in the sustainability of the New Abnormal. They are simply unaware of the parting of the ways depicted in the cartoon. They have persuaded themselves that the natural rate of

**Cartoon 4 Parting of the Ways**

interest is zero, which is why they adopted ZIP in the first place. They are unaware of the fact that the natural rate of interest measured by the return on fixed assets is positive and large. Their reference to the "New Normal" in meetings, official documents, and professional discourse may have anesthetized them to the dangers of the New Abnormal. They are oblivious to the dangers of carrying on with the New Abnormal and cannot see what lies beyond what appears to be a long, twisty, and uncertain road ahead.

It does not matter for our purposes whether policy makers believe in the New Abnormal or whether they see themselves as in the cartoon, facing a dilemma between continuing with the status quo or risking the hazards in the return to macroeconomic normality. However, if they are aware of the dilemma, they may find the following discussion enlightening.

Ending the New Abnormal involves three hurdles. First and foremost, the central bank must begin the process by ending ZIP and by raising its policy rate. As we have seen, this in itself is deflationary. If wages and prices were perfectly flexible the transition between points $a$ and $b$ in Figure 10.4 would be painless. In practice, however, a recession would be induced during the transition. Also, asset prices, including housing, would decrease, just as they increased under ZIP. The more credible is the intention to end ZIP, and the more advance warning is provided through forward guidance, the less painful will be the cost of transition. The US experience during 2016–19 suggests that ending ZIP does not have to involve a painful transition. As noted in Chapter 5, the response of financial markets to this reversal of ZIP suggests that it was not expected to be permanent. Indeed, this expectation was vindicated when the Federal Reserve starting cutting its policy rate during the second half of 2019. It is therefore important to establish that there will be no return to ZIP.

The details of ending ZIP in terms of gradualism versus shock treatment need not detain us here. What matters is to convince the public that ZIP has ended forever. There is no going back.

Ending ZIP and normalizing interest rates is the "easy part" of exiting the New Abnormal. Far more difficult are the implications of ending ZIP for the debt trap, and especially in those countries where debt-to-GDP ratios exceed 100 percent. There is a tension between resolving the debt trap on the one hand, and resolving the problem of kinetic inflation on the other, because inflation erodes debt-to-GDP ratios. For example, Japan's debt-to-GDP ratio in 2021 is 260 percent. If kinetic inflation is 300 percent (as guesstimated above), Japan's debt-to-GDP ratio would tumble towards 60 percent. Indeed, inflation is an effective cure for the debt trap. See, for example, in Chapter 5 how Israel reduced its debt-to-GDP ratio from 300 percent in the 1970s through inflation especially during 1980–5. Hyperinflation in Weimar Germany, Austria, and Hungary in the 1920s wiped out the public debt accumulated during World War One.

Suppose that kinetic inflation happened to be zero. Since ending ZIP is deflationary, the debt trap worsens for two reasons. First, the cost of debt service is positive. Second, the decrease in the price level reduces nominal GDP, which raises the debt-to-GDP ratio arithmetically. Suppose in Figure 10.4 $P_1$ is 15 percent smaller than $P_0$ and the debt-to-GDP ratio under ZIP is 100 percent. The decrease in the price level increases the debt-to-GDP ratio to 117.6 percent. In general, this price deflation effect should be netted out against kinetic inflation. In the Japanese case, kinetic inflation is so large that it dominates the price deflation effect of ZIP. However, elsewhere matters might be different, especially in countries that have not engaged in massive QE. If kinetic inflation happened to be 15 percent, it would cancel out the price deflation effect in our numerical example.

In our analysis of the debt trap in Chapter 2, we distinguished between two cases. In the first, the real rate of economic growth exceeds the real rate of interest (or, where the rate of growth in nominal GDP exceeds the nominal rate of interest). In the second, the real rate of economic growth is less than the real rate of interest. In the first case the post-ZIP debt-to-GDP ratio exceeds its ZIP counterpart, but it is stable for given primary deficits as a percentage of GDP. The primary fiscal deficit rate under ZIP remains economically feasible post-ZIP, but if the post-ZIP debt-to-GDP ratio happens to be too large politically, policy makers need to cut the primary deficit rate. In the second case, the debt-to-GDP ratio is explosive. The primary fiscal deficit rate under ZIP is no longer economically feasible. It has to be cut, and if the debt-to-GDP ratio under ZIP is large, it may even be necessary to operate a primary fiscal surplus.

In the second case the debt trap is catastrophic. Policy makers will be under enormous pressure to inflate their way out of the debt trap, or simply renege. Just as indebted private corporations have negotiated "haircuts," so might policy makers. Historically, inflation has been the preferred option. There are numerous examples in which policy makers have reneged on external debt, but there are no precedents where they have initiated haircuts on internal debt. The latter might be the lesser evil because inflation imposes other economic and social costs. Also, inflation is more difficult to control. Haircutting inevitably undermines public confidence in public debt, but so does inflation. In this second case, policy makers should seriously consider haircutting as a practical option.

If they do, we are left with the problem of kinetic inflation. This problem also faces policy makers in countries where the real rate of economic growth exceeds the real rate of interest. This is the easiest of the three problems to solve. Under ZIP the economy is caught in the liquidity trap and there is no inflation. Ending ZIP activates kinetic inflation, which is largely induced by the cumulative effect of quantitative easing on base money ($M_0$). To resolve the problem of kinetic inflation, central banks should simply reverse their QE; they should sell back to the public the assets purchased under QE. Since thus far QE has primarily involved long-term treasury bonds, reversing QE will tend to normalize yield curves by raising long-term interest rates relative to short-term interest rates. Just as QE flattened yield curves, so reversing QE will unflatten them.

The analysis so far has ignored existential risk, which according to Chapters 4 and 5 is responsible for the widening gap between the natural rate of interest, as measured by the return on fixed assets, and long-term interest rates. Ending the New Abnormal is expected to eliminate existential risk, which should express itself in closing this gap. This happens because business investment increases despite the increase in interest rates. The gap narrows from both directions: the cost of capital increases because market rates of interest are positive, and the return on fixed assets decreases in response to the increase in business investment. Just as ZIP drove a wedge between the natural rate of interest and market rates of interest because it induced existential risk, so should this process be reversed when ZIP is terminated. The wedge shrinks with the disappearance of existential risk.

Therefore, at point $a$ in Figure 10.4 real GDP is likely to be smaller than at point $b$ because existential risk prevails at point $a$ but not at point $b$, i.e. aggregate supply is larger post-ZIP. Also, the gap between the natural rate of interest and the market rate at point $a$ is expected to be larger than at point $b$. Because aggregate supply is larger post-ZIP, schedule $D_1$ in Figure 10.4 will be to the right of where it is drawn. It will intersect schedule $S_1$ above point $b$, so that the post-ZIP market rate of interest exceeds $i_1$ and the post-ZIP money stock exceeds $M_1$.

In Figure 10.5 we illustrate the effect of eliminating existential risk, where point $b$ replicates point $b$ in Figure 10.3. The increase in aggregate supply resulting from the elimination of existential risk shifts schedule $MM_1$ to the left (because at the same rate of interest $P$ must be smaller). It also shifts schedule $CC_0$ to the left

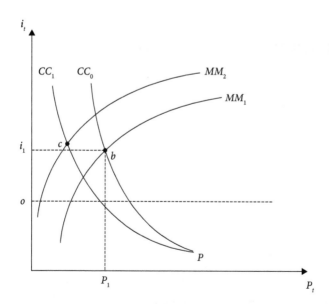

**Fig. 10.5** Elimination of Existential Risk

($CC_1$). In the new equilibrium at point $c$, the rate of interest is higher at point $c$ than at point $b$, and the price level is lower. As expected, the elimination of existential risk raises the rate of interest and decreases the price level because business investment increases, which increases aggregate supply.

## Cryptocurrencies and Existential Risk

Although economists differ on many issues, there has been a surprising negative consensus regarding Bitcoin and cryptocurrencies in general. Eight Nobel laureates in economics (Wikipedia) consider Bitcoin to be a bubble phenomenon, which sooner or later must burst. I shall argue that Bitcoin is a product of the New Abnormal; it is a child of its time. But for the New Abnormal, Bitcoin would probably not have survived since its invention in 2009, and as the New Abnormal became increasingly abnormal, the market for cryptocurrencies has become increasingly active. Although volatile, the price of Bitcoin has steadily increased (Figure 10.6), and the market for cryptocurrencies has become more competitive as the number of cryptocurrencies has expanded (Table 10.2). By far the most important cryptocurrency is the first, Bitcoin.

Money has three functions: it is a medium of exchange, a unit of account, and a store of value. Cryptocurrencies fulfill these functions but in different ways to conventional money. They are a poor medium of exchange for most transactions because blockchain technology is cumbersome and takes time. Even

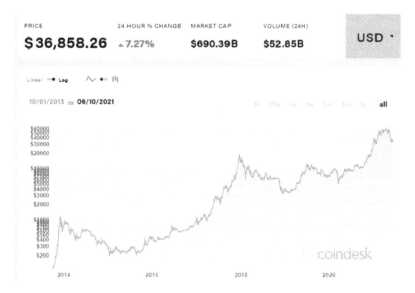

**Fig. 10.6** The Price of Bitcoin (logarithm)
Source: Coindesk, June 10, 2021.

**Table 10.2** Market Value of Cryptocurrencies
($b, January 28, 2021)

| Cryptocurrency | Market value |
| --- | --- |
| Bitcoin | 610.6 |
| Ethereum | 154.1 |
| Tether | 24.8 |
| Polkadot | 16.5 |
| XRP | 12.5 |
| Cardano | 11.3 |
| Total | 962.9 |

for large transactions in which time is less important, it is cheaper to transfer funds by other means, such as electronic transfer. Payment by cryptocurrency has two main advantages: it is anonymous and safe. Like Paypal, internet payment by cryptocurrency ensures that payors receive the goods or assets they have purchased from payees. Cryptocurrencies are also a poor medium of exchange because central banks restrict their function. For example, the Bank of France does not allow banks to credit accounts resulting from cryptocurrency transactions. On the other hand, the French tax authority requires capital gains from cryptocurrency transactions to be reported for tax purposes. The same applied in Israel until February 2021, when a court ruling required banks to accept capital gains in shekels from cryptocurrency transactions.

Central banks naturally wish to retain their monopoly over their fiat money, as predicted by Hayek (1990). If cryptocurrency replaced central bank money, central banks would obviously lose their income from seigniorage. However, in some countries transactions and pricing in cryptocurrency is permitted. See the growing list of outlets and service providers, in Wikipedia, that take payment in cryptocurrency, including Wikipedia itself. Not only do central banks have an ambivalent attitude towards cryptocurrency, so do tax authorities because transactions are anonymous. Through the OECD, tax authorities have fought a successful battle against tax evasion in tax havens and against numbered bank accounts. If cryptocurrencies replace fiat money, tax evasion will become viral. It is most probably no coincidence that cryptocurrencies have developed in parallel to the OECD's success.

It might be argued that cryptocurrency is a poor store of value because its price has been so volatile. On the other hand, its price has tended to increase since 2014 at an annual rate of 50 percent (Figure 10.6), whereas inflation undermines central bank money as a store of value. As documented in Chapter 5, central banks have consciously increased money supply through ZIP and unprecedented QE. Thanks to the liquidity trap the inflationary implications of ZIP have remained kinetic, but threaten to be unleashed when ZIP ends. By contrast, the supply of cryptocurrency is inherently inelastic. For example, Satoshi Nakamoto, who launched Bitcoin (BTC) in 2009, set an upper limit of 21 million BTC. As of January 2021, 18.6 million BTC are in existence and one new BTC is mined every 10 minutes, which implies that the rate of growth of BTC is currently about 2 percent per year. At this rate, the upper limit of 21 million is expected to be reached by 2140, during which time the rate of growth of BTC will gradually tend to zero. Miners of BTC currently retain 6.26 BTC per block (block reward), which decreases and tends to zero as the upper limit of 21 million is approached. Their newly mined cryptocurrency is traded in the Mount Gox cryptocurrency exchange in Japan, which acts as a clearing house for all cryptocurrency accounts. Other cryptocurrencies, including those listed in Table 10.2, follow the same blockchain protocols as Bitcoin. For example, although Ethereum (ETH) has no upper limit, it limits the mining of new ETH.

Whereas the supply of BTC is more or less known in advance, the supply of cryptocurrency as a whole is not because, as noted in Table 10.2, the cryptocurrency industry is open to new entrants. Ten years ago, there was only Bitcoin. Today there are at least ten major cryptocurrencies. The long-run marginal cost of a unit of BTC depends on the price of electricity, which varies by country. As of February 2018, the cost of mining BTC was estimated (by Elite Fixtures) at $4758 in the US, $8402 in the UK, $1852 in Ukraine, and $2177 in Belarus. Just as the mining cost of gold constrained the supply of gold under the Gold Standard, so does the mining cost of cryptocurrency constrain its supply. These constraints do not, of course, apply to fiat money, as the New Abnormal has demonstrated.

Cryptocurrency is perceived to be a more reliable if more volatile long-term store of value than central bank money. To hedge against existential risk, cryptocurrency serves as a more reliable anchor than central bank money. It also serves as a more reliable hedge than gold because cryptocurrency may be used in transactions whereas gold cannot. BTC is better than gold, and is replacing gold as the traditional safe haven. Matters might have been different but for the New Abnormal.

Whereas Bitcoin is a decentralized payments system that does not require a reliable agent or third party such as Paypal to guarantee successful exchanges, other cryptocurrencies enable decentralized financing (DeFi). For example, Compound enables the payment of interest on loans in cryptocurrency; Uniswap and Sushiswap enable transactions between cryptocurrencies and fiat money; UMA (not to be confuse with UMA of the unpleasant monetary arithmetic) enables transactions in cryptocurrency derivatives such as forward transactions; and Chainlink enables cryptocurrency options as well as options between crypto and fiat money. These DeFi facilities imply that cryptocurrencies are imperfect substitutes, which explains why their prices are imperfectly correlated. Hence, between January 1 and February 17, 2021 the following price increases were recorded:

Bitcoin 77 percent, Etherium 146 percent, Chainlink 183 percent, Compound 203 percent, UMA 241 percent, and Uniswap 302 percent.

In summary, the cryptocurrency market is evolving rapidly, and is expected to undergo much change, rationalization and consolidation in the years to come. It is more than a currency market; through DeFi, it is maturing into a sophisticated, decentralized clearing house involving derivative contracts, which may be compared to their counterparts in fiat currencies.

Figure 10.7 depicts macroeconomic equilibrium when the public holds cryptocurrency as well as central bank money. Panel I is based on Figure 10.3 in Chapter 2 where the demand for money in real terms varies inversely with the nominal rate of interest (i) and the supply of money varies directly with the nominal rate of interest. The demand schedule for money shifts to the right with real GDP, and the supply schedule for money shifts to the right with base money, and to the left with the rate of interest set by the central bank. Prior to the availability of cryptocurrency, the supply of money equals the demand for money at point $a$ at which the market rate of interest is $i_0$.

In panels II and III the real stock of cryptocurrency is measured on the horizontal axis. It is defined as the nominal stock of cryptocurrency ($C = QP_c$), where Q denotes the stock of BTC and $P_c$ its price. For simplicity Q is assumed to be fixed for reasons discussed below that are related to the "mining irrelevance theorem" (Schilling and Uhlig 2019). Just as the demand for money varies inversely with the

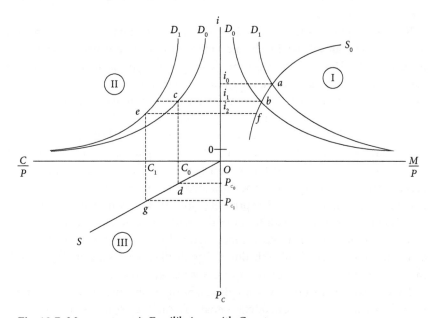

**Fig. 10.7** Macroeconomic Equilibrium with Cryptocurrency

rate of interest because it does not bear interest, so does the demand for cryptocurrency, which like money, becomes infinitely elastic, and for the same reasons, as the rate of interest tends to zero.

The demand schedule for cryptocurrency is initially represented by schedule $D_0$ in panel II. If cryptocurrency is an imperfect substitute for central bank money, the demand schedule for the latter will contract to schedule $D_1$ in panel I. At the new equilibrium in panel I (point $b$) the rate of interest will be lower at $i_1$, and the demand for cryptocurrency will be $C_1$ rather than $C_0$. The rate of interest naturally decreases because, although base money and the rate of interest of the central bank remain unchanged, the quantity of cryptocurrency has increased.

In panel III, $P_c$ denotes the price of cryptocurrency in the same units of the general price level (P), e.g. dollars in the US and sterling in the UK. Schedule OS plots the relation between the demand for cryptocurrency and its price, assuming that the units of cryptocurrency (Q) are fixed. If the number of units is increased, schedule OS becomes flatter and the price of cryptocurrency decreases given the demand. Since the demand for cryptocurrency is $C_1$, its price is $P_{c1}$. Hence, Say's Law is turned on its head; demand creates its own supply. This is why new cryptocurrency need not be mined to increase supply; letting the price rise is cheaper than mining cryptocurrency, as noted by Schilling and Uhlig. In principle, just one unit of cryptocurrency would be enough to support a large demand for cryptocurrency. Hence, points $b$, $c$, and $d$ in Figure 10.9 constitute an equilibrium. If the long-run cost of mining cryptocurrency is $P_{c0}$, this equilibrium will be permanent because there is no incentive for new mining companies to enter the cryptocurrency market.

If technical progress reduces the long-run cost of mining so that Q increases, schedule OS became flatter, in which event the price of cryptocurrency decreases relative to $P_{c0}$. However, because the demand for cryptocurrency in terms of value remains unchanged at $C_0$, the equilibrium ($b$, $c$, $d$) remains unchanged. As expected, mining shocks are irrelevant for macroeconomic equilibrium.

Suppose next that existential risk increases so that the demand schedule for cryptocurrency increases from schedule $D_0$ in panel II to schedule $D_1$. The new equilibrium would be represented by points $e$, $f$, and $g$ in Figure 10.7. Notice that the market rate of interest is lower than $i_2$ because the increase in the supply (equals demand) for cryptocurrency has increased from $C_0$ to $C_1$, and its price has increased from $P_{c0}$ to $P_{c1}$. The price of cryptocurrency is driven up in this way by existential risk, which tends to lower the market rate of interest. Since $P_{c1}$ exceeds the mining cost of cryptocurrency, new mining companies are expected to enter the industry. As a result, schedule OS gradually becomes flatter (Q gradually increases) until the price of cryptocurrency is restored to $P_{c0}$.

The price of cryptocurrency is also driven by other phenomena, apart from the flight from fiat money induced by existential risk. An increase in the "darknet" (encrypted online content not indexed by conventional search engines) would have the same qualitative effect as an increase in existential risk, as would an increase in the demand for cryptocurrency for purposes of tax evasion. On the other hand, a sudden surge in the price of cryptocurrency is unlikely to be induced by these factors, and is more likely to be related to nervousness about existential risk. Indeed, existential risk is priced in the cryptocurrency market; the price of cryptocurrency serves as a measure of existential risk. This would imply that in early 2021 the insurance premium against existential risk doubled during 2020.

In summary, cryptocurrency is directly comparable to gold in that it has to be mined to be produced. It can't be "printed" like fiat money. Just as goldmines vary by their efficiency, so cryptocurrency mines vary with the cost of electricity. The difference is that, whereas the locations of goldmines depend on nature, the locations of cryptocurrency mines do not. They can be set up in countries such as Belarus or Iceland where electricity is cheap. If cryptocurrencies ever replace central bank money, it would be equivalent to a return to the Gold Standard. This would be ironical because the Gold Standard was abandoned as a "barbarous relic" (Keynes 1923, p 172) to be replaced by a fiat money standard, which would be operated scientifically and responsibly. A Cryptocurrency Standard would be just as barbarous insofar as it depends on computer technology and the cost of electricity. However, there is a major difference between a Gold Standard and Cryptocurrency Standard as long as fiat money continues to be used. Because the price of cryptocurrency in terms of fiat money ($P_c$) is perfectly flexible, and is freely determined by market forces, whereas the general price level of goods and services in terms of fiat money ($P$) is not perfectly flexible, the physical quantity of cryptocurrency ($Q$) is irrelevant for macroeconomic equilibrium. Indeed, the nominal value of cryptocurrency ($C$) is determined by demand, as in Figure 10.7.

Cryptocurrency would turn into a barbarous relic, however, if fiat money ceased to exist altogether. In this limiting case the price of cryptocurrency ($P_c$) would replace the general price level, and it would cease to be perfectly flexible for the same reasons that the general price level is imperfectly flexible. A pure Cryptocurrency Standard would condemn the economy to depend on the technology of crypto-mining technology. A pure Cryptocurrency Standard should remain a theoretical possibility, provided central bankers can restore faith in their currencies in the aftermath of the New Abnormal.

## Exit Strategy from the New Abnormal: Practice

In this section we apply the general principles discussed above in the design of an exit strategy from the New Abnormal to specific countries. We distinguish between economies with minimal background morbidity where debt-to-GDP ratios and kinetic inflation are small, and economies with extensive background morbidity. In the nature of things, the latter, such as Japan, descended into ZIP a long time ago, while the former, such as Australia, adopted ZIP more recently. Our premise is that ZIP and the New Abnormal are unsustainable despite the fact the Japan has survived 23 years under ZIP. In any case, survival under ZIP comes at a price; background morbidity eventually becomes chronic.

In the absence of background morbidity, the escape from ZIP turns out to be relatively simple. If the public expects ZIP to persist, it will persist. If the public expects ZIP to end, it will end. There are many examples in macroeconomic history where expectations become self-fulfilling. Inflations have been stopped almost overnight by coordinated monetary policy and fiscal policy, such as in Israel in 1985. Once the public truly believes that these policies are going to be implemented, their success becomes self-fulfilling. If central banks announce with conviction that it intends to raise interest rates, it will happen with minimal collateral damage.

We are not concerned here with economic recovery in the aftermath of the Covid-19 pandemic. Our concern instead is with the future prospects of the New Abnormal in the aftermath of the Covid-19 pandemic, and made worse by it (Chapter 9). Perhaps one comment about economic recovery is worth making. There is a great difference between economic crises induced by natural disasters, such as Covid-19, and economic crises that are man-made, such as the Great Depression in the 1930s and the Subprime Crisis. Man-made disasters occur because the economy is structurally unhealthy. Economic recovery from man-made crises is hard and long because their root causes remain. For example, there is no consensus about the root causes of the Subprime Crisis. Some blame the failure of liberal market economics and the Old Normal, while others blame structural failure including conflicts of interest between bankers, regulators, and politicians, popularized in movies such as "The Big Short" and "Inside Job." Because the root causes of man-made crises are never clear-cut, and vested interest groups oppose reform, it is impossible to be sure that they won't recur.

Economic recovery from natural disasters is easier, faster, and more durable because their root cause is clear-cut, and their occurrence is unrelated to the structural health of the economy. Once the disaster has passed, the root cause is removed, and life returns to normal. Natural disasters such as earthquakes, volcanic eruptions, tsunamis, floods, and droughts take their toll in the short run, but the regional and national economies involved recover leaving almost no trace of the disaster, as predicted by neoclassical growth theory. Empirical studies broadly support this hypothesis (Xiao 2011, Cavallo et al 2013, Grinberger and Felsenstein 2014).

Pandemics such as Covid-19 are not regional, and may even be global. Because pandemics are inherently less frequent than natural disasters such as earthquakes etc., there is almost no empirical evidence on economic recovery from pandemics. Nevertheless, there is no reason to suspect that, as far as economic recovery is concerned, pandemics are inherently different to earthquakes etc.

Figures 10.8 and 10.9 compare the effects on GDP of the January 2010 earthquake in Haiti, which killed 250,000 people, and the 2009 debt crisis in Greece. Haiti was also devastated by Hurricane Matthew in 2016. This comparison may not be fair. Nevertheless, in Greece GDP has not recovered, whereas in Haiti GDP decreased by 5 percent in 2010, but more than recovered subsequently. Haiti got over its earthquake, but Greece continues to struggle.

The gross provincial product (GPP) of Fukushima (Japan) had been in decline prior to the tsunami and related nuclear disaster of May 2011. In 2010 the GPP of Fukushima was ¥7177.2 billion (at 2011 prices). GPP in 2011 decreased by almost 9 percent. In 2012 GPP was 2 percent below its pre-disaster level; by 2013 it was almost 5 percent greater, and by 2016 it was 10.3 percent greater. Although

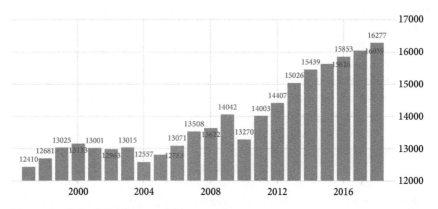

**Fig. 10.8**  GDP of Haiti: Natural Disaster 2010
(Gourdes millions at constant prices)
*Source:* The Institute of Statistics and Information, Haiti

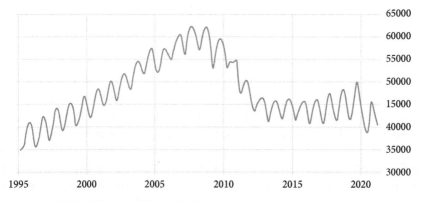

**Fig. 10.9**  GDP of Greece: Manmade Disaster 2009
(Euro millions at constant prices)
*Source:* National Statistical Service of Greece

Japan as a whole continued to suffer from its prolonged man-made "lost decade," as described in Chapter 8, the economy in Fukushima recovered quickly.

Economists, who should have known better, compared the negative economic growth in 2020 with the Great Depression of the 1930s. Worse still, they proposed Keynesian pump-priming to promote post-Covid-19 economic recovery as if the natural causes of negative economic growth in 2020 could be compared to the man-made causes of the Great Depression. Economic growth in 2020 would not have been negative but for the Covid-19 pandemic. Once Covid-19 has been eliminated, economic recovery should happen spontaneously (as it appears to be happening in Israel, Chapter 9). There is no need for grandiose economic recovery programs.

Finally, it is implicitly assumed that in the post-Covid recovery the underlying rate of growth per capita up to 2019 will eventually be restored as predicted by the neoclassical growth model (Chapter 2). By contrast, endogenous growth theory predicts that economic growth per capita may increase as a result of technical progress in RNA technology, communications, and logistics induced by the pandemic. Although there is no reason to suppose that Covid-19 harmed long-term growth prospects, there are reasons to hope that economic growth per capita will be faster after the recovery than it was up to 2019.

## Debt Arithmetic

Recall once more the fiscal arithmetic from Chapter 2 and simulated in Table 10.1. For increased transparency, however, the role of monetization and seigniorage is ignored. Hence, equation (3.1) is simplified by ignoring segniorage to:

$$d(t) = \left(d_0 - \frac{defp}{g-i}\right) e^{(i-g)t} + \frac{defp}{g-i} \tag{5.1}$$

where $d_0$ denotes the initial debt-to-GDP ratio, defp denotes the primary fiscal deficit relative to GDP, g denotes the rate of growth of nominal GDP and i denotes the nominal rate of interest, and $g-i = q-r$. Under ZIP, i = 0. If the primary fiscal deficit does not change over time and nominal income growth is positive (g > 0), equation (5.1) implies that the debt-to-GDP ratio tends to defp/g regardless of the initial level of debt. If, for example, the initial level of debt is 100 percent of annual GDP ($d_0$ = 1), the primary fiscal deficit is 2 percent of annual GDP and nominal income grows at 1 percent per year, the debt-to-GDP ratio will stabilize at 200 percent of GDP (d tends to 2). The debt-to-GDP ratio eventually doubles. It will more than double if the primary fiscal deficit is larger than 2 percent or if nominal income grows more slowly than 1 percent. If the initial debt-to-GDP ratio is less than 200 percent, it will increase over time until it eventually stabilizes at 200 percent. If, instead, the initial debt-to-GDP ratio exceeds 200 percent, it will decrease over time until it stabilizes at 200 percent.

It is important to distinguish between two cases. In the first, the debt-to-GDP ratio grows but stabilizes at some high level, as in the numerical example. In the second, it grows but does not stabilize; it tends to infinity. The first case arises when the rate of interest is less than the rate of growth of nominal income ($i < g$). The second arises when the rate of interest exceeds that rate of growth of nominal income ($i > g$). Equivalently, the first case arises when the real rate of interest is less than the real rate of growth of GDP, and the second case arises when the real rate of interest exceeds the real rate of economic growth.

Some numerical illustrations are reported in Table 10.3 when nominal GDP grows at 2 percent per year ($g = 0.02$). In the first row, the rate of interest is zero (ZIP), and the debt-to-GDP ratio eventually increases from 100 percent to 150 percent after initially increasing by 1 percent per year. The initial fiscal deficit equals the primary fiscal deficit because the rate of interest is zero due to ZIP. The long-term debt-to-GDP ratio does not depend on its initial level $d_0$. Had this initial level been 50 percent instead of 100 percent, it would have taken longer to reach 150 percent of GDP. Had the initial level exceeded 150 percent, the debt-to-GDP ratio would have decreased until it converged on 150 percent. In the second row, the rate of interest is 1 percent ($i = 0.01$), hence ZIP is terminated, but the primary fiscal deficit remains 3 percent of GDP. However, the initial fiscal deficit exceeds the primary fiscal deficit by 1 percent of GDP because the cost of debt service is no longer zero. Because the rate of interest is less than the growth rate of nominal GDP the debt-to-GDP ratio eventually stabilizes at 300 percent of GDP, which is

Table 10.3 Numerical Illustrations of Equation (5.1)

| $d_0$ | defp | i | $d^*$ | $\dot{d}_0/d_0$ | $def_0$ | defp* |
|---|---|---|---|---|---|---|
| 1 | 0.03 | 0 | 1.5 | 0.01 | 0.03 | 0.02 |
| 1 | 0.03 | 0.01 | 3 | 0.02 | 0.04 | 0.01 |
| 1 | 0.04 | 0 | 2 | 0.02 | 0.04 | 0.02 |
| 1 | 0.02 | 0 | 1 | 0 | 0.02 | 0.02 |
| 1.5 | 0.04 | 0 | 2 | 0.013' | 0.04 | 0.03 |
| 1 | 0.03 | 0.02 | ∞ | 0.03 | 0.06 | 0 |
| 1 | 0.03 | 0.03 | ∞ | 0.04 | 0.07 | −0.01 |
| 1.5 | 0.04 | 0.03 | ∞ | 0.03' | 0.09 | −0.015 |

$g = 0.02$. $d^*$ denotes the long-term debt-to-GDP ratio. Column 5 reports the initial rate of growth in the debt-to-GDP ratio. Column 6 reports the initial fiscal deficit as a percent of GDP. The final column reports the primary fiscal deficit which stabilizes the debt-to-GDP ratio at $d_0$.

double its counterpart in row 1. This illustrates the sensitivity of the debt-to-GDP ratio to even small increases in the rate of interest.

In rows 3–5 ZIP is reinstated. Row 3 illustrates the effect of an increase in the primary fiscal deficit to 4 percent of GDP instead of 3 percent in row 1. The debt-to-GDP ratio stabilizes at 200 percent of GDP instead of 150 percent in row 1. Row 4 shows that, if the primary fiscal deficit as a percent of GDP (2 percent) equals the difference between the nominal rate of growth and the rate of interest, the debt-to-GDP ratio remains at its initial level (100 percent). Comparing rows 5 and 3 shows that the rate of growth of the debt-to-GDP ratio varies inversely with its initial level. Fat people put on weight more slowly than slim people (Chapter 2).

In rows 6–9 the rate of interest is positive once more and, unlike in row 2, nominal GDP does not grow faster than the rate of interest. In these conditions the debt-to-GDP ratio ceases to be stable. Hence d* tends to infinity at a rate which varies directly with the primary fiscal deficit.

In row 4 it may be small comfort to know that the debt-to-GDP ratio will eventually stabilize at 300 percent of GDP. To stabilize the current debt-to-GDP ratio, the primary fiscal deficit as a percentage of GDP must be:

$$defp^* = (g - i)\, d_0 \tag{5.2}$$

as reported in the final column of Table 10.3. Notice that in the unstable case (rows 6 and 7) it is necessary to run primary fiscal surpluses, which vary directly with the current debt-to-GDP ratio and the difference between the rates of interest and economic growth.

In Table 10.3 it has been assumed that nominal income growth does not depend on the rate of interest. If tighter monetary policy reduces nominal income growth either by reducing inflation and/or by inducing recession, rows 6–9 will understate the destabilizing effects of ending ZIP. Indeed, if g decreases when i is increased the termination of ZIP tends to be doubly explosive.

In summary, the current debt-to-GDP ratio matters even in the stable case because it may stabilize at a level that is too high. The unstable case arises when the nominal rate of interest exceeds that growth rate in nominal income. When ZIP is terminated, the fiscal deficit increases dramatically relative to the primary fiscal deficit. If the rate of interest exceeds the rate of growth in nominal GDP, primary fiscal surpluses are necessary to prevent the debt-to-GDP ratio from exploding.

We conclude by reviewing the prospects of ending the New Abnormal in selected countries, starting with Japan with the least prospects and finishing with New Zealand with the most.

## Japan

As Chapter 8 made clear, the prospects of Japan ever ending the New Abnormal are zero. The simulations (carried out by the OECD) described in Chapter 8 showed that large primary fiscal surpluses (up to 5 percent of GDP) are required to prevent its current debt-to-GDP ratio of 260 percent from doubling by 2050. Whereas it took Israel 35 years to outgrow a debt-to-GDP ratio of almost 300 percent (resulting from the Yom Kippur War), there has been almost no economic growth in Japan during the last 35 years. Hence, Japan cannot outgrow its massive debt-to-GDP ratio. The deep structural reforms required to end the New Abnormal are beyond the cultural and political capabilities of the Japanese. Also, the Bank of Japan dare not end ZIP because it is caught in a debt trap; the cost of debt service would increase the debt-to-GDP ratio even further.

Japan is a special case because it has been entangled in the New Abnormal for a generation. Sooner or later, Japan will crash out of the New Abnormal apocalyptically. Japan is turning into the "sick man" of Asia.

## United States

Although there is no need for grandiose post Covid-19 economic recovery programs, one of President Biden's first initiatives was to launch such a recovery program. The US is one of the countries that came out badly from the Covid-19 crisis (Chapter 9). Its fiscal deficit increased from 4.6 percent of GDP in 2019 to 14.9 percent in 2020 (Table 9.7 in Chapter 9) and its public debt, which was already 107 percent of GDP in 2019, peaked at 136 percent in 2020 before decreasing to 122 percent of GDP by the third quarter of 2021. Also, 2020 saw massive increases in QE by the Federal Reserve. As chairperson of the Federal Reserve, Janet Yellen took the audacious first steps, by ending ZIP in 2016, to lead the US and the world out of the New Abnormal. In 2021, as Secretary of the Treasury, she sang its praises. "The world has changed. In a very low interest-rate environment like we're in, what we're seeing is that even though the amount of debt relative to the economy has gone up, the interest burden hasn't....But right now, with interest rates at historical lows, the smartest thing we can do is to act big." (Janet Yellen, Congressional Hearing, January 19, 2021).

Ending the New Abnormal is not on the agenda of the US. Projections in March 2021 of the Congressional Budget Office indicate the debt-to-GDP ratio stabilizing during the 2020s, but doubling by 2050. In summary, the US appears to be on a Japanese-style trajectory into further entanglement with the New Abnormal.

Whereas Japan has passed the point of no return, the same does not apply to the US, which does not face the need for deep structural reforms. The US economy is capable of growing itself out of the New Abnormal, as it outgrew a similar debt-to-GDP ratio after World War Two, provided fiscal policy is prudent. The fiscal deficit as a percent of GDP needs to be smaller than the rate of economic growth for at least a decade. It should commit itself to restoring a debt-to-GDP ratio of 50 percent of GDP, as in the 1980s. This commitment should be made public.

Apart from normalizing fiscal policy, the Federal Reserve needs to normalize monetary policy. There are two aspects to this: ending ZIP and reversing QE. The Federal Reserve has already acquired experience with ending ZIP in 2016. By September 2019 the federal funds rate was heading for 3 percent. The US economy took this normalization in its stride. It can do so again, but it will be harder because its debt-to-GDP ratio is almost double what it was in 2016. Since ending ZIP would release the US economy from the liquidity trap, kinetic inflation is in danger of becoming actual. To prevent this development, the Federal Reserve would have to engage in reverse QE; by selling the assets it acquired under QE it would mop up the excess liquidity, which generated kinetic inflation.

The public should be engaged in this normalization policy by announcing it in advance. We saw in Chapter 5 that it took several years before capital markets adjusted to the New Abnormal. Perhaps this was inevitable because the authorities in Japan and elsewhere did not intend the New Abnormal to be a permanent feature of their political economy. Capital markets as well as labor and foreign exchange markets will adjust more rapidly to normalization policy because there is a fundamental asymmetry to gradual entrapment by the New Abnormal and its instigated reversal through normalization.

## United Kingdom

An unsung benefit of Brexit has been the superior vaccination roll-out against Covid-19 in the UK relative to the EU (Chapter 9). But for Brexit the UK would have joined other EU countries in the inept "common vaccination policy" operated by the eurocrats in Brussels. Economic recovery from Covid-19 in the UK is therefore expected to precede economic recovery in the EU. Also, the cumulative death toll from Covid-19 is expected to be greater in the EU than in the UK.

Another advantage of the UK compared with members of the eurozone (19 out of 27 members of the EU) is that it has its own central bank. It is easier for one central bank, such as the Bank of England, to end ZIP than it is for the 19 members of the eurozone, whose monetary policy is decided by the European Central Bank (ECB). Just as the ECB lagged behind the Bank of England when it adopted ZIP in 2013, so is it likely to lag behind the Bank of England if and when it ends ZIP.

In many respects, the UK and the US share common New Abnormal features. They both adopted ZIP in 2009. They had large and similar fiscal deficits in 2020

(14.3 and 14.4 percent). Their debt-to-GDP ratios in 2020 were large (97 and 129 percent), and their central banks engaged in massive QE. The main difference is that, whereas the Biden administration shows no sign of fiscal prudence and every intention of continuing with ZIP, matters are more nuanced in the UK. Therefore, the UK is a more likely candidate than the US for exiting the New Abnormal. However, there is currently no such policy in prospect.

If this prospect were to change, the UK would need to follow the prescriptions advocated for the US. It would have to cut the primary fiscal deficit as a percentage of GDP, while it grew out of its large debt-to-GDP ratio. The Bank of England would have to end ZIP and engage in reverse QE to prevent kinetic inflation from becoming actual.

## Eurozone

The 19 members of the eurozone cannot end ZIP individually because they share the same currency, the euro. The ECB alone determines interest rate policy through a complex political process. Members of the eurozone operate independent fiscal policies. According to the Maastricht Treaty (1992), members should strive to achieve debt-to-GDP ratios of 60 percent. In 2020 the largest debt-to-GDP ratio (according to Eurostat) was in Greece (205.6 percent), with Italy in a second place (155.8 percent). The lowest was in Estonia (18.2 percent), with Bulgaria in second place (25 percent). The average debt-to-GDP ratio in the eurozone stood at 98 percent. Eastern European countries are well below the average. See Table 7 in Chapter 9 for other eurozone countries.

These huge disparities naturally create enormous economic and political tensions within the eurozone. Countries with low debt-to-GDP ratios consider that countries with large debt-to-GDP ratios are living at their expense. As long as interest rates are zero the costs of servicing these debts are relatively small. Since there is no effective mechanism for enforcing the Maastricht target of 60 percent, these disparities are likely to continue widening. The Greek debt crisis (2009) established the precedent that, to prevent Greece from leaving the eurozone, key members such as Germany and France were prepared to bail out Greece. In return, Greece deflated; its GDP decreased by 25 percent between 2009 and 2014 (Figure 10.9). In 2020 GDP was less than what it was in 2000. Greece continues to pay an enormous price for remaining in the eurozone.

Since ECB adopted ZIP in 2013, countries such as Greece, Italy, and France have found it easier to service their debts. This explains, for example, why despite its increased indebtedness a second debt crisis has not occurred in Greece. But for ZIP, there would most probably have been debt crises in Italy and France. Since the integrity of the eurozone is a keystone in the political economy of the EU, it is most unlikely that the ECB will end ZIP. Indeed, the ECB is a prisoner of the euro; to stave off debt crises in countries such as Greece, France, and Italy it must persist with ZIP, otherwise it would trigger debt crises in these countries.

In summary, the eurozone is a special case on its own. The political objective of preventing the collapse of the euro means that the debts of debtors will continue to grow, and the ECB will continue to ease their debt burden by operating ZIP. The prospects of ending the New Abnormal in the eurozone are related to the continued existence of the euro. The prospects for crashing out of the New Abnormal loom large.

## European Union Excluding Eurozone

Eight members of the EU are not members of the eurozone, five of which are Eastern European (Poland, Czech Republic, Hungary, Bulgaria, and Romania) and Sweden, Denmark, and Croatia. Perhaps it is no coincidence that these countries have small debt-to-GDP ratios. As of May 2021, ZIP applied in these countries with the exception of Croatia and Romania. Denmark, Bulgaria, and Croatia belong the the European Exchange Rate Mechanism II (ERM II) countries; they have independent currencies but they seek to stabilize their exchange rates with respect to the euro in case they wish to join the eurozone in the future. If these countries remain in ERM II, their destiny is expected to be similar to other less-indebted members of the eurozone. This leaves Poland, Sweden, Czech Republic, and Hungary as potential candidates for normalizing monetary policy. Since these countries have small debt-to-GDP ratios they are not caught in a debt trap, which makes it easier to end ZIP.

Some of these countries, such as Hungary and Poland, are newcomers to ZIP; they adopted ZIP with the outbreak of Covid-19. The central bank of the Czech Republic adopted ZIP in 2013 and began to raise its interest rate at the end of 2017. It re-adopted ZIP with the outbreak of Covid-19, by which time the policy rate of interest reached 2 percent. Ending ZIP in these countries should be as straightforward as the Czech experience at the end of 2017.

Matters are different in Sweden, which adopted ZIP in 2009 (Chapter 5). Nevertheless, they are still straightforward because there is no debt trap and there has been no quantitative easing.

## Australia, New Zealand, and Israel

These countries are not debt-trapped because they have small debt-to-GDP ratios (Table 7 in Chapter 9). They are also relative newcomers to ZIP. Australia joined in 2019, New Zealand in 2020, and Israel in 2014. As explained in Chapter 5 the

Bank of Israel adopted ZIP because it sought to weaken the exchange rate of the shekel. Most probably the same reasoning lay behind the Reserve Bank of Australia's decision to adopt ZIP in 2019. The decision of the Reserve Bank of New Zealand coincided with the outbreak of Covid-19 in March 2020.

In Chapter 2 we explained that, according to relative interest rate parity theory, interest rate policy has only a temporary effect on the exchange rate, in contrast to absolute interest rate parity theory, according to which the effect on the exchange rate should be permanent. The descent into ZIP weakened exchange rates temporarily but not permanently according to relative interest parity theory. Therefore, to terminate ZIP, central bankers should not fear that raising their policy rates will appreciate exchange rates permanently. This issue in positive economics is quite separate to the normative question of whether central banks should target exchange rates.

## Crashing out of the New Abnormal

In summary, despite the theoretical assertion that the New Abnormal cannot last forever, Japan, the US, and eurozone members are politically committed to its perpetuation. This commitment does not mean that the New Abnormal will continue to survive. Rather it means that, instead of an orderly exit from the New Abnormal, a chaotic exit is in prospect. Crashing out of the New Abnormal will be similar to crashing out of the Gold Standard in the 1930s or out of the Bretton Woods system in the early 1970s. In the case of the New Abnormal, crashing out will most probably begin with inflation. Kinetic inflation will cease to be kinetic. Subsequently, ZIP will no longer be feasible, as a result of which the service cost of public debt will increase. The liquidity trap, which generated kinetic inflation under ZIP, will cease to operate because the nominal rate of interest is no longer zero. Debt-to-GDP ratios will increase further. If interest rates increase by less than nominal GDP growth (because inflation and real economic growth are not sufficiently high), the debt-to-GDP ratio explodes. If, instead, inflation is sufficiently high, the debt-to-GDP ratio eventually stabilizes at an even higher level than before the crash. In either case the government will have to run fiscal surpluses if this is politically feasible. If inflation is sufficiently hyper, the debt-to-GDP ratio will decrease. The economic disruption will be great.

In August 2020 the yields to maturity on US Treasury bonds reached their nadir (ten years, 0.52 percent; twenty years, 0.96 percent; thirty years, 1.19 percent). In Chapter 5 we noted that it took a long time for investors to internalize the fact that the Federal Reserve's zero interest policy was here to stay. The same applied in the UK, Japan, and elsewhere. As of June 2021, these yields had edged up by slightly more than a percentage point. Meanwhile, the yields on gilt-edged securities edged up too, but by less. The same applied in Israel. Although these developments suggest that investors are less certain about the sustainability of the New Abnormal than in 2020, they nevertheless expect it to persist.

As this book goes to press (February 2022) there is growing concern about the resurgence of inflation, especially in the US where the consumer price index increased by almost 8 percent over the previous year. The inflation rates reported in Table 10.4 were of the order of only 1 percent a year ago. Could these inflation rates be the first omen of the outbreak of kinetic inflation, and the beginning of the end of the New Abnormal? Since securing his second term in office as Chairman of the Federal Reserve in January 2022, Jerome Powell has initiated reverse quantitative easing and has hinted (January 26) that he will raise the rate of interest in face of inflationary pressure (7 percent year-on-year in December 2021). Market sentiment embodied in the term structure of interest rates does not appear to think so. The term structure has not steepened as might be expected if ZIP is about to end, or if the US is about to crash out of the New Abnormal. The yield to maturity on 10-year treasury bonds, which bottomed out at 0.55 percent in July 2020 was 1.82 percent in early February 2022, compared to 1.71 percent in March 2021. The yield to maturity on 10-year index-linked treasury bonds in early February 2022 was −1 percent, suggesting that the expected rate of inflation over the next 10 years is 2.82 percent. Thus far the bond market has not discounted the end of ZIP and the New Abnormal.

Similar, but weaker, developments have occurred in the UK; yields on gilts have firmed and inflation has increased. A comparison of ten-year index-linked gilts with ordinary gilts suggests that expected inflation has increased from less than 1 percent in 2020 to 3.2 percent in November 2021. Inflation has also increased in the eurozone, but yields to maturity on treasury bonds have remained low and flat as the European Central Bank continues with its New Abnormal monetary policy. In other countries, such as Australia and Israel, inflation was higher in 2021 than in 2020 and treasury bond yields increased. A comparison of ten-year index linked bonds in Israel (−1.61 percent in November 2021) with ordinary bonds suggests that expected inflation increased from less than 1 percent in 2020 to 2.43 percent by November 2021.

The exception in Table 10.4 continues to be Japan, where inflation remains nonexistent and bond yields are flat. The New Abnormal seems safe in Japan. It may be safe too in the US and elsewhere. The reappearance of inflation may be related to the recovery of the world economy from Covid-19 discussed in Chapter 9. If so, the New Abnormal is not on the verge of collapse.

Whereas buildings and aircraft crash within minutes, economic crashes are protracted. After the dust has settled, inflation, aided by fiscal surpluses, should have eroded debt-to-GDP ratios to Maastricht orders of magnitude (60 percent of GDP). If inflation targets remain in the range of 1 to 2 percent, the policy rates of central banks should be in the range of 2 to 3 percent. If economic growth recovers to 2 percent per annum, primary fiscal deficits should be 0.6 percent of GDP (equation 3.5) and fiscal deficits should range between 1.2 and 2.4 percent of GDP.

**Table 10.4** Yields on Treasury Bonds and Inflation

|  | Yields to Maturity | | Annual Inflation |
|---|---|---|---|
|  | 10 years | 30 years |  |
| US | 1.55 | 1.92 | 6.2 |
| UK | 0.91 | 1.38 | 3.1 |
| Euro Zone | −0.22 | 0.025 | 4.1 |
| Japan | 0.06 | 0.67 | 0.2 |
| Australia | 1.76 | 2.08[a] | 3.0 |
| Israel | 1.42 | 1.96[a] | 2.3 |

Notes: a: 15 years. Data refer to mid November 2021 for yields to maturity and October for CPI inflation.

After the dust has settled, existential risk will disappear. Consequently, the gap between the natural rate of interest and the policy rate of the central bank (minus inflation) which opened up under the New Abnormal will begin to contract through increased business investment. During this adjustment process, economic growth will be unusually strong. The years of lost economic growth under the New Abnormal induced by existential risk will be made up during this adjustment period.

Faulty financial and economic architectures, like buildings, remain intact until they collapse. After their collapse, soul-searching commences and early warnings are belatedly identified. My purpose has been to identify these early warnings in advance.

## Synopsis

The development of cryptocurrencies is inextricably intertwined with the New Abnormal. Investors hedge existential risk by holding cryptocurrency. They will be protected against inflation, bankruptcies, and bank failures if the US, Japan, and eurozone countries crash out of the New Abnormal. The price of cryptocurrency embodies an existential risk premium.

If cryptocurrency coexists with fiat money, the "mining irrelevance theorem" states that the market value of cryptocurrency does not depend on mining costs (mainly electricity) or its supply. Cryptocurrency enhances macroeconomic price flexibility because its price is more flexible than the general price level. If cryptocurrency eventually replaces fiat money, macroeconomic theory will have to be reconstructed.

Under zero interest policy (ZIP), the cost of public debt service is low. As a result, debt-to-GDP ratios tend to be stable; they increase but eventually stabilize at a high level, which varies inversely with the rate of growth of nominal GDP and varies directly with the primary fiscal deficit. Ending ZIP raises the cost of debt service. If the rate of interest is less than the rate of growth of nominal GDP, the debt-to-GDP ratio stabilizes at a higher level. If it exceeds the rate of growth of nominal GDP, the debt-to-GDP ratio explodes.

In the explosive case, it is necessary to run fiscal surpluses to stabilize debt-to-GDP ratios. In the stable case, it is necessary to cut primary fiscal deficits to stabilize debt-to-GDP ratios at levels that are politically feasible. In these cases, countries are caught in a "debt trap."

According to Ricardian equivalence theory, public debt is regarded by tax payers as a future liability. Hence, an increase in public debt is equivalent to a current increase in taxes (discounted). Accordingly, what matters is not public debt per se, but the burden of government measured by the primary fiscal surplus (taxes minus government consumption). This theory assumes, inter alia, that capital markets are perfect. Empirical evidence shows that, although some aspects of the theory are corroborated, public debt and current taxes are not perfectly equivalent. Hence, debt-to-GDP ratios matter.

Economic recovery from natural disasters such as Covid-19 tends to be quicker and more complete than economic recovery from man-made disasters such as the Subprime Crisis because the root causes of the former disappear naturally whereas the root causes of man-made disasters tend to persist. Greece has not recovered from its 2009 man-made debt crisis, whereas Haiti recovered rapidly from the devastating earthquake of 2010 and Fukushima province recovered rapidly from the tsunami of 2011.

Countries that fail to exit the New Abnormal in an orderly fashion will crash out of it destructively. Kinetic inflation will cease to be kinetic. Subsequently, ZIP will no longer be feasible, as a result of which the service cost of public debt will increase. The liquidity trap, which generated kinetic inflation under ZIP, will cease to operate because the nominal rate of interest is no longer zero. Debt-to-GDP ratios will increase further. If interest rates increase by less than nominal GDP growth (because inflation and real economic growth are not sufficiently high), the debt-to-GDP ratio explodes. If, instead, inflation is sufficiently high, the debt-to-GDP ratio eventually stabilizes at an even higher level than before the crash. In either case the government will have to run fiscal surpluses if this is politically feasible. If inflation is sufficiently hyper, the debt-to-GDP ratio will decrease. The economic disruption will be great.

Japan is so burdened by public debt and its prospects for deep structural reforms are so weak that it is politically and economically unfeasible to exit the New Abnormal in an organized fashion. At some point Japan will crash out of the New Abnormal through hyperinflation and economic chaos.

Although the US under the Biden administration has no intention of exiting the New Abnormal and its entanglement with it is scheduled to deepen, the US is capable of achieving an orderly exit from the New Abnormal. At the present rate, however, it is on a Japanese-style trajectory, as a result of which it threatens to pass a point-of-no-return. Unlike Japan, the US can outgrow its high debt-to-GDP ratio (130 percent of GDP). In the end the US might crash-out of the New Abnormal, which would be deleterious, and not just for the US.

Members of the eurozone determine their own fiscal policy while monetary policy is decided by the European Central Bank (ECB). This combination is incentive-incompatible because the Maastrict Treaty guidelines for fiscal policy are honored in the breach. But for ZIP, the cost of debt service in Greece, Italy, Spain, and France would have been prohibitive. Hence ZIP has prevented a second debt crisis in Grecce, as well as debt crises in Italy, Spain, and France. To save the integrity of the euro, ECB has to persist with ZIP. It will do so until members of the eurozone crash out of ZIP and the New Abnormal.

For countries with relatively small debt-to-GDP ratios, especially newcomers to the New Abnormal such as Australia, New Zealand, and Israel, exiting the New Abnormal mainly involves ending ZIP. To do so, they must cease targeting their exchange rates, which is why they descended into ZIP in the first place. Also, they should not fear that raising their policy rates from zero under ZIP to more than one percent will be recessive. If business investment is slack when the return on capital is at least 10 percentage points greater than the cost of capital, it will not be slacker if this difference is 9 percent or even 8 percent. On the contrary, ending ZIP will reduce existential risk to the benefit of business investment.

In the nature of things, some countries will crash out of the New Abnormal while others will manage orderly exits. To insulate themselves from the surrounding chaos, the latter should allow their exchange rates to float freely.

Like buildings, faulty financial and economic architectures remain intact until they collapse. After their collapse, soul-searching commences and early warnings are belatedly identified. My purpose has been to identify these early warnings in advance.

## Postscript

Since completing my manuscript in 2021 my prediction that an outbreak of kinetic inflation will force an end to Zero Interest Policy seems to be materializing. Unfortunately, the central banks of the US, the UK, Canada and shortly the European Central Bank are crashing out of the New Abnormal instead of preparing for a soft landing. These are early days yet. As interest rates normalize, debt interest will increase and the debt-trap will tighten. Maybe it is too soon to declare victory of the Old Normal over the New, as well as the triumph of macroeconomic orthodoxy over heterodoxy. The New Abnormal will probably be judged as a historical aberration created by academia and policy makers alike.

# References

Ahrenfeldt L.J., Otavova M., Christensen K., and Lindahl-Jacobsen R. (2020) Sex and age differences in Covid-19 mortality in Europe. *Wiener Klinische Wochenschrift*, https://doi.org/10.1007/s00508-020-01793-9.

Amariglio J., Cullenberg S., and Ruccio D.F. (2001) *Postmodernism, Economics and Knowledge*. Routledge, London.

Bacchetta P. and Benhima K. (2015) The demand for liquid assets, corporate saving, and international capital flows. *Journal of the European Economic Association*, 13: 1101–35.

Baldwin F. and Allison A. (2015) *Japan: the Precarious Future*. New York University Press, NY.

Bark D.L. and Gress D.R. (1993) *A History of West Germany: From Shadow to Substance 1945-1963*. Second edition, Blackwell, Oxford.

Bar-Nathan M., Beenstock M., and Haitovsky Y. (1998) The market for housing in Israel. *Regional Science and Urban Economics*, 28: 21–50.

Barsky E., Justiniano A., and Melosi L. (2014) The natural rate of interest and its usefulness for monetary policy. *American Economic Review*, 104: 37–43.

Becker G.S. (1992) *A Treatise on the Family*. Second edition, Harvard University Press.

Beenstock M. (1978) *The Foreign Exchanges: Theory, Modelling and Policy*. Macmillan, London.

Beenstock M. (1980) *A Neoclassical Analysis of Macroeconomic Policy*. Cambridge University Press.

Beenstock M. (1983) Rational expectations and the effect of exchange rate intervention on the exchange rate. *Journal of International Money and Finance*, 3: 319–31.

Beenstock M. (1984) *The World Economy in Transition*. Second edition, Allen and Unwin, London.

Beenstock M. and Felsenstein D. (2015) Spatial spillover in housing construction. *Journal of Housing Economics*, 28: 42–58.

Beenstock M. and Ilek A. (2010) Wicksell's classical dichotomy: is the natural rate of interest independent of the money rate of interest? *Journal of Macroeconomics*, 32: 366–77.

Beenstock M., Reingewertz Y., and Paldor N. (2016) The historic tracking of climate change models. *International Review of Forecasting*, 32: 1234–46.

Beenstock M. and Felsenstein D. (2019) *The Econometric Analysis of Nonstationary Spatial Panel Data*. Springer Nature, Switzerland.

Beenstock M. and Xieer D. (2020) The natural and unnatural histories of Covid-19 contagion. *Covid Economics*, April, 10: 92–120.

Ben Bassat A. (2001) *The Israeli Economy 1985 – 1998: from Government Intervention to Market Economics*. Am Oved, Tel Aviv (Hebrew).

Ben Porath Y. (1986) *The Israeli Economy: Maturing through Crises*. Harvard University Press, Cambridge MA.

Berck P. and Villas-Boas S.B. (2016) A note on the triple difference in economic models. *Applied Economics Letters*, 23: 239–42.

Berg B.A. (2004) *Markov Chain Monte Carlo Simulation and their Statistical Analysis*. World Scientific Press, Singapore.

Bismut C. and Ramajo I. (2019) Nominal and real interest rates in OECD countries: an eclectic approach. Center for Environmental Economics, Montpellier University, working paper 2019-22.

Blanchard O.J. and Gali J. (2007) Real wage rigidities and the New Keynesian Model. *Journal of Money Credit and Banking*, 39: 35–65.

Böhm-Bawerk E. (1889) *Capital and Interest: Positive Theory of Capital*. Libertarian Press, S.Holland, IL (1959).

Borio C., Disyatat P. and Rungcharoenkitkul P. (2019) What anchors the natural rate of interest? Bank for International Settlements, Working Paper 777.

Brand C., Bielecki C. and Penalver A. (2018) The natural rate of interest: estimates, drivers and challenges to monetary policy. European Central Bank, Occasional paper 217.

Bruno M. and Fischer S. (1990) Seigniorage, operating rules and the high inflation trap. *Quarterly Journal of Economics*, 105: 353–74.

Bruno M. and Sachs J. (1985) *The Economics of Worldwide Stagflation*. Blackwell, Oxford.

Caballero R.J., Farhi E., and Gourinchas P.O. (2008) An equilibrium model of global imbalances and low interest rates. *American Economic Review*, 98: 358–93.

Caballero R.J., Farhi E., and Gourinchas P.O (2016) Safe asset scarcity and aggregate demand. *American Economic Review*, 106: 513–18.

Cameron C. and Trivedi P. (2005) *Microeconometrics*. Cambridge University Press.

Canova F. (2007) *Methods for Applied Macroeconomic Research*. Princeton University Press, Princeton and Oxford.

Cargill T. and Sakamoto T. (2008) *Japan since 1980*. Cambridge University Press.

Carvalho C., Ferrero A. and Nechio F. (2016) Demographics and real interest rates: inspecting the mechanism. *European Economic Review*, 88: 208–26.

Cavallo E., Galiani S., Noy I., and Pantano J. (2013) Catastrophic natural disasters and economic growth. *Review of Economics and Statistics*, 95: 1549–61.

Chan-Lee J.H. and Sutch H. (1985) *Profits and Rates of Return in OECD Countries*, Working Paper 20, OECD, Paris. https://doi.org/10.1787/468348810348.

Chudik A., Pesaran M.H. and Tosetti E. (2011) Weak and strong cross-section dependence in large panels. *Econometrics Journal*, 14: C45-C90.

Cochrane J.H. (2005) *Asset Pricing*. Second edition, Princeton University Press, Princeton New Jersey.

Colciago A., Samarina A., and de Haan J. (2019) Central bank policies and income and wealth inequality: a survey. *Journal of Economic Surveys*, 33: 1199–231.

Cowell F. (2011) *Measuring Inequality*, Oxford University Press.

Daley D.J. and Gani J. (1999) *Epidemic Modelling: An Introduction*, Cambridge University Press.

De Leeuw F. and Gramlich E. (1968) The Federal Reserve – MIT econometric model. Federal Reserve Bulletin, 54: 11–40.

Defoe D. (1722) *A Journal of the Plague Year*. Oxford University Press (2010), Oxford.

DeJong P.J. and Dave C. (2007) *Structural Macroeconometrics*. Princeton University Press, Princeton and Oxford. 2nd edition 2012

Diamond P.W. and Dybvig P.H. (1983) Bank runs, deposit insurance and liquidity. *Journal of Political Economy*, 91: 401–19.

Doherty N.A. and Garven J.R. (1995) Insurance cycles: interest rates and the capacity constraint model. *Journal of Business*, 68: 383–404.

Duffie D. (1996) *Dynamic Asset Pricing Theory*. Princeton University Press, Princeton, New Jersey.

Elder M. (2015) METI and industrial policy in Japan. In *Japan's Managed Globalization*, Schaeda U. and Grimes W. (eds), M.E. Sharpe.

Elkayam D. and Segal G. (2018) Estimated natural rate of interest in an open economy: the case of Israel. Bank of Israel, Research Department, Discussion Paper.

Engle R. and Granger C.W.J. (1987) Cointegration and error correction: representation, estimation and testing. *Econometrica*, 35: 251–276.

Ericcson N.R. and Irons J.S. (1994) *Exogeneity*. Oxford University Press, Oxford.

Filipovic J. (2020) *OK Boomer, Let's Talk: How my Generation got Left Behind*. One Signal Publihers/ Astia, New York.

Fleming J.M. (1962) Domestic financial policies under fixed and floating exchange rates. *IMF Staff Papers*, 9: 369–79.

Foley D.F. and Sidrausky M. (1970) Portfolio choice, investment and growth. *American Economic Review*, 60: 44–67.

Friedman M. (1953) The methodology of positive economics. In *Essays in Positive Economics*, University of Chicago Press, 3–43.

Friedman M. (1969) *The Optimal Quantity of Money and Other Essays*. Aldine, Chicago.

Fuller S. (2015) *Knowledge: the Philosophical Quest in History*. Routledge, London and New York.

Funabashi H. (2012) Why the Fukushima nuclear disaster is a man-made calamity. *International Journal of Japanese Sociology*, 21: 65–75.

Goodhart C. and Pradhan M. (2020) *The Great Demographic Reversal: Ageing Societies, Waning Inequality and Inflation Renewal*. Springer International, Switzerland.

Gordon R.G. (2016) *The Rise and Fall of American Growth: The US Standard of Living Since the Civil War*. Princeton University Press, Princeton and Oxford.

Gourieroux, C., Montfort A. and Renault E. (1993) Indirect inference. *Journal of Applied Econometrics*, 8: S85–S118.

Grinberger A.Y. and Felsenstein D. (2014) Bouncing back or bouncing forward? Simulating urban resilience. *Urban Design and Planning*, 167: 115–24.

Hale T., Webster S., Pethnick A. et al (2020) Oxford Covid-19 Government Tracker. Blavatnik School of Government, Oxford University.

Hamilton J. (1994) *Time Series*. Princeton University Press.

Hansen L.P. and Sargent T. (1991) *Rational Expectations Econometrics*. Westview Press, Boulder.

Harvey A. and Jaeger A. (1993) Detrending, stylized facts and business cycles. *Journal of Applied Econometrics*, 8: 231–47.

Haugh M. (2005) What does 'face' mean to the Japanese? Understanding the import of 'face' in Japanese business transactions. In *Asian Business Discourse(s)*, Bargiela-Chiappini F. and Gotti M. (eds), Peter Long, Switzerland, 211–39.

Haugh M. and Watanabe Y. (2009) *Analyzing Japanese 'face-in-interaction': insights from intercultural business meetings*. In *Face, Communication and Social Interaction*, Bargiela-Chiappini F. and Haugh M. (eds), Equinox Publishing, London, 78–95.

Hayek F.A. (1990) *The Denationalization of Money; the Argument Refined*. Third edition, Hobart Paper (Special) 70, Institute for Economic Affairs, London.

Hendry D.F. (1995) *Dynamic Econometrics*. Oxford University Press.

Hicks J. (1937) Mr Keynes and the Classics: a suggested interpretation. *Econometrica*, 5: 147–59.

Hodrick R. and Prescott E.C. (1997) Postwar US business cycles: an empirical investigation. *Journal of Money, Credit and Banking*, 29: 1–16.

Holsboer J.H. (2000) The impact of low interest rates on insurers. *Geneva Papers on Risk and Insurance*, 25: 38–58.

Holston K., Laubach T., and Williams J.C. (2016) Measuring the natural rate of interest: international trends and determinants. Federal Reserve Bank of San Francisco. Working Paper 2106–11.

International Monetary Fund (2020) The great lockdown: dissecting the economic effects. *World Economic Outloook*. IMF, October, Chapter 2.

Ito T., Patrick H., and Weinstein D. (2008) *Reviving Japan's Economy*. MIT Press, Cambidge MA.

Johansen S. (1995) *Likelihood-based Inference in Cointegrated Vector Autoregressive Models*. Oxford University Press.

Johnson C.A. (1982) *MITI and the Japanese Miracle*. Stanford University Press, Stanford CA.

Johnson H.G. (1967) Money in a one-sector neoclassical growth model. *Essays in Monetary Economics*. Allen & Unwin, London, 143–78.

Johnson P. and Duberley E. (2000) *Understanding Management Research: An Introduction to Epistemology*. SAGE Publications, London.

Johnstone B. (1999) *We were burning: Japanese and the Forging of the Electronic Age*. Basic Books, New York.

Kahneman D. and Tversky A. (1979) Prospect theory: an analysis of decisions under risk. *Econometrica*, 47: 263–91.

Kaldor N. (1956) Alternative theories of distribution. *Review of Economic Studies*, 23: 83–100.

Kalecki M. (1938) The determinants of distribution of the national income. *Econometrica* 6: 97–112.

Karlinsky A. and Kobak D. (2021) The world mortality dataset: tracking excess mortality across countries during the Covid-19 pandemic. megR$_X$iv, https://doi.org/10.1101/2021. 01.21.21250604.

Katz R. (1998) *Japan the System that Soured: the Rise and Fall of the Japanese Economic Miracle*. Eastgate Book, M.E. Sharpe, New York.

Katzner D. (2007) The workings of the Japanese economy. In *Crisis or Recovery in Japan: State and Industrial Economy*, Bailey D., Coffey D. and Tomlinson P. (eds), Edward Elgar, Cheltenham, Chapter 2.

Kendig H., McDonald P., and Piggot J. (2016) *Population Ageing and Australia's Future*. ANU Press, Canberra.

Kenen P.B. (1960) International liquidity and the balance of payments of a reserve-currency country. *Quarterly Journal of Economics*, 74: 572–86.

Kermack W.O. and McKendrick A.G. (1927) A contribution to the mathematical theory of epidemics. *Proceedings of the Royal Society of London, A*, 115: 700–721.

Keynes J.M. (1923) *A Tract on Monetary Reform*. Macmillan, London.

Keynes J.M. (1930) *A Treatise on Money*. Harcourt Brace, London.

Keynes J.M. (1936) *The General Theory of Employment, Interest and Money*. Macmillan, London.

Kim J-Y. and Nan S-H. (1998) The concept and dynamics of face: implications for organizational behavior in Asia. *Organization Science*, 9: 522–34.

Klein L.R. and Goldberger A.S. (1955) *An Econometric Model for the US: 1929–1952*. North Holland, Amsterdam.

Koo R.C. (2009) *The Holy Grail of Macroeconomics: Lessons from Japan's Great Recession*. John Wiley (Asia), Singapore.

Krugman P. (1998) It's baaack: Japan's slump and the return of the liquidity trap. *Brookings Papers on Economic Activity*, 2: 137–205.

Kuhn T.S. (1970) *The Structure of Scientific Revolutions*. Second edition, University of Chicago Press, Chicago. Illinois.

Kydland F.R. and Prescott E.C. (1982) Time to build and aggregate fluctuations. *Econometrica*, 50: 1345–70.

Kydland F.E, and Prescott E.C. (1991) Business cycles: real facts and a monetary myth. *Quarterly Review*, Federal Reserve Bank of Minneapolis, 14: 3–18.

Kydland F.R. and Prescott E.C. (1996) The computation experiment: an econometric tool. *Journal of Economic Literature*, 10: 69–85.

Laubach T. and Williams J. (2003) Measuring the natural rate of interest. *Review of Economics and Statistics*, 85: 1063–70.

Le V.P.M, Meenagh D., Minford P., and Wickens M. (2011) How much nominal rigidity is there in the US Economy? Testing a New Keynesian DSGE model using indirect inference. *Journal of Economic Dynamics and Control*, 35: 2078–104.

Lebra T.S. (1976) *Japanese Patterns of Behavior*. The University Press of Hawai, Honolulu.

Lucas R.E. (1976) Econometric policy evaluation: a critique. *The Phillips Curve and Labor Markets*, Brunner K. and Meltzer A. (eds), Carnegie-Rochester Conference Series on Public Policy, Vol 1.

Maddala G.S. (2001) *Introduction to Econometrics*. Third edition, John Wiley & Sons, Chichester.

Malliaris A.G. and Brock W.A. (1988) *Stochastic Methods in Economics and Finance*. N. Holland, Amsterdam.

Manski C.F. (1995) *Identification Problems in the Social Sciences*. Harvard University Press, Cambridge MA.

Manski C.F. (2008) *Identification for Prediction and Decision*. Harvard University Press, Cambridge MA.

Marx M., Mojon B., and Velde F.R. (2018) Why have interest rates fallen far below the return on capital? Federal Reserve Bank of Chicago, Working Paper 2018–01.

Matsumoto D.R. (1996) *Unmasking Japan: Myths and Realities about the Emotions of the Japanese*. Stanford University Press, Stanford CA.

McCallum B.T. (1976) Rational expectations and the natural rate hypothesis: some consistent estimates. *Econometrica*, 44: 43–52.

McCallum B.T. and Nelson E. (1999) A optimizing IS-LM specification for monetary policy and business cycle analysis. *Journal of Money, Credit and Banking*, 31: 296–316.

McCloskey D.N. (1985) *The Rhetoric of Economics*. University of Wisconsin Press, Madison, Wisconsin.

McCloskey D.N. (1994) *Knowledge and Persuasion in Economics*. Cambridge University Press, Cambridge.

Meenagh D., Minford P., Wickens M., and Xu Y. (2019) Testing DSGE models by indirect inference: a survey of recent findings. *Open Economies Review*, 30: 593–620.

Meigs A.J. (1962) *Free Reserves and the Money Supply*. University of Chicago Press, Chicago.

Minford P. and Peel D.A. (2019) *Advanced Macroeconomics: A Primer*. Second edition, Edward Elgar.

Miyagawa T., Takizawa M., Tonoji K., and Fukao K. (2018) Declining rate of return on capital and the role of intangibles in Japan. In *Productivity Dynamics in Emerging and Industrialized Countries*, Das D.K. (ed), Routledge, India, Chapter 8.

Modigliani F. and Sutch R. (1966) Innovations in interest rate policy. *American Economic Review*, 56: 178–97.

Mokyr J. (2002) *The Gifts of Athena: Historical Origins of the Knowledge Economy*. Princeton University Press, Princeton, New Jersey.

Morgan M. (1990) *The History of Econometric Ideas*. Cambridge University Press.

Mundell R.A. (1963) Capital mobility and stabilization policy under fixed and floating exchange rates. *Canadian Journal of Economics and Political Science*, 19: 475–85.

National Insurance Institute (2019) *Report on Poverty and Social Inequality*. Jerusalem (Hebrew).

Nozick R. (1974) *Anarchy, State and Utopia*. Basic Books, New York.

O'Driscoll G.P. (1977) The Ricardian Nonequivalence Theorem. *Journal of Political Economy*. 85: 207–10.

OECD (2018) *Economic Outlook*. OECD, Paris, Issue 1, p 28.

OECD (2019) *Economic Surveys Japan*. OECD, Paris.

OECD (2019) *Pensions at a Glance 2018*. OECD, Paris.

OECD (2021) *Economic Outlook*, OECD, Paris.

Ogawa N., Matsakura R., and Lee S-H. (2016) Declining fertility and the rising cost of children and elderly in Japan and other selected Asian countries: an analysis based on the NTA approach. Chapter 5 in *Population Ageing and Australia's Future*, Kendig H., McDonald P. and Piggot J. (eds), Australian National University Press, Canberra.

Ohno K. (2017) *The History of Japanese Economic Development: The Origins of Private Dynamism and Policy Competence*. Routledge, London.

Olden A. and Møen J. (2020) The triple difference estimator. Discussion paper, Norwegian School of Business.

Omori R., Matsuyama R., and Nakata Y. (2020) The age distribution of mortality from novel coronavirus disease (Covid-19) suggests no large difference in susceptibility by age. *Nature Scientific Reports*, https://doi.org/10.1030/s41590-020-73777-8.

Parkin M. and Bade R. (1988) *Modern Macroeconomics*. Second edition, Philip Allan, Oxford.

Patinkin D. (1966) *Money, Interest and Prices: An Integration of Monetary and Value Theory*. Second edition, Harper & Rowe, New York and Evanston.

Patinkin D. (1976) *Keynes' Monetary Thought: A Study of its Development*. Duke University Press, Durham NC.

Patrick H. (1986) Japan's high technology industrial policy in comparative context. In *Japan's High Technology Industries: Lessons and Limitations of Industrial Policy*, H. Patrick and L. Meissner (eds), Seattle, University of Washington Press.

Pesaran M.H. (1978) *The Limits to Rational Expectations*. Blackwell, Oxford.

Phelps E.S. (1968) Money-wage dynamics and labor market equilibrium. *Journal of Political Economy*, 76: 678–711.

Pirsig R.M. (1974) *Zen and the Art of Motorcycle Maintenance*. Bantam Books, New York.

Poole W. (1970) Optimal choice of monetary policy in a simple stochastic macro model. *Quarterly Journal of Economics*, 84: 197–216.

Popper K.R. (1963) *Conjectures and Refutations: The Growth of Scientific Knowledge*. Routledge and Kegan Paul, London.

Porter M. (1990) *The Competitive Advantage of Nations*. New York, the Free Press.

Prescott E.C. (1986) Theory ahead of business cycle measurement. *Federal Reserve Bank of Minneapolis Quarterly Review*, 10: 9–22.

Rawls J. (1971) *A Theory of Justice*. Belknap Press, Cambridge MA.

Razin A. (2018) *Israel and the World Economy*. MIT Press, Cambridge MA.

Robertson D.H. (1939) Mr Keynes and the rate of interest. *Essays in Monetary Theory*, chapter 1, P.S. King and Son, London.

Romer D. (2019) *Advanced Macroeconomics*. Fifth edition, McGraw Hill, New York.

Romer P. (2016) The trouble with macroeconomics. *The Economist*, 22/9/2016.

Roser M., Morelli S., Hassal J., and Atkinson A.B. (2019) *Chartbook of Economic Inequality.* Third edition, Harvard Dataverse.

Ruccio D. (1991) Postmodernism and economics. *Journal of Post Keynesian Economics,* 13: 495–510.

Ruccio D.F. and Amariglio J. (2004) *Postmodern Moments in Modern Economics.* Princeton University Press, Princeton NJ.

Samuelson P.A. (1997) Credo of a lucky textbook author. *Journal of Economic Perspectives,* 11: 153–160.

Sargent T.J. (1979) *Macroeconomic Theory.* Academic Press.

Sargent T.J. and Wallace N. (1981) Some unpleasant monetarist arithmetic. Federal Reserve Bank of Minneapolis, *Quarterly Review,* 3: 1–17.

Schilling L. and Uhlig H. (2019) Some simple Bitcoin economics. *Journal of Monetary Economics.* 106: 16–26.

Sims C. (1980) Macroeconomics and reality. *Econometrica,* 48: 1–48.

Singleton K.J. (2006) *Empirical Dynamic Asset Pricing: Model Specification and Econometric Assessment.* Princeton University Press, Princeton and Oxford.

Smets F. and Wouters R. (2003) An estimated dynamic stochastic general equilibrium model for the euro zone. *Journal of the European Economic Association,* 1: 1123–75.

Smets F. and Wouters R. (2007) Shocks and frictions in US business cycles: a Bayesian DSGE approach. *American Economic Review,* 97: 586–606.

Smith L.B. (1969) A model of the Canadian housing and mortgage markets. *Journal of Political Economy,* 96: 795–816.

Smithers A. (2013) *The Road to Recovery: How and Why Economic Policy Must Change.* John Wiley & Sons, Chichester.

Soreczky A. (2013) Was the Bank of Israel's Foreign Exchange Intervention effective? *Bank of Israel Review,* 86: 7–45. (Hebrew).

Stern N. (2006) *The Economics of Climate Change.* Cambridge University Press.

Summers L. (1989) The Ishihara – Morita brouhaha. *International Economy,* December, 3: 49-55.

Sutton G.D., Mihaljek D., and Subelyte A. (2017) Interest rates and house prices in the United States and around the world. Bank for International Settlements Working Paper 665.

Svensson L.E.O. (2000) Open-economy inflation targeting. *Journal of International Economics,* 50: 155–83.

Takayama N. (2016) Funded pensions: the Japanese experience and its lessons. IPLE Seminar at CASS, Beijing.

Taylor J.B. (1993) Discretion versus policy rules in practice. *Carnegie Rochester Conference Series on Public Policy,* 39: 195–214.

Taylor P. (2014) *The Next America: Boomers, Millennials and the Looming Generation Slowdown.* Public Affairs, New York.

Thurow L. (1992) *Head-to-Head: the Coming Economic Battle among Japan, Europe and America.* William Morrow, New York.

Triffin R. (1960) *Gold and the Dollar Crisis: The Future of Convertibility.* Yale University Press, New Haven CT.

Vines D. and Wills S. (2018) The rebuilding macroeconomic theory project: an analytical assessment. *Oxford Review of Economic Policy,* 34: 1–42.

Vines D. and Wills S. (2018) The financial system and the natural real rate of interest: towards a new benchmark theory model. *Oxford Review of Economic Policy,* 34: 252–68.

Walsh C.E. (2017) *Monetary Theory and Policy*. Fourth edition, MIT Press, Cambridge MA.

Watanabe H.R. (2019) *The Japanese Economy*. Agenda Publishing, Newcastle-upon-Tyne.

Watanabe N. (1996) Private pension plans in Japan. *Securing Employer-based Pensions: An International Perspective*, Bodie Z., Mitchell O.S. and Turner J.A. (eds), chapter 4, University of Pennsylvania Press.

Weinstein D.E., Kayshap A.K., and Hamada K. (2011) *Japan's Bubble, Deflation and Long-term Stagnation*. MIT Press, Cambridge MA.

Weiss T. (2015) The rate of return on capital in Germany: an empirical study. 19th FMM Conference "The Spectre of Stagflation? Europe in the World Economy", Berlin. https://www.boeckler.de/pdf/v.2015-10-24-weiss.

Wickens M.R. (1982) The efficient estimation of econometric models with rational expectations. *Review of Economic Studies*, 49: 55–67.

Wicksell K. (1898) *Interest and Prices: A Study of the Causes Regulating the Value of Money*. Macmillan, London (1936).

Wicksell K. (1949) *Lectures on Political Economy*. Volume 2, George Routledge, London.

Wicksell K. (1958) *Selected Papers on Economic Theory*, Chapter 2. George Allen & Unwin, London. Subsequently published by A.M. Kelly, New York (1969) and Routledge, London (2018).

Wicksell K. (1898) Ludwig van Mises, The Theory of Money and Credit, in *Selected Essays in Economics*, chapter 33, volume 2, B. Sandelin (ed), Routledge 1999.

Winter J. and Teitelbaum M. (2013) *The Global Spread of Fertility Decline: Population Fear and Uncertainty*. Yale University Press, New Haven Ct.

Wood S. (2020) Covid lockdown and the economics of valuing lives. *The Spectator*, October 3.

Woodford M. (2003) *Interest and Prices: Foundations of a Theory of Monetary Policy*. Princeton University Press, Princeton NJ.

Wren-Lewis S. (2018) Ending the microfoundations hegemony. *Oxford Review of Economic Policy*, 34: 55–69.

Wynne M.A. and Zhang R. (2017) Estimating the natural rate of interest in an open economy. Federal Reserve Bank of Dallas, Working paper 16.

Xiao Y. (2011) Local economic impacts of natural disasters. *Journal of Regional Science*, 51: 804–20.

Yitzhaki S. and Schechtman E. (2013) *The Gini Methodology: A Primer on a Statistical Methodology*. Springer, New York.

Yoshikawa H. (2008) *Japan's Lost Decade*. House Press, Tokyo.

Yule G.U. (1897) On the theory of correlation. *Journal of the Royal Statistical Society*, 60: 812–854.

Yule G.U. (1926) Why do we sometimes get nonsense correlations between time series? A study in sampling and the nature of time series. *Journal of the Royal Statistical Society*, 89: 1–64.

Zeira J. (2021) *The Economy of Israel: A Story of Success and Costs*. Princeton University Press.

# General Index

Tables and figures are indicated by an italic *t* and *f* following the page number.

# Index of Names

Tables and figures are indicated by an italic *t* and *f* following the page number.